THE BEST
AMERICAN
MAGAZINE
WRITING

2004

THE BEST AMERICAN MAGAZINE WRITING 2004

American Society of Magazine Editors

Perennial Currents

An Imprint of HarperCollins*Publishers*

Contents

xi *Introduction by Susan Orlean*

xv *Acknowledgments*

2 "The Dark Art of Interrogation"
by Mark Bowden
PUBLISHED IN *The Atlantic Monthly*
FINALIST—Public Interest

52 "The Marriage Cure"
by Katherine Boo
PUBLISHED IN *The New Yorker*
WINNER—Feature Writing

90 "The Killer Elite" (Part I)
by Evan Wright
PUBLISHED IN *Rolling Stone*
WINNER—Reporting

124   "The League of Extraordinary Gentlemen"
                             by Tucker Carlson
                             PUBLISHED IN *Esquire*
                             FINALIST—Feature Writing

148   "Housewife Confidential"
                             by Caitlin Flanagan
                             PUBLISHED IN *The Atlantic Monthly*
                             FINALIST—Reviews and Criticism

166   "The Stovepipe"
                             by Seymour M. Hersh
                             PUBLISHED IN *The New Yorker*
                             WINNER—Public Interest

192   "*Columbia*'s Last Flight"
                             by William Langewiesche
                             PUBLISHED IN *The Atlantic Monthly*
                             FINALIST—Reporting

254   "The David Kelly Affair"
                             by John Cassidy
                             PUBLISHED IN *The New Yorker*
                             FINALIST—Reporting

302   "The Vulgarian in the Choir Loft"

by Andrew Corsello

PUBLISHED IN *GQ*

FINALIST—Essays

316   "The Red Bow"

by George Saunders

PUBLISHED IN *Esquire*

WINNER—Fiction

330   "Newshound"

by Calvin Trillin

PUBLISHED IN *The New Yorker*

FINALIST—Profile Writing

358   "A Sudden Illness"

by Laura Hillenbrand

PUBLISHED IN *The New Yorker*

WINNER—Essays

382   "Wynton's Blues"

by David Hajdu

PUBLISHED IN *The Atlantic Monthly*

FINALIST—Profile Writing

410 "The $20 Theory of the Universe"
by Tom Chiarella
PUBLISHED IN *Esquire*
FINALIST—Leisure Interests

422 "My Big Fat Question"
by Michael Wolff
PUBLISHED IN *New York Magazine*
WINNER—Columns and
Commentary

432 "The Confessions of Bob Greene"
by Bill Zehme
PUBLISHED IN *Esquire*
WINNER—Profile Writing

460 "The Only Meaning of the Oil-Wet Water"
by Dave Eggers
PUBLISHED IN *Zoetrope: All-Story*
FINALIST—Fiction

494 "The Falling Man"
by Tom Junod
PUBLISHED IN *Esquire*
FINALIST—Feature Writing

517   Contributors

523   2004 National Magazine Award Finalists

533   1966–2004 National Magazine Award Winners

541   ASME Board of Directors 2003–2004

542   ASME Mission Statement

Introduction

When I was a kid, I lived for *Life*. Generally speaking, I read like a maniac—romantic novels by the armload, comic strips by the ton, even whatever inappropriate nonfiction treatises like *Ideal Marriage, Its Physiology and Technique* that my parents happened to have lying around. But what I burned for, what I launched hair-pulling and arm-pinching fights with my brother and sister for, was dibs on each issue of *Life* that slid through our mail chute once a month and landed with a solid thud just inside our front door. Yes, of course, I did turn first to the funny picture-of-the-month on the inside back page, but then I read—devoured—the whole magazine. What entranced me so completely was the tone and pace of the stories in *Life*. Newspapers made declarations; books contemplated; magazines, by contrast, seemed involved in a human-tempo conversation about the world and what was in it. *Life* considered country doctors' lives; embryonic development; skateboarding; skyjacking; Biafra; the Beatles; dropout wives; and runaway kids, all in an unhurried but animated voice. Like fiction, it evoked a world; better than fiction, it was true. Reading the magazine lifted me out of my Midwestern suburban-girl reality and deposited me in, say, a North Vietnamese prison, Winston Churchill's casket, the Selma civil-rights march, a space walk. To me, this was a miracle. I think that I learned more—and more willingly—by reading *Life* and the other publications my family got (*Look, Time, Newsweek, The New Yorker, Reader's Digest, National Geographic, Architectural Digest*) than through any other medium, including school. I fell in love with that tone of spry, engrossed inquiry that *Life* first introduced me to, and it made me fall thoroughly and enduringly in love with magazines.

I really do think that magazines are kind of a miracle. Every week or month, they present a rich, well-realized, enterprising view of the human condition; they evoke an imagined community of fellow readers; they provide visual, intellectual, and emotional sustenance through reportage, fiction, art, photography, and essays—all for a few bucks. Technically speaking, the cost-benefit ratio of a magazine purchase is really excellent. As a matter of fact, according to a recent survey by Northwestern University's Media Management Center, the dominant magazine reader experience—the thing that drives people to read magazines—is "I get value for my time and money." (In case you're wondering, other comments about magazines in that same survey included "It makes me smarter"; "I trust it"; "I learn things first here"; and "The stories absorb me." Of course, there are a few slightly less laudatory opinions, such as "This magazine irritates me" and "It leaves me feeling bad.")

Magazines popped up in the United States in the eighteenth century, put down roots in the nineteenth, and flourished—indeed, exploded—in the twentieth. Their success followed the growth in the nation's literacy, or, quite likely, was instrumental in it. Books were daunting to new readers, while magazines appeared more manageable; by the 1940s, almost everyone in America had read a magazine, and popular ones like *Saturday Evening Post* had a gigantic audience. The form seemed ideally calibrated to the way people wanted to read—with some immediacy, some currency, but with something more than the disposability of a newspaper, and something less than the ponderousness of a book.

This is not, by any means, an us-versus-them polemic about the superiority of magazines over other species of the printed word. I am awed by good newspapers and read them avidly; I love books, read them passionately, and even write them occasionally. But magazines still thrill me the most. Maybe some of it is because of the surprise they deliver—each issue arriving packed with stories you didn't expect and couldn't have imagined. And also because of the sum-of-the-parts aspect of magazines, the way each issue orchestrates the work of so many people and such disparate elements. Of course, my real love for magazines is in writing for them. The size and shape required of a magazine story, the elasticity and the openness of the format, the quick turnaround between writing and publishing, the feel you have of your readers (far more than you have when writing a book), is, to me, the ideal way to work. In fact, with the possible exception of serving as the queen of a peaceful, prosperous, impossibly beautiful tropical island, there is no job I (and, I suspect, most journalists) would rather have than that of a writer for a good magazine.

From the beginning, magazines—even the silliest of them—were instruments of instruction. Rather than just recording the world, they tried to illuminate it, to expand on sheer facts in order to offer information on how to live amid those facts. Which brings us to, at last, this collection of the best magazine pieces of the year. These were published in a year when the world wasn't in great shape, and by and large, they try to explicate what underlies the bad shape we're in. War preoccupied the world this year, and accordingly it preoccupied magazines, and several of these pieces—including work by Seymour Hersh, Mark Bowden, Michael Wolff, and John Cassidy—are efforts to investigate how this war came to be, and the culture of war-mongering that supported it. Using that same approach of the painstaking investigation, several other pieces here take on different tragedies—the last flight of the shuttle *Columbia*, an unknown victim of September 11, even the excruciating personal collapse of columnist Bob Greene. There are portrayals of things that are more individual: the grinding disappointments in the lives of poor people, the bewildering cocoon of illness, the daunting and sometimes almost comic complexities of modern marriage. There are sharp and funny recountings of bad personal behavior, of singing in public, and of falling in love.

What this wide spread of stories share is a wonderful ambition and intent to talk to readers, to offer them the outcome of the opportunity that is uniquely afforded writers—to go out into the world and try to understand it better, and return to tell the tale. It is a great mission and a challenging one, especially as the world grows more chaotic and scarier and that much harder to explain. But that's exactly why magazines remain important, and grow more important all the time, and why their effort is so admirable and so worth noting each year. That's why little suburban kids hair-pull and arm-pinch to get to magazines the moment they fall through the mail slot and announce with a thud that they are delivering a new installment of this ongoing journalistic conversation, and why millions of people count on them regularly to be a clear window—maybe the clearest window—onto the world.

—*Susan Orlean*

Acknowledgments

Ever since Ben Franklin published America's first magazine, *The General Magazine and Historical Chronicle*, in 1741, magazines have been amazing instruments of change, information and inspiration. And for 40 years now, the American Society of Magazine Editors has been honoring the best of the best. The collection you are holding in your hands represents some of the finalists and winners of the 2004 National Magazine Awards. This Academy Award–like celebration of superior writing and editing is run by ASME in association with the Columbia University Graduate School of Journalism.

As you read from our selected favorites, keep in mind the words of the late, great actor Sir Peter Ustinov, who said, "Acting is incredibly easy. Writing is incredibly more mysterious and personal." Our fifth annual volume features the work of established All-Star authors as well as relative newcomers, not to mention the talents of gifted editors who worked to bring out their writers' best efforts.

ASME was founded forty years ago by editors who shared the following mission: to acquaint the general public with the work of magazine editors and the special character of magazines as a channel of communication, to encourage and reward outstanding and innovative achievement, to attract young people of talent to editorial work, to inform and support magazine editors on matters of mutual interest, and to safeguard the First Amendment.

This thought-provoking and entertaining compendium would not have been possible without ASME's exceptional executive director, Marlene Kahan, who not only expertly orchestrates the awards program but worked with Mark Bryant, our editor at HarperCollins, to select the pieces that follow. We are also grateful to Columbia's Dean, Nicholas Lemann, and Columbia's National Magazine Award director, Robin Blackburn, for their great advice and collaboration. A special thanks as well to all the editors who stand proudly behind their writers' bylines. If you enjoy reading this collection, by all means run out, buy more of your favorite magazines, and perhaps try some you've never read before.

—*Susan Ungaro*
Editor-in-Chief, *Family Circle*
President, ASME (2002–2004)

THE BEST
AMERICAN
MAGAZINE
WRITING

2004

The Atlantic Monthly

FINALIST, PUBLIC INTEREST

The Dark Art of Interrogation

Mark Bowden's richly reported, haunting story lays out the methods of modern torture used on prisoners around the globe. It forces the reader to contemplate the argument that such techniques are not simply necessary but are in fact a morally justifiable way of fighting terrorism in a post-9/11 world.

Mark Bowden

The Dark Art of Interrogation

The most effective way to gather intelligence and thwart terrorism can also be a direct route into morally repugnant terrain. A survey of the landscape of persuasion.

Rawalpindi, Pakistan

On what may or may not have been a Saturday, on what may have been March 1, in a house in this city that may have been this squat two-story white one belonging to Ahmad Abdul Qadoos, with big gray-headed crows barking in the front yard, the notorious terrorist Khalid Sheikh Mohammed was roughly awakened by a raiding party of Pakistani and American commandos. Anticipating a gunfight, they entered loud and fast. Instead they found him asleep. He was pulled from his bed, hooded, bound, hustled from the house, placed in a vehicle, and driven quickly away.

Here was the biggest catch yet in the war on terror. Sheikh Mohammed is considered the architect of two attempts on the World Trade Center: the one that failed, in 1993, and the one that succeeded so catastrophically, eight years later. He is also believed to have been behind the attacks on the U.S. embassies in Kenya and Tanzania in 1998, and on the USS *Cole* two years later, and behind the slaughter last year of the *Wall Street Journal* reporter Daniel Pearl, among other things. An intimate of Osama bin Laden's, Sheikh Mohammed has been called the operations chief of al-Qaeda, if such a formal role can be said to exist in such an informal organization. Others have suggested that an apter designation might be al-Qaeda's "chief franchisee." Whatever the analogy, he is one of the terror organization's most important figures, a burly, distinctly modern, cosmopolitan thirty-seven-year-old man fanatically devoted to a medieval form of Islam. He was born to Pakistani parents, raised in Kuwait, and educated in North Carolina to be an engineer before he returned to the Middle East to build a career of bloody mayhem.

Some say that Sheikh Mohammed was captured months before the March 1 date announced by Pakistan's Inter-Services Intelligence (ISI). Abdul Qadoos, a pale, white-bearded alderman in this well-heeled neighborhood, told me that Sheikh Mohammed was not there "then or ever." The official video of the takedown appears to have been faked. But the details are of minor importance. Whenever, wherever, and however it happened, nearly everyone now agrees that Sheikh Mohammed is in U.S. custody, and has been for some time. In the first hours of his captivity the hood came off and a picture was taken. It shows a bleary-eyed, heavy, hairy, swarthy man with a full black moustache, thick eyebrows, a dark outline of beard on a rounded, shaved face, three chins, long sideburns, and a full head of dense, long, wildly mussed black hair. He stands before a pale tan wall whose paint is chipped, leaning slightly forward, like a man with his hands bound behind him, the low cut of his loose-fitting white T-shirt exposing matted curls of hair on his chest, shoulders, and back. He is looking down and to the right of the camera. He appears dazed and glum.

Sheikh Mohammed is a smart man. There is an anxious, searching quality to his expression in that first post-arrest photo. It is the look of a man awakened into nightmare. Everything that has given his life meaning, his role as husband and father, his leadership, his stature, plans, and ambitions, is finished. His future is months, maybe years, of imprisonment and interrogation; a military tribunal; and almost certain execution. You can practically see the wheels turning in his head, processing his terminal predicament. How will he spend his last months and years? Will he maintain a dignified, defiant silence? Or will he succumb to his enemy and betray his friends, his cause, and his faith?

If Sheikh Mohammed felt despair in those first hours, it didn't show. According to a Pakistani officer who sat in on an initial ISI questioning, the al-Qaeda sub-boss seemed calm and stoic. For his first two days in custody he said nothing beyond confirming his name. A CIA official says that Sheikh Mohammed spent those days "sitting in a trancelike state and reciting verses from the Koran." On the third day he is said to have loosened up. Fluent in the local languages of Urdu, Pashto, and Baluchi, he tried to shame his Pakistani interrogators, lecturing them on their responsibilities as Muslims and upbraiding them for cooperating with infidels.

"Playing an American surrogate won't help you or your country," he said. "There are dozens of people like me who will give their lives but won't let the Americans live in peace anywhere in the world." Asked if Osama bin Laden was alive, he said, "Of course he is alive." He spoke of meeting with bin Laden in "a mountainous border region" in December. He seemed smug about U.S. and British preparations for war against Saddam Hussein. "Let the Iraq War begin," he said. "The U.S. forces will be targeted inside their bases in the Gulf. I don't have any specific information, but my sixth sense is telling me that you will get the news from Saudi Arabia, Qatar, and Kuwait." Indeed, in the following months al-Qaeda carried out a murderous attack in Saudi Arabia.

On that third day, once more hooded, Sheikh Mohammed was driven to Chaklala Air Force base, in Rawalpindi, and turned over to U.S. forces. From there he was flown to the CIA interrogation center in Bagram, Afghanistan, and from there, some days later, to an "undisclosed location" (a place the CIA calls "Hotel California")—presumably a facility in another cooperative nation, or perhaps a specially designed prison aboard an aircraft carrier. It doesn't much matter where, because the place would not have been familiar or identifiable to him. Place and time, the anchors of sanity, were about to come unmoored. He might as well have been entering a new dimension, a strange new world where his every word, move, and sensation would be monitored and measured; where things might be as they seemed but might not; where there would be no such thing as day or night, or normal patterns of eating and drinking, wakefulness and sleep; where hot and cold, wet and dry, clean and dirty, truth and lies, would all be tangled and distorted.

Intelligence and military officials would talk about Sheikh Mohammed's state only indirectly, and conditionally. But by the time he arrived at a more permanent facility, he would already have been bone-tired, hungry, sore, uncomfortable, and afraid—if not for himself, then for his wife and children, who had been arrested either with him or some months before, depending on which story you believe. He would have been warned that lack of cooperation might mean being turned over to the more direct and brutal interrogators of some third nation. He would most likely have been locked naked in a cell with no trace of daylight. The space would be filled night and day with harsh light and noise, and would be so small that he would be unable to stand upright, to sit comfortably, or to recline fully. He would be kept awake, cold, and probably wet. If he managed to doze, he would be roughly awakened. He would be fed infrequently and irregularly, and then only with thin, tasteless meals. Sometimes days would go by between periods of questioning, sometimes only hours or minutes. The human mind craves routine, and can adjust to almost anything in the presence of it, so his jailers would take care that no semblance of routine developed.

Questioning would be intense—sometimes loud and rough, sometimes quiet and friendly, with no apparent reason for either. He would be questioned sometimes by one person, sometimes by two or three. The session might last for days, with interrogators taking turns, or it might last only a few minutes. He would be asked the same questions again and again, and then suddenly be presented with something completely unexpected—a detail or a secret that he would be shocked to find they knew. He would be offered the opportunity to earn freedom or better treatment for his wife and children. Whenever he was helpful and the information he gave proved true, his harsh conditions would ease. If the information proved false, his treatment would worsen. On occasion he might be given a drug to elevate his mood prior to interrogation; marijuana, heroin, and sodium pentothal have been shown to overcome a reluctance to speak, and methamphetamine can unleash a torrent of talk in the stubbornest subjects, the very urgency of the chatter making a complex lie impossible to sustain. These drugs could be administered surreptitiously with food or drink, and given the bleakness of his existence, they might even offer a brief period of relief and pleasure, thereby creating a whole new category of longing—and new leverage for his interrogators.

Deprived of any outside information, Sheikh Mohammed

would grow more and more vulnerable to manipulation. For instance, intelligence gleaned after successful al-Qaeda attacks in Kuwait and Saudi Arabia might be fed to him, in bits and pieces, so as to suggest foiled operations. During questioning he would be startled regularly by details about his secret organization—details drawn from ongoing intelligence operations, new arrests, or the interrogation of other captive al-Qaeda members. Some of the information fed to him would be true, some of it false. Key associates might be said to be cooperating, or to have completely recanted their allegiance to *jihad*. As time went by, his knowledge would decay while that of his questioners improved. He might come to see once-vital plans as insignificant, or already known. The importance of certain secrets would gradually erode.

Isolated, confused, weary, hungry, frightened, and tormented, Sheikh Mohammed would gradually be reduced to a seething collection of simple needs, all of them controlled by his inter-rogators.

The key to filling all those needs would be the same: *to talk*.

Smacky-Face

We hear a lot these days about America's over-powering military technology; about the professionalism of its warriors; about the sophistication of its weaponry, eavesdropping, and teleme-try; but right now the most vital weapon in its arsenal may well be the art of interrogation. To counter an enemy who relies on stealth and surprise, the most valuable tool is information, and often the only source of that information is the enemy himself. Men like Sheikh Mohammed who have been taken alive in this war are classic candidates for the most cunning practices of this dark art. Intellectual, sophisticated, deeply religious, and well trained, they present a perfect challenge for the interrogator. Getting at the information they possess could allow us to thwart major attacks, unravel their organization, and save thousands of lives. They and their situation pose one of the strongest arguments in modern times for the use of torture.

Torture is repulsive. It is deliberate cruelty, a crude and ancient tool of political oppression. It is commonly used to terrorize people, or to wring confessions out of suspected criminals who may or may not be guilty. It is the classic shortcut for a lazy or incompetent investigator. Horrifying examples of torturers' handiwork are catalogued and publicized annually by Amnesty International, Human Rights Watch, and other organizations that battle such abuses worldwide. One cannot help sympathizing with the innocent, powerless victims showcased in their literature. But professional terrorists pose a harder question. They are lockboxes containing potentially life-saving information. Sheikh Mohammed has his own political and religious reasons for plotting mass murder, and there are those who would applaud his principled defiance in captivity. But we pay for his silence in blood.

The word "torture" comes from the Latin verb *torquere,* "to twist." *Webster's New World Dictionary* offers the following primary definition: "The inflicting of severe pain to force information and confession, get revenge, etc." Note the adjective "severe," which summons up images of the rack, thumbscrews, gouges, branding irons, burning pits, impaling devices, electric shock, and all the other devilish tools devised by human beings to mutilate and inflict pain on others. All manner of innovative cruelty is still commonplace, particularly in Central and South America, Africa, and the Middle East. Saddam Hussein's police force burned various marks into the foreheads of thieves and deserters, and routinely sliced tongues out of those whose words offended the state. In Sri Lanka prisoners are hung upside down and burned with hot irons. In China they are beaten with clubs and shocked with cattle prods. In India the police stick pins through the fingernails and fingers of prisoners. Maiming and physical abuse are legal in Somalia, Iran, Saudi Arabia, Nigeria,

Sudan, and other countries that practice *sharia*; the hands of thieves are lopped off, and women convicted of adultery may be stoned to death. Governments around the world continue to employ rape and mutilation, and to harm family members, including children, in order to extort confessions or information from those in captivity. Civilized people everywhere readily condemn these things.

Then there are methods that, some people argue, fall short of torture. Called "torture lite," these include sleep deprivation, exposure to heat or cold, the use of drugs to cause confusion, rough treatment (slapping, shoving, or shaking), forcing a prisoner to stand for days at a time or to sit in uncomfortable positions, and playing on his fears for himself and his family. Although excruciating for the victim, these tactics generally leave no permanent marks and do no lasting physical harm.

The Geneva Convention makes no distinction: it bans any mistreatment of prisoners. But some nations that are otherwise committed to ending brutality have employed torture lite under what they feel are justifiable circumstances. In 1987 Israel attempted to codify a distinction between torture, which was banned, and "moderate physical pressure," which was permitted in special cases. Indeed, some police officers, soldiers, and intelligence agents who abhor "severe" methods believe that banning all forms of physical pressure would be dangerously naive. Few support the use of physical pressure to extract confessions, especially because victims will often say anything (to the point of falsely incriminating themselves) to put an end to pain. But many veteran interrogators believe that the use of such methods to extract information is justified if it could save lives—whether by forcing an enemy soldier to reveal his army's battlefield positions or forcing terrorists to betray the details of ongoing plots. As these interrogators see it, the well-being of the captive must be weighed against the lives that might be saved by forcing him to talk. A method that produces life-saving information without doing lasting harm to anyone is not just preferable; it appears to be morally sound. Hereafter I will use "torture" to mean the more severe traditional outrages, and "coercion" to refer to torture lite, or moderate physical pressure.

· · ·

There is no clear count of suspected terrorists now in U.S. custody. About 680 were detained at Camp X-Ray, the specially constructed prison at Guantánamo, on the southeastern tip of Cuba. Most of these are now considered mere foot soldiers in the Islamist movement, swept up in Afghanistan during the swift rout of the Taliban. They come from forty-two different nations. Scores of other detainees, considered leaders, have been or are being held at various locations around the world: in Pakistan, Saudi Arabia, Egypt, Sudan, Syria, Jordan, Morocco, Yemen, Singapore, the Philippines, Thailand, and Iraq, where U.S. forces now hold the top echelon of Saddam Hussein's dismembered regime. Some detainees are in disclosed prisons, such as the facility at Bagram and a camp on the island of Diego Garcia. Others—upper-tier figures such as Sheikh Mohammed, Abu Zubaydah, Abd al-Rashim al-Nashiri, Ramzi bin al-Shibh, and Tawfiq bin Attash—are being held at undisclosed locations.

It is likely that some captured terrorists' names and arrests have not yet been revealed; people may be held for months before their "arrests" are staged. Once a top-level suspect is publicly known to be in custody, his intelligence value falls. His organization scatters, altering its plans, disguises, cover stories, codes, tactics, and communication methods. The maximum opportunity for intelligence gathering comes in the first hours after an arrest, before others in a group can possibly know that their walls have been breached. Keeping an arrest quiet for days or weeks prolongs this opportunity. If March 1 was in fact the day of Sheikh Mohammed's capture, then the cameras and the headlines were an important intelligence failure. The arrest of the senior al-Qaeda figure Abu Anas Liby, in Sudan in February of 2002, was not made public until a month later, when U.S. efforts to have him transferred to custody in Egypt were leaked to the *Sunday Times* of London. So, again, there is no exact count of suspected terrorists in custody. In September of last year, testifying before the House and Senate Intelligence Committees, Cofer Black, the State Department's coordinator for counterterrorism, said that the number who have been detained was about 3,000.

All these suspects are questioned rigorously, but those in the top ranks get the full coercive treatment. And if official and unofficial government reports are to be believed, the methods work. In report after report hard-core terrorist leaders are said to be either cooperating or, at the very least, providing some information—not just vague statements but detailed, verifiable, useful intelligence. In late March, *Time* reported that Sheikh Mohammed had "given U.S. interrogators the names and descriptions of about a dozen key al-Qaeda operatives believed to be plotting terrorist attacks on America and other western countries" and had "added crucial details to the descriptions of other suspects and filled in important gaps in what U.S. intelligence knows about al-Qaeda's practices." In June, news reports suggested that Sheikh Mohammed was discussing operational planning with his captors and had told interrogators that al-Qaeda did not work with Saddam Hussein. And according to a report in June of last year, Abu Zubaydah, who is said to be held in solitary confinement somewhere in Pakistan, provided information that helped foil a plot to detonate a radioactive bomb in the United States.

Secretary of Defense Donald Rumsfeld said in September of last year that interrogation of captured terrorist leaders had yielded "an awful lot of information" and had "made life an awful lot more difficult for an awful lot of folks." Indeed, if press accounts can be believed, these captured Islamist fanatics are all but dismantling their own secret organization. According to published reports, Sheikh Mohammed was found in part because of information from bin al-Shibh, whose arrest had been facilitated by information from Abu Zubaydah. Weeks after the sheikh's capture Bush Administration officials and intelligence experts told *The Washington Post* that the al-Qaeda deputy's "cooperation under interrogation" had given them hopes of arresting or killing the rest of the organization's top leadership.

How much of this can be believed? Are such reports wishful thinking, or deliberate misinformation? There is no doubt that intelligence agencies have scored big victories over al-Qaeda in the past two years, but there is no way to corroborate these stories. President Bush himself warned, soon after 9/11, that in war mode his Administration would closely guard intelligence sources and methods. It would make sense to claim that top al-Qaeda leaders had caved under questioning even if they had not. Hard men like Abu Zubaydah, bin al-Shibh, and Sheikh Mohammed are widely admired in parts of the world. Word that they had been broken would demoralize their followers, and would encourage lower-ranking members of their organization to talk; if their leaders had given in, why should they hold out?

To some, all this jailhouse cooperation smells concocted. "I doubt we're getting very much out of them, despite what you read in the press," says a former CIA agent with experience in South America. "Everybody in the world knows that if you are arrested by the United States, nothing bad will happen to you."

Bill Cowan, a retired Marine lieutenant colonel who conducted interrogations in Vietnam, says, "I don't see the proof in the pudding. If you had a top leader like Mohammed talking, someone who could presumably lay out the whole organization for you, I think we'd be seeing sweeping arrests in several different countries at the same time. Instead what we see is an arrest here, then a few months later an arrest there."

These complaints are all from people who have no qualms about using torture to get information from men like Sheikh

Mohammed. Their concern is that merely using coercion amounts to handling terrorists with kid gloves. But the busts of al-Qaeda cells worldwide, and the continuing roundup of al-Qaeda leaders, suggest that some of those in custody are being made to talk. This worries people who campaign against all forms of torture. They believe that the rules are being ignored. Responding to rumors of mistreatment at Bagram and Guantánamo, Amnesty International and Human Rights Watch have written letters and met with Bush Administration officials. They haven't been able to learn much.

Is the United States torturing prisoners? Three inmates have died in U.S. custody in Afghanistan, and reportedly eighteen prisoners at Guantánamo have attempted suicide; one prisoner there survived after hanging himself but remains unconscious and is not expected to revive. Shah Muhammad, a twenty-year-old Pakistani who was held at Camp X-Ray for eighteen months, told me that he repeatedly tried to kill himself in despair. "They were driving me crazy," he said. Public comments by Administration officials have fueled further suspicion. An unnamed intelligence official told *The Wall Street Journal*, "What's needed is a little bit of smacky-face. Some al-Qaeda just need some extra encouragement." Then there was the bravado of Cofer Black, the counterterrorism coordinator, in his congressional testimony last year. A pudgy, balding, round-faced man with glasses, who had served with the CIA before taking the State Department position, Black refused to testify behind a screen, as others had done. "The American people need to see my face," he said. "I want to look the American people in the eye." By way of presenting his credentials he said that in 1995 a group of "Osama bin Laden's thugs" were caught planning "to kill me."

Describing the clandestine war, Black said, "This is a highly classified area. All I want to say is that there was 'before 9/11' and 'after 9/11.' After 9/11 the gloves came off." He was referring to the overall counterterrorism effort, but in the context of detained captives the line was suggestive. A story in December of 2002 by the *Washington Post* reporters Dana Priest and Barton Gellman described the use of "stress and duress" techniques at Bagram, and an article in *The New York Times* in March described the mistreatment of prisoners there. That month Irene Kahn, the secretary-general of Amnesty International, wrote a letter of protest to President Bush.

> The treatment alleged falls clearly within the category of torture and other cruel, inhuman or degrading treatment or punishment which is absolutely prohibited under international law . . . [We] urge the US government to instigate a full, impartial inquiry into the treatment of detainees at the Bagram base and to make the findings public. We further urge the government to make a clear public statement that torture and other cruel, inhuman or degrading treatment of suspects in its custody will not be tolerated under any circumstances, and that anyone found to have engaged in abuses will be brought to justice.

In June, at the urging of Amnesty and other groups, President Bush reaffirmed America's opposition to torture, saying, "I call on all governments to join with the United States and the community of law-abiding nations in prohibiting, investigating, and prosecuting all acts of torture . . . and we are leading this fight by example." A slightly more detailed response had been prepared two months earlier by the Pentagon's top lawyer, William J. Haynes II, in a letter to Kenneth Roth, the executive director of Human Rights Watch. (My requests for interviews on this subject with the Pentagon, the White House, and the State Department were declined.) Haynes wrote,

> The United States questions enemy combatants to elicit information they may possess that could help the coalition

win the war and forestall further terrorist attacks upon the citizens of the United States and other countries. As the President reaffirmed recently to the United Nations High Commissioner for Human Rights, United States policy condemns and prohibits torture. When questioning enemy combatants, US personnel are required to follow this policy and applicable laws prohibiting torture.

As we will see, Haynes's choice of words was careful—and telling. The human-rights groups and the Administration are defining terms differently. Yet few would argue that getting Sheikh Mohammed to talk doesn't serve the larger interests of mankind. So before tackling the moral and legal questions raised by interrogation, perhaps the first question should be, What works?

Acid Tests and Monkey Orgasms

The quest for surefire methods in the art of interrogation has been long, ugly, and generally fruitless. Nazi scientists experimented on concentration-camp inmates, subjecting them to extremes of hot and cold, to drugs, and to raw pain in an effort to see what combination of horrors would induce cooperation. The effort produced a long list of dead and maimed, but no reliable ways of getting people to talk.

In 1953 John Lilly, of the National Institute of Mental Health, discovered that by placing electrodes inside the brain of a monkey, he could stimulate pain, anger, fear—and pleasure. He placed one inside the brain of a male monkey and gave the monkey a switch that would trigger an immediate erection and orgasm. (The monkey hit the switch roughly every three minutes, thus confirming the gender stereotype.) The idea of manipulating a brain from the inside promptly attracted the interest of the CIA, which foresaw, among other things, the possibility of sidestepping a reluctant informant's self-defenses. But Lilly dropped the line of research, pointing out that merely inserting the electrodes caused brain damage.

These experiments and others are recorded in detail in John Marks's somewhat overheated book *The Search for the "Manchurian Candidate": The CIA and Mind Control* (1979) and in George Andrews's book M*KULTRA: The CIA's Top Secret Program in Human Experimentation and Behavior Modification* (2001). Andrews summarized information revealed in congressional probes of CIA excesses. Marks was more sensational. In the spirit of the times, he tended to interpret the Agency's interest in behavioral science, hypnosis, and mind-altering drugs as a scheme to create zombie-like secret agents, although it appears that the real goal was to make people talk.

There was a lot of hope for LSD. Discovered by accident in a Swiss pharmaceutical lab in 1943, it produced powerful mind-altering effects in very small doses. It was more powerful than mescaline, which had its own adherents, and could easily be administered without the victim's knowledge, slipped into food or drink. The hope was that an informant in such an artificially open-minded state would lose sight of his goals and sense of loyalty and become putty in the hands of a skilled interrogator. Studies on LSD began at a number of big universities, and as word of the drug's properties spread, it started to attract a broad range of interest. Theologians, scholars, and mental-health workers visited the Maryland Psychiatric Research Institute, just outside Baltimore, to turn on and tune in, and similar programs began in Boston, New York, Chicago, and other cities. Almost twenty years ago I interviewed a number of those who took part in these experiments; all of them were apparently motivated only by professional curiosity. The CIA's role was kept quiet. But the most notorious of its efforts at LSD experimentation involved Frank Olson, an Army scientist who was dosed without his knowledge and subsequently committed suicide. The U.S. Army conducted field tests of LSD as an interrogation tool in 1961 (Operation Third Chance), dosing nine foreigners and an American soldier named James Thornwell, who had been accused of stealing classified documents. Thornwell subsequently sued the government and was awarded $650,000. Most of these efforts led to little more than scandal and embarrassment. The effects of the drug were too wildly unpredictable to make it useful in interrogation. It tended to amplify the sorts of feelings that inhibit cooperation. Fear and anxiety turned into terrifying hallucinations and fantasies, which made it more difficult to elicit secrets, and added a tinge of unreality to whatever information was divulged. LSD may have unlocked the mind in some esoteric sense, but secrets tended to ride out the trip intact.

Experiments were also conducted with heroin and psychedelic mushrooms, neither of which reliably delivered up the secrets of men's souls. Indeed, drugs seemed to enhance some people's ability to be deceptive. Scopolamine held out some early hope, but it often induced hallucinations. Barbiturates were promising, and were already used effectively by psychiatrists to help with therapy. Some researchers advocated electroshock treatments, to, as it were, blast information from a subject's brain. Drugs such as marijuana, alcohol, and sodium pentothal can lower inhibitions, but they do not erase deep-seated convictions. And the more powerful the drug, the less reliable the testimony. According to my intelligence sources, drugs are today sometimes used to assist in critical interrogations, and the preferred ones are methamphetamines tempered with barbiturates and cannabis. These tools can help, but they are only as effective as the interrogator.

Better results seemed to come from sensory deprivation and solitary confinement. For most people severe sensory deprivation quickly becomes misery; the effects were documented in the notorious 1963 CIA manual on interrogation, called the *Kubark Manual*. It remains the most comprehensive and detailed explanation in print of coercive methods of questioning—given the official reluctance to discuss these matters or put them in writing, because such things tend to be both politically embarrassing and secret. Treatises on interrogation in the public domain are written primarily for police departments and address the handling of criminal defendants—with all the necessary concern for protecting a defendant's rights. Unearthed in 1997, through the Freedom of Information Act, by the *Baltimore Sun* reporters Gary Cohn, Ginger Thompson, and Mark Matthews, the *Kubark Manual* reveals the CIA's insights into the tougher methods employed by the military and intelligence agencies. Much of the practice and theory it details is also found unchanged in the 1983 *Human Resource Exploitation Training Manual,* usually known as the *Honduras Manual*—which the CIA had tried to soften with a hasty edit prior to releasing it. The manual was shaken loose at the same time by Cohn and Thompson. And the more summary discussions of technique in later U.S. Army manuals on interrogation, including the most recent, also clearly echo *Kubark.* If there is a bible of interrogation, it is the *Kubark Manual.*

The manual cites a 1954 study at the National Institute of Mental Health (again led by John Lilly) in which two volunteers attempted to see how long they could stay suspended in water wearing blackout masks and hearing only the sound of their own breathing and "some faint sounds of water from the piping." Neither lasted more than three hours. According to the study, "Both passed quickly from normally directed thinking through a tension resulting from unsatisfied hunger for sensory stimuli and concentration upon the few available sensations to provide reveries and fantasies and eventually to visual imagery somewhat resembling hallucinations." John Marks reported in his book that in a similar experiment a volunteer kicked his way out of a sensory-deprivation box after an hour of tearful pleas for release had been ignored.

The summary of another experiment concluded,

The results confirmed earlier findings. 1) The deprivation of sensory stimuli induces stress; 2) the stress becomes unbearable for most subjects; 3) the subject has a growing need for physical and social stimuli; and 4) some subjects progressively lose touch with reality, focus inwardly, and produce delusions, hallucinations, and other pathological effects.

But these effects didn't trouble everyone. One man's misery is another man's mind-altering experience. Some people found they liked sensory-deprivation tanks; indeed, in later years people would pay for a session in one. Lilly was fond of injecting himself with LSD and then closing himself off in his tank—a series of experiments made famous in the 1980 film *Altered States*. In Canada a scientist put a fifty-two-year-old woman identified only as Mary C. in a sensory-deprivation chamber for thirty-five days. She never asked to be let out.

One thing all these experiments made clear was that no matter what drugs or methods were applied, the results varied from person to person. So another major area of inquiry involved trying to define certain broad personality types and discover what methods would work best for each. The groups were ridiculously general—the *Kubark Manual* lists "The Orderly-Obstinate Character," "The Greedy-Demanding Character," "The Anxious, Self-Centered Character"—and the prescriptions for questioning them tended to vary little and were sometimes silly (the advice for questioning an Orderly-Obstinate Character recommends doing so in a room that is especially neat). The categories were useless. Everyone, and every situation, is different; some people begin a day greedy and demanding and end it orderly and obstinate.

The one constant in effective interrogation, it seems, is the interrogator. And some interrogators are just better at it than others.

"You want a good interrogator?" Jerry Giorgio, the New York Police Department's legendary third-degree man, asks. "Give me somebody who people like, and who likes people. Give me somebody who knows how to put people at ease. Because the more comfortable they are, the more they talk, and the more they talk, the more trouble they're in—the harder it is to sustain a lie."

Though science has made contributions, interrogation remains more art than science. Like any other subject, Sheikh Mohammed presented his interrogators with a unique problem. The critical hub of a worldwide secret network, he had a potential road map in his head to the whole shadow world of *jihad*. If he could be made to talk, to reveal even a few secrets, what an intelligence bonanza that would be! Here was a man who lived to further his cause by whatever means, who saw himself as morally, spiritually, and intellectually superior to the entire infidel Western world, a man for whom capitulation meant betraying not just his friends and his cherished cause but his very soul.

What makes a man like that decide to talk?

Alligator Clips

Bill Cowan spent three and a half years fighting the war in Vietnam. He was a young Marine captain assigned to the Rung Sat Special Zone, a putrid swamp that begins just south of Saigon. Miles and miles of thick, slurping mud that swallowed soldiers to their waists, it is populated by galaxies of mosquitoes and other biting insects, snakes, crocodiles, and stands of rotting mangrove. It is intersected by the saltwater rivers of the Mekong Delta, and features occasional stretches of flat, open farmland. The Marines knew that several battalions of Vietcong were in the Rung Sat. The enemy would lie low, building strength, and then launch surprise attacks on South Vietnamese or U.S. troops. The soldiers in Cowan's unit played cat-and-mouse with an enemy that melted away at their approach.

So when he captured a Vietcong soldier who could warn of ambushes and lead them to hidden troops but who refused to speak, wires were attached to the man's scrotum with alligator clips and electricity was cranked out of a 110-volt generator.

"It worked like a charm," Cowan told me. "The minute the crank started to turn, he was ready to talk. We never had to do more than make it clear we could deliver a jolt. It was the fear more than the pain that made them talk."

Fear works. It is more effective than any drug, tactic, or torture device. According to unnamed scientific studies cited by the *Kubark Manual* (it is frightening to think what these experiments might have been), most people cope with pain better than they think they will. As people become more familiar with pain, they become conditioned to it. Those who have suffered more physical pain than others—from being beaten frequently as a child, for example, or suffering a painful illness—may adapt to it and come to fear it less. So once interrogators resort to actual torture, they are apt to lose ground.

"The threat of coercion usually weakens or destroys resistance more effectively than coercion itself," the manual says.

> The threat to inflict pain, for example, can trigger fears more damaging than the immediate sensation of pain . . . Sustained long enough, a strong fear of anything vague or unknown induces regression, whereas the materialization of the fear, the infliction of some form of punishment, is likely to come as a relief. The subject finds that he can hold out, and his resistances are strengthened.

Furthermore, if a prisoner is subjected to pain after other methods have failed, it is a signal that the interrogation process may be nearing an end. "He may then decide that if he can just hold out against this final assault, he will win the struggle and his freedom," the manual concludes. Even if severe pain does elicit information, it can be false, which is particularly troublesome to interrogators seeking intelligence rather than a confession. Much useful information is time-sensitive, and running down false leads or arresting innocents wastes time.

By similar logic, the manual discourages threatening a prisoner with death. As a tactic "it is often found to be worse than useless," the manual says, because the sense of despair it induces can make the prisoner withdraw into depression—or, in some cases, see an honorable way out of his predicament.

Others disagree.

"I'll tell you how to make a man talk," a retired Special Forces officer says. "You shoot the man to his left and the man to his right. Then you can't shut him up."

John Dunn found the truth to be a little more complicated. In his case the threat of execution forced him to bend but not break. He was a U.S. Army intelligence officer in the Lam Dong Province of Vietnam, in March of 1968, when he was captured by the Vietcong. He and other captives were marched for weeks to a prison camp in the jungle, where initially he was treated quite well. The gentle treatment lulled him, Dunn says, and contributed to his shock when, in his first interrogation session, he was calmly told, "We don't need you. We did not sign the Geneva Convention, and you are not considered a prisoner of war anyway. You are a war criminal. If you don't cooperate with us, you will be executed."

He was sent back to his hammock to think things over. Dunn had never considered himself a superaggressive soldier, a "warrior type," and had never imagined himself in such a situation. His training for captivity had been basic. He had been instructed to tell his captors only his name, rank, and serial number. Anything beyond that was considered a breach of duty—a betrayal of his country, his role as a soldier, and his personal honor. Faced with death, Dunn weighed his devotion to this simple code. He felt it was unrealistic. He wrestled to come up with a solution that would keep him alive without completely compromising his dignity. He figured there were certain details about his life and service that were not worth dying to protect. Some things needed to be kept secret, and others did not. Struggling with shame, he decided to answer any questions that did not intrude on that closed center of secrecy. He would not tell them he was an intelligence officer. ("Not out of patriotism," he says. "Out of fear, strictly self-preservation.") He would not reveal accurate details about fortifications around his company's headquarters, in Di Linh. He would not tell them about upcoming plans, such as the Phoenix Program (an assassination program targeting Vietcong village leaders), and above all, he would not make any public statements. But he would talk. The threat of execution in his case was not "worse than useless." It shook Dunn to his core.

In a subsequent session he talked, but not enough to satisfy his captors. Again and again he refused to make a public statement. Starved, sore, and still frightened, Dunn was told, "You will be executed. After dark."

When the sun set, the interrogator, his aide, and the camp commander came for Dunn with a group of soldiers. They unlocked his chain, and he carried it as they led him away from the encampment into the jungle. They stopped in front of a pit they had dug for his grave and put a gun to his head. The interrogator gave him one more chance to agree to make a statement.

"No," Dunn said. He had gone as far as he was willing to go.

"Why do you want to die?" he was asked.

"If I must, I must," Dunn said. He felt resigned. He waited to be killed.

"You will not be executed," the camp commander said abruptly, and that was that.

Judging by Dunn's experience, the threat of death may be valuable to an interrogator as a way of loosening up a determined subject. But, as with pain, the most important factor is fear. An unfrightened prisoner makes an unlikely informer.

·   ·   ·

If there is an archetype of the modern interrogator, it is Michael Koubi. The former chief interrogator for Israel's General Security Services, or Shabak, Koubi probably has more experience than anyone else in the world in the interrogation of hostile Arab prisoners, some of them confirmed terrorists and religious fanatics—men, he says, "whose hatred of the Jews is unbridgeable." He has blue eyes in a crooked face: time, the greatest caricaturist of all, has been at work on it for more than sixty years, and has produced one that is lean, browned, deeply lined, and naturally concave. His considerable nose has been broken twice, and now ends well to the right of where it begins, giving him a look that is literally off-center. His wisdom, too, is slightly off-center, because Koubi has been given a uniquely twisted perspective on human nature. For decades he has been experimenting with captive human beings, cajoling, tricking, hurting, threatening, and spying on them, steadily upping the pressure, looking for cracks at the seams.

I met Koubi at his home on the beach in Ashkelon, just a short drive north of the border with the Gaza Strip, in whose prisons he worked for much of his career. He is comfortably retired from his Shabak job now, a grandfather three times over, and works for the municipal Inspection and Sanitation Department. There are still many things he is not free to discuss, but he is happy to talk about his methods. He is very proud of his skills, among them an ability to speak Arabic so fluently that he can adopt a multitude of colloquial flavors. Koubi came to his career as an interrogator through his love of language. He grew up speaking Hebrew, Yiddish, and Arabic, and he studied Arabic in high school, working to master its idiom and slang. He also had a knack for reading the body language and facial expressions of his subjects, and for sensing a lie. He is a skilled actor who could alternately befriend or intimidate a subject, sometimes turning on a dime. Blending these skills with the tricks he had learned over the years for manipulating people, Koubi didn't just question his subjects, he orchestrated their emotional surrender.

To many, including many in Israel, Koubi and the unit he headed are an outrage. The games they played and the tactics they employed are seen as inhumane, illegal, and downright evil. It is hard to picture this pleasant grandfather as the leader of a unit that critics accuse of being brutal; but then, charm has always been as important to interrogation work as toughness or cruelty—perhaps more important. Koubi says that only in rare instances did he use force to extract information from his subjects; in most cases it wasn't necessary.

"People change when they get to prison," Koubi says. "They may be heroes outside, but inside they change. The conditions are different. People are afraid of the unknown. They are afraid of being tortured, of being held for a long time. Try to see what it is like to sit with a hood over your head for four hours, when you are hungry and tired and afraid, when you are isolated from everything and have no clue what is going on." When the captive believes that *anything* could happen—torture, execution, indefinite imprisonment, even the persecution of his loved ones—the interrogator can go to work.

Under pressure, he says, nearly everyone looks out first and foremost for No. 1. What's more, a very large part of who a man is depends on his circumstances. No matter who he is before his arrest, his sense of self will blur in custody. Isolation, fear, and deprivation force a man to retreat, to reorient himself, and to reorder his priorities. For most men, Koubi says, the hierarchy of loyalty under stress is 1) self, 2) group, 3) family, 4) friends. In other words, even the most dedicated terrorist (with very rare exceptions), when pushed hard enough, will act to preserve and protect himself at the expense of anyone or anything else. "There's an old Arab saying," Koubi says. "'Let one hundred mothers cry, but not my mother—but better my mother than me.'"

With older men the priorities shift slightly. In middle age the family often overtakes the group (the cause) to become the second most important loyalty. Young men tend to be fiercely committed and ambitious, but older men—even men with deeply held convictions, men admired and emulated by their followers—tend to have loves and obligations that count for more. Age frays idealism, slackens zeal, and cools ferocity. Abstractions lose ground to wife, children, and grandchildren. "Notice that the leaders of Hamas do not send their own sons and daughters, and their own grandchildren, to blow themselves up," Koubi says.

So it is often the top-level men, like Sheikh Mohammed, who are easier to crack. Koubi believes that having the al-Qaeda leader's wife and children in custody gives his interrogators powerful leverage. The key is to find a man's weak point and exploit it.

For Koubi the three critical ingredients of that process are preparation, investigation, and theater.

Preparing a subject for interrogation means softening him up. Ideally, he has been pulled from his sleep—like Sheikh Mohammed—early in the morning, roughly handled, bound, hooded (a coarse, dirty, smelly sack serves the purpose perfectly), and kept waiting in discomfort, perhaps naked in a cold, wet room, forced to stand or to sit in an uncomfortable position. He may be kept awake for days prior to questioning, isolated and ill-fed. He may be unsure where he is, what time of day it is, how long he has been or will be held. If he is wounded, as Abu Zubaydah was, pain medication may be withheld; it is one thing to cause pain, another to refuse to relieve it.

Mousa Khoury, a Palestinian businessman, knows the drill all too well. A slender thirty-four-year-old man with a black goatee and thinning hair, he is bitter about the Israeli occupation and his experiences in custody. He has been arrested and interrogated six times by Israeli forces. He was once held for seventy-one days.

"My hands were cuffed behind my back, and a potato sack was over my head," he says. "My legs were cuffed to a tiny chair. The chair's base is ten centimeters by twenty centimeters. The back is ten centimeters by ten centimeters. It is hard wood. The front legs are shorter than the back ones, so you are forced to slide forward in it, only your hands are bound in the back. If you sit back, the back of the chair digs into the small of your back. If you slump forward, you are forced to hang by your hands. It is painful. They will take you to the toilet only after screaming a request one hundred times." He could think about only one thing: how to make the treatment stop. "Your thoughts go back and forth and back and forth, and you can no longer have a normal stream of consciousness," he says.

Preparing an interrogator means arming him beforehand with every scrap of information about his subject. U.S. Army interrogation manuals suggest preparing a thick "dummy file" when little is known, to make it appear that the interrogator knows more than he does. Nothing rattles a captive more than to be confronted with a fact he thought was secret or obscure. It makes the interrogator seem powerful, all-knowing. A man's sense of importance is wounded, and he is slower to lie, because he thinks he might be caught at it. There are many ways that scraps of information—gathered by old-fashioned legwork or the interrogation of a subject's associates—can be leveraged by a clever interrogator into something new. Those scraps might be as simple as knowing the names of a man's siblings or key associates, the name of his girlfriend, or a word or phrase that has special meaning to his group. Uncovering privileged details diminishes the aura of a secret society, whether it is a social club, a terrorist cell, or a military unit. Joining such a group makes an individual feel distinct, important, and superior, and invests even the most mundane of his activities with meaning. An interrogator who penetrates that secret society, unraveling its shared language, culture, history, customs, plans, and pecking order, can diminish its hold on even the staunchest believer. Suspicion that a trusted comrade has betrayed the group—or the subject himself—undermines the sense of a secretly shared purpose and destiny. Armed with a few critical details, a skilled interrogator can make a subject doubt the value of information he has been determined to withhold. It is one thing to suffer in order to protect a secret, quite another to cling to a secret that is already out.

This is how a well-briefed interrogator breaches a group's defenses.

•   •   •

Koubi believes that the most important skill for an interrogator is to know the prisoner's language. Working through interpreters is at best a necessary evil. Language is at the root of all social connections, and plays a critical role in secret societies like Hamas and al-Qaeda. A shared vocabulary or verbal shorthand helps to cement the group.

"I try to create the impression that I use his mother tongue even better than he does," Koubi says. "No accent, no mistaken syntax. I speak to him like his best friend speaks to him. I might ask him a question about a certain word or sentence or expression, how it is used in his culture, and then demonstrate that I know more about it than he does. This embarrasses him very much."

Once a prisoner starts to talk, rapid follow-up is needed to sort fact from fiction, so that the interrogator knows whether his subject is being cooperative or evasive, and can respond accordingly. Interrogation sessions should be closely observed (many rooms designed for this purpose have one-way mirrors), and in a well-run unit a subject's words can sometimes be checked out before the session is over. Being caught so quickly in a lie demonstrates the futility of playing games with the interrogator, and strengthens his hand. It shames and rattles the subject. When information checks out, the interrogator can home in for more details and open up new avenues of exploration.

Religious extremists are the hardest cases. They ponder in their own private space, performing a kind of self-hypnosis. They are usually well educated. Their lives are financially and emotionally tidy. They tend to live in an ascetic manner, and to look down on nonbelievers. They tend to be physically and mentally strong, and not to be influenced by material things—by either the incentives or the disincentives available in prison. Often the rightness of their cause trumps all else, so they can commit any outrage—lie, cheat, steal, betray, kill—without remorse. Yet under sufficient duress, Koubi says, most men of even this kind will eventually break—most, but not all. Some cannot be broken.

"They are very rare," he says, "but in some cases the more aggressive you get, and the worse things get, the more these men will withdraw into their own world, until you cannot reach them."

Mousa Khoury, the Palestinian businessman who has been interrogated six times, claims that he never once gave in to his jailers. Koubi has no particular knowledge of Khoury's case, but he smiles his crooked, knowing smile and says, "If someone you meet says he was held by our forces and did not cooperate at all, you can bet he is lying. In some cases men who are quite famous for their toughness were the most helpful to us in captivity."

Interrogation is also highly theatrical. The *Kubark Manual* is very particular about setting the stage.

The room in which the interrogation is to be conducted should be free of distractions. The colors of the walls, ceiling, rugs, and furniture should not be startling. Pictures should be missing or dull. Whether the furniture should include a desk depends not upon the interrogator's convenience but rather upon the subject's anticipated reaction to the connotations of superiority and officialdom. A plain table may be preferable. An overstuffed chair for the use of the interrogatee is sometimes preferable to a straight-backed, wooden chair because if he is made to stand for a lengthy period or is otherwise deprived of physical comfort, the contrast is intensified and increased disorientation results.

The manual goes on to recommend lighting that shines brightly in the face of the subject and leaves the interrogator in shadow. There should be no phone or any other means of contact with those outside the room, to enhance concentration and the subject's feeling of confinement. In Koubi's experience it was sometimes helpful to have associates loudly stage a torture or beating session in the next room. In old CIA interrogation training, according to Bill Wagner, a retired agent, it was recommended that mock executions take place outside the interrogation room.

A good interrogator is a deceiver. One of Koubi's tricks was to walk into a hallway lined with twenty recently arrested, hooded, uncomfortable, hungry, and fearful men, all primed for interrogation, and shout commandingly, "Okay, who wants to cooperate with me?" Even if no hands, or only one hand, went up, he would say to the hooded men, "Okay, good. Eight of you. I'll start with you, and the others will have to wait." Believing that others have capitulated makes doing so oneself much easier. Often, after this trick, many of the men in the hall would cooperate. Men are herd animals, and prefer to go with the flow, especially when moving in the other direction is harsh.

In one case Koubi had information suggesting that two men he was questioning were secretly members of a terrorist cell, and knew of an impending attack. They were tough men, rural farmers, very difficult to intimidate or pressure, and so far neither man had admitted anything under questioning. Koubi worked them over individually for hours. With each man he would start off by asking friendly questions and then grow angrier and angrier, accusing the subject of withholding something. He would slap him, knock him off his chair, set guards on him, and then intervene to pull them off. Then he would put the subject back in the chair and offer him a cigarette, lightening the mood. "Let him see the difference between the two atmospheres, the hostile one and the friendly one," Koubi says. Neither man budged.

Finally Koubi set his trap. He announced to one of the men

that his interrogation was over. The man's associate, hooded, was seated in the hallway outside the room. "We are going to release you," Koubi said. "We are pleased with your cooperation. But first you must do something for me. I am going to ask you a series of questions, just a formality, and I need you to answer 'Yes' in a loud, clear voice for the recorder." Then, in a voice loud enough for the hooded man outside in the hall to hear, but soft enough so that he couldn't make out exactly what was being said, Koubi read off a long list of questions, reviewing the prisoner's name, age, marital status, date of capture, length of detainment, and so forth. These were regularly punctuated by the prisoner's loud and cooperative "Yes." The charade was enough to convince the man in the hall that his friend had capitulated.

Koubi dismissed the first man and brought in the second. "There's no more need for me to question you," Koubi said. "Your friend has confessed the whole thing." He offered the second prisoner a cigarette and gave him a good meal. He told him that the information provided by his friend virtually ensured that they would both be in prison for the rest of their lives . . . unless, he said, the second prisoner could offer him something, anything, that would dispose the court to leniency in his case. Convinced that his friend had already betrayed them both, the second prisoner acted promptly to save himself. "If you want to save Israeli lives, go immediately," he told Koubi. "My friends went with a car to Yeshiva Nehalim [a religious school]. They are going to kidnap a group of students . . ." The men were found in Erez, and the operation was foiled.

There are other methods of keeping a prisoner confused and off balance, such as rapidly firing questions at him, cutting off his responses in mid-sentence, asking the same questions over and over in different order, and what the manual calls the "Silent" technique, in which the interrogator "says nothing to the source, but looks him squarely in the eye, preferably with a slight smile on his face." The manual advises forcing the subject to break eye contact first. "The source will become nervous, begin to shift around in his chair, cross and recross his legs, and look away," the manual says. "When the interrogator is ready to break silence, he may do so with some quite nonchalant questions such as 'You planned this operation a long time, didn't you? Was it your idea?'"

Then there is "Alice in Wonderland."

> The aim of the Alice in Wonderland or confusion technique is to confound the expectations and conditioned reactions of the interrogatee . . . The confusion technique is designed not only to obliterate the familiar but to replace it with the weird . . . Sometimes two or more questions are asked simultaneously. Pitch, tone, and volume of the interrogators' voices are unrelated to the import of the questions. No pattern of questions and answers is permitted to develop, nor do the questions themselves relate logically to each other.

If this technique is pursued patiently, the manual says, the subject will start to talk "just to stop the flow of babble which assails him."

Easily the most famous routine is "Good Cop/Bad Cop," in which one interrogator becomes the captive's persecutor and the other his friend. A lesser-known but equally effective technique is "Pride and Ego," "Ego Up/Ego Down," or (as the more pretentious *Kubark Manual* puts it) "Spinoza and Mortimer Snerd," in which the "Ego Down" part involves repeatedly asking questions that the interrogator knows the subject cannot answer. The subject is continually berated or threatened ("How could you not know the answer to that?") and accused of withholding, until, at long last, he is asked a simple question that he can answer. An American POW subjected to this technique has said, "I know it seems strange now, but I was positively grateful to them when they switched to a topic I knew something about."

CIA psychologists have tried to develop an underlying theory for interrogation—namely, that the coercive methods induce a gradual "regression" of personality. But the theory is not convincing. Interrogation simply backs a man into a corner. It forces difficult choices, and dangles illusory avenues of escape.

A skillful interrogator knows which approach will best suit his subject; and just as he expertly applies stress, he continually opens up these avenues of escape or release. This means understanding what, at heart, is stopping a subject from cooperating. If it is ego, that calls for one method. If it is fear of reprisal or of getting into deeper trouble, another method might work best. For most captives a major incentive to keep quiet is simply pride. Their manhood is being tested, not just their loyalty and conviction. Allowing the subject to save face lowers the cost of capitulation, so an artful interrogator will offer persuasive rationales for giving in: others already have, or the information is already known. Drugs, if administered with the subject's knowledge, are helpful in this regard. If a subject believes that a particular drug or "truth serum" renders him helpless, he is off the hook. He cannot be held accountable for giving in. A study cited in George Andrews's book *MKULTRA* found that a placebo—a simple sugar pill—was as effective as an actual drug up to half of the time.

Koubi layered his deception so thick that his subjects never knew exactly when their interrogation ended. After questioning, captives usually spent time in a regular prison. The Israelis had bugged the prison with a system that was disguised well enough to *appear* hidden but not well enough to avoid discovery. In this way prisoners were led to believe that only certain parts of the prison were bugged. In fact, all of the prison was bugged. Conversations between prisoners could be overheard anywhere, and were closely monitored. They were an invaluable source of intelligence. Prisoners who could hold out through the most intense interrogation often let their guard down later when talking to comrades in jail.

To help such inadvertent confessions along, Koubi had yet another card to play. Whenever an interrogated subject was released to the general prison, after weeks of often grueling questioning, he was received with open arms by fellow Palestinians who befriended him and congratulated him for having endured interrogation. He was treated like a hero. He was fed, nursed, even celebrated. What he didn't know was that his happy new comrades were working for Koubi.

Koubi calls them "birdies." They were Palestinians who, offered an incentive such as an opportunity to settle with their families in another country, had agreed to cooperate with Shabak. Some days or weeks after welcoming the new prisoner into their ranks, easing his transition into the prison, they would begin to ask questions. They would debrief the prisoner on his interrogation sessions. They would say, "It is very important for those on the outside to know what you told the Israelis and what you *didn't* tell them. Tell us, and we will get the information to those on the outside who need to know." Even prisoners who had managed to keep important secrets from Koubi spilled them to his birdies.

"The amazing thing is that by now the existence of the birdies is well known," Koubi says, "and yet the system still works. People come out of interrogation, go into the regular prison, and then tell their darkest secrets. I don't know why it still works, but it does."

Big Daddy Uptown

Most professional interrogators work without the latitude given the CIA, the FBI, or the military in the war on terror. A policeman's subjects all have to be read their Miranda rights, and cops who physically threaten or abuse suspects—at least nowadays—may find themselves in jail. Jerry Giorgio, the legendary NYPD interrogator, has operated within these rules for nearly forty years. He may not know all the names of the CIA and military techniques, but he has probably seen most of them at work. Known as "Big Daddy Uptown," Giorgio now works for the New York County district attorney in a cramped office in Lower Manhattan that he shares with two others. He is a big man with a big voice, thinning gray hair, a broad belly, and wide, searching greenish-brown eyes. He is considered a wizard by his former colleagues in the NYPD. "All of us of a certain generation came out of the Jerry Giorgio school of interrogation," says John Bourges, a recently retired Manhattan homicide detective.

"Everybody knows the Good Cop/Bad Cop routine, right?" Giorgio says. "Well, I'm always the Good Cop. I don't work with a Bad Cop, either. Don't need it. You want to know the truth? The truth is—and this is important—everybody down deep *wants* to tell his or her story. It's true. No matter how damaging it is to them, no matter how important it is for them to keep quiet, they want to tell their story. If they feel guilty, they want to get it off their chest. If they feel justified in what they did, they want to explain themselves. I tell them, 'Hey, I know what you did and I can prove it. Now what are you going to do about it? If you show remorse, if you help me out, I'll go to bat for you.' I tell them that. And if you give them half a reason to do it, they'll tell you everything."

The most important thing is to get them talking. The toughest suspects are those who clam up and demand a lawyer right at the start. Giorgio believes that once he gets a suspect talking, the stream of words will eventually flow right to the truth. One murderer gave him three voluntary statements in a single day, each one signed, each one different, each one slightly closer to the truth.

The murderer was Carlos Martinez, a hulking former football player who in May of 1992 killed his girlfriend, Cheryl Maria Wright, and dumped her body in New York, right at the Coliseum overlook off the Henry Hudson Parkway. Since many young female murder victims are killed by their boyfriends, Giorgio started looking for Wright's. Martinez phoned Giorgio when he heard that the detective wanted to ask him some questions. Giorgio had pictures of Wright with Martinez, and in all the pictures the young beau had a giant head of Jheri curls. But he showed up in Giorgio's office bald. The detective was immediately more suspicious; a man who worries that somebody might have seen him commit a crime generally tries to alter his appearance.

Here is how Giorgio summarizes what turned out to be a very long and fruitful conversation:

"I was at home last night," Martinez said. "She did call me."

"Really, why?"

"She wanted me to pick her up. I told her, 'I'm watching the Mets game; I can't pick you up.'"

That was it. Giorgio acted very pleased with this statement, thanked Martinez, wrote it up, and asked the young man to sign it. Martinez did.

Then Giorgio stared at the statement and gave Martinez a quizzical look.

"You know, Carlos, something about this statement doesn't look right to me. You two had been going out for, what? Seven years? She calls you and asks you to pick her up at night where she's just gotten off work. It's not a safe neighborhood, and you tell her no? You mean a ball game on TV was more important to you?"

The question was cunning. The detective knew that Martinez was trying to make a good impression; he definitely didn't want to leave Giorgio with any unresolved issues to play in his mind. So it concerned him that his first statement didn't sound right. Giorgio's question also touched Martinez's sense of chivalry, an important quality for many Hispanic men. It wouldn't do to be seen as ungentlemanly. Here was a young woman who had just been brutally killed. How would it look to her family and friends if he admitted that she had called and asked him for a ride and he had left her to her fate—for a ball game on TV? The question also subtly suggested an out: The neighborhood wasn't safe. People got hurt or killed in that neighborhood all the time. Maybe

Martinez could admit that he had seen Cheryl on the night of the murder without directly implicating himself. No one ever accused the former footballer of being especially bright. He rose to Giorgio's bait immediately.

He said, "Jerry, let me tell you what really happened." ("Note," Giorgio says proudly, "already I'm *Jerry*!") Martinez now said that he had left his place to pick Wright up after work, but they had gotten into an argument. "She got mad at me and told me she didn't need a ride, so I waited until she got on the bus, and then I left." ("Look, now he's the picture of chivalry!" Giorgio says happily.)

"Let me take that down," Giorgio said, again acting pleased with the statement. He wrote it out neatly and asked Martinez to look it over and sign it. Martinez did.

Again Giorgio squinted at the paper. "You know, Carlos, something is still not right here. Cheryl was a strikingly beautiful girl. People who saw her remembered her. She's taken that bus home from work many nights, and people on that bus know who she is. And you know what? Nobody who rode that bus saw her on it last night."

(This was, in Giorgio's words, "pure bullshit." He hadn't talked to anybody who rode that bus. "Sometimes you have to just take a chance," he says.)

Again Martinez looked troubled. He had not allayed the detective's suspicions. So he tried again. "Okay, okay," he said. "This is really it. Let me tell you what really happened. Cheryl called, and I left to pick her up, but I ran into a friend of mine—I can't tell you his name—and we picked her up together. Then Cheryl and I got in this argument, a big fight. My friend got fed up. So we drove away, up Broadway to 181st Street, and stopped at the McDonald's there. He pulled out a gun, my friend, and he told me to get out of the car. 'Wait here,' he told me. 'I'm going to get rid of your problem.' Then he left. I waited. Then he came back. He said he had gotten rid of my problem."

Giorgio nodded happily and started to write up statement No. 3. He acted troubled over the fact that Martinez refused to name the friend, and the young man quickly coughed up a name. Giorgio's lieutenant, who had been watching the session through a one-way mirror, immediately got to work tracking down Martinez's friend. By the time the third statement had been written up, signed, and nestled neatly on top of the other two, Giorgio had a new problem to pose to Martinez: it seemed that his friend was in South Carolina, and had been for some time.

"We never did get to finish the fourth statement," Giorgio says. "Martinez's family had hired a lawyer, and he called the station forbidding us to further question his client." It was, of course, too late.

Captain Crunch Versus the Tree Huggers

On a spring morning in the offices of Amnesty International, in Washington, D.C., Alistair Hodgett and Alexandra Arriaga were briefing me on their organization's noble efforts to combat torture wherever in the world it is found. They are bright, pleasant, smart, committed, attractive young people, filled with righteous purpose. Decent people everywhere agree on this: torture is evil and indefensible.

But is it always?

I showed the two an article I had torn from that day's *New York Times,* which described the controversy over a tragic kidnapping case in Frankfurt, Germany. On September 27 of last year a Frankfurt law student kidnapped an eleven-year-old boy named Jakob von Metzler, whose smiling face appeared in a box alongside the story. The kidnapper had covered Jakob's mouth and nose with duct tape, wrapped the boy in plastic, and hidden him in a wooded area near a lake. The police captured the suspect when he tried to pick up ransom money, but the suspect wouldn't reveal where he had left the boy, who the police thought might still be alive. So the deputy police chief of Frankfurt, Wolfgang Daschner, told his subordinates to threaten the suspect with torture. According to the suspect, he was told that a "specialist" was being flown in who would "inflict pain on me of the sort I had never experienced." The suspect promptly told the police where he'd hidden Jakob, who, sadly, was found dead. The newspaper said that Daschner was under fire from Amnesty International, among other groups, for threatening torture.

"Under these circumstances," I asked, "do you honestly think it was wrong to even *threaten* torture?"

Hodgett and Arriaga squirmed in their chairs. "We recognize that there are difficult situations," said Arriaga, who is the group's director of government relations. "But we are opposed to torture under any and all circumstances, and threatening torture is inflicting mental pain. So we would be against it."

Few moral imperatives make such sense on a large scale but break down so dramatically in the particular. A way of sorting this one out is to consider two clashing sensibilities: the warrior and the civilian.

The civilian sensibility prizes above all else the rule of law. Whatever the difficulties posed by a particular situation, such as trying to find poor Jakob von Metzler before he suffocated, it sees abusive government power as a greater danger to society. Allowing an exception in one case (saving Jakob) would open the door to a greater evil.

The warrior sensibility requires doing what must be done to complete a mission. By definition, war exists because civil means have failed. What counts is winning, and preserving one's own troops. To a field commander in a combat zone, the life of an uncooperative enemy captive weighs very lightly against the lives of his own men. There are very few who, faced with a reluctant captive, would not in certain circumstances reach for the alligator clips, or something else.

"It isn't about getting mad, or payback," says Bill Cowan, the

Vietnam interrogator. "It's strictly business. Torturing people doesn't fit my moral compass at all. But I don't think there's much of a gray area. Either the guy has information you need or not. Either it's vital or it's not. You know which guys you need to twist."

The official statements by President Bush and William Haynes reaffirming the U.S. government's opposition to torture have been applauded by human-rights groups—but again, the language in them is carefully chosen. What does the Bush Administration mean by "torture"? Does it really share the activists' all-inclusive definition of the word? In his letter to the director of Human Rights Watch, Haynes used the term "enemy combatants" to describe those in custody. Calling detainees "prisoners of war" would entitle them to the protections of the Geneva Convention, which prohibits the "physical or mental torture" of POWs, and "any other form of coercion," even to the extent of "unpleasant or disadvantageous treatment of any kind." (In the contemptuous words of one military man, they "prohibit everything except three square meals, a warm bed, and access to a Harvard education.") Detainees who are American citizens have the advantage of constitutional protections against being held without charges, and have the right to legal counsel. They would also be protected from the worst abuses by the Eighth Amendment, which prohibits "cruel and unusual punishment." The one detainee at Guantánamo who was discovered to have been born in the United States has been transferred to a different facility, and legal battles rage over his status. But if the rest of the thousands of detainees are neither POWs (even though the bulk of them were captured during the fighting in Afghanistan) nor American citizens, they are fair game. They are protected only by this country's international promises—which are, in effect, unenforceable.

What are those promises? The most venerable are those in the Geneva Convention, but the United States has sidestepped this agreement in the case of those captured in the war on terror. The next most important would be those in the Universal Declaration of Human Rights, which asserts, in Article 5, "No one shall be subjected to torture or to cruel, inhuman or degrading treatment or punishment." There is also the Convention Against Torture, the agreement cited by Bush in June, which would seem to rule out any of the more aggressive methods of interrogation. It states, in Article I, "For the purposes of this Convention, torture means any act by which severe pain or suffering, whether physical or mental, is intentionally inflicted on a person." Again, note the word "severe." The United States is avoiding the brand "torturer" only by sleight of word.

The history of interrogation by U.S. armed forces and spy agencies is one of giving lip service to international agreements while vigorously using coercion whenever circumstances seem to warrant it. However, both the Army and the CIA have been frank in their publications about the use of coercive methods. The *Kubark Manual* offers only a few nods in its 128 pages to qualms over what are referred to, in a rare euphemism, as "external techniques": "Moral considerations aside, the imposition of external techniques of manipulating people carries with it the grave risk of later lawsuits, adverse publicity, or other attempts to strike back." The use of the term "strike back" here is significant; it implies that criticism of such unseemly methods, whether legal, moral, or journalistic, would have no inherent validity but would be viewed as an enemy counterattack.

Bill Wagner, the former CIA agent, remembers going to the Agency's three-week interrogation course at "The Farm," in Williamsburg, Virginia, in 1970. Until it was shut down, a few years later, it was considered the Agency's "premier course," Wagner says, and only the best recruits were invited to take it. "To say you had been through it was a real feather in your cap."

Volunteers played the role of captives in return for guaranteed space in a future session of the coveted course. They were deprived of sleep, kept doused with water in cold rooms, forced to sit or stand in uncomfortable positions for long periods, isolated from sunlight and social contacts, given food deliberately made unappetizing (oversalted, for instance, or tainted with a green dye), and subjected to mock executions. At least 10 percent of the volunteers dropped out, even though they knew it was just a training exercise. Wagner says that many of those who had served as victims later refused to take the course and victimize others. "They lost their stomach for it," he says.

Several years after Wagner took the course, he says, the Agency dropped it entirely. The scandals of the Nixon years put the CIA under unprecedented scrutiny. Over the next three decades spying schools and most human-intelligence networks were gradually dismantled. The United States itself was losing its stomach for hands-on intelligence gathering—and with it, interrogation.

. . .

Nobody experienced the effects of this shift more dramatically than Keith Hall, who earned the nickname Captain Crunch before he lost his job as a CIA agent. Now he describes himself as "a poster child for political correctness." He is a pugnacious brick of a man, who at age fifty-two is just a thicker (especially in the middle) version of the young man who joined the Marines thirty years ago. After his discharge he earned a master's degree in history and international relations; he took a job as a police officer, because he craved a more physical brand of excitement than academia had to offer. His nickname comes from this craving.

The CIA hired Hall immediately after he applied, in 1979, because of his relatively rare combination of academic and real-world credentials. He was routed into the Investigation and Analysis Directorate, where he became one of the Agency's covert operators, a relatively small group ("about forty-eight guys, total," Hall says) known as the "knuckle-draggers." Most CIA agents, especially by the 1980s, were just deskmen.

Hall preferred traveling, training, and blowing things up, even though he felt that the rest of the Agency looked down its patrician nose at guys like him. When the U.S. Embassy in Beirut was bombed, on April 18, 1983, eight of the seventeen Americans killed were CIA employees. There were going to be plenty of official investigations, but the Agency wanted one of its own. Hall was selected to carry it out.

"They flew me to Langley on one of their private planes, and delivered me to the seventh floor," he says. "They told me, 'We want you to go to Beirut and find out who blew up the embassy and how they did it. The President himself is going to be reading your cables. There is going to be some retribution here.'"

Hall was honored, and excited. This was a mission of singular purpose, of the highest priority, and he knew he was expected to get results. Having been a police officer and a Marine, he knew that the official investigations had to build a case that might someday stand up in court. His goal was not to build a case but just to find out who did it.

He slept on rooftops in Beirut, changing the location every two nights. It was a dangerous time to be an American—especially a CIA officer—there, and Hall kept moving. He worked with the Lebanese Special Security Force, and set up a computer in the police building.

Hall says he took part without hesitation in brutal questioning by the Lebanese, during which suspects were beaten with clubs and rubber hoses or wired up to electrical generators and doused with water. Such methods eventually led him to the suspected "paymaster" of the embassy bombing, a man named Elias Nimr. "He was our biggest catch," Hall says—a man with powerful connections. "When I told the Lebanese Minister of Defense, I watched the blood drain out of his face."

Nimr was a fat, pampered-looking twenty-eight-year-old, used to living the good life, a young man of wealth, leisure, and power. He came to the police building wearing slacks, a shiny sport shirt, and Gucci shoes. He had a small, well-trimmed moustache at the center of his soft, round face, and wore gold on his neck, wrists, and fingers. When he was marched into the building, Hall says, some of the officers "tried to melt into the shadows" for fear of eventual retribution. Nimr was nonchalant and smirking in his initial interview, convinced that when word got back to his family and connections, he would promptly be released.

When Hall got a chance to talk to him, he set out to disabuse Nimr. "I'm an American intelligence officer," he said. "You really didn't think that you were going to blow up our embassy and we wouldn't do anything about it, did you? You really should be looking inside yourself and telling yourself that it's a good idea to talk to me. The best way to go is to be civilized . . . I know you think you are going to walk right out of here in a few minutes. That's not going to happen. You're mine. I'm the one who will make the decisions about what happens to you. The only thing that will save your ass is to cooperate." Nimr smiled at him dismissively.

The next time they met, Nimr wasn't in such good shape. In this case his connections were failing him. No one had roughed him up, but he had been kept standing for two days. Hall placed him in a straight-backed metal chair, with hot floodlights in his face. The agent sat behind the light, so that Nimr couldn't see him. Nimr wasn't as cocky, but he was still silent.

At the third interrogation session, Hall says, he kicked Nimr out of his chair. It was the first time anyone had physically abused him, and he seemed stunned. He just stared at Hall. He hadn't eaten since his arrest, four days earlier. But he still had nothing to say.

"I sent him back to his cell, had water poured over him again and again while he sat under a big fan, kept him freezing for about twenty-four hours. He comes back after this, and you can see his mood is changing. He hasn't walked out of jail, and it's beginning to dawn on him that no one is going to spring him."

Over the next ten days Hall kept up the pressure. During the questioning sessions he again kicked Nimr out of his chair, and both he and the Lebanese captain involved cracked him occasionally across the shins with a wooden bat. Finally Nimr broke. According to Hall, he explained his role in the bombing, and in the assassination of Lebanon's President. He explained that Syrian intelligence agents had been behind the plan. (Not everyone in the CIA agrees with Hall's interpretation.)

Soon afterwards Nimr died in his cell. Hall was back in Washington when he heard the news. He assumed that Nimr had been killed to prevent him from testifying and naming others involved in the plot. Armed with tapes of Nimr's confession, Hall felt he had accomplished his mission; but several months after finishing his report he was fired. As he understood it, word had leaked out about torture sessions conducted by a CIA agent, and the U.S. government was embarrassed.

None of the men charged was ever prosecuted for the bombing. Hall believes that the United States may have paid dearly for backing away from his investigation and letting the matter drop. William Buckley, who was Hall's station chief, was subsequently kidnapped, tortured, and killed. He was among fourteen Western civilians kidnapped in Beirut in 1984. In October of the previous year, 241 American servicemen were killed in the bombing of their barracks at the Beirut airport. Some analysts believe that all these atrocities were committed by the same group, the one Hall believes he unearthed in his investigation. Still bitter about it nineteen years later, Hall says, "No one was punished for it, except me!"

Hall sees the loss of his career as dramatic proof that the CIA sold out to the "tree huggers" two decades ago, and points with scorn to a directive from President Bill Clinton that effectively barred intelligence agents from doing business with unsavory characters. The full-scale U.S. retreat from the uglier side of espionage is well documented—but has, by all accounts, been sharply reversed in the aftermath of 9/11.

"People are being very careful, very legal, and very sensible," one former top intelligence official says. "We are not inflicting intense pain, or doing anything damaging or life-threatening. We are once again asking, 'How do you take people down a series of steps in such a way that it has an impact?' That's the only game in town."

Despite the hue and cry over mistreatment of prisoners at Guantánamo, two former Pakistani inmates there—Shah Muhammad and Sahibzada Osman Ali—told me that except for some roughing up immediately after they were captured, they were not badly treated at Camp X-Ray. They both felt bored, lonely, frustrated, angry, and helpless (enough for Shah Muhammad to attempt suicide), but neither believed that he would be harmed by his American captors, and both regarded the extreme precautions (shackles, handcuffs, hoods) that so outraged the rest of the world as comical. "What did the American soldiers think I could do to them?" asked Sahibzada, who stands about five feet eight and weighs little more than 150 pounds. Indeed, the lack of fear at Camp X-Ray no doubt made it more difficult to sort out foot soldiers from dedicated terrorists.

The perfect model of an interrogation center would be a place where prisoners lived in fear and uncertainty, a place where they could be isolated or allowed to mingle freely, as the jailer wished, and where conversations anywhere could be overheard. Interrogators would be able to control the experience of their subjects completely, shutting down access to other people, or even to normal sensation and experience, or opening that access up. Subjects' lives could be made a misery of discomfort and confusion, or restored to an almost normal level of comfort and social interaction within the limitations of confinement. Hope could be dangled or removed. Cooperation would be rewarded, stubbornness punished. Interrogators would have ever growing files on their subjects, with each new fact or revelation yielding new leads and more information—drawn from field investigations (agents in the real world verifying and exploring facts gathered on the inside), the testimony of other subjects, collaborators spying inside the prison, and surreptitious recordings. The interrogators in this center would have the experience and the intuition of a Jerry Giorgio or a Michael Koubi.

Serious interrogation is clearly being reserved for only the most dangerous men, like Sheikh Mohammed. So why not lift the fig leaf covering the use of coercion? Why not eschew hypocrisy, clearly define what is meant by the word "severe," and amend bans on torture to allow interrogators to coerce information from would-be terrorists?

•　　•　　•

This is the crux of the problem. It may be clear that coercion is sometimes the right choice, but how does one allow it yet still control it? Sadism is deeply rooted in the human psyche. Every army has its share of soldiers who delight in kicking and beating bound captives. Men in authority tend to abuse it—not all men, but many. As a mass, they should be assumed to lean toward abuse. How does a country best regulate behavior in its dark and distant corners, in prisons, on battlefields, and in interrogation rooms, particularly when its forces number in the millions and are spread all over the globe? In considering a change in national policy, one is obliged to anticipate the practical consequences. So if we formally lift the ban on torture, even if only partially and in rare, specific cases (the attorney and author Alan Dershowitz has proposed issuing "torture warrants"), the question will be, How can we ensure that the practice does not become commonplace—not just a tool for extracting vital, life-saving information in rare cases but a routine tool of oppression?

As it happens, a pertinent case study exists. Israel has been a target of terror attacks for many years, and has wrestled openly with the dilemmas they pose for a democracy. In 1987 a commission led by the retired Israeli Supreme Court justice Moshe Landau wrote a series of recommendations for Michael Koubi and his agents, allowing them to use "moderate physical pressure" and "nonviolent psychological pressure" in interrogating prisoners who had information that could prevent impending terror attacks. The commission sought to allow such coercion only in "ticking-bomb scenarios"—that is, in cases like the kidnapping of Jakob von Metzler, when the information withheld by the suspect could save lives.

Twelve years later the Israeli Supreme Court effectively revoked this permission, banning the use of any and all forms of torture. In the years following the Landau Commission recommendations, the use of coercive methods had become widespread in the Occupied Territories. It was estimated that more than two thirds of the Palestinians taken into custody were subjected to them. Koubi says that only in rare instances, and with court permission, did he slap, pinch, or shake a prisoner—but he happens to be an especially gifted interrogator. What about the hundreds of men who worked for him? Koubi could not be present for all those interrogations. Every effort to regulate coercion failed. In the abstract it was easy to imagine a ticking-bomb situation, and a suspect who clearly warranted rough treatment. But in real life where was the line to be drawn? Should coercive methods be applied only to someone who knows of an immediately pending attack? What about one who might know of attacks planned for months or years in the future?

"Assuming you get useful information from torture, then why not always use torture?" asks Jessica Montell, the executive director of B'Tselem, a human-rights advocacy group in Jerusalem. "Why stop at the bomb that's already been planted and at people who know where the explosives are? Why not people who are building the explosives, or people who are donating money, or transferring the funds for the explosives? Why stop at the victim himself? Why not torture the victims' families, their relatives, their neighbors? If the end justifies the means, then where would you draw the line?"

And how does one define "coercion," as opposed to "torture"? If making a man sit in a tiny chair that forces him to hang painfully by his bound hands when he slides forward is okay, then what about applying a little pressure to the base of his neck to aggravate that pain? When does shaking or pushing a prisoner, which can become violent enough to kill or seriously injure a man, cross the line from coercion to torture?

Montell has thought about these questions a lot. She is thirty-five, a slender woman with scruffy short brown hair, who seems in perpetual motion, directing B'Tselem and tending baby twins and a four-year-old at home. Born in California, she emigrated to Israel partly out of feelings of solidarity with the Jewish state and partly because she found a job she liked in the human-rights field. Raised with a kind of idealized notion of Israel, she now seems committed to making the country live up to her ideals. But those ideals are hardheaded. Although Montell and her organization have steadfastly opposed the use of coercion (which she considers torture), she recognizes that the moral issue involved is not a simple one.

She knows that the use of coercion in interrogation did not end completely when the Israeli Supreme Court banned it in 1999. The difference is that when interrogators use "aggressive methods" now, they know they are breaking the law and could potentially be held responsible for doing so. This acts as a deterrent, and tends to limit the use of coercion to only the most defensible situations.

"If I as an interrogator feel that the person in front of me has information that can prevent a catastrophe from happening," she says, "I imagine that I would do what I would have to do in order to prevent that catastrophe from happening. The state's obligation is then to put me on trial, for breaking the law. Then I come and say these are the facts that I had at my disposal. This is what I believed at the time. This is what I thought necessary to do. I can evoke the defense of necessity, and then the court decides whether or not it's reasonable that I broke the law in order to avert this catastrophe. But it has to be that I broke the law. It can't be that there's some prior license for me to abuse people."

In other words, when the ban is lifted, there is no restraining lazy, incompetent, or sadistic interrogators. As long as it remains illegal to torture, the interrogator who employs coercion must accept the risk. He must be prepared to stand up in court, if necessary, and defend his actions. Interrogators will still use coercion because in some cases they will deem it worth the consequences. This does not mean they will necessarily be punished. In any nation the decision to prosecute a crime is an executive one. A prosecutor, a grand jury, or a judge must decide to press charges, and the chances that an interrogator in a genuine ticking-bomb case would be prosecuted, much less convicted, is very small. As of this writing, Wolfgang Daschner, the Frankfurt deputy police chief, has not been prosecuted for threatening to torture Jakob von Metzler's kidnapper, even though he clearly broke the law.

•   •   •

The Bush Administration has adopted exactly the right posture on the matter. Candor and consistency are not always public virtues. Torture is a crime against humanity, but coercion is an issue that is rightly handled with a wink, or even a touch of hypocrisy; it should be banned but also quietly practiced. Those who protest coercive methods will exaggerate their horrors, which is good: it generates a useful climate of fear. It is wise of the President to reiterate U.S. support for international agreements banning torture, and it is wise for American interrogators to employ whatever coercive methods work. It is also smart not to discuss the matter with anyone.

If interrogators step over the line from coercion to outright torture, they should be held personally responsible. But no interrogator is ever going to be prosecuted for keeping Khalid Sheikh Mohammed awake, cold, alone, and uncomfortable. Nor should he be.

The New Yorker

WINNER, FEATURE WRITING

The Marriage Cure

In Katherine Boo's "Marriage Cure," we meet two women from Oklahoma City who have signed up for a course in how to get and stay married, part of the Bush administration's prescription for curing poverty. Without Boo ever explicitly underlining her story, we come to understand the inadequacy of this solution, and the barrier between these likable, hardworking women and the middle-class life they so earnestly desire. The piece is a marvel of deep reporting, beautifully understated writing, stylishly articulated perceptions and empathy.

Katherine Boo

The Marriage Cure

Is wedlock really a way out of poverty?

One July morning last year in Oklahoma City, in a public-housing project named Sooner Haven, twenty-two-year-old Kim Henderson pulled a pair of low-rider jeans over a high-rising gold lamé thong and declared herself ready for church. Her best friend in the project, Corean Brothers, was already in the parking lot, fanning away her hot flashes behind the wheel of a smoke-belching Dodge Shadow. "Car's raggedy, but it'll get us from pillar to post," Corean said when Kim climbed in. At Holy Temple Baptist Church, two miles down the road, the state of Oklahoma was offering the residents of Sooner Haven three days of instruction on how to get and stay married.

Kim marvelled that Corean, who is forty-nine, seemed to know what to wear on such occasions. The older woman's lacquered fingernails were the same shade as her lipstick, pants suit, nylons, and pumps, which also happened to be the color of the red clay dust that settled on Sooner Haven every summer. The dust stained the sidewalks and gathered in the interstices of a high iron security perimeter that enclosed the project's hundred and fifty modest houses.

This forbidding fence, and the fact that most of the adults inside it were female, sometimes prompted unkind comparisons with the old maximum-security women's prison five minutes up the road. But Kim and Corean believed that they could escape Sooner Haven, and so were only mildly irked by what one of their neighbors called "our cage." Besides, other low-income areas had fierce borderlines, too. The distance between Sooner Haven and Holy Temple Baptist Church edged the territories of the street gangs Hoover Crip, Grape Street Crip, and Rolling Twenties. Kim's brother had been murdered by a gang, but she couldn't keep track of their ever-mutating names, boundaries, and affiliations. And Corean had refused to learn, even when Hoover Crip members started shooting at one of her five children. It was Corean's contention that you could be in the ghetto and not of it. Ignoring the stunts of heavily armed neighbors kept your mind free for more enriching pursuits, such as the marriage class for which Corean had roused her young friend from bed this morning.

Oklahoma has rarely found itself in the vanguard of antipoverty thinking, but the class to which the two women were heading embodies a vigorous new idea—something known locally, and archly, as "the marriage cure." Traditionally, singleness has been viewed as a symptom of poverty. Today, however, a politically heterodox cadre of academics is arguing that singleness—and, particularly, single parenthood—is one of poverty's primary causes, for which matrimony might be a plausible tonic. For the past few years, the state of Oklahoma has been converting this premise into policy. In an initiative praised by the Bush Administration, which aims to seed marriage-promotion programs nationwide, the state has deputized public-relations firms, community leaders, and preachers (among them the pastor at Holy Temple Baptist Church) to take matrimony's benefits to the people. Last summer, that marriage drive reached Sooner Haven. "Come learn about relationships!" said the recruiter who knocked on the housing project's beat-up doors.

Kim happened to be available for edification, having recently quit a job that she had found depressing: selling home-security systems over the phone. The script she'd had to memorize still banged around her brain. "What? You can't afford twenty-nine ninety-nine a month but can afford to run the risk of being robbed and losing everything you've worked hard for in life? Or, even worse, a family member? You say God will protect you, but maybe my call to you today is God's way of telling you that the world he created does possess an element of danger, and he wants you to be as safe as you can be. It is quite possible that God has a reason for my call to you today."

"Most of the people I called were old and scared already," Kim said, sighing. "I wasn't putting enough heart into my rebuttals."

Many of Kim's contemporaries are single mothers and thus eligible for welfare between jobs. But for Kim, who is unmarried, childless, and on a strict regime of Depo-Provera contraceptive injections, the decision to quit a job before lining up the next one had harsh repercussions. She was hungry, and hoped that marriage class would come with free lunch. In any event, it would give her respite from her unit at Sooner Haven, which, despite her liberal use of paper doilies, ceramic angels, and lavender-scented candles, was no longer a pleasant place to spend a day. The roof leaked, and an overnight storm had flooded her living room and kitchen. Still, food and sanctuary were not the extent of Kim's interest in marriage class. She had recently fallen, as she put it, "heart over heels" in love.

Kim has moist brown eyes, a body that neighborhood males call "ripe" and "aching for my love time," and a bleeding ulcer that an emergency-room doctor ascribes, not implausibly, to stress. It is her habit to think with a fist on her chin, and the puzzle that engrosses her is how to live a life less indigent and criminal than the one in which she was raised. The youngest of seven children, she was the first of her four sisters to forgo having babies as a teen-ager. She hoped as well to be the first to go to college, and had recently taken a series of tests for a general-equivalency diploma. Although she didn't know anyone from a background like hers who had obtained a college degree, she didn't see why a smart woman couldn't pull it off. For several years, she'd been trying to do the precise opposite of what people around her had done, in the hope of eventually attaining what she termed "a healthy, wealthy, normal-lady life." Marriage, like staying out of jail, struck her as a vital part of normal-lady living.

The man she'd chosen (although he had yet to be informed of his selection) was a tall, soft-spoken construction worker named Derrick, whom she had first spoken to at the International House of Pancakes. He was a graduate of a two-year college and had a one-year-old son "he actually does for." And, unlike her previous boyfriend, he didn't use or sell drugs.

· · ·

Kim keeps the things that matter to her next to her mattress, in a cardboard box stamped "Fragile—Eggs." In addition to a handmade card that her father sent from prison on her eighteenth birthday, and a tangle of blond hair extensions that her mother had mailed when Kim turned twenty-two, the box held several poems that Kim had written about the meagreness of what people around her termed love. Many of the men she knew called their women "bitch" when their male friends came to visit, and they hit those women when the male friends went away. After sex, they wanted to leave, pretending not to hear when a girl offered to turn on the hot plate and make breakfast biscuits from scratch. "You know how they wrassle you down and it's wham wham wham, and then when they come they go, 'Say my name!'?" she asked. "It's all about their egos, and that's all I ever knew. But the first time I slept with Derrick he asked, 'Is this O.K., does this feel right?' And, after, I just burst out crying. Because when he held me I felt, this is it—this is the something I've been missing my whole life." Holding on to this something was a feat for which her life's experience had provided no strategy, and she hoped that the marriage class to which she was headed might suggest one.

Corean found it moving that, even among city girls like Kim, who had been nourished on rappers named Kingpin Skinny Pimp, Dirty, and Lord-knows-what-all, the word "love" retained the gentle, Barbara Cartland contours of her own Deep South girlhood. But Corean, who had separated from her husband twelve years ago, was not the romantic she had once been; she applauded Kim's optimism but didn't share it.

So why bother with a three-day seminar at a church whose ceiling, after asbestos removal, appeared to consist of the pelts of a thousand plush toys? Corean Brothers, so outwardly composed that her kids called her the Reverend Doctor Mom, was feeling a little wobbly. In the fall, the youngest of her five babies would enter his final year in high school, and while her grown children were regular, affectionate presences in her life, the cause to which she had devoted herself since her divorce no longer seemed to require her full-time vigilance. Corean had two sets of grandchildren, by her eldest son. But he frequently quarrelled with the mothers of the babies, and Corean saw her four grandchildren only intermittently. She busied herself with what she called her "private ministry": visiting nursing-home residents and penitentiary inmates; helping Sooner Haven's younger women, Kim among them, with their monthly budgets or workplace disputes. Still, the days now contained enough hours for a reasonable woman to fret about her future.

Lately, besides the symptoms of menopause, a "burning kind of numbness" had been snaking up her arms. Ineligible for Medicaid and unable to afford private insurance, she improvised treatments, just as she'd improvised over the years to keep her children from noticing when a child-support payment didn't come. Her annual income was five thousand dollars, but, except for ten months when she and her husband first separated, she had not received welfare. "The child support was supposed to have covered us, but when it stopped coming I couldn't afford a lawyer," she said. "So I did what you do when you're a girl from the sticks—you just make do." Amid the four-o'clocks and marigolds in her flower bed, and in defiance of housing-authority rules, she had planted peppers and cantaloupe. She decorated her children's bedrooms with thrift-shop items and roadside salvage. With the castoffs of a woman whose house she cleaned, she sent each child to school sharply dressed.

The standards of parenting at Sooner Haven are not uniformly exacting. One exasperated resident recently named her newborn De Las' One. But it was generally acknowledged in the complex that Corean Brothers had been blessed with mother wit. "I even found great pleasure in hard work," read a passage from Ecclesiastes which she had underlined and asterisked five times in the disintegrating Living Bible that now accompanied her to Holy Temple church. "The pleasure was, indeed, my only reward for all my labors."

Her husband had remarried six months after the divorce; Corean had had one second date in twelve years. Mornings now, she interrogated the mirror with new ruthlessness, curious about whether Preparation H could, as she'd heard, reduce the puffiness around one's eyes. If five children had altered her face for the worse, they had at least erased the evidence of her malnourished childhood as a Central Florida field hand. "You're ninety pounds with two bricks in your pockets," boys had teased her then. Now she was shaped like a Coke bottle, and Coke-colored, too—red and gold glints in dark-brown skin. Her cheekbones were still high, her eyes were alive with humor.

One unacknowledged consolation of struggling in the inner city is the lack of time one has to indulge romantic discontent. It was letting go of her children, more than losing her husband, that had caused the Reverend Doctor Mom to notice that she was alone.

. . .

Many Oklahoma City maps end where the Sooner Haven neighborhood begins. Pizza places won't deliver here, and local strip malls have been abandoned, their display windows given over to the leaflets of undercapitalized entrepreneurs ("Nile Princess Home Braidz 4 Less"). The neighborhood feels connected to the world around it mainly on Sunday mornings, when residents who have moved up and out return to its churches to pray. Nonetheless, the community is an apt setting for a test of whether the government can persuade low-income citizens to marry.

Using federal money to raise the marriage rate among the poor—the House recently approved a three-hundred-million-dollar White House plan to help states experiment toward this goal—is an effort to complete what the Administration considers the unfinished business of the 1996 federal welfare-reform law. And Oklahoma turns out to be a quintessential post-welfare state. In the past eight years, its public-assistance rolls dropped ninety-one per cent—among the country's most substantial declines—but widespread work hasn't brought widespread economic security. Median household income remains among the lowest in the country, and out-of-wedlock childbearing rates are among the country's highest. While a considerable amount of social-science data suggest that two-parent families are good for children, marriage promoters also see matrimony as a means of decreasing crime and welfare dependence in neighborhoods like Sooner Haven. In a recent homage to Oklahoma's marriage-promotion pioneers, Wade Horn, the Bush Administration's marriage-promotion guru, wrote, "If marriage is good for communities, why should government be shy about promoting and strengthening it?"

The 2000 census recorded a decline in marriage rates across all demographic groups, but the least likely to marry are African-Americans, who are also increasingly overrepresented on national welfare rolls. As Orlando Patterson, of Harvard, a scholar of black marriage patterns, recently observed, African-Americans remain "among the most unpartnered and estranged individuals in the world."

Kim Henderson dreamed of a sunset wedding in a neighborhood park. Corean Brothers's fantasy was simpler still: she'd hire Oklahoma's fastest-talking preacher and hold matrimonial history's briefest reception, in order to get more swiftly to the honeymoon action. "It's been twelve years," she said, laughing. "I am a religious woman, but not a dead one." The two women were not especially concerned that their romantic ambitions could interest the government. Outsiders were always coming to Sooner Haven to sell opportunity, prying into the residents' business while doing so. Some of the people in the project believed that these help-brokers were counterfeit, that laws had been set in place to push blacks down while helping other minorities prosper. Over-the-clothesline conversation turned periodically to "the tax-free Asians"—North Vietnamese who, according to rumor, were welcomed to America (after fighting and killing black G.I.s) and exempted from income taxes, which explained how they came to own all those nail salons. Corean and Kim weren't certain about the Asians, but they did believe in the existence of opportunity for black people, somewhere. And it was as likely to be found at Holy Temple Baptist Church as anywhere else.

They arrived at marriage class thirty minutes late but were enthusiastically welcomed. Despite door-to-door solicitation in Sooner Haven and announcements in neighboring churches and social-service agencies, the total turnout was five, not counting the church secretary, a Sooner Haven single mother who, in a barely audible voice, described her divorce as "living death." Kim and Corean chose seats at the far end of a long Formica table, near the exit.

The government's evangelist, Pastor George E. Young, was tall, with a gleaming pate and a cell phone holstered to his khakis. When he folded his arms across his chest after making a point, the women giggled at his resemblance to Mr. Clean. "I am not naïve enough to think this class will stop you from having men over," he said as he distributed state-sponsored workbooks of what Oklahoma calls "empirically informed, empirically tested, regularly updated" information on how to make and keep a decent marriage. "What I am hoping is that, when the man does come over, you will have a different conversation."

The curriculum was rich with statistics and poll results, which Pastor Young displayed by overhead projector on a cracked cinder-block wall. What do couples fight about before marriage? (Money, jealousy, future in-laws.) What do couples fight about after marriage? (Money, communication, children, sex.) What percentage of married people feel unhappy in the relationship? (Most.) The data are bleak by design; the social scientists on whom Oklahoma relies believe that a crucial part of making and keeping a marriage is disabusing oneself of sentimental notions. Marriage is not sexual and emotional bliss between soul mates, they contend; it is a job requiring as much patience, self-sacrifice, and discipline as any other.

The students found the statistics depressing and the flow-charts in the workbooks unfathomable, but Pastor Young was neither of those things, and in three days of class only one student dozed off, briefly, following a Crock-Pot lunch. Christ built his church upon a rock, Young told the students; a marriage requires a similarly unyielding foundation. Value the ability to fight decently and nonviolently, he said, because, "believe me, there will be storms."

Hence, a pillar of the course was a "speaker-listener" technique intended to promote calm, productive conflict resolution. To demonstrate, Young played a state-supplied video of couples working through the sort of conflicts that are seldom encountered in Sooner Haven. (Spouse hogs home computer. Spouse procrastinates about cleaning guest bedroom.) This cultural disconnect was perhaps predictable, as the curriculum used in Oklahoma was actually developed a quarter of a century ago for engaged or married couples. The curriculum's creators, the Colorado psychologists Scott Stanley and Howard Markman, say that their course encourages not just healthy marriages but individuals who are "less reliant on government services including welfare, health care, mental health care, and earning and saving more money." However, testing of the approach has been conducted only minimally in inner-city settings. Marriage education in places like Sooner Haven is, like marriage itself, a venture in optimism.

"I'm not going to lie and say it's easy," Pastor Young, who is in his second marriage, told the class. "So I know some of you will wonder whether it's worth it. But when you know how it feels to go home at night, to have them there every night, to have them trusting you, and to know you trust them back . . ." For a moment, he seemed to lose his place in the lesson plan. "To find that person and have that feeling—that is worth struggling toward, it's worth crying over. It is the worthiest of personal goals."

. . .

From his counselling, Pastor Young has come to share the belief of many marriage-initiative advocates: that men more than women need convincing on this point. Thus he sees it as an unhappy but unavoidable fact that women are this social policy's beasts of burden. Having already complied with social and economic pressures to work, poor women were now being asked to do something that their government had so far failed at: push their male counterparts into the cultural and economic mainstream.

Kim and Corean found the couples squabbling on the videos

"kind of petty" but enjoyed practicing the problem-solving techniques that the couples demonstrated. Pairing off for role-playing, the students learned to refrain from saying to a man who disappointed them, "You're an oily, two-timing toad," and to say instead, "When you did x, in situation y, I felt z." They practiced swallowing their rage, articulating their grievances specifically and respectfully, recognizing when a fight might turn violent, and listening with open minds to imaginary mates. Acting the part of a neglected wife and mother, Kim channelled her loneliness so convincingly that Pastor Young blinked back tears—an achievement that left Kim beaming.

"But in real life I'm still back at the beginning," Kim said after the exercise. "I mean, how do you get to the point of even having a bad marriage, when every time you start to say the word 'love' he starts talking about basketball?"

"My thing is: how do you get a man to talk about marriage when you're pretty sure he's still sleeping with his baby's mother?" a nurse's aide asked, expressing a problem so familiar at Sooner Haven that it is known by the term "baby-mama drama." "And then how do you tell if he wants to marry you for the right reasons?" the nurse's aide went on. "When I wear my white uniform, guys around here know I'm working and chase me down the street to get their hands on my paycheck."

"You have to ask to be treated as you deserve," Pastor Young said. "If you don't demand respect from the males, you won't get it."

"Here's what troubles me," Corean said, as another transparency lit up the wall. "Look at all those couples who say they're stable but not happy. I am enjoying these exercises, and I agree our society has too much divorce, but it doesn't seem right to me that a woman should stick with a man when she's miserable, or settle for one who doesn't make her happy. Why isn't it better to be alone?"

"Two parents means two paychecks," Kim said, frowning. On a ledger, as a pooling of resources, marriage made sense. But Kim's experience with males, like that of the other women in the class, pointed toward a more complex calculation. None of the women were on welfare, and all were determined not to be. And while they wanted men for companionship, sex, and the sort of honest, intimate conversation they were enjoying in marriage class, they weren't entirely sure that men were useful to their efforts at self-improvement. All but one of the women in the room had grown up without a father in the home. At least two had been sexually abused in the first ten years of their lives. Those who had children had been left by the children's fathers. Three had been beaten by men they had loved, and two had been involved with violent criminals. In short, it required an imaginative leap to believe that a committed relationship with a man would rescue a woman from poverty. At Sooner Haven, relationships with men were often what stopped an ambitious woman from escaping.

As an urban preacher, Pastor Young grasped this paradox better than the developers of the curriculum he delivered, so he was not shattered when the first tangible result of his marriage instruction was the termination of what had been the most enduring relationship in the group. The nurse's aide, riding to the second day's class with Corean and Kim, passed her unemployed boyfriend's house and noticed another woman's car parked outside. Following an antic period of discovery, and with the encouragement of her classmates, the nurse sent the boyfriend of two years packing.

"Matthew 19:30 tells us the first will be last and the last will be first," Pastor Young said on the final day, as phone numbers were exchanged and sugar cookies were spirited into pocketbooks for later. "You think you are last now, you may be last in the eyes of the world, but if you only believe and live that you are worthy to be who you are, you will be first. You will eke out some respect and happiness from this life." He closed his Bible and sighed.

"I wish I could get more men into this room, instead of asking you all to go out and be the messengers for what a meaningful, committed relationship might be," he went on. "But for now it's up to you to go out and teach the men."

.　　.　　.

Waiting at the bus stop on a withering August afternoon, Kim Henderson shook the front of her white blouse, in the vain hope of keeping sweat stains at bay. She wanted to look nice, as she was bound for one of Oklahoma City's upmarket shopping malls. After her retirement from burglar-alarm telemarketing, she had papered the mall's boutiques with job applications. But while she attended marriage class her phone was cut off, owing to an outstanding fifty-nine-dollar bill. Since there was now no way for prospective employers to reach her, and since she had no money to buy toilet paper, let alone pay her phone bill, she had decided to take a bus to the mall and go from shop to shop, asking if anyone had tried to call her about a job.

The mall was a long ride from Sooner Haven. Derrick owned a Pontiac Grand Am that he might have let her use, but Kim hadn't seen or heard from him in ten days. She thought he might be working at a construction site outside Oklahoma City, or might be preoccupied with his baby son. "Derrick's a good person," she said determinedly. "And just because I'm not sure of the reason doesn't mean he doesn't have one."

When a bus turned down her street, she stepped off the curb, but the bus did not slow down. Half an hour later, a second bus cruised by her outstretched, dollar-waving hand. It is an unhappy fact of Oklahoma City life that bus drivers bypass would-be riders in very poor neighborhoods, and blacks in less poor ones. Kim's grandmother, who had died the previous year, bequeathed Kim an aged blue Oldsmobile. But Kim had passed the car on to her mother, who lives in Arkansas. "She's sixty and had to walk all this way to the school cafeteria where her job is at," Kim explained. Recently, several of her girlfriends had applied to a program at the Oklahoma City human-services office, which gave them five hundred dollars to get a car for work. Her friends are eligible for such aid because they are single mothers. Childless Kim must rely on buses.

Kim has tried to develop constructive ways of venting her frustration. She had kept a journal until a relative discovered it and passed it around. She tried to talk into an imaginary tape recorder, but that made her feel crazy. Lately, she had settled on the "weird but hopefully less pathetic" technique of translating her anxieties and hopes into unmetered, bluesy song. "Help may not come just when I want it to," she sang to the street, "but when it comes it might not be too late."

After an hour, a bus pulled over. It took her to the center-city bus depot, which is situated in front of the county jail. Waiting for a transfer bus under a billboard for Crawley 24-Hour Bail Bonds, Kim was propositioned by a man wheeling a baby carriage and smoking a Black & Mild cigar. Kim cut him off in mid-fantasy. "Don't you know me? I'm Frank's daughter, which makes you my cousin. And you know Frank would kill you for this."

The cousin with the carriage peeled away, and another suitor stepped forward. When she told the new guy that she had a boyfriend, he laughed, and said, "Well, then, he must not love you, honey, if he be making you take the damn bus."

"Like flies to apple pies," Corean liked to say of Kim's ability to attract male interest, but Kim's options usually fell short of marriage-class standards. This was a hitch in the uplift-by-marriage method which even Pastor Young understood. "Kim wants to get out of her situation by working, going to school, maybe getting married," he said once, when Kim was out of earshot. "But she lives in an isolated neighborhood where most of the males have abandoned hope in schools, legit jobs, the system. The way they tell it to me, they see three ways to get out of the ghetto: through professional sports, through rapping, and through crime." Half of Oklahoma's black men are out of the labor force, according to the 2000 census. In the neighborhoods around Sooner Haven, the figure is higher still.

An older man in an orange jumpsuit was now standing before Kim, balancing a broom on his shoulder. "Now, for my part, I believe you have a beautiful face and a nice body," he said. "Are you over eighteen? I'll be getting out of the halfway house in several months and I'd like to buy you a steak."

Kim sometimes laughed about being a "creep magnet," but Derrick's unexplained absence had lately sapped her humor. Her father had repeatedly pulled vanishing acts, too—into drink and into prison. For most of her life, Kim's mother had compensated, watching her little girl's back as best she could, but two years ago her mother left Oklahoma City to work in Arkansas.

Before Kim adopted her normal-lady plan, she had had a crew of girlfriends with whom she could share her thoughts on love and men. When the connecting bus arrived at the center-city depot, one of them—Amanda—was on it. Amanda's T-shirt said, in large type, "I promise to be a good girl," and, in small type, "if you promise to be a bad boy." Seeing Kim, she reached into a tight back pocket and produced a photograph of a newborn. "Ashley—I had her six weeks ago Saturday."

Kim's eyes darted to her friend's flat belly. "I know," Amanda said proudly, "I didn't gain any weight with her at all. Now, get this: When my time came, I was seven centimetres dilated and didn't have nobody with me, and still they kicked me out of St. Anthony Hospital, because they claimed my Medicaid card didn't clear. I had to go clear across the city to Mercy hospital by myself—dag, I thought I would never make it. Funny, my Medicaid card cleared there."

Kim wants to have two children, but only when she's married and has financial stability. This plan struck some of her acquaintances as foolish; they thought only white women waited until they were too old to keep up with a toddler. Kim believed that, at twenty-two, she still had time. But in lonely stretches like this one her hunger for the companionship of a baby grew so acute that she borrowed acquaintances' children, took them to Wal-Mart, and had photographs taken of them in her arms.

"Now my new boyfriend wants me to have his baby, too," Amanda was saying when the bus pulled into Penn Square Mall.

The manager of a store that sells jelly beans in ninety-nine flavors said, "Kim Henderson—yes, I remember your name. You had a good application, but we couldn't get through on the phone, so we hired someone else."

If we had wanted an interview, the managers at Trendz and American Eagle and nine other stores said, we would have called you.

"But after I left my application my phone got cut off. That's why I came today. I was an assistant manager at Subway."

If we decide we want you, the managers said, we'll call you.

The mall smelled of cinnamon buns, reminding Kim that she hadn't eaten. At one store, she reached for the manager's hand and begged, "The person who comes all this way just to see if you've called, that's a person who is going to work her behind off for you when you hire her." She then learned that the job required her to work until 9 P.M. There is no regular bus service to Sooner Haven or its environs after dark.

"I feel like an ant," Kim said, leaving the fourteenth store. "A little nothing that bus drivers and supervisors can't see." A ten-dollar bill fell from the purse of a middle-aged shopper walking ahead of her. Kim scooped it up and returned it to the woman, lowering her lashes to hide the fact that her eyes had filled with tears. "If I don't get a job soon, I don't know what I'll do." Kim broke down outside a boutique called the Buckle, which sells sun hats and turquoise-encrusted belts. On her earlier visit, she had steered clear of the store, along with J. Crew, because she thought that her clothes might be too ghetto. Blowing her nose, she glanced inside. "Maybe if I pretend that I did apply there, and the staff thinks they lost my application, they'll be nice to me."

The gambit worked. A supervisor couldn't find Kim's name in a loose-leaf binder of rejected applications, gave Kim two minutes to summarize her qualifications, and then scheduled a phone interview with the manager for that night at eight o'clock. Kim recited Corean's number. When she returned to the bus stop outside the mall, the heat still blasted, but she bounced on and off the curbside like an overwound toy. "The ant has an interview!" she sang.

A slim white woman emerged from Dillard's department store with four shopping bags, a Burberry satchel, and, dangling from her wrist, a silver peace-sign charm. Kim suddenly grew still. "I'd like to be elegant someday, too," she said quietly. "But if I ever did get a healthy, wealthy life, I wonder if my children would grow up looking down at people like me."

When a bus that would have taken her home accelerated past, Kim practiced answers to potential interview questions: "I have a genuine interest in fashion and have been working a cash register since I was fourteen." When the next bus cruised by, she tried a trick that she'd recently invented to manage depression, recalling in detail the happiest days of her life. "Here's one I like—my mom's birthday, in April, 1990. We had nothing to eat, we were suffering at the time, and the thing to know about my mom is that the only pleasure she ever really had in life was bingo—Lucky Star Casino, Will Rogers Bingo Hall, she played everywhere, and sometimes took me along to play a card, too. One of those places had a special deal for regulars—you play free on every Wednesday in the month of your birthday. She went out, and when she came back we were going to bed. She rustled us up and told us to open the door. She'd played U-Pick-Em and won twenty-five hundred dollars in cash and a big old stereo, which was sitting there outside. All eight of us busted out crying. Back then, we thought a hundred dollars was everything, so with twenty-five hundred dollars we could hardly imagine it, we thought we were millionaires. I got a pink-and-blue winter parka, and jeans from the old Fifty-Percent-Off Store. Mom bought some serious groceries and then gave us each ten dollars to spend however we wanted. I went to the 7-Eleven and bought Good & Plenty."

Another bus was coming through the shopping plaza. Kim stepped forward, signalling furiously. When it swerved around her, she sank to the curb. The bus was not only the seventh one to pass her that day; it was the last bus to Sooner Haven until morning. In terms of landmass, Oklahoma City is the third-largest metropolis in America, and she was a five-hour walk from home.

A pretty woman in a tear-and-sweat-soaked blouse will eventually be noticed by somebody. A Chevy Impala pulled over, driven by a black woman not much older than Kim. "I know, I used to have to take the bus, too," said the driver, who, as it turned out, was an assistant supervisor at a gift store in the mall. "I'll drive you home." She went past the alabaster state capitol and into the northeast quadrant, where Sooner Haven is situated, and where TV crews were covering a shooting from the parking lot of a carryout called Leo's BBQ. "It as bad as they say around here?" the woman asked Kim when they reached the project's gates.

"If you go outside and try to be known, you're going to have trouble," said Kim, her optimism not yet flattened by the Buckle manager, who would not keep her appointment. "But if you live all low and invisible you'll more than likely be O.K."

.   .   .

One fall morning, Corean accompanied her youngest son, Fella, who is eighteen, to parent-teacher day at his magnet school. Fella, suffering from a football injury, limped along in a knee brace. Even so, he could outpace a mother in toe-strangling secondhand shoes. A few paces behind her son, Corean watched a group of lithe classmates embrace him, fretting over his readiness for next week's game. Corean is the rare mother of an Oklahoma high-school footballer who doesn't know what position her boy plays. But in a drawer by her bed she has every standardized-test score he's brought home since preschool.

When Corean reached the school entrance, the girls had dispersed, and her son, looking stricken, was being marched down the hall by an apple-cheeked teacher. "Who-o-o-o," the teacher called out, "is the mother of this spectacular child?"

Other mothers turned to look as the instructor caught Corean in an armlock. "I have been waiting to meet you, Mrs. Brothers. I love your kid, and the smarts aren't the half of it. You've raised one way-cool human being."

A pleasure to teach, a treasure to know: in every classroom Corean entered, she received happy news about her son. Alerted to forthcoming assignments on Gilgamesh and "Silas Marner," clutching a quiz marked 97, Corean retreated as soon as politeness allowed. She was still not entirely at home in school. Her father, an epileptic and an alcoholic, had disappeared when she was six, abandoning a wife and ten children in a Florida shanty without electricity or running water. When she was in seventh grade, her mother had the first of a series of strokes. A year later, Corean quit school and became, at fourteen, a laborer in orange groves and snap-bean fields. In those days, she ate so much red dirt and Argo starch that she acquired a taste for them. (She came to tolerate fatback pork, too, but not the consequent tapeworms that dangled pinkly from one's nose.) She had failed to fulfill one promise she made to herself then—that her own children would be spared the experience of poverty. But she saw to it that each received the education that she had pined for.

Once, Fella was mistaken for a gangbanger, and his blue bandanna for a cocky display of Crip colors. Such underestimations crushed Corean; they just made Fella work harder at his calculus. Intent on being a doctor, he was stricter with himself than his teachers tended to be—an independence that Corean generally admired. But, returning home to Sooner Haven from parent-teacher day, she felt a shadow slip across her sense of satisfaction.

Did a boy become self-reliant because the people who could have helped him didn't?

Fella was an A student at a good math-and-science high school, and a state champion in church oratory. Corean had hoped that his achievement would bring him scholarships and a first-rate college education. But as Pastor Young, a former high-school basketball player, observed from his pulpit, colleges recruit inner-city boys with athletic talent, not inner-city boys with good grades. (The vast majority of black students at selective colleges are from middle- or upper-class families.) Fella wasn't big enough to be a serious college football player. "It's fun, I like it," he said. "But the human brain, the science of it—that's what amazes me." He was already a third of his way through his senior year, however, and had yet to be advised about college by overworked guidance counsellors, whose numbers had been reduced by a state budget crisis. "I don't know about any colleges, really," Fella said, "though if I don't get scholarships I can't blame anyone but me. They say the money's out there. I just can't say for sure where it is."

When her older children were finishing high school, Corean had sensed a similar lack of official attention to their futures, and knew less than Fella about how to counter it. Those children were now employed and independent, and, except for the old-est—her rebel son, who held down two jobs as a nursing-home aide—were strong in the church. But Shandy, twenty, who is a receptionist and writes plays in her free time, had recently dropped out of community college, unable, on her salary, to cover the tuition. Dana, twenty-five years old and very bright, had managed to get an associate's degree at Oklahoma State University and now worked the desk at a local Hertz Rent-A-Car. When Corean fell behind on her phone or electricity bills, Dana would be at her door, waving a check. But Dana's plan of saving enough money to complete her B.A. and go to law school seemed to be perpetually deferred. The help that her children needed now, to become the people Corean believed they might be, seemed beyond the ken of a low-income, eighth-grade-dropout single mother.

.   .   .

When she was eighteen, Corean left fruit-picking for the Job Corps, a Great Society program for the poor which had an opening in Oklahoma City. She became a certified nurse's aide. She also met a funny, conscientious man who worked on a loading dock. She did what the Holy Temple pastor was now recommending, and married. Over the years, she emptied bedpans in a nursing home and cleaned houses for the affluent, but her earnings—forty-five dollars a day for housekeeping—didn't cover day-care costs. Eventually, she became a stay-at-home mother. Then her husband, who had become a truck driver for Frito-Lay, declared bankruptcy. "Financially, he was struggling, and with the kids I could only take day work," Corean said. "He was angry at me for not pulling my weight, income-wise, while I believed the kids needed me at home. The fights just tore us apart."

Occasionally, for memory's sake, she drives by a brick house on an elm-lined street three miles from Sooner Haven, where her family spent its happiest years. A basketball hoop rises from a square of concrete in the back yard, and lace curtains hang in the window of the bedroom where, one night, her husband beat her. "Black as I am," she remembered, "I was blue."

When she cleaned houses in one of Oklahoma City's better neighborhoods, Corean had studied the ways that rich women argued with their husbands—how they had raised their eyebrows and their voices instead of their fists. After the beating, she told her husband to leave. "I still loved him, and once I secured my physical safety I hoped we could work through the anger, try to talk about reconciliation," she said. But almost as soon as her husband left he began dating. "At the divorce hearing, the judge said to me, 'You didn't bother to get a lawyer?' But I had five kids, aged four to fifteen, and I had four hundred dollars in rent, and food and water and electricity and the phone and whatnot. My husband did have a lawyer, a good one, so what happened happened, and off I went to Sooner Haven, where my kids, who love their father, were angry at me for a very long time."

In those days, the Sooner Haven duplex was crowded. Now, with the older kids gone and Fella staying late for football practice every weekday, it felt unnervingly roomy. Corean was pleased when Dana came by after work. Over dinner, they discussed a college classmate of Dana's who had announced her engagement, then they turned to Corean's dating prospects. As she had little discretionary income, Corean's most regular outings were walks she took in a nearby city park. On one of those walks, she had struck up a conversation with an educated man who owned a lawn-care business. But he seemed to lose interest when he picked her up several days later for a dinner date. "I think he was shook up when he realized I lived in the projects," she said. Still, it was a date, something she'd never got from the singles gatherings she'd attended at her church for a decade. Often, not one male was in attendance.

"There's a short supply, no question," Dana said, "and a shorter supply for women who aren't going to let the man be the master, shut their mouths, and do what he tells them to do. But I'm not going to settle. I do believe that somewhere in this great big world God has someone in mind for me, someone wonderful who won't cheat on me. But, in the meantime, I've got plans for my life. If he's not bringing anything to the table, then he's just bringing me down." Her voice grew teasing. "But you, Reverend Doctor, you're getting old. You gotta get on it, make your *moo-oove*."

"Well, it used to be all I had to say was 'Five kids' and most men would turn tail and run," Corean replied. "But now I'm exploring my options, don't you worry." She looked down at her hands. "But even when you do find a man it's still a game of chance. I thought I was being careful the first time, but that didn't protect me from getting hurt."

Later that night, Corean shut off all the lights in the house except the one she needed to fold the laundry she'd taken in from her clothesline. In fact, she did know a decent man who wanted to marry her. He had given her a papier-mâché jewelry box and a ceramic rhinoceros, which sat on her dresser, but there was a reason she hadn't mentioned him to Dana.

Corean believed in maintaining appearances. "People may be looking for an excuse to write you off," she'd warned her children. "Don't give them the curse words or dirty clothes to help them do it." Corean knew exactly how those children would react when they learned that the Reverend Doctor Mom, while doing charity work at a faraway prison, had had her head turned by a three-time felon.

.   .   .

"Have my eyebrows grown out too scrungy?" Kim asked Derrick, as she dressed for work one autumn morning. Derrick placed his water glass on the cardboard box marked "Fragile—Eggs" and stared into her heart-shaped face. "They don't look so rough," he concluded after a moment. Kim exhaled; brow waxing and other vanities were not in her monthly budget.

Kim had recently obtained another telemarketing gig, a job whose chief requisite was the ability to absorb a gale force of customer hostility and whose chief benefit, by Kim's lights, was that she could get to it without taking the bus. Instead, every weekday, a colleague named Tiphani dropped her newborn at day care near Sooner Haven and then picked up Kim. In a cavernous warehouse in the northwest section of the city, they worked the phones from 3 P.M. to 11 P.M., after which Tiphani drove Kim home.

Kim's task was to persuade people in California and Ohio and New York to switch their local phone service to A. T. & T. She was not actually employed by A. T. & T. Her employer was an A. T. & T. subcontractor that paid two hundred dollars a week to start. But

Tiphani said that after they memorized A. T. & T.'s catalogue of products—call waiting, call forwarding, and so on—they'd have an edge on other people who wanted a job at the bona-fide A. T. & T. In the meantime, Kim found the work preferable to frightening old people into buying home security, and preferable as well to the offer that she'd received recently, while walking down the street, "to play pool and do adult activities" under the auspices of a neighborhood fixture called Da Pimp.

Some women Kim knew posed for pornographers, or slept with men in exchange for money, clothes, and diapers. But the run-in with Da Pimp reminded Kim of why escaping the city's underworld was worth a stress ulcer. She had grown up around gangbangers, warrant dodgers, and woman beaters. "When I was young, I loved school so much I cried when I couldn't go on weekends," she said. "School, and not my crazy home, was the only place I could find peace."

But in the legit world Kim kept botching things. In the six weeks between leaving her burglar-alarm job and taking the new one, she had applied for emergency food stamps and been denied. Corean eventually accompanied her to the welfare office and pleaded her case, successfully, but in the meantime Kim bounced several checks to Wal-Mart. Oklahoma penalties for bad checks are stiff, and are a politically popular income-generator for the District Attorney's office. For writing a twelve-dollar-and-eighteen-cent check, she now faced a hundred-and-fourteen-dollar penalty, including "victim restitution" to Wal-Mart and a fee to the D.A. And then there were two more bounced checks, and, as the letter from the D.A. said, if she didn't come up with four hundred and ninety-five dollars and fifty-three cents in ten days she could face a year-long jail sentence.

Corean pointed out that the District Attorney's wife, a plastic surgeon and former Miss Oklahoma, had just pleaded guilty to illegally obtaining narcotics, for which she received community service and permission to resume doing nose jobs. But Kim, who had seen her own father and brother face less forbearing jurists, did not anticipate lenient treatment.

Kim was guzzling Hawaiian Punch to soothe her ulcer, but at least Derrick had reappeared. Back in the summer, she suspected that he was keeping her from his friends and family. Now he introduced her warmly, saying, "This ain't my girl. This is my woman." He came over with candles when her gas and electricity were cut off. And when his toddler son took his first steps they were toward Kim.

Corean worried about how hard Kim was falling. "Maybe you don't get the love you need from your family, then you grow up and go out all desperate to find it," she said. "And if and when you don't find the right thing you try to tell yourself the wrong thing is right." But Kim was mindful of Pastor Young's advice— "It's up to you to go out and teach the men"—and she began to express her wish for commitment. "I don't want to pressure you," she said to Derrick, "but I care about you so much and feel serious about this relationship."

"I know, baby," he invariably replied, but she didn't know what to do next to nudge things closer to a sunset wedding. The problem-solving techniques that she'd learned in marriage class did, however, help her to learn more about her would-be husband. Using the "When you do x, I feel y" technique in order to convey her frustration at his failure to help her resolve her problem with the courts and the world's largest retailer, she learned that his construction job paid two hundred and fifty dollars a week, and that he didn't think often about marriage. He thought more about how to pay for his son's food and diapers while avoiding the repossession of his Grand Am, which he'd bought before he lost a job as a supervisor at Coca-Cola, and which was crucial to keeping his new, less remunerative job, "building houses in the middle of nowhere."

As Kim made the bed and prepared to leave for work, Derrick peered into her freezer. A bag of lima beans hung limply from a shelf. He closed the door and gave Kim a gentle goodbye kiss. From her screen door, Kim watched him climb into the Grand Am, crank the radio louder than befitted the partner of a healthy-wealthy woman, and wheel through Sooner Haven's gates.

She checked her watch. Tiphani should have arrived by now to take her to work, but the only cars in the parking lot were a Cutlass Supreme, whose vinyl top appeared to be suffering from multiple stab wounds, and a wheelless Toyota bearing the bumper sticker "Americans Kick Ass."

For Kim, given the bad-check problem, losing a day's pay would be financially disastrous. She tried to focus on a giveaway magazine called *American Baby,* which contained an article she loved: "They say here the five most important values to give your children are trust, patience, respect, empathy—is that how you pronounce it? And then the last one, self-reliance. That's the one where you teach your child that he can't depend on hardly anyone for anything, because in the end they're probably going to let you down."

Suddenly, Tiphani hollered from the parking lot, and *American Baby* hit the floor. Kim bolted out of her rusted screen door, the most eager cold-caller in the city.

·   ·   ·

The visiting room at Great Plains Correctional Facility holds six plastic chairs, a wall painting of a leafy lane (prisoners pose for snapshots in front of it), and a slew of posted rules that remind Corean of the ones she enforced in her own home when her kids were adolescents. "Only handholding is allowed!" the signs say. "Any other form of contact and your visit will be terminated."

Great Plains sits on the prairie an hour's drive west of Oklahoma City, a journey that provided a workout for Corean's Dodge Shadow. But the family of Steven Bruner, the inmate whom Corean was now visiting, lived even farther away. Five years ago, they'd asked Corean, a family friend, to check on him when they couldn't. Since then, her car had occasionally given up before it reached the facility, and more than once she had felt unwelcome in the white, working-class towns surrounding Great Plains. Still, on the nights before her visits, she would catch herself spreading skirts on her bed, wondering whether Steven would prefer the leopard-print or the pink one with pleats.

In northeast Oklahoma City, the question "Where he away at?" is widely understood to mean, In what prison is he serving time? Nearly one in ten black men is a prison inmate—one of the highest incarceration rates in the country. Steven, who started his criminal career at fifteen, had passed most of his adult life behind bars. Now he was thirty-eight, with maximum-security forearms and a broader range of reading interests than most other men Corean knew. Since his first imprisonment, educational and vocational programs for prisoners had been drastically curtailed, but he had availed himself of what remained, learning to inlay carpets with animal faces and craft ceramic knickknacks. He visited the library three times a week, the maximum permitted. And, three years after Corean first began talking to him about her faith, he became, to her delight, a Christian.

Corean struggled to explain even to herself how a bleak room separated from the outside world by three layers of razor wire, two sturdy gates, motion detectors, and a phalanx of armed guards (one of them assigned to sit beside her and Steven) had become a place where she could relax. Steven couldn't help get Fella into college. He couldn't even hold her. Their conversations, given the presence of the guard, were often self-conscious and sometimes, given the limited range of events in their respective lives, outright boring. Still, Steven listened with unwearied attention, a luxury Corean hadn't known since her divorce: "Well, Steven, the mechanic looked at the car and did the fan with some black tape, but when he fixed the brakes he didn't bleed them, so they still pump all the way down to the floor. I'll take it in when I have some change in my pocket. Anyway, I did try to fix the radio myself, took a pair of tweezers ..."

"You don't have to take it in to get the brakes fixed. When you go home, get yourself some brake fluid at the auto-parts store, open the engine, and put it in the big round mouth."

"There's a lot of round things in that motor, you know darn well."

"There's a little screw on the side, and it's connected to the square—look, take a photo of the engine, send it to me, and I'll show you what's what. You'll see, it ain't hard."

Corean stretched her legs, letting her foot graze the instep of his state-issue sneaker.

Corean still termed their relationship a friendship, and she had told him not to count on her, but it had been some time since she'd signed a letter to him the way she'd signed the first, "Cordially, Corean." Steven wore his desires on his chest. A fellow-inmate, using a piece of wire and some ingenuity, had tattooed there the words "Corean's Playground." Only after she'd seen the tattoo did she choose to learn the particulars of his sentence: assaulting an undercover police officer with a car, fifty years.

Steven confronted the difficulty of the relationship as visiting time drew to a close. "If you decide to wait for me, I worry that you're doing time, same as I am—just marking off days—and I don't know if that's right. I mean, I want you to . . ." He stopped and shook his head. "You know. But I'd be lying if I said I could make the argument on your end."

.   .   .

Back home, sitting outside in a plastic chair just like those at the prison, Corean took no pleasure in the spectacular red and yellow pansies growing in her garden. She was staring grimly through Sooner Haven's fence. She could see two of her young grandchildren standing in a yard across the busy street. She had been barred from seeing the children because their mother was once again feuding with Corean's son. The toddlers, oblivious of the commands of a woman who was minding them, were staring right back at Corean through the fence. Inside her house, Corean had bibs and placemats on which their names had been emblazoned, and Dr. Seuss books, and a tiny bucket and shovel for digging in the garden. But this evening they were fenced off from her, as Steven was. She figured that this was what people meant by a midlife crisis—the sense that everything you wanted was just outside your reach.

Fella, home with the flu, sensed his mother's mood. A do-rag on his head and a black-and-white composition book in his hand, he came outside and plopped his large self on his mother's small lap. "Mommeee," he said, "I need your help with this speech." This spectacle prompted some little girls who were playing by the fence to shriek with laughter, and Corean couldn't help but laugh, too.

When she came home after prison, Fella unbuckled his mother's sandals, unasked, and pressed her swelling feet. After football practice or the late shift at the Taco Bueno, he often joined her in the house's one lighted room, where they compared their days until they drifted into sleep. Corean remembered how, when she was a child, hardship had turned members of her family against each other, and was grateful for her own family's closeness. But she also knew that single mothers could be seduced by it. Husbandless, they treated their Danas as confidantes and their Fellas as stand-in partners, and were shattered when those companions left them behind.

Eventually, Dana arrived for dinner, and conversation turned to Fella's college plans. He'd found a book and some pamphlets on scholarship options and discovered that in-state tuition could be covered by an Oklahoma program for poor children with good grades. He also saw that four years of college fees and books would leave his mother with nothing to live on, even if he avoided paying room and board by living at home.

When Corean imagined Fella at college, she saw him as being

relaxed. "I don't see him fretting over how his mom can pay the phone bill—I see him free to study, and having enough change to take a girl out to lunch if he likes," she said. When Fella pictured himself at college, he dreamed of a dorm, not a tiny bedroom in Sooner Haven. And after reviewing his scholarship options he had decided it would behoove him to unearth some Native American roots.

In the neighborhood, the "Indian option" was an opportunity discussed with as much avidity as marriage. Cherokee, Shawnee, and Kickapoo reservations encircle Oklahoma City, and many city residents suspect that they are of mixed heritage. Those families which are able to document sufficient Native American blood can secure housing, health-care, and scholarship benefits far in excess of those available to families who are simply poor. "Benefits offered through official Native American status!" a video available from a Web site called Blackindians.com trumpets. Corean and her children knew several people who had pursued those benefits.

When Corean was young, her older siblings had told her that her high cheekbones were the Cherokee legacy of their father. Her paternal grandmother had thrilled Corean's siblings by demonstrating that she could sit on her hair. "Black hair just doesn't grow that long," Corean said. But to prove the rumor and secure Fella a scholarship required producing ancestral birth certificates to which tribal codes had been affixed. Corean's father had taken his family history with him when he vanished; all she really knew was that he was born in a southwest-Georgia peanut-farming town and died in another, four miles away. Still, as housekeeping work paid so poorly and no economically advantageous marriage was in the offing, this avenue of opportunity tempted her, and possessed an irony she appreciated. "I feel bad to say this," she told Fella and Dana, "but my father might be more help to this family dead than he ever was alive."

As the dinner dishes were washed and put away, Corean's children dropped the Indian option and began chiding their mother about her strictness. "No playing cards in the house, having to come in for family prayers and singing every night, not even a phone call from a boy until we turned sixteen—you were so mean when I was a teen-ager, it was pathetic," Dana said, wringing out a dish towel. "By the time I was seventeen, I was so itching to get away from you I bought my own tissue and soap and stored it in a box beneath my bed. And, when I finally did get my own place, me and the preacher's daughter went and got ourselves a bottle of Bacardi and we cut up, I can assure you."

Corean said what she always said in the face of her children's mock recriminations: "When I see the Lord, I'm telling Him, look, if I messed up, I messed up trying." And that was the thing about the Indian idea. It reminded a make-do woman that there was usually something else left to try.

.   .   .

"They're all telling me, 'I'm here for you, we love you, I'll never let you go, our baby,' but it's too late," went a poem that Kim had written and placed in her cardboard box. "My feet is slowly walking the sand under the water." Her "Fragile—Eggs" depository now rested beside a concave orange-brown couch in the small home where her father, disabled by a stroke after leaving prison, lived. Kim was "in hiding" there, fearing that she would be arrested on the bad-check-writing charge. She still went to work every day, even when her friend Tiphani quit, forcing Kim back onto the bus. But the D.A.'s office knew that Kim lived in Sooner Haven. She gave up her unit and moved in with her father, three miles away.

Before leaving Sooner Haven, she had received the results of her general-equivalency exam. She'd aced everything except math. A teacher at a local community college had offered to help her master the math and apply for college. But the tutoring conflicted with Kim's telemarketing hours, which were non-negotiable. "Still, I've come this far, I'm not going to give up," she said. She now owed around nine hundred dollars in fines from the bounced checks. Increasingly fearful of doing jail time, she had decided to take out a loan from "a guy named Dave, whose whole business is helping people who have hot-check charges against them."

Kim still wanted to be Derrick's wife, and he had agreed to move in with her when they had the means for an apartment. Marriage class had helped her grasp the work involved in achieving a deeper level of commitment; in addition, it reinforced her sense that the child she longed for should have two parents. But steady proximity to Derrick had also given her a sense of how married life would and wouldn't change her general circumstances. Her father's couch was too narrow for two, so when she slept with Derrick now it was at his mother's apartment, where he was living to save money. "He goes to work in the early morning, I get home after midnight, and sometimes we both work six or seven days a week because of his son and my debts. So even when we coördinate our schedules we're tired. We play this video game called Tetris and go to sleep."

Some nights while Kim was trying to pitch A. T. & T.'s services to residents of Long Beach or Dayton or Scarsdale, the computers connected her to women who, she suspected, were struggling even harder than she was to get by—women who didn't want to switch phone carriers, who just wanted to keep another voice on the end of the line. Sometimes Kim's supervisor listened in, and he would cut off the call. But when he wasn't listening Kim asked the women about their jobs, the men who disappointed them, the bills they couldn't pay. She learned the callers' names, gave them her own, promised to stay in touch.

·   ·   ·

One frigid morning, Corean's daughter Shandy, who was weak from mononucleosis, drove Corean to the Oklahoma City

Greyhound station. The previous week, Corean had taken Shandy to the hospital, a specialist, and the pharmacy, bouncing checks all the way. Shandy, although she was employed, could not afford health insurance. "I know what happened to Kim, but I was fearing major medical," Corean said. "If you're poor, the government will cover you until you're eighteen, and then after you're sixty-five. That's forty-seven years on your own." Unless, she added, eyes bright, "you are an Indian."

A ticket from Oklahoma City to the Georgia peanut fields of her father's birth cost sixty-nine dollars but the journey took seven buses and two days. Outside the Oklahoma City limits, Corean stared through the window at the designated capitals of a series of Indian nations—capitals that, from her vantage, looked suspiciously like gas stations selling off-brand beer.

It felt odd not to have a child in tow. "This is the future," she said. "I best get used to it." The strangeness was tempered by the fact that on the Greyhound people treated her with more respect than she was used to getting in the project—even when, in the Ozarks, drug-enforcement dogs were unleashed on the passengers' luggage. One bus driver reserved the front seat—farthest from the toilet smells—for Corean and an enormous pink church hat with dotted-swiss netting which she carried along with her Bible. "It's obvious you're a lady," he said. At the edge of the Mississippi delta, another driver pulled to the side of the road and held her elbow as she climbed stiffly off the bus. A minute later, she returned triumphant, brandishing a six-and-a-half-foot stalk of sugarcane. She hadn't seen cane since she was a child in the fields.

"People are quite friendly and interesting when you get out in the world," she said, feeling almost regretful when the bus pulled up to a secondhand-furniture store ("No Cash, No Credit, No Problem") that doubled as the bus depot of Sylvester, Georgia.

W. E. B. Du Bois, in "The Souls of Black Folk," called this part of southwest Georgia "perhaps the richest slave kingdom the modern world ever knew." As the proprietor of the furniture store watched her things, Corean set out on foot through the shabby downtown toward the county courthouse. The entrance hall, lined with framed portraits of white civic leaders, was being mopped by a black female prison crew, one of whom directed her to the public-records office. There, she was no longer the first lady of the cross-country Greyhound bus. A records search showed that her father had no birth certificate, let alone a tribal number. "Lotta poor folks just had their babies in the woods and didn't tell no one," a young black clerk tried to console her, directing her to the Corinthian-columned public library across the street. In the genealogy room there, two elderly white couples were paging through books like "Men of Mark in Georgia" and tapping intently into a stretch of new computers. "Before this, we were in Salt Lake City, doing the Mormon Church records," one of the men said to the other. "We have it nailed down to 1830." The burning numbness in her arm had kept Corean awake for two nights. She sat at a table before a pile of thick brown books, trying to make sense of twentieth-century county censuses. Decade after decade, her father's family—her family—had not been counted. Corean got a second wind in the evening when she called home to check on Fella. "Harvard, Yale, I don't know about them. I guess those are places for the extremely wealthy," she said. "But if we could pay for the best school in Oklahoma, and then medical school …"

The next day, Corean gave a man fifteen dollars to drive her to Albany, Georgia, just west of Sylvester. Her father had gone there after he left his wife and children in the citrus fields, and had died there in 1981. If he was an Indian, she reasoned, some deed or public filing might have noted his tribe. Approaching the courthouse, she met a black man in a cowboy hat who was emerging from a new BMW. He turned out to be a Cherokee chief, a successful exerciser of the Indian option, which she took to be an excellent omen.

Once her sugarcane had been scanned by a metal detector and

scrutinized by a puzzled security squad, she set up shop in the county office of public records. Around her, young couples on lunch breaks were applying for marriage licenses. Corean bore down on a drawer of black plastic microfilm cannisters. She queried clerks who consulted databases, after which she paged through land records and worn manila files. And after several hours she realized only this: that her father had no records of deeds, no liens, no civil or criminal suits, no taxes owed nor businesses owned. Whether black or Indian, the man had been destitute enough, and law-abiding enough, to leave no trace in the public record.

She asked a secretary for the local phone book. Her family's surname was Smith, and as she scanned the pages she found a given name, Daisy, that sounded familiar. She phoned, and soon an old car arrived at the courthouse to take her to the pink cinderblock home of Miss Daisy, a woman she'd never met, who turned out to be her father's only sister.

There were four generations of women in Daisy's house. A seven-week-old girl, born to a single mother, slept beside a toddler wearing a T-shirt that said "Just Be Glad I'm Not Your Child." Daisy, a birdlike octogenarian, sat on a plaid recliner surrounded by Ragú spaghetti-sauce jars filled with tobacco-flecked spit. She had recently suffered a stroke, and was attended by a visiting speech therapist. "You can hardly swallow, Miss Daisy. Spit out the chaw so we can do this." When the therapist moved between Daisy and an NBC soap opera called "Passions," Daisy extended a wasted arm and tapped the woman out of the way.

Corean sat uneasily on the edge of the couch, asking questions about her father and the grandma who could sit on her hair. The younger women had also grown up believing they were part Cherokee, but they, too, had no proof. It was only when Corean was leaving that she noticed on a shelf behind the television a leatherette family Bible as worn as her own. Forgetting her manners, she seized it. In the centerfold she found what she suspected: a family tree filled out by a meticulous hand. One name differed from the others.

"Anyone know this Suzanna Sunbeam?" Corean's voice was hoarse, the way it got when she prayed too extravagantly on Sundays. The women shook their heads.

"Aaaaaz-uh," croaked the old woman, her eyes fixed on the TV screen. She didn't say anything else until "Passions" broke for a commercial. Then she said, "Suzanna was the Indian girl."

Corean clapped her hands, elated. "I knew it would be in the family Bible," she said. "I felt it!" But after a series of hugs among newfound relatives, themselves enamored of the Indian option, Corean returned to the family Bible and registered that Suzanna Sunbeam was not her father's mother but her grandmother's mother, which meant that there wasn't enough Indian blood in Corean's son Fella to do his doctor dreams a lick of good.

The signage in the Albany bus station where Corean fanned herself late that night was much as it had been in 1961, when the station was a staging area of the civil-rights movement. Probably then, as now, men kicked cardboard boxes of worldly goods across the station's greasy floor. But now the people in the station, waiting and working and scrawling "Lil Bit wuz here" on the historic bathroom wall, were black. Waiting for the bus, Corean opened her Bible. "And when we obey Him, every path He leads us on is fragrant with His loving kindness." Eventually, the belly of a Greyhound opened to receive a stalk of sugarcane destined for furtive planting in Sooner Haven.

· · ·

When she returned to Oklahoma, Corean applied to be a guinea pig in a pharmaceutical trial, to earn thirteen hundred dollars for Fella's tuition. After a physical, the testers rejected her, saying she was too ill and tired. Shortly afterward, she discovered that the mother of two of her grandchildren was living in a house where people with guns came and went. Corean hurried the toddlers back to Sooner Haven and did her best to raise them, despite losing financial help from Dana, who had been laid off from her longtime job. In the spring, Fella graduated with honors and found work moving furniture at a warehouse. He would stay in Oklahoma City for college.

One afternoon, Kim stopped to visit. She had paid off her bad-check charges and earned an award for being the third-most-productive salesperson in her office—just before the prospect of a National Do Not Call Registry led her employer to cut its workforce in half. Worried, she had applied for another job, as an aide to the homebound elderly. "It's only six dollars an hour, and no commissions," she said, "but some money's better than none." She and Derrick now shared a small apartment with a lockbox in a closet, for saving dimes and quarters. "This year," they told each other, "we're going to make something of ourselves."

Corean also saw Pastor Young, who was conducting another marriage seminar at Sooner Haven, and preaching to a larger crowd. "We're learning how to do this as we go, but we're getting there," he said. One day soon, he predicted, the training would produce its first wedding.

It could be Kim's, Corean thought. She suspected that it wouldn't be her own. Lately, she had been pulling back from Steven—"fading out," as he put it. "Anyway, when he's released, who knows if he will even want me," she said sadly. "Who knows what a person wants when he has choices." She still attended the mostly female singles meetings at her church, trying to heed what her kids said about not hiding her light under a bushel. But she was more broke than ever, the toddlers were exhausting, and the brakes on her car had given out. So most days she stayed inside the fence.

Rolling Stone

WINNER, REPORTING

The Killer Elite (Part 1)

A landmark piece of combat reportage, "The Killer Elite" offers a viscerally honest look at the war in Iraq. In his two months of riding with the men of Bravo Company, Evan Wright experienced everything from the gory horrors to the daily discomforts of Marines at war. Many reporters volunteered to be embedded, but Wright gets beyond the soldiers' political views and taste in music to tell their inner story.

Evan Wright

The Killer Elite (Part 1)

Meet the Marines of Bravo Company— proud, hardened professionals who deal in that most specialized of American exports: ultraviolence. The true story of bullets, bombs and a Marine platoon at war in Iraq

The invaders drive north through the Iraqi desert in a Humvee, eating candy, dipping tobacco and singing songs. Oil fires burn on the horizon, set during skirmishes between American forces and pockets of die-hard Iraqi soldiers. The four Marines crammed into this vehicle—among the very first American troops who crossed the border into Iraq—are wired on a combination of caffeine, sleep deprivation, excitement and tedium. While watching for enemy fire and simultaneously belting out Avril Lavigne's "I'm With You," the twenty-two-year-old driver, Cpl. Joshua Ray Person, and the vehicle team leader, twenty-eight-year-old Sgt. Brad Colbert—both Afghan War veterans—have already reached a profound conclusion about this campaign: that the battlefield that is Iraq is filled with "fucking retards." There's the retard commander in their battalion who took a wrong turn near the border, delaying the invasion by at least an hour. There's another officer, a classic retard, who has already begun chasing through the desert to pick up souvenirs thrown down by fleeing Iraqi soldiers: helmets, Republican Guard caps, rifles. There are the hopeless retards in the battalion-support sections who screwed up the radios and didn't bring enough batteries to operate the Marines' thermal-imaging devices. But in their eyes, one retard reigns supreme: Saddam Hussein—"We already kicked his ass once," says Person, spitting a thick stream of tobacco juice out his window. "Then we let him go, and he spends the next twelve years pissing us off even more. We don't want to be in this shit-hole country. We don't want to invade it. What a fucking retard."

The war began twenty-four hours ago as a series of explosions that rumbled across the Kuwaiti desert beginning at about six in the morning on March 20th. Marines sleeping in holes dug into the sand twenty miles south of the border with Iraq sat up and gazed into the empty expanse, their faces blank as they listened to the distant rumblings. There were 374 men camped out in the remote desert staging area, all members of the First Reconnaissance Battalion, which would lead the way during considerable portions of the invasion of Iraq, often operating behind enemy lines. These Marines had been eagerly anticipating this day since leaving their base at Camp Pendleton, California, more than six weeks before. Spirits couldn't have been higher. Later that first day, when a pair of Cobra helicopter gunships thumped overhead, flying north, presumably on their way to battle, Marines pumped their fists in the air and screamed, "Yeah! Get some!"

"Get some!" is the unofficial Marine Corps cheer. It's shouted when a brother Marine is struggling to beat his personal best in a fitness run. It punctuates stories told at night about getting laid in whorehouses in Thailand and Australia. It's the cry of exhilaration after firing a burst from a .50-caliber machine gun. *Get some!* expresses in two simple words the excitement, fear, feelings of power and the erotic-tinged thrill that come from confronting the extreme physical and emotional challenges posed by death, which is, of course, what war is all about. Nearly every Marine I've met is hoping this war with Iraq will be his chance to get some.

Marines call exaggerated displays of enthusiasm—from shouting "Get some!" to waving American flags to covering their bodies with Marine Corps tattoos—"moto." You won't ever catch Sgt. Brad Colbert, one of the most respected Marines in First Recon and the team leader I would spend the war with, engaging in any moto displays. They call Colbert the Iceman. Wiry and fair-haired, he makes sarcastic pronouncements in a nasal whine that sounds a lot like David Spade. Though he considers himself a "Marine Corps killer," he's also a nerd who listens to Barry Manilow, Air Supply and practically all the music of the 1980s except rap. He is passionate about gadgets—he collects vintage videogame consoles and wears a massive wristwatch that can only properly be "configured" by plugging it into his PC. He is the last guy you would picture at the tip of the spear of the invasion of Iraq.

The vast majority of the troops will get to Baghdad by swinging west onto a modern superhighway built by Hussein as a monument to himself and driving, largely unopposed, until they reach the outskirts of the Iraqi capital. Colbert's team in First

Recon will reach Baghdad by fighting its way through some of the crummiest, most treacherous parts of Iraq. Their job will be to screen the advance of a Marine battle force, the 7,000-strong Regimental Combat Team One (RCT 1), through a 115-mile-long agricultural-and-urban corridor that runs between the cities of An Nasiriyah and Al Kut filled with thousands of well-armed fedayeen guerrilla fighters. Through much of this advance, First Recon, mounted in a combination of seventy lightly armored and open-top Humvees and trucks, will race ahead of RCT 1, uncovering enemy positions and ambush points by literally driving right into them. After this phase of the operation is over, the unit will move west and continue its role as ambush hunters during the assault on Baghdad.

Reconnaissance Marines are considered among the best trained and toughest in the Corps. Maj. Gen. James Mattis, commander of the Marine ground forces in Iraq, calls those in First Recon "cocky, arrogant bastards." They go through much of the same training as do Navy SEALS and Army Special Forces. They are physical prodigies who can run twelve miles loaded with 150-pound packs, then jump in the ocean and swim several more miles, still wearing their boots, fatigues and carrying their weapons and packs. They are trained to parachute, scuba dive, snowshoe, mountain climb and rappel from helicopters. Many of them are graduates of Survival Evasion Resistance Escape School, a secretive training facility where Recon Marines, fighter pilots, Navy SEALs and other military personnel in high-risk jobs are put through a simulated prisoner-of-war camp with student inmates locked in cages, beaten (within prescribed limits) and subjected to psychological torture overseen by military psychiatrists—all with the intent of training them to resist enemy captivity. Paradoxically, despite all the combat courses Recon Marines are put through (it takes a couple of years for them to cycle through every required school), almost none are trained to drive Humvees and fight in them as a unit. Traditionally, their job is to sneak behind enemy lines in small teams, observe from afar and avoid contact with the enemy. What they are doing in Iraq—seeking out ambushes and fighting through them—is something they only started training for around Christmas, a month before being deployed to Kuwait. Cpl. Person, the team's primary driver, doesn't even have a military operator's license for a Humvee and has only practiced driving in a convoy at night a handful of times.

Gen. Mattis, who had other armored-reconnaissance units available to him—ones trained and equipped to fight through enemy ambushes in specialized, armored vehicles—says he choose First Recon for one of the most dangerous roles of the campaign because "what I look for in the people I want on the battlefield are not specific job titles but courage and initiative." By the time the war is declared over, Mattis will praise First Recon for having been "critical to the success of the entire campaign." The Recon Marines will face death nearly every day for a month, and they will kill a lot of people, a few of whose deaths Sgt. Colbert and his fellow Marines will no doubt think about and perhaps even regret for the rest of their lives.

•   •   •

Colbert's first impression of Iraq is that it looks like "fucking Tijuana." It's a few hours after his team's dawn crossing into Iraq. We are driving through a desert trash heap, periodically dotted with mud huts, small flocks of sheep and clusters of starved-looking, stick-figure cattle grazing on scrub brush. Once in a while you see wrecked vehicles: burnt-out car frames, perhaps left over from the first Gulf War, a wheel-less Toyota truck resting on its axles. Occasionally there are people, barefoot Iraqi men in robes. Some stand by the road, staring. A few wave.

"Hey, it's ten in the morning!" says Person, yelling in the direction of one of the Iraqis we pass. "Don't you think you ought to change out of your pajamas?"

Person has a squarish head and blue eyes so wide apart his Marine buddies call him Hammerhead or Goldfish. He's from Nevada, Missouri, a small town where "NASCAR is sort of like a state religion." He speaks with an accent that's not quite Southern, just rural, and he was proudly raised working-poor by his mother. "We lived in a trailer for a few years on my grandpa's farm, and I'd get one pair of shoes a year from Wal-Mart." Person was a pudgy kid in high school who didn't play sports, was on the debate team and played any musical instrument—from guitar to saxophone to piano—he could get his hands on.

Becoming a Marine was a 180-degree turn for him. "I'd planned to go to Vanderbilt on a scholarship and study philosophy," he says. "But I had an epiphany one day. I wanted to do my life for a while, rather than think it." It often seems like the driving force behind this formerly pudgy, nonathletic kid's decision to enter the Corps and to join one of its most elite, macho units was so he could mock it, and everything around him. A few days before moving out of its desert camp in Kuwait to begin the invasion, his unit was handed letters sent by schoolchildren back home. Person opened one from a girl who wrote that she was praying for peace. "Hey, little tyke," Person shouted. "What does this say on my shirt? 'U.S. Marine!' I wasn't born on some hippie-faggot commune. I'm a death-dealing killer. In my free time I do push-ups until my knucles bleed. Then I sharpen my knife."

As the convoy charges north into the desert, Person sings A Flock of Seagulls' "I Ran (So Far Away)." He says, "When I get out"—he's leaving the Marines in November—"I'm going to get a Flock of Seagulls haircut, then I'm going to become a rock star."

"Shut up, Person," Colbert says, peering intently at the dust-blown expanse, his M-4 rifle pointed out the window. Colbert and Person get along like an old married couple. Being a rank lower than Colbert, Person can never directly express anger to him, but on occasions when Colbert is too harsh and Person's feelings are hurt, the driving of the Humvee suddenly becomes erratic. There are sudden turns, and the brakes are hit for no reason. It will happen even in combat situations, with Colbert suddenly in the role of wooing his driver back with retractions and apologies. But generally, they seem to really like and respect each other. Colbert praises Person, whose job specialty is to keep the radios running—a surprisingly complex and vital job for the team—calling him "one of the best radio operators in Recon."

Obtaining Colbert's respect is no small feat. He maintains high standards of personal and professional conduct and expects the same from those around him. This year he was selected as team leader of the year in First Recon. Last year he was awarded a Navy Commendation for helping to take out an enemy missile battery in Afghanistan, where he led one of the first teams of Marines on the ground. Everything about him is neat, orderly and crisp. He grew up in an ultramodern house designed by his father, an architect. There was shag carpet in a conversation pit. One of his fondest memories, he tells me, was that before parties, his parents would let him prepare the carpet with a special rake. Colbert is a walking encyclopedia of radio frequencies and encryption protocols and can tell you the exact details of just about any weapon in the U.S. or Iraqi arsenal. He once nearly purchased a surplus British tank, even arranged a loan through his credit union, but backed out only when he realized just parking it might run afoul of zoning laws in his home state, the "communist republic of California."

But there is another side to his personality. His back is a garish wash of heavy-metal tattoos. He pays nearly $5,000 a year in auto-motorcycle insurance due to outrageous speeding tickets; he routinely drives his Yamaha R1 racing bike at 130 miles per hour. He admits to a deep-rooted but controlled rebellious streak that was responsible for his parents sending him to military academy when he was in high school. His life, he says, is driven by a simple philosophy: "You don't want to ever show fear or back down, because you don't want to be embarrassed in front of the pack."

With Colbert located in the front passenger seat, providing security off the right side of the vehicle, left-side security is provided by Cpl. Harold Trombley, a nineteen-year-old who mans the SAW machine gun in the rear passenger seat. Trombley is a thin, dark-haired and slightly pale kid from Farwell, Michigan. He speaks in a soft yet deeply resonant voice that doesn't quite fit his boyish face. One of his eyes is bright red from an infection caused by the continual dust storms. He has spent the past couple of days trying to hide it so he doesn't get pulled from the team. Technically, he is a "paper Recon Marine," because he has not yet completed Basic Reconnaissance course. But it's not just his youth and inexperience that keep Trombley on the outside, it's also his relative immaturity. He caresses his weapon and says things like, "I hope I get to use her soon." Other Marines make fun of him for using such B-movie war dialogue. They're also suspicious of his tall tales. He claims, for example, that his father was a CIA operative, that most of the men in the Trombley family died mysterious, violent deaths—the details of which are vague and always shifting with each telling. He looks forward to combat as "one of those fantasy things you always hoped would really happen." In December, a month before his deployment, Trombley got married. (His bride's father, he says, couldn't attend the wedding, because he died in a "gunfire incident" a while before.) He spends his idle moments writing down lists of possible names for the sons he hopes to have when he gets home. "It's up to me to carry on the Trombley name," he says.

Despite some of the other Marines' reservations about Trombley, Colbert feels he has the potential to be a good Marine. Colbert is always instructing him—teaching him how to use different communications equipment, how best to keep his gun clean. Trombley is an attentive pupil, almost a teacher's pet at times, and goes out of his way to quietly perform little favors for the entire team, like refilling everyone's canteens each day.

The other team member in the vehicle is Cpl. Gabriel Garza, a twenty-one-year-old from Sebastian, Texas. He stands half out of the vehicle, his body extending from the waist up through a turret hatch. He mans the Mark-19 automatic grenade gun, the vehicle's most powerful weapon, mounted on top of the Humvee. His job is perhaps the team's most dangerous and demanding. Sometimes on his feet for as long as twenty hours at a time, he has to constantly scan the horizon for threats. Garza doesn't look it, but the other Marines credit him with being one of the strongest men in the battalion, and physical strength rates high among them. He modestly explains his reputation for uncanny strength by joking, "Yeah, I'm strong. I've got retard strength."

•   •   •

Colbert's team is part of a twenty-three-man platoon in Bravo Company. Along with First Recon's other two line companies—Alpha and Charlie—as well as its support units, the battalion's job is to hunt the desert for Iraqi armor, while other Marines seize oil fields to the east. During the first forty-eight hours of the invasion, Colbert's team finds no tanks and encounters hundreds of surrendering Iraqi soldiers—whom Colbert does his best to avoid, so as not to be saddled with the burden of searching, feeding and detaining them, which his unit is ill-equipped to do. Fleeing soldiers, some of them still carrying weapons, as well as groups of civilian families stream past Colbert's vehicle parked by a canal on his team's second night in Iraq. Colbert delivers instructions to Garza, who is keeping watch on the Mark-19: "Make sure you don't shoot the civilians. We are an invading army. We must be magnanimous."

"Magna-nous?" Garza asks. "What the fuck does that mean?"

"Lofty and kinglike," Colbert answers.

Garza considers this information. "Sure," he says. "I'm a nice guy."

Colbert and Person mostly pass the time monitoring the sins committed by a Recon officer they nickname Captain America. Colbert and other Marines in the unit accuse Captain America of leading the men on wild-goose chases, disguised as legitimate missions. Captain America is a likable enough guy. If he corners you, he'll talk your ear off about all the wild times he had in college, working as a bodyguard for rock bands such as U2, Depeche Mode and Duran Duran. His men feel he uses these stories as a pathetic attempt to impress them, and besides, half of them have never heard of Duran Duran.

Before First Recon's campaign is over, Captain America will lose control of his unit and be investigated for leading his men into committing war crimes against enemy prisoners of war. A battalion inquiry will clear him, but here in the field, some of his men fantasize about his death. "All it takes is one dumb guy in charge to ruin everything," says one. "Every time he steps out of the vehicle, I pray he gets shot."

Aside from Captain America's antics, there's an inescapable sense among Colbert's team that this is going to be a dull war. All that changes when they reach Nasiriyah on their third day in Iraq.

. . .

On March 23rd, Colbert's team, in a convoy with the entire First Recon Battalion, cuts off from the backcountry desert trails and heads northwest to Nasiriyah, a city of about 300,000 on the Euphrates River.

By late afternoon, the battalion becomes mired in a massive traffic jam of Marine vehicles about thirty kilometers south of the city. The Marines are given no word about what's happening ahead, though they get some clue when, before sundown, they begin to notice a steady flow of casualty-evacuation helicopters flying back and forth from Nasiriyah. Eventually, traffic grinds to a halt. The Marines turn off their engines and wait.

During the past four days, no one on the team has slept for more than two hours a night, nor has anyone had a chance to remove his boots. Everyone wears bulky chemical-warfare protection suits and carries gas masks. When they do sleep, in holes dug at each stop, they are required to keep their boots on and wear their protective suits. They live on MREs (meals ready to eat), which come in plastic bags about half the size of a phone book. Inside there are about half a dozen foil packets containing a meat or vegetarian entree, such as meatloaf or pasta. More than half the calories in an MRE come from candy and junk food such as cheese pretzels and toaster pastries. Many Marines supplement this diet with massive amounts of freeze-dried coffee—they often just eat the crystals straight from the packet—chewing tobacco and over-the-counter stimulants including ephedra.

Colbert constantly harps on his men to drink water and to take naps whenever there is a chance, even questioning them on whether their pee is yellow or clear. When he comes back from taking a shit, Trombley turns the tables on him.

"Have a good dump, Sergeant?" he asks.

"Excellent," Colbert answers. "Shit my brains out. Not too hard, not too runny."

"That sucks when it's runny and you have to wipe fifty times," Trombley says conversationally.

"I'm not talking about that." Colbert assumes his stern teacher's voice. "If it's too hard or too soft, something's not right. You might have a problem."

"It should be a little acid," Person says, offering his own medical observation. "And burn a little when it comes out."

"Maybe on your little bitch asshole from all the cock that's been stuffed up it," Colbert snaps.

Hearing this exchange, another Marine in the unit says, "Man, the Marines are so homoerotic. That's all we talk about."

Another big topic is music. Colbert attempts to ban any references to country music in his vehicle. He claims that the mere mention of country, which he deems "the Special Olympics of music," makes him physically ill.

The Marines mock the fact that many of the tanks and Humvees stopped along the road are emblazoned with American flags or moto slogans such as "Angry American" or "Get Some." Person spots a Humvee with the 9/11 catchphrase "Let's Roll!" stenciled on the side.

"I hate that cheesy patriotic bullshit," Person says. He mentions Aaron Tippin's "Where the Stars and Stripes and Eagles Fly." "Like how he sings those country white-trash images. 'Where eagles fly.' Fuck! They fly in Canada, too. Like they don't fly there? My mom tried to play me that song when I came home from Afghanistan. I was like, 'Fuck, no, Mom. I'm a Marine. I don't need to fly a little flag on my car to show I'm patriotic.'"

"That song is straight homosexual country music, Special Olympics-gay," Colbert says.

Colbert's team spends the night by the highway. Late in the night, we hear artillery booming up ahead in the direction of Nasiriyah. The ground trembles as a column of massive M1A1 tanks rolls past, a few feet from where the Marines are resting. Out of the darkness, someone shouts, "Hey, if you lay down with your cock on the ground, it feels good."

A couple of hours after sunrise on the 24th, they tune in to the BBC on a shortwave radio that Colbert carries in the Humvee and hear the first word of fighting up the road in Nasiriyah. A while later, Colbert's platoon commander, Lt. Nathan Fick, holds a briefing for the three other team leaders in the twenty-three-man platoon. Fick, who's twenty-five, has the pleasant good looks of a former altar boy, which he is. The son of a successful Baltimore attorney, he went through Officer Candidate School after graduating from Dartmouth. This is his second deployment in a war. He commanded a Marine infantry platoon in Afghanistan. But like Colbert and the six other Marines in the platoon who also served in Afghanistan, he saw very little shooting.

Fick tells his men that the Marines have been taking heavy casualties in Nasiriyah. Yesterday, the town was declared secure. But then an Army supply unit traveling near the city came under attack from an Iraqi guerrilla unit of Saddam Hussein loyalists called fedayeen. These fighters, Fick says, wear civilian clothes and set up positions in the city among the general populace, firing mortars, rocket-propelled grenades (RPGs) and machine guns from rooftops, apartments and alleys. They killed or captured twelve soldiers from the Army supply unit, including a woman. Overnight, a Marine combat team from Task Force Tarawa attempted to move into the city across the main bridge over the Euphrates. Nine Marines lost their lives, and seventy more were injured.

First Recon has been ordered to the bridge to support Task Force Tarawa, which barely controls its southern approach. Fick can't tell his men exactly what they're going to do when they get to the bridge, as the plans are still being drawn up at a higher level. What he does tell the men is that their rules of engagement have changed. Until now, they've let armed Iraqis pass, sometimes even handing them food rations. Now, Fick says, "Anyone with a weapon is declared hostile. If it's a woman walking away from you with a weapon on her back, shoot her."

At 1:30 P.M., the 374 Marines of First Recon form up on the road and start rolling north toward the city. Given the news of heavy casualties during the past twenty-four hours, it's a reasonable assessment that everyone in the vehicle has a better than average chance of getting killed or injured in Nasiriyah.

The air is heavy with a fine, powdery dust that hangs like dense fog. Cobras clatter directly overhead, swooping low with the grace of flying sledgehammers. They circle First Recon's convoy, nosing down through the barren scrubland on either side of the road, hunting for enemy shooters. Before long, we are on our own. The helicopters are called off because fuel is short. The bulk of the Marine convoy is held back until the Iraqi forces ahead are put down. One of the last Marines we see standing by the road pumps his fist as Colbert's vehicle drives past and shouts, "Get some!"

We drive into a no man's land. A burning fuel depot spews fire and smoke. Garbage is strewn on either side of the road as far as the eye can see. The convoy slows to a crawl, and the Humvee fills with a black cloud of flies.

"Now, *this* looks like Tijuana," says Person.

"And this time I get to do what I've always wanted to do in T.J.," Colbert answers. "Burn it to the ground."

There is a series of thunderous, tooth-rattling explosions directly to the vehicle's right. We are even with a Marine heavy-artillery battery set up next to the road, firing into Nasiriyah, a few kilometers ahead. There's a mangled Humvee in the road. The windshield is riddled with bullet holes. Nearby are the twisted hulks of U.S. military-transport trucks, then a blown-up Marine armored vehicle. Marine rucksacks are scattered on the road, clothes and bedrolls spilling out.

We pass a succession of desiccated farmsteads—crude, square huts made of mud, with starving livestock in front. The locals sit outside like spectators. A woman walks past with a basket on her head, oblivious to the explosions. No one has spoken for ten minutes, and Person cannot repress the urge to make a goofy remark. He turns to Colbert, smiling. "Hey, you think I have enough driving hours now to get my Humvee license?"

We reach the bridge over the Euphrates. It is a long, broad concrete structure. It spans nearly a kilometer and arches up gracefully toward the middle. On the opposite bank, we glimpse Nasiriyah. The front of the city is a jumble of irregularly shaped two- and three-story structures. Through the haze, the buildings appear as a series of dim, slanted outlines, like a row of crooked tombstones.

Nasiriyah is the gateway to ancient Mesopotamia, the Fertile Crescent lying between the Euphrates, just above us, and the Tigris, a hundred kilometers north. This land has been continuously inhabited for 5,000 years. It was here that humankind first invented the wheel, the written word and algebra. Scholars believe that Mesopotamia was the site of the Garden of Eden. After three days in the desert, the Marines are amazed to find themselves in this pocket of tropical vegetation. There are lush groves of palm trees all around, as well as fields where tall grasses are growing. As Marine artillery rounds explode around us, Colbert keeps repeating, "Look at these fucking trees."

While two First Recon companies are instructed to set up positions on the banks of the Euphrates, Bravo Company waits at the foot of the bridge, about 200 meters away from the river's edge. No sooner are we settled than machine-gun fire begins to rake the area. Incoming rounds make a zinging sound, just like they do in Bugs Bunny cartoons. They hit palm trees nearby, shredding the fronds, sending puffs of smoke off the trunks. Marines from Task Force Tarawa to our right and to our left open up with machine guns. First Recon's Alpha and Charlie companies begin blasting targets in the city with their heavy guns.

Enemy mortars start to explode on both sides of Colbert's vehicle, about 150 meters distant. "Stand by for shit to get stupid," Person says, sounding merely annoyed. He adds, "You know that feeling before a debate when you gotta piss and you've got that weird feeling in your stomach, then you go in and kick ass?" He smiles. "I don't have that feeling now."

Marine helicopters fly low over a palm grove across the street, firing rockets and machine guns. It looks like we've driven into a Vietnam War movie. As if on cue, Person starts singing a Creedence Clearwater Revival song. This war will need its own theme music, he tells me. "That fag Justin Timberlake will make a soundtrack for it," he says, adding with disgust, "I just read that all these pussy faggot pop stars like Justin Timberlake and Britney Spears were going to make an anti-war song. When I become a pop star, I'm just going to make pro-war songs."

While Person talks, there's a massive explosion nearby. An

errant Marine artillery round hits a power line and detonates overhead, sending shrapnel into a vehicle ahead of ours. A group of six Marines is also hit. Two are killed immediately; the four others are injured. Through the smoke, we can hear them screaming for a medic. Everyone takes cover in the dirt.

I lie as flat on the ground as possible. I look up and see a Marine cursing and wiggling, trying to pull down his chemical-protection suit. The pants don't have zippers in the front. You have to unhook suspenders and wrestle them down, especially tough when you're lying sideways. It's a Marine in Colbert's platoon, one of his closest friends, Sgt. Antonio Espera, 30. Espera grew up in Riverside, California, and was, by his own account, truly a "bad motherfucker"—participating in all the violent pastimes available to a young Latino from a broken home and raised partially in state facilities. With his shaved head and deep-set eyes, he's one of the scariest-looking Marines in the platoon, but Espera makes no show of trying to laugh off his fear. He's wrestling his penis out of his pants so he can take a leak while lying on his side. "I don't want to fucking piss on myself," he grunts.

The Marines took a combat-stress class before the war. An instructor told them that twenty-five percent of them can expect to lose control of their bladders or bowels when they take fire. Before the war started, many in First Recon tried to get Depend diapers—not just for embarrassing combat accidents, but in case they have to wear their chemical-warfare protection suits for twenty-four to forty-eight hours after an actual attack. These never arrived, so they piss and shit frantically whenever they can.

The guy on my other side is another Bravo team leader, Sgt. Larry Sean Patrick, 28, of Lincolntown, North Carolina, and he's looked up to about as much as Colbert is. I ask him what the hell we're doing just waiting around while the bombs fall. His response is sobering. He tells me the platoon is about to be sent on a suicide mission. "Our job is to kamikaze into the city and collect casualties," he says.

"How many casualties are there?" I ask.

"Casualties?" he says. "They're not there yet. We're the reaction force for an attack that's coming across the bridge. We go in during the fight to pick up the wounded."

I don't know why, but the idea of waiting around for casualties that don't exist yet strikes me as more macabre than the idea of actual casualties.

Yet despite how much it sucks here—by this bridge, taking heavy fire—it's kind of exciting, too. I had almost looked down on the Marines' shows of moto, the way they shouted "get some" and acted all excited about being in a fight. But the fact is, there's a definite sense of exhilaration every time there's an explosion and you're still there afterward. There's another kind of exhilaration, too. Everyone is side by side facing the same big fear: death. Usually, death is pushed to the fringes of things you do in the civilian world. Most people face their end pretty much alone, with a few family members if they are lucky. Here, the Marines face death together, in their youth. If anyone dies, he will do so surrounded by the very best friends he believes he will ever have.

As mortars continue to explode around us, I watch Garza pick through an MRE. He takes out a packet of Charms candies and hurls it into the gunfire. Marines view Charms as almost infernal talismans. A few days earlier, in the Humvee, Garza saw me pull Charms out of my MRE pack. His eyes lighted up and he offered me a highly prized bag of cheese pretzels for my candies. He didn't explain why. I thought he just really liked Charms until he threw the pack he'd just traded me out the window. "We don't allow Charms anywhere in our Humvee," Person said, in a rare show of absolute seriousness. "That's right," Colbert said, cinching it. "They're fucking bad luck."

A fresh pair of Marine gunships flies overhead, firing rockets into a nearby grove of palm trees. Bravo Marines leap up after one of the helicopters fires a TOW missile that sends up a large orange fireball from the trees. "Get some!" the Marines shout.

For nearly six hours, we are pinned down, waiting, we think, to storm into Nasiriyah. But after sunset, plans are changed, and First Recon is called back from the bridge to a position four kilometers into the trash-strewn wastelands south of the city. When the convoy stops in relative safety, away from the bridge, Marines wander out of the vehicles in high spirits. First Recon's Alpha Company killed at least ten Iraqis across the river from our position. They come up to Colbert's vehicle to regale his team with exploits of their slaughter, bragging about one kill in particular, a fat fedayeen in a bright-orange shirt. "We shredded him with our .50-cals," one says.

It's not just bragging. When Marines talk about the violence they wreak, there's an almost giddy shame, an uneasy exultation in having committed society's ultimate taboo, and doing it with state sanction.

"Well, good on you," Colbert says to his friend.

Person stands by the road pissing. "Man, I pulled my trousers down, and it smells like hot dick. That sweaty hot-cock smell. I kind of smell like I just had sex." Despite the cold, Bravo's Sgt. Rudy Reyes, 31, from Kansas City, Missouri, has stripped off his shirt and is washing his chest with baby wipes, every muscle gleaming in the flickering light of a nearby oil fire.

Reyes doesn't quite fit the image of the macho brute. He reads Oprah's magazine and waxes his legs and chest. Other members of the unit call him "fruity Rudy" because he is so beautiful. "It doesn't mean you're gay if you think Rudy's hot. He's just so beautiful," Person tells me. "We all think he's hot."

The Recon Marines are told they will be pushing north through Nasiriyah at dawn, along a route they've deemed "sniper alley." At midnight, Espera and I share a last cigarette. We climb under a Humvee for cover and lie on our backs, passing it back and forth.

"I've been so up and down today," Espera says. "I guess this is how a woman feels." He's extremely worried about driving through Nasiriyah in a few hours and even admits to having second thoughts about coming to Iraq at all. "I asked a priest if it's OK to kill people in war," he tells me. "He said it's OK as long as you don't enjoy it. Before we crossed into Iraq, I fucking hated Arabs. I don't know why. But as soon as we got here, it's just gone. I just feel sorry for them. I miss my little girl. I don't want to kill anybody's children."

Past midnight, Marine artillery booms into the city. Back in the Humvee, Trombley once again talks about his hopes of having a son with his new young bride when he returns home.

"Never have kids, Corporal," Colbert lectures. "One kid will cost you $300,000. You should never have gotten married. It's always a mistake." Colbert often proclaims the futility of marriage. "Women will always cost you money, but marriage is the most expensive way to go. If you want to pay for it, Trombley, go to Australia. For a hundred bucks, you can order a whore over the phone. Half an hour later, she arrives at your door, fresh and hot, like a pizza."

Despite his bitter proclamations about women, if you catch Colbert during an unguarded moment, he'll admit that he once loved one girl who jilted him, a junior-high-school sweetheart whom he dated on and off for ten years and was even engaged to until she left him to marry one of his closest buddies. "And we're still all friends," he says, sounding almost mad about it. "They're one of those couples that likes to takes pictures of themselves doing all the fun things they do and hang them up all over their goddamn house. Sometimes I just go over there and look at the pictures of my ex-fiancée doing all those fun things I used to do with her. It's nice having friends."

Just after sunrise, First Recon's seventy-vehicle convoy rolls over the bridge on the Euphrates and enters Nasiriyah. It's one of those sprawling Third World mud-brick-and-cinder-block cities that probably looks pretty badly rubbled even on a good day. This morning, smoke curls from collapsed structures. Most buildings facing the road are pockmarked and cratered. Cobras fly overhead spitting machine-gun fire. Dogs roam the ruins.

The convoy stops to pick up a Marine from another unit who is wounded in the leg. A few vehicles come under machine-gun and RPG fire. The Recon Marines return fire and redecorate an apartment building with about a dozen grenades fired from a Mark-19. In an hour, we clear the outer limits of the city and start to head north. Dead bodies are scattered along the edges of the road. Most are men, enemy fighters, some with weapons still in their hands. The Marines nickname one corpse Tomato Man, because from a distance he looks like a smashed crate of tomatoes in the road. There are shot-up cars and trucks with bodies hanging over the edges. We pass a bus, smashed and burned, with charred human remains sitting upright in some windows. There's a man with no head in the road and a dead little girl, too, about three or four, lying on her back. She's wearing a dress and has no legs.

We drive on, pausing a few kilometers ahead for the battalion to call in an airstrike on an Iraqi armored vehicle up the road. Next to me, Trombley opens up an MRE and furtively pulls out a pack of Charms. "Keep it a secret," he says. He unwraps the candies and stuffs them into his mouth.

•　　•　　•

At ten in the morning, first Recon is ordered off Highway 7, the main road heading north out of Nasiriyah, and onto a narrow dirt trail, to guard the main Marine fighting force's flanks. There's a dead man lying in a ditch where we turn off the highway. Two hundred meters past the corpse, there's a farmhouse with a family out front, waving as we drive by. At the next house, two old ladies in black jump up and down, whooping and clapping. A bunch of bearded men shout, "Good! Good! Good!" The Marines wave back. In the span of a few minutes, they have gone from kill-anyone-that-looks-dangerous mode to smiling and waving as if they're on a float in the Rose Bowl parade.

"Stay frosty, gents," Colbert warns. "No matter what you see, we're in back-country now, and we're all alone."

The road has dwindled down to a single narrow lane. We crawl along at a couple of miles per hour. There are farmhouses every few hundred meters. The Marines stop and toss bright-yellow humanitarian food packages at clusters of civilians. As kids run out to grab them, Colbert waves: "You're welcome. Vote Republican." He gazes at the "ankle biters" running after the food rations and says, "I really thank God I was born American. I mean, seriously, it's something I lose sleep over."

The demeanor of the civilians we pass has suddenly changed. They've stopped waving. Many avoid eye contact with us altogether. Over the radio, we hear that RCT 1 is in contact with enemy forces at a town a few kilometers to the north. As we continue along the road, we begin to notice that villagers on the other bank of the canal are fleeing in the opposite direction. Two villagers approach a Humvee behind Colbert's and warn the Marines through hand gestures that something bad lies ahead.

The convoy stops. We are at a bend in the road, with a five-foot-high berm to the left. Shots are fired directly ahead of us. "Incoming rounds," Person announces.

"Damn it," says Colbert. "I have to take a shit."

Instead, Colbert picks up a 203 round—an RPG—kisses the nose of it and slides it into the lower chamber of his gun. He opens the door and climbs up the embankment to observe a small cluster of homes on the other side. He signals for all the Marines to come out of the vehicle and join him on the berm. Marines from another platoon fire into the hamlet with rifles, machine guns and Mark-19s. But Colbert does not clear his team to fire. He can't discern any targets. About two kilometers up the road, where First Recon's Alpha Company is stopped, suspected fedayeen open up with machine guns and mortars. Alpha takes no casualties. The battalion calls in an artillery strike on the fedayeen positions.

The team gets back in the Humvee. Trombley sits in the back seat eating spaghetti directly out of a foil MRE pack, squeezing it into his mouth from a hole in the corner. "I almost shot that man," he says excitedly, referring to a farmer in the hamlet on the other side of the berm.

"Not yet," Colbert says. "Put your weapon on safety."

Nobody speaks for a solid ten minutes. A vicious sandstorm is kicking up. Fifty-to-sixty-mile-per-hour winds buffet the side of the vehicle. Visibility drops, and the air fills with yellow dust. The battalion is hemmed in on narrow back roads with enemy shooters in the vicinity.

RCT 1 is now waiting outside a town about six kilometers ahead. Its commander has reported taking fire from the town, and First Recon plans to bypass it. Colbert explains the situation to his men.

"Why can't we just go through the town?" Trombley asks.

"I think we'd get smoked," Colbert says.

Fifteen minutes later, we start moving north. Everyone in Colbert's vehicle believes we are taking a route that bypasses the hostile town, Al Gharraf. Then word comes over the radio of a change in plan. We are driving straight through.

Colbert's vehicle comes alongside the walls of the town, which looks like a smaller version of Nasiriyah. The street we are on, now paved, bears left. As Person makes the turn, the wall of a house directly to my right and no more than three meters from my window erupts with muzzle flashes and the clatter of machine-gun fire. The vehicle takes twenty-two bullets, five of them in my door. The light armor that covers much of the Humvee (eighth-inch steel plates riveted over the doors) stops most of them, but the windows are open and there are gaps in the armor. A bullet flies past Colbert's head and smacks into the frame behind Person's. Another round comes partially through my door.

We have barely entered the city, and it's a two-kilometer drive through it. Ahead of us, a Bravo Marine driving in an open Humvee takes a bullet in his arm.

The shooting continues on both sides. Less than half an hour before, Colbert had been talking about stress reactions in combat. In addition to the embarrassing losses of bodily control that twenty-five percent of all soldiers experience, other symptoms include time dilation, i.e., time slowing down or speeding up; vividness, a starkly heightened awareness of detail; random thoughts, the mind fixating on unimportant sequences; memory loss; and, of course, your basic feelings of sheer terror.

In my case, hearing and sight become almost disconnected. I see more muzzle flashes next to the vehicle but don't hear them. In the seat beside me, Trombley fires 300 rounds from his machine gun. Ordinarily, if someone was firing a machine gun that close to you, it would be deafening. His gun seems to whisper.

The look on Colbert's face is almost serene. He's hunched over his weapon, leaning out the window, intently studying the walls of the buildings, firing bursts from his M-4 and grenades from the 203 tube underneath the main barrel. I watch him pump in a fresh grenade, and I think, "I bet Colbert's really happy to be finally shooting a 203 round in combat." I remember him kissing the grenade earlier. Random thoughts.

I study Person's face for signs of panic, fear or death. My fear is he'll get shot or freak out, and we'll get stuck on this street. But Person seems fine. He's slouched over the wheel, looking through the windshield, an almost blank expression on his face. The only thing different about him is he's not babbling his opinions on Justin Timberlake or some other pussy faggot retard who bothers him.

Trombley pauses from shooting out his window and turns around with a triumphant grin. "I got one, Sergeant!" he shouts.

Colbert ignores him. Trombley eagerly goes back to shooting at people out his window. A gray object zooms toward the windshield and smacks into the roof. The Humvee fills with a metal-on-metal scraping sound, which I do hear. Earlier that day Colbert had traded out Garza for a Mark-19 gunner from a different unit. The guy's name is Cpl. Walt Hasser, 23, from Taylorstown, Virginia. Hasser's legs twist sideways. A steel cable has fallen or been dropped over the vehicle. Another one falls on it and scrapes across the roof.

Colbert calls out, "Walt, are you OK?" There's silence. Person turns around, taking his foot off the gas pedal.

The vehicle slows and wanders slightly to the left. "Walt?" Person calls.

"I'm OK!" he says, sounding almost cheerful. Person has lost his focus on moving the vehicle forward. We slow to a crawl. Person later says that he was worried one of the cables dropped on the vehicle might have been caught on Hasser. He didn't want to accelerate and somehow leave him hanging from a light pole by his neck in downtown Gharraf.

"Drive, Person!" Colbert shouts.

Person picks up the pace, and there is silence outside. We are still in the town, but no one seems to be shooting at us.

"Holy shit! Did you see that? We got fucking lit up!" Colbert is beside himself, laughing and shaking his head. "Holy shit!"

Trombley turns to Colbert, again seeking recognition. "I got one, Sergeant. His knee exploded, then I cut him in half!"

"You cut him in half?" Colbert asks. "That's great, Trombley!"

"Before we start congratulating ourselves," Person says, "we're not out of this yet."

We pass a mangled, burned car on the right, then Person makes a left into more gunfire. Set back from the road are several squat cinder-block buildings, like an indusdistrict. I see what looks like white puffs of smoke streaking out from them: more enemy fire. Person floors the Humvee. Colbert and Trombley start shooting again.

"I got another one!" Trombley shouts.

There's a white haze in the distance: the end of the city. We fly out onto a sandy field that looks almost like a beach. There's so much sand blowing in the air—winds at still at about sixty miles per hour—it's tough to see anything. There's gunfire all around. The Humvee drives about twenty meters into the sand, then sinks into it. Person floors the engine, and the wheels spin. The Humvee has sunk up to the door frames in tar. It's a sobka field. Sobka is a geological phenomenon peculiar to the Middle East. It looks like desert on top, with a hard crust of sand an inch or so thick, which a man could possibly walk on, but break through the crust and beneath it's the La Brea tar pits, quicksand made of tar.

Colbert jumps out and runs to the other Recon vehicles, lined up now, shooting into the city. He runs down the lines of guns, shouting, "Cease fire! Assess the situation!"

Back at Colbert's Humvee, one of his superiors pounds on the roof and shouts, "Abandon the Humvee!" He adds, "Thermite the radios!" He is referring to a kind of intense-heat grenade used to destroy sensitive military equipment before abandoning it.

Colbert jumps up behind him. "Fuck, no! I'm not thermiting anything. We're driving this out of here!"

He dives under the wheel wells with bolt cutters, slicing away the steel cables, a gift of the defenders of Gharraf, wrapped around the axle. A five-ton support truck backs up, its driver taking fire, and Marines attach towing cables to our axle. Within half an hour, Colbert's vehicle is freed and limping to Recon's camp, a few kilometers distant, for the night.

The Bravo Marines spend half an hour recounting every moment of the ambush. Aside from the driver in the other platoon who was shot in the arm, no one was hit. They laugh uproariously about all the buildings they blew up. Privately, Colbert confesses to me that he had absolutely no feelings going through the city. He almost seems disturbed by this. "It was just like training." he says. "I just loaded and fired my weapon from muscle memory. I wasn't even aware what my hands were doing."

That night we are rewarded with the worst sandstorm we have have experienced in Iraq. Under a pitch-black sky, sand and pebbles kicked up by sixty-mile-per-hour winds pelt sleeping bags like hail. Then it rains. Lightning flashes intermingle with Marine artillery rounds sailing into the city. Just before turning in, I smell a sickly-sweet odor. During chemical-weapons training before the war, we were taught that some nerve agents emit unusual, fragrant odors. I put on my gas mask and sit in the dark Humvee for twenty minutes before Person tells me what I'm smelling is a cheap Swisher Sweet cigar that Espera is smoking underneath his Humvee.

•　　•　　•

The next morning at dawn, Lt. Fick tells his Marines, "The good news is, we will be rolling with a lot of ass today. RCT 1 will be in front of us for most of the day. The bad news is, we're going through four more towns like the one we hit yesterday."

There are wild dogs everywhere along the highway. "We ought to shoot some of these dogs," Trombley says.

"We don't shoot dogs," Colbert says.

"I'm afraid of dogs," Trombley mumbles.

I ask him if he was ever attacked by a dog when he was little.

"No," he answers. "My dad was once. The dog bit him, and my dad jammed his hand down his throat and ripped up his stomach. I did have a dog lunge at me once on the sidewalk. I just threw it on its side, knocked the wind out of him."

"Where did we find this guy?" Person asks.

We drive on.

"I like cats," Trombley offers. "I had a cat that lived to be sixteen. One time he ripped a dog's eye out with his claw."

We pass dead bodies in the road again, men with weapons by their sides, then more than a dozen trucks and cars burned and smoking by the road. Many have a burned corpse or two of Iraqi soldiers who died after crawling five or ten meters away from the vehicle before they expired, hands still grasping forward on the pavement. Just north of here, at another stop, Marines in Fick's vehicle machine-gun four men in a field who appear to be stalking us. It's no big deal. Since the shooting started in Nasiriyah forty-eight hours ago, firing weapons and seeing dead people has become almost routine.

• • •

We stop next to a green field with a small house set back from the road. Marines from a different unit suspect that gunshots came from the house. A Bravo Marine sniper observes the house for forty-five minutes. He sees women and children inside, nobody with guns. For some reason, a handful of Marines from the other unit opens fire on the house. Soon, Marines down the line join in with heavy weapons.

One of Recon's own officers, whom the Marines have nicknamed Encino Man because of his apelike appearance, steps out of his command vehicle. He is so eager to get in the fight, it seems, he forgets to unplug his radio headset, which jerks his head back as the cord, still attached to the dash unit, tightens. Colbert, who believes the house contains only noncombatants, starts screaming, "Jesus Christ! There's fucking civilians in that house! Cease fire!"

Encino Man pops off a 203 grenade that falls wildly short of the house. Colbert, like other Marines in Bravo, is furious. Not only do they believe this Recon officer is firing on civilians, but the guy also doesn't even know how to range his 203.

Colbert sits in the Humvee, trying to rationalize the events outside that have spiraled beyond his control: "Everyone's just tense. Some Marine took a shot, and everyone has just followed suit."

Before this event can be fully resolved—some Marines insist gunshots did come from the house—First Recon is sent several kilometers up the road to the edge of another town, Ar Rifa. Colbert's team stops thirty meters from the town's outer walls. The winds have died down, but dust is so think in the air that it looks like twilight at noon. An electrical substation is on fire next to Colbert's vehicle, adding its own acrid smoke. Shots come from the town, and Colbert's team fires back.

But a different crisis is brewing a few vehicles down. Encino Man, who an hour ago attempted to fire on the house Colbert believed contained civilians, commits what his men believe is a more dangerous blunder. Operating under the belief that a team of fedayeen is nearby, Encino Man attempts to call in an artillery strike almost directly on top of Bravo's position. A few enlisted Marines in Bravo confront the officer. One calls Encino Man a "dumb motherfucker" to his face.

Fick attempts to intervene on the side of the enlisted Marines, and the officer threatens him disciplinary action. The artillery strike never occurs. But the incident aggravates growing tensions between First Recon's officers and its enlisted men, who are beginning to fear that some of their leaders are dangerously incompetent.

After night falls outside of Rifa, another bad day in Iraq ends with a new twist: a friendly-fire incident. A U.S. military convoy moving up the road in complete darkness mistakenly opens fire on First Recon's vehicles. Inside his Humvee, Sgt. Colbert sees the "friendly" red tracer rounds coming from the appraoching convoy and orders everyone down. One round slices through the rear of the Humvee, behind the seat where Trombley and I are sitting.

Later, we find out from Fick that we were shot up by Navy Reservist surgeons on their way to set up a mobil shock-trauma unit on the road ahead. "Those were fucking doctors who do nose and tit jobs," Fick tells the men.

.   .   .

A half-hour after the friendly-fire incident. First Recon is ordered to immediately drive forty kilometers through back roads to the Qal'at Sukkar airfield, deep behind enemy lines. "Well, I guess we won't be sleeping tonight," Colbert says.

The drive takes about three hours. On the way, the men are informed that they will be setting up an observation post on the field to prepare for a parachute assault that British forces are going to execute at dawn. But plans change again at sunrise. At 6:20, after the Bravo Marines have slept for about ninety minutes, Colbert is awakened and told his men have ten minutes to race onto the airfield, six kilometers away, and assault it.

At 6:28, Colbert's team is in the Humvee driving with thirty other Recon vehicles down a road they've never even studied on a map. They're told over the radio they will face enemy tanks.

"Everything and everyone on the airfield is hostile," Colbert says, passing on a direct order from his commander.

Next to me in the rear seat, Trombley says, "I see men running."

"Are they armed?" Colbert asks.

"There's something," Trombley says.

I look out Trombley's window and see a bunch of camels.

"Everyone's declared hostile," Colbert says. "Light them up."

Trombley fires a burst or two from his SAW. "Shooting motherfuckers like it's cool," he says, amused with himself.

The Humvees race onto the airfield and discover it's abandoned, nothing but crater-pocked airstrips. Nevertheless, they've beaten the British to it. The landing is called off.

"Gentlemen, we just seized an airfield," Colbert says. "That was pretty ninja."

An hour later, the Marines have set up a camp off the edge of the airfield. They are told they will stay here for a day or longer. This morning, the sun shines and there's no dust in the air. For the first time in a week, many of the Marines take their boots and socks off. They unfurl camo nets for shade and lounge beside their Humvees. A couple of Recon Marines walk over to Trombley and tease him about shooting camels.

"I think I got one of those Iraqis, too. I saw him go down."

"Yeah, but you killed a camel, too, and wounded another one."

The Marines seem to have touched a nerve.

"I didn't mean to," Trombley says defensively. "They're innocent."

A couple of hours later, two Bedouin women arrive at the edge of Bravo's perimeter. Bedouins are nomadic tribespeople who roam the desert, living in tents, herding sheep and camels. One of the women is dressed in a purple robe and appears to be in her thirties. She is pulling a heavy object wrapped in a blanket and is accompanied by an old woman with blue tribal tattoos on her wrinkled face. They stop on top of a berm about twenty meters away and start waving. Robert Timothy Bryan, a Navy Corpsman who functions as the platoon's medic, walks over to them.

Later, he'll say that he's not sure why he even walked up to the women. In recent days, Marines have grown weary of Iraqi civilians, who have begun accosting them, begging for food, cigarettes, sometimes even chanting the one English word they all seem to be learning: "Money, money, money." When he reaches them, he notices that the younger woman seems highly distraught, gesturing and moving her mouth, but no words come out. Her breasts are exposed, her robes having fallen open while she was dragging her bundle across the fields. As Bryan approaches, she frantically unrolls its contents, revealing what appears to be a youth's bloody corpse. The boy looks about fourteen. Then he opens his eyes. Bryan kneels down. There are four small holes, two on each side of his stomach.

Bryan begins treating him immediately. In the field, several men appear walking a seventeen-year-old with blood streaming down his right leg. The two Bedouin boys were shot with rounds from a Marine SAW. Trombley is the only Marine who fired his SAW that morning. There were no other Marines in the area for twenty kilometers.

Bryan assesses the boys' condition, cursing loudly as other Marines approach. "These fucking jackasses," he says. "Trigger-happy motherfuckers."

The woman in purple, the mother, kneels, putting her hands in the air, still talking with no sounds coming out. The old lady, who turns out to be the grandmother, stands up, cigarette dangling from her lips, and covers her daughter's breasts as more Marines walk up. None of the Bedouins—there are about eight sitting around watching Bryan examine the boy—seems the least bit angry. When I walk over, the grandmother offers me a cigarette.

The younger boy's name is Naif. His brother, still hobbling around on his bloody shot leg, is Latif. The boys had gone out to the family's herd of camels, which had been frightened by the Marine Humvees and started running. The boys were chasing after them when they were shot. One was carrying a stick.

Each of the four holes in Naif's body is an entry wound, meaning the four bullets zoomed around inside his slender stomach and chest cavity, ripping apart his organs.

Bryan continues cursing his fellow Marines. "We're *Recon* Marines," he says. "We're paid to observe. We don't shoot unarmed children."

Bravo Marines are now milling around, trying to help. They hold up ponchos over the two wounded boys, shielding them from the sun. But there's not much else to do. Bryan determines that the younger boy has hours to live unless he can be med-evacked. But Lt. Col. Steve Ferrando, the battalion commander, has sent a Marine bearing news that the request has been denied. Just then, an unmanned spy plane flies low overhead. "We can afford to fly fucking Predators," Bryan says, "but we can't take care of this kid?"

Just then, Colbert comes up the hill. He sees the mother, the kid, the brother with the bloody leg, the family, the Marines holding up the ponchos.

"This is what Trombley did," Bryan says. A Marine at the front of the convoy says he passed the same shepherds and it was obvious to him that they were not hostile. "Twenty Marines drove past those kids and didn't shoot," he says.

"Don't say that," Colbert says. "Don't put this on Trombley. I'm responsible for this. It was my orders."

Colbert kneels down over the kid and starts crying. He doesn't lose control or anything dramatic. His eyes just water, and he says, "What can I do here?"

"Apparently fucking nothing," Bryan says.

Within a couple of minutes, the Recon Marines have come up with a plan. They load the boy onto a stretcher to carry him into the camp. With Colbert and Bryan carrying the front of the stretches, they lead the entire entourage of Marines and Bedouin tribespeople underneath the camouflage nets of the battalion headquarters. "What the hell is going on here?" Sgt. Maj. John Sixta, First Recon's highest-ranking enlisted man, walks up, veins pulsing on his head as he confronts what seems to be a mutinous breakdown of military order.

"We brought him here to die," Bryan says defiantly.

"Get him the fuck out of here," the sergeant major bellows.

Ten minutes after they carry the Bedouin boy off, Ferrando has a change of heart. He orders his men to bring the Bedouins to the shock-trauma unit, twenty kilometers south. Some Marines believe Ferrando reversed himself to heal the growning rift between the officers and enlisted men in the battalion. As Bryan climbs onto the back of an open truck with the wounded boys and most of their clan, a Marine walks up to him and says, "Hey, Doc. Get some."

Colbert walks off, privately inconsolable. "I'm going to have to bring this home with me and live with it," he says. "Pilots don't see what they do when they drop bombs. We do." He goes back to the Humvee, sits Trombley down and tells him he is not responsible for what happened: "You were following my orders." Already there are rumors spreading of a possible judicial inquiry into the shooting. "Is this going to be OK, I mean with the investigation?" Trombley asks Colbert.

"You'll be fine, Trombley."

"No. I mean for you, Sergeant." Trombley grins. "I don't care what happens, really. I'm out in a couple of years. I mean for you. This is your career."

"I'll be fine." Colbert stares at him. "No worries."

(After an inquiry, Trombley and Bravo Company are cleared of any wrongdoing.)

Something's been bothering me about Trombley for a day or two, and I can't help thinking about it now. I was never quite sure if I should believe his claim that he cut up those two Iraqis in Gharraf. But he hit those two shepherds, one of whom was extremely small, at more than 200 meters, from a Humvee bouncing down a rough road at forty miles per hour. However horrible the results, his work was textbook machine-gun shooting, and the fact is, from now on, every time I ride with Colbert's team, I feel a lot better when Trombley is by my side with the SAW.

Esquire

FINALIST, FEATURE WRITING

The League of Extraordinary Gentlemen

Who would ever think to invite Tucker Carlson, one of the whitest and most conservative men in America, on a peace mission to Liberia? The trip, brainchild of Al Sharpton, results in Carlson's hilarious story about a handful of America's black leaders who set out to make order out of chaos in a war-torn land. They fail completely, but they do succeed in embracing—figuratively and, eventually, literally—their misfit friend.

Tucker Carlson

The League of Extraordinary Gentlemen

Recently, an eminent, varied, large, and unlikely delegation of Americans, led by the Reverend Al Sharpton, went to Africa to heal a wounded continent. They took the whitest man in America with them.

Five minutes before we boarded the plane to Africa, Al Sharpton called the group into a circle to pray. It struck me as a fine idea. Sharpton's plan to lead a delegation of American civil-rights activists into the middle of the Liberian civil war clearly was going to require some divine support. And that was assuming we even got there. A man in the departure lounge at JFK had just finished telling me a long and disturbing story about Ghana Airways, the carrier we had chosen for the eleven-hour flight over. Apparently, much of its fleet was in Italy at the moment, impounded for debt. The rest was aging, creaky, and, given the virtually bankrupt condition of the company, spottily maintained. "Ghana Airways probably won't even exist a month from now," the man said. I was all for praying.

Fourteen of us gathered across from the gate one afternoon in late July and held hands. On my left was Sanford Rubenstein, Abner Louima's lawyer in the NYPD brutality case. On my right was His Eminence Franzo W. King, D.D., archbishop and lead sax player of the St. John Coltrane African Orthodox Church in San Francisco. Across the circle was former D. C. mayor Marion Barry's wife, Cora Masters Barry, and three guys from the Nation of Islam, two of them named James Muhammad. Cornel West, the writer and scholar, led the prayer. "Lord, keep us safe," West intoned as we bowed our heads. "But more important, keep us soulful."

No one looked more soulful than West himself, who was dressed, as always, like a slightly flashy undertaker: white shirt, black three-piece suit, silver pocket watch and chain. He could have been on his way to meet the next of kin. In fact, he was coming from a jazz club. West had stayed in the city until 4:00 A.M. before returning to his "crib in Jersey" (Princeton, New Jersey, where he teaches), then catching a ride to the airport. Along the way, he'd neglected to pack. West boarded the flight for Ghana with two books and a tiny carry-on the size of a woman's cosmetic case. That was it. He had no suitcases or garment bags or luggage of any kind. Nor did he have any real idea where we were going or how long we might be there. "When are we coming back?" he asked me as we walked down the ramp onto the plane.

It was not an idle question. By the morning we left, Sharpton's office had released only three days of what was supposed to be a weeklong itinerary. From what I could tell, the plan was to fly to Ghana and charter a plane from there to Liberia, where Sharpton would meet with indicted-war-criminal president Charles Taylor and talk peace. Of course, Sharpton doesn't have the standing to negotiate anything on behalf of anybody other than himself. But to get hung up on this fact is to miss the improvisational brilliance of this trip. And besides, Sharpton had actually spoken to Colin Powell about it just two days before. The State Department had raised no objection.

Once Sharpton had completed whatever it was he planned to do with Charles Taylor, we were going to leave Liberia, presumably again by charter, and head back to Ghana. Unless plans changed and we decided to fly down to South Africa for an audience with Nelson Mandela. Or something like that. At the end, we'd come home.

Those were all the details I got, and they were hard earned. I'd first heard about the trip only five days before, when Rachel Noerdlinger, Sharpton's spokeswoman, sent me a two-sentence e-mail: "Rev. is planning to head to Liberia this Sat. and if you want to go, call Minister Akbar Muhammad for travel details." She added that if I wanted my visa expedited, I should call a number in Brooklyn and "ask for Brian."

I called Brian first. He was friendly enough and seemed to know a lot about embassies. But when he declined to reveal his last name, I decided against sending him my passport. Next I called Akbar Muhammad. Muhammad is the international representative of the Nation of Islam and a longtime assistant to Louis Farrakhan. He was recruited into the Nation in 1960 by Malcolm X himself. A few years ago, when it looked as if Farrakhan might die of prostate cancer, Muhammad was considered a likely successor. In the Nation of Islam, Akbar Muhammad is a big deal. In his spare time, he runs a travel agency in St. Louis.

Muhammad agreed to purchase my plane tickets and set up hotel and travel arrangements, all for a 2.5 percent processing fee. Rachel Noerdlinger seemed surprised when I told her about it. "You gave your *credit card* to Akbar Muhammad?" she said. "The entire Nation of Islam is going to be buying clothes on you. Louis Farrakhan's going to get a new house on your MasterCard." Actually, she assured me, "they'd get their ass in trouble if they did that."

Not that the possibility really bothered me. Sure, it would be a hassle if Louis Farrakhan bought a new house on my Master-Card. But what a story. The trip had the same sort of appeal: an African war zone. With Al Sharpton. Accompanied by a busload of black nationalists and Abner Louima's lawyer. It was hard to say exactly what it all added up to, apart from a pretty interesting scene. That was enough for me.

Midway across the Atlantic, the captain informed us that we'd be making an unscheduled stop in the Azores to refuel. It was the middle of the night when we landed on Santa Maria Island, a ten-mile-long rock with a gas pump. We were sitting on the runway in the dark when *I Love Lucy* came on.

Due to budget cuts, Ghana Airways does not provide headphones. This means that all in-flight entertainment must be piped through the plane's PA system. The effect is to make even the chirpiest dialogue sound like an Official Announcement. I knew Ricky was saying something to Lucy about her spending habits, but I couldn't shake the feeling he was talking about emergency exits and flotation devices.

Suddenly, a commotion broke out in business class. The Reverend Al Sampson, the pastor of Fernwood United Methodist Church in Chicago and a longtime friend of Sharpton's, had collared a flight attendant and was berating him about the choice of entertainment. "We're going to Africa," Sampson said, very agitated. "This is *Ghana Airways*. And you put this on? We shouldn't have to watch *I Love Lucy* in the year 2003."

The flight attendant was squatting in the aisle, doing his best to listen politely. He was obviously confused. Julianne Malveaux, the liberal commentator and PBS host, who happened to be sitting nearby, jumped in. "This is *offensive*," she said.

Overwhelmed, the flight attendant left to get his superior, who arrived at a half trot. The discussion continued at high volume for the rest of the episode. Sampson never explained precisely what was so disturbing about *I Love Lucy*. His main point seemed to be that it was a show "with no cultural context," which I took to mean that it had too many white people.

He was still stewing when we arrived in Ghana at five in the morning. On the bus to the hotel, someone mentioned a story that had run on Black Entertainment Television about Sharpton's trip to Africa. Apparently it was unflattering. Sampson made the connection immediately.

"Who owns *I Love Lucy*?" he said. "Viacom. And what's part of Viacom? BET. BET is part of Viacom."

"That's right," said someone from the back of the bus.

Sampson nodded sagely. "So you know that the disinformation is just beginning."

It was a tantalizing introduction, and I wanted to hear more. Unfortunately, before Sampson could flesh out the BET—Viacom—Ricky Ricardo nexus, we had arrived at the hotel. After a shower and a change of clothes, we were off again.

As a rule, the civil-rights establishment is not punctual. But even by the standards of the chronically late, Sharpton is chronically late. Like all politicians, he tends to schedule an impossible number of events in a single day. But that's only part of the problem. Habit accounts for the rest. After spending so many years on the road, with so little cash, so far from the edge of respectability, Sharpton has lost the ability to travel like a legitimate person. In Sharpton's world, itineraries are merely suggestions. It's a measure of his awesome natural talent that he's able to get anything done at all. He's that disorganized.

One of the few commitments that Sharpton never misses is church on Sunday. He attends a service no matter where he happens to be. If you know Sharpton primarily through his political activism—or his history as a Tawana Brawley adviser or FBI informant or James Brown protégé—it can be hard to believe that he's actually a Christian clergyman. Doubts disappear when you hear him preach.

Sharpton preaches like a man who has been doing it since before he could read or write. (He was only four when he gave his first sermon on John 14 in front of nine hundred people at the Washington Temple Church of God in Christ in Brooklyn.) His sermons are as extemporaneous as his schedule. Not a word is written down; everything is subject to change. Often he switches the topic of a sermon midway through in response to what he feels from the crowd. Sometimes he bursts into song.

Most surprising of all, there's a fair amount of religion in Sharpton's preaching. He quotes at length from the Bible, talks without embarrassment about Jesus and redemption and heaven and hell. He believes in the supernatural and says so. He's probably the only Democratic presidential candidate this year who is comfortable discussing faith healing, prophesies, and speaking in tongues, all of which he has seen and is convinced are real.

Sharpton was scheduled to preach at Calvary Baptist Church in downtown Accra the first morning of the trip. We arrived more than an hour late. Annoyed, the pastor interrupted Sharpton's sermon after just five minutes. For the rest of the service, the congregation sang. Archbishop King of the Church of Coltrane stood in front of the altar in full clerical regalia playing the saxophone. Two local men played the congas. Women danced in the aisles. Cornel West hugged me for the second time that morning. After a few minutes, Sharpton got a call on his satellite phone and went outside.

It was Jewel Taylor, the first lady of Liberia, calling from Monrovia once again to offer the spare bedroom in the presidential palace for our scheduled visit the next day. Sharpton was polite but skeptical. "We'll call her tomorrow morning," he said once he got off the phone. "If she doesn't answer, we'll know what that means."

• • •

At some point during our flight across the Atlantic, Charles Taylor had lost control of his country. Two rebel armies—Liberians United for Reconciliation and Democracy, known as LURD; and the Movement for Democracy in Liberia, known as MODEL—appeared to have taken everything but downtown Monrovia. LURD was said to be within ten miles of Taylor's home.

Liberia has been in a state of low-grade revolution since at least 1980, when a twenty-eight-year-old master sergeant named Samuel Doe executed virtually the entire leadership of the country, most of them descendants of freed American slaves. President Doe himself met his end ten years later, when he had the misfortune of being captured by a guerrilla leader known as General Prince Johnson. Johnson force-fed Doe his own penis, then cut off his ears and rolled him around Monrovia in a wheelbarrow until he died, videotaping the whole thing for posterity. The country went downhill from there. Taylor knew he had little hope for mercy if LURD made it to his house.

Which, it occurred to me, might explain why he seemed so eager to have Sharpton come visit. When you're facing slow death by acetylene torch, even a third-tier American presidential candidate can look like a lifeline. If Taylor did have to meet his enemies face-to-face, Sharpton might help him talk his way out of being castrated. In Africa as in Brooklyn, Sharpton is famous for being a good talker.

A similar thought had occurred to LURD, as I discovered when I called CNN's producer in Liberia. The network had asked me to bring a box of audio equipment to the CNN crew in Monrovia, which had essentially been stranded in the city when commercial air service was suspended the week before. The producer wasn't bullish on Sharpton's prospects of success. LURD was well aware he was coming, he said. They viewed the trip as an effort to prop up Taylor. LURD might try to kill Sharpton at the airport, the producer explained, or possibly at one of the roadblocks on the long drive into the city. It "would be brave" to come to Liberia tomorrow, he said.

The producer said one other thing. Actually, he didn't come right out and say it, because foreign correspondents, particularly Australian ones, almost never admit they're afraid, even when they're bleeding or on fire or falling out of airplanes. But the tone of his voice indicated that Monrovia was getting unruly. He and the other foreign press were hunkered in the U. S. embassy compound. Outside, Taylor's troops were fighting street battles with LURD forces. Many of the soldiers on both sides were barely in their teens. Some of the LURD forces were dressed in women's clothes—wedding dresses, blond wigs, high heels—and were deranged from huffing gasoline. It sounded like an uncomfortable scene.

If Sharpton was aware of what was happening in Liberia, he didn't show it. He just nodded when Akbar Muhammad explained that we'd be taking an ambulance plane into Monrovia after breakfast. He didn't flinch when told that LURD had just seized the airport. None of it seemed to bother him.

An hour later we drove to a hotel in Accra, where representatives of LURD, MODEL, and the Taylor government were holding "peace talks." The talks had been going on for six weeks, during which time, all sides agreed, nothing had been accomplished. Sharpton had decided it would be a good venue for his diplomatic skills.

Late in the afternoon, about thirty Liberian factional represen-
tatives and exile leaders filed into a room off the lobby of the
M Plaza Hotel. Sharpton was sitting at the head table, alongside
Archbishop King, Rev. Sampson, Cornel West, and Marjorie
Harris, the capable, good-natured director of Sharpton's National
Action Network. The idea was for Sharpton to moderate a discus-
sion among all sides, as a disinterested third party. I believe that
was the idea.

The secretary general of the National Patriotic Party, Taylor's
man in Accra, spoke first. "The U. S. has been the drum major
behind problems in Liberia," he began. With that in mind, the
United States government should take steps to atone for its sins,
mostly by not helping anybody who might be seeking to replace
Charles Taylor. That, said the secretary general, would be
"rewarding rebellion."

A representative from an anti-Taylor group immediately
objected. His name was Mohammed Kromah, and he identified
himself as the head of something called the Union of Liberian
Associations in the Americas. When not conducting diplomacy in
West Africa, Kromah is a supervisor at the Maryland Department
of Human Resources in Baltimore. Kromah, like most Liberians
outside the Taylor government, had seen relatives and friends die
in the endless cycle of wars and was desperate for U.S. interven-
tion. He spoke passionately about the historic ties between the
United States and Liberia. He pleaded for American troops to
come and end the killing. Finally, Al Sampson cut him off.

Sampson, a heavyset man in his sixties who is partial to gold
chains and safari suits, began by describing himself as "the man
who was ordained by Martin King." Then he launched into what
was perhaps the most patronizing lecture that I have ever personally witnessed. Addressing Kromah, Sampson explained that
the very idea of sending U.S. troops to Liberia was immoral.
African-American soldiers fighting in Africa? That would be
"black-on-black violence." Indeed, it would constitute a kind of

civil war within the African diaspora. "The problem is," Sampson thundered, "we ain't seeing each other as brothers."

That was for sure. Apart from skin tone, Sampson has more in common with Trent Lott than with the people he was haranguing. The average Liberian, it turns out, does not share the same assumptions as the average black Methodist minister from Chicago. "He doesn't understand," Mohammed Kromah said to me later. "Being brothers because we're all black. It sounds good. But when there were riots in Los Angeles after Rodney King, did they ask gang leaders to get together and talk? No, they took them to court. They sent police."

It was a good point, but Kromah had to wait a long time to make it. The Reverend Sampson was just getting started. By the time he got to our upcoming trip to the war zone, he had a far-away look in his eyes.

"Nobody in the White House is prepared to step into Liberia tomorrow to live or die," Sampson said. But we are. Because we cannot *know* the hour that God will call us home. We cannot *know* when our work on this earth is done. We can only do our duty. As Martin did. As Malcolm did. As Ron Brown did. For, like them, we have been to the mountaintop. And we are unafraid."

Or something like that. My notes trail off after the first *die*. I was too mesmerized to keep writing. Sampson seemed delighted by the idea of buying it in Liberia. You could tell he was imagining the headlines back home: "Spiritual Leader Slain on Quest for Peace: Chicagoland Minister Leaves Legacy of Healing."

I wasn't on board. For one thing, I hadn't been to the mountaintop yet. For another, my kids would miss me if I got killed. And since when did Ron Brown, Clinton's commerce secretary, get inducted into the pantheon of civil-rights martyrs?

By dinner, details of the chaos in Liberia were all over CNN, but as far as I know, no one in the group piped up to suggest that flying in might be a bad idea. I didn't. Around midnight I headed back to my room, feeling slightly ill. As I passed through the lobby, I saw Archbishop King sitting alone against a wall. I liked King. It's easy to mock a man who has founded a religion based on John Coltrane, who considers *A Love Supreme*, whatever its merits as a jazz album, to be holy scripture. It's hard to take a man like that too seriously, and I confess that my first instinct was not to. But after spending a week with him, I can report that His Eminence Franzo W. King is a genuinely spiritual man.

He certainly talks like one. King tends to speak in riddles and dictums and parables, and at an almost inaudible volume. One day I told him that I considered some person or other a bit of a phony. King looked at me intently for a moment, then put his hand on the back of my head and pulled my ear to his lips. "Is a tree phony because it loses its leaves in winter?" he whispered.

I suspect that Archbishop King did a ton of acid at some point. Either that or he really is a mystic. I'm still not sure, and that night I didn't care. I wanted to know what he thought of our impending trip to Monrovia. He didn't answer the question directly, of course. Instead he quoted John Coltrane: "During Vietnam, they asked Coltrane what he thought of the war. He said, 'I'm against all wars.'" King looked at me and nodded slowly. I nodded back, then said goodnight and went to bed.

·   ·   ·

In the end, the question of whether or not to go to Monrovia was settled by the pilot of the ambulance plane. The next morning he refused to fly in, on the grounds that we'd get killed. Apparently he hadn't been to the mountaintop yet, either.

Sharpton accepted the news like the flexible traveler he is and immediately began planning peace talks of his own at our hotel. The logistics weren't complicated, since much of the leadership of LURD happened to be staying on the same floor. They were all over the hotel at all hours and very hard to miss. They were the sinister ones with guns. I didn't meet anyone affiliated with

LURD who didn't look as if he'd just returned from a long but enjoyable day of summary executions.

One morning I was sitting in the lobby interviewing Ruth Perry, who for a brief time during the 1990s was the president of Liberia and lived to tell about it. With her was a fellow Liberian named Marie Parker. Parker was also unusually lucky, having made the last charter flight out of Monrovia the day before. While her plane taxied down the runway, LURD troops lobbed mortars onto the tarmac. Looking out the window, she saw a child decapitated by shrapnel.

As Mrs. Parker told her story and Mrs. Perry gasped, a tall man dressed entirely in black approached the table, pulled up a chair, and sat down. He did not remove his sunglasses. He introduced himself as Lieutenant General Donzo of LURD. The outline of a handgun stood out in relief against his leg. He smiled at the women. They glared back.

Unprompted, Donzo gave the three of us an update on the fighting in Monrovia. "Mr. Taylor cannot escape," he said. "We will catch him. Mr. Taylor is on a suicide mission now. We could run the whole city in seventy-two hours."

Donzo grinned and fiddled with his cell phone, which he said he used to command his fourteen-year-old transvestite gas-sniffing troops in the field. It was a newish Nokia, with Internet service and a built-in camera. Aiming it across the room, he took a picture of an air-conditioning unit to show off the picture quality. Donzo claimed to be thirty-five, but I'd bet my car he was at least ten years younger.

I remembered a piece of propaganda I had seen, produced by the Taylor government, that accused LURD soldiers of practicing cannibalism and human sacrifice. I was glad when Lieutenant General Donzo left the table.

Sharpton wanted every member of the delegation at the first round of his peace talks, scheduled for 9:00 P.M. in a conference room at the hotel. LURD agreed to come, though it wasn't clear whether its members understood what they were coming to. (LURD's deputy secretary general told me that he was looking forward to talking to "Ashcroft" at the meeting.) Cornel West had high hopes nonetheless. "This is going to set the tone for the post-cold-war era," he said with real enthusiasm.

The LURD guys were precisely on time. They walked in as a group with their heads down, like tenth graders late for class, and sat together in the third row. Representatives from Taylor's government were supposed to come, too, but at the last minute they didn't show, claiming they were caught in traffic.

Undaunted, Sharpton reached Sam Jackson, Taylor's unusually slick minister of economic affairs, on his cell phone. Sharpton carried on the conversation while the rest of the room listened. "These brothers have come to the table," he said, referring to the LURD guys, who were still sitting with their heads down. "They're willing to talk. You've got to respond." Jackson said he'd call back with an offer.

Cornel West, meanwhile, had started a one-man teach-in, a complex rap on the struggle for indigenous self-determination in the postcolonial era. It sounded a lot like a graduate seminar on Third World politics. "The alternative to bloodshed is dialogue," West said. "The dialogue has to be one where reasons have weight. The Liberian people will have to take their future in their own hands. What we all want to avoid is some sort of imperial imposition."

Before it was over, I'm fairly sure West had used the term *dialectic* several times, possibly even *paradigm*. The LURD guys obviously didn't understand a word of it. They sat in perfect silence for the duration. At one point, a cell phone went off in the LURD row, ringing the theme from *Woody Woodpecker*. No one answered it.

Sam Jackson called back at 9:40 with Taylor's latest offer, which sounded suspiciously like the offer he'd been making all along: If the United States was willing to send peacekeepers to

Monrovia, Taylor would leave the country within a day and allow an interim government, with representatives from both rebel factions, to take his place.

Sharpton sounded skeptical: "If Taylor equivocates, I will blast him all over the world as a liar." Jackson offered his strongest reassurances. All right, said Sharpton, "I'll get Cornel and them to draft a statement." The deal was almost done.

All that remained was to convince the LURD delegation. In theory, it should have been easy. The points Taylor had agreed to—U.S. troops, exile in Nigeria, an interim government—were precisely those that LURD said it was fighting for. The problem wasn't with details. It was with comprehension. The LURD guys were utterly confused.

Sharpton tried his best. He explained the deal at least three times, each time with increasing vehemence. By the end, he was preaching, every sentence ending with the rhetorical "Is that right?" Unfortunately, the typical African warlord doesn't know much about the customs of the American black church. Sharpton's call-and-response routine left them even more bewildered.

Finally, the leader of the LURD delegation stopped Sharpton to ask a question. (He may have even raised his hand.) Does the deal include a cease-fire? Do we have to stop fighting? he wanted to know.

Sharpton looked as if he were going to drop dead of exasperation. "*Of course there's got to be a cease-fire!*" You morons.

I imagine it had been a long time since anyone had spoken that way to LURD leaders and lived to tell about it. The meeting broke up shortly after. Sharpton dismissed the LURD contingent like a class. "We'll be back to you in a few hours," he said. "We got your numbers." They shuffled out obediently.

There were several more meetings over the next few days. For a short time it looked as though Sharpton might have achieved a breakthrough. LURD seemed to figure out most of what was going on. Taylor appeared to be getting more flexible. On the third day, the State Department sent a foreign-service officer from the Africa desk in Washington to brief Sharpton on Liberian politics. (Sharpton had spoken again to Colin Powell.) I ran into him at lunch. "I don't have a position on the Sharpton Plan, official or unofficial," he said.

Then it all fell apart. Predictably, the plan unraveled when it reached the LURD troops. They didn't want to stop fighting. When called by their commanders from the hotel coffee shop in Ghana and told about the cease-fire, the pantyhose-clad guerrillas in Monrovia simply hung up the phone. As any parent knows, fourteen-year-olds can be hard to control.

·   ·   ·

Suddenly, the bring-peace-to-Liberia portion of the trip was over. There was talk of heading to Johannesburg to see Nelson Mandela, but no one could find his number. We spent the next few days sightseeing, visiting a refugee camp, and following Sharpton as he made campaignlike stops around Accra, including a remarkably contentious interview on Good Evening, Ghana. The rest of the time, we sat around talking about religion, death, and politics.

The Nation of Islam guys turned out to be terrific conversationalists, the two James Muhammads in particular. They were sharp and informed and extremely polite. The most striking thing about them, though, was how relentlessly normal they seemed. Both had been loyal members of the Nation of Islam for more than twenty years. Presumably they believed, as NOI doctrine teaches, that the white race is intrinsically evil and will be incinerated by an enormous spaceship currently hovering above the earth. You'd never guess it from talking to them.

The first James Muhammad, James G., was at the time the editor of the *Final Call*, NOI's weekly newspaper and a forum for every conceivable crackpot racialist view. In his heart, James G. may be convinced that Jewish doctors are injecting black babies with AIDS, but he could not have been nicer to me. Almost every morning he called or came by my room to make sure I was awake. Once we got home, he sent me digital pictures of the trip. He ended his e-mail with a smiley face.

The second James Muhammad, James L. (formerly James 10X), was if anything even gentler and more friendly. An accountant in the dean's office at Yale, he confided to me that his first love was photojournalism. "If I could come back as anything, I'd be a *National Geographic* photographer," he said.

I decided that it was their sincere belief in black supremacy that made the James Muhammads such good company. From their point of view, I was an irredeemable White Devil, cursed by Allah and marked for destruction. They had nothing to prove to me; I was like the retarded kid. We got along great. At the end of the trip, James L. pronounced me an honorary member of the Nation of Islam: Tucker X.

Only occasionally were there reminders that the Nation of Islam is not a mainstream religious organization. One afternoon, I called the CNN news desk and learned that Uday and Qusay Hussein had been killed by American troops in Iraq. At dinner I mentioned the news to Akbar Muhammad. He looked crestfallen. "That's unfortunate," he said. Akbar had known the Hussein boys, as well as their father. He reminisced about their time together in prewar Baghdad.

As the NOI's chief diplomat, Akbar seemed to spend most of his time traveling to the world's most repressive dictatorships. I forgot to ask him if he'd made it to North Korea, but he'd been just about everywhere else. Occasionally he'd drop references to "Brother Qaddafi" or the meal he had recently shared with Robert Mugabe, the lunatic of Zimbabwe.

On our final day in Ghana, Akbar mentioned another old friend, Idi Amin. Amin had slipped into a coma that week at a hospital in Jedda, Saudi Arabia, and wasn't expected to recover. This put Akbar in a sentimental mood. He told me about the first time he met Idi. It was 1977. The two had strolled through downtown Kampala, which at the time was "safe and quiet." If Amin dies, Akbar said, and CNN decides to run an obituary, "maybe you can present the other side."

Sharpton laughed when I told him about the conversation. He seemed amused by the Nation of Islam, whose theology he summarized as "no booze, pork, or white women." Sharpton is widely regarded by white people as a racist, and it is true that he used to make references to "crackers" in his speeches. ("I ain't never worked for a cracker in my life," he once boasted.) He doesn't talk like that anymore. Sharpton still rails against the White Power Structure, but these days he reserves his harshest rhetoric for black people.

During a speech at the W. E. B. DuBois center in Accra, Sharpton came off as something approaching conservative. He described black gang members as "savages" engaged in "crass, despicable, irresponsible behavior." He all but denounced hip-hop culture and the "irrelevant Negroes" it produces. "DuBois didn't come here to teach Ghanaians how to break-dance or call their grandmother 'bitch,'" Sharpton said. Decency, hard work, academic excellence—that, said Sharpton, is the path to dignity and self-improvement.

Al Sampson, meanwhile, continued to do a spot-on impression of the early Malcolm X. I made it to breakfast one morning just in time to catch him in mid-rant. If you're looking for a single cause of all the world's problems, Sampson was saying, look no further than the white race. He glanced up and saw me, the physical embodiment of eons of injustice and oppression. "When are you going to stop trashing the universe?" he said.

I should have laughed it off, but it was just too early. What a vicious, ignorant thing to say, I replied.

Ignorant? he said. Are you saying I have a low IQ?

Before I could answer, Sampson began to tick off a list of white crimes against humanity, beginning with the slave trade. As it happened, Sharpton was planning to visit a slavery museum that very day. I'll be watching you when we get there, Sampson said. "I want to see if you even cry."

I was close to the snapping point. After days of needling from Sampson, I was being poisoned by a toxic buildup of dislike. I longed for the cathartic release that would come from leaping across the table and smashing his nose. I must have telegraphed it, because both James Muhammads immediately tried to calm me down. "Come on back, now," said James L. "Come on back." Archbishop King didn't say anything, but walked over and gave me a hug.

Sampson was trying to make me feel guilty. It wasn't obvious to me at the time. The idea that I'd be responsible for the sins (or, for that matter, share in the glory of the accomplishments) of dead people who happened to share my skin tone has always confused me. Racial solidarity wasn't a working concept in my southern-California hometown. Most people barely had last names, much less ethnic identities. I grew up feeling about as much connection to nineteenth-century slave owners as I did to bus drivers in Helsinki or astronomers in Tirana. We're all capable of getting sunburned. That's it.

I tried a couple of times to explain this to Rev. Sampson. But "your people," he'd say, did this or that appalling thing. I don't have any "people," I'd reply. Beyond my immediate family, I don't speak for anybody. The deceased bad guys you're talking about, we just look alike.

Either he didn't get it, or he didn't believe me. Day after day, Sampson kept it up, trying his best to make me feel bad about myself for being a universe trasher. I never did. Ultimately, I'm just not a guilty white person. Maybe that's why Sharpton and I got along so well. We talked for hours over the course of the week, about everything from marriage to the Iowa caucuses. By the end, I'd settled at least one question: Sharpton doesn't hate whites after all. He just hates white liberals.

·   ·   ·

"You've dealt with inoffensive Negroes," Sharpton roared, imagining that he was talking to Terry McAuliffe or some other Democratic-party official. "Now you've got to deal with Al Sharpton." Sharpton knows that many white Democrats are embarrassed that he exists. The street-hustler wardrobe, Tawana Brawley, *the hair*—he is a public-relations disaster for the Democratic party, a living explanation of why suburbanites vote Republican. The thought fills him with pleasure, because it means that he has the power to make white Democrats uncomfortable every time he speaks.

Which is why he can hardly wait for the Democratic National Convention next summer in Boston. "Let me put it this way: I can speak inside or outside. They can choose the venue. But either way, I'm speaking in prime time." Either speech, he points out, will almost certainly be carried live on the networks.

"The only people who don't respect me are white liberals," he said one night at dinner. Some have dismissed him outright as a buffoon (he became furious just thinking about it); others have merely patted him on the head and tried to send him on his way. That's how it felt, anyway. He saw it happen to Jesse Jackson, who started out as an independent man of the Left and wound up a party hack, summoned to the Clinton White House periodically like a servant to perform.

They got Jackson little by little, Sharpton believes, mostly by giving him things: money, jobs for his friends, the use of private airplanes. Within a year or two, Jackson was an employee. Sharpton considers it a profound political lesson. "I saw what happened to Jesse. I was there. They're assuming I want what Jesse wanted."

If so, they're wrong. Sharpton has never taken federal grants. He doesn't want patronage. He's happy to fly commercial. "What can they give me? A couple hundred grand in voter-registration money? Please. I don't need that. I don't need *anything* from them. They can't control me. That's why they hate me."

What does Al Sharpton want? He didn't even pause when I asked. "What we want is *them*." By *them* Sharpton means every white liberal in the leadership of the Democratic party who has ever assumed a high-handed tone with him, put him off for a meeting, or in any way acted supercilious or superior in his presence. That's a lot of people. Sharpton says he'll start by demanding control over the chairmanship of the party. From there, he'd like a hand in picking next year's vice-presidential nominee. After that, we'll see.

Sharpton understands he may not get everything he wants. *They* might continue to patronize him. That's fine, too. He could always pull a Nader and go third party. "That's up to them," he said between bites of chicken. "If I buy a suit and the pants split, I need to get it fixed or get a new suit. My butt is out. My behind is getting cold in the wind." The question you have to ask at that point, he said, is: "Do I need to get a new suit? Or do you have a needle and thread?"

Sharpton has thought all of this through in some detail. He's fairly certain Democratic leaders consider him incapable of formulating a serious strategy. "I've got a plan. They never thought of that. They're used to—at best—a shakedown."

And that's only Sharpton's plan for the next year. He said he intends to come up with new demands by 2006, when Senator Hillary Clinton comes up for reelection. New York is one place Sharpton has uncontested influence. He could cause Senator Clinton a significant headache if he ran against her in the primary or withheld his endorsement in the general election. Like his convention speech, that thought pleases him.

None of this has escaped Bill Clinton's notice. Clinton called

Sharpton in July to set up a meeting. Sharpton assumes the former president wanted to get a sense of what the demands might be. When the meeting takes place, Sharpton said, "I won't give up anything. It's not to my advantage for him to figure me out."

In the end, of course, Sharpton isn't really running for president of the United States. He's running for president of black America. In some ways, with the rest of the traditional civil-rights leadership aging or retired, he has already won.

•   •   •

We left for the slavery museum later that morning. It was about a hundred miles up the coast by bus. Akbar Muhammad sat in the front with a microphone, acting as our tour guide. As we rolled through an outdoor market, he ruminated on the tragedy of the modern African diet. Until colonization, he explained, Africans did not eat pork. "It was the white man who brought the pig."

The travelogue/history lesson went on for about an hour. Finally Akbar paused. He rooted around in his bag and produced a cassette. "I hope you don't mind," he said, popping it into the dash. "This is one of my favorite tapes."

I don't know what I expected. A speech by Minister Farrakhan, maybe, or the Protocols of the Elders of Zion, as read by Amiri Baraka. And then it started. *Strumming my pain with his fingers.* Akbar cranked it up. Sharpton picked up the tune. *Singing my life with his words.* Cornel West started to dance in his seat. *Killing me softly with his song, killing me softly. With his song.* The whole bus was singing with Roberta Flack now, the James Muhammads taking the lead. Akbar rewound the song and played it again. After that we listened to Lou Rawls.

The slavery museum was at Cape Coast Castle, a massive former British customs house, which for more than a hundred years was used as a holding pen for slaves bound for the Americas. Single file and in silence, we walked down stone steps into the slave dungeon. Inside, it was as dark as a cave but hotter, with a single barred window fifteen feet up the wall. Akbar explained that the shallow channel carved into the floor had been the slaves' only latrine. He asked us to observe a moment of silence in their memory. We stood in a circle holding hands with our heads down. Someone began to sing a Negro spiritual, a cappella. Then the sobbing started.

It began, I think, with Cornel West. Soon it had spread to Sharpton and Akbar, and even to the notably white Sandy Rubenstein, who told me later that he was overcome by the thought of his own forebears enslaved by Pharaoh. Within a minute, the stone walls echoed with the sounds of a dozen people weeping, wailing, and gasping for breath. Al Sampson sounded as if he was about to die.

I felt like a voyeur. I closed my eyes while crying men shouted out the names of deceased ancestors. Someone passed out candles, and the group sang "We Shall Overcome." Sharpton, Cornel West, Sampson, and Akbar closed the ceremony with prayers. West thanked God for Sharpton, whom he described as a leader "in the tradition of John Coltrane, Curtis Mayfield, and Gladys Knight." I was sweating profusely.

Cornel West, I noticed, was not. I looked at him closely as he prayed. Though it was at least 100 degrees in the dungeon, he had not taken off his coat or loosened his tie. (I never once saw him do either.) He had on the same clothes he'd been wearing when we boarded the plane in New York six days before. They looked perfect. There was not a speck of lint or dandruff or dust on his suit. His shoes were shined, the creases in his trousers crisp. His shirt was so white it looked luminescent. The next day I broke down and asked him how, with no change of clothes, he managed to stay so clean. He laughed cryptically but didn't answer. I began to suspect that I was witnessing some sort of supernatural event, a low-grade miracle. I still can't think of a better explanation.

Finally we emerged from the dungeon and stood around squinting in the sunlight. Al Sampson walked over to where I was standing. His face was puffy from crying. He put his hands on my shoulders. For a moment I was certain he was going to bite me. Instead, he looked into my eyes and smiled. "I love you, man," he said.

From that moment until we parted at the baggage claim at JFK, Sampson treated me like an old friend.

.   .   .

We left Ghana the next day, or tried to. True to its reputation, Ghana Airways was thirteen hours late leaving Accra. No sooner had we reached altitude than the pilot announced we'd be making an unscheduled stop in Banjul, Gambia, for more fuel. On the ground in Gambia, Marjorie Harris, Sharpton's closest aide, called New York from her satellite phone to check in. There were a lot of messages. The most pressing was from the family of James Davis, a New York City councilman who had been shot to death the day before at City Hall. Davis's family wanted Sharpton's support—not just his moral support, but money to pay for the funeral, as well as related "expenses." Harris opposed the idea. The office was already in debt. Not two months before, one of Sharpton's cars had been repossessed for late payments.

Sharpton said he had no choice but to send the Davis family money. "I can't believe he didn't have insurance, but I guess he didn't." Harris appeared to be completely unconvinced. "We've got to help," Sharpton said. And so he agreed to. He looked tired, but also resigned. The president, he knows, is never off duty.

The Atlantic Monthly

FINALIST, REVIEWS
AND CRITICISM

Housewife Confidential

Caitlin Flanagan's prose cuts through the clutter of modern domestic life in ways both blisteringly funny and warmly empathetic. Her columns transcend the commonplace and, with honesty and style, refract our preoccupation with the states of our unions.

Caitlin Flanagan

Housewife Confidential

A tribute to the old-fashioned housewife, and to Erma Bombeck, her champion and guide

My mother's copy of *The Settlement Cook Book* (1948 edition) begins, as cookbooks used to, with instructions on the proper way to run a household. To air a room: "Lower the upper sash of one window and raise the lower sash of an opposite window." To remove a glue stain: "Apply vinegar with a cloth." There are sections on the feeding of infants and of invalids: "Use the daintiest dishes in the house. Place a clean napkin on the tray and, if possible, a fresh flower." My reaction to these household rules—and especially to the daily schedules for small children, which suggest thrilling mini-narratives of carefully lived days, of cooked cereal at seven o'clock and diluted orange juice at nine o'clock—is in the nature of avidity. The way a lonely man in a motel room pores over *Playboy*, I pore over descriptions of ironing and kitchen routines; I have never made a solution composed of one part bleach and nine parts warm water, but the idea of such a solution and its many practical uses—wiping down an emptied refrigerator once a month, sanitizing a kitchen sink—commands my riveted attention. The notion of a domestic life that purrs along, with routines and order and carefully delineated standards, is endlessly appealing to me. It is also quite foreign, because I am not a housewife. I am an "at-home mother," and the difference between the two is vast.

Consider the etymology. When a woman described herself as a "housewife," she was defining herself primarily through her relationship to her house and her husband. That children came along with the deal was simply assumed, the way that airing rooms and occasionally cooking for invalids came along with the deal. When a housewife subjected herself and her work to a bit of brutally honest examination, she may have begun by assessing how well she was doing with the children, but she may just as well have begun by contemplating the nature and quality of her housework. If it had been suggested to her that she spend the long, delicate hours between three and six o'clock squiring her children to the array of enhancing activities pursued by the modern child, she would have laughed. Who would stay home to get dinner on? More to the point, why had she chosen a house so close to a playground if the children weren't going to get out of her hair and play in it? The kind of childhood that many of us remember so fondly—with hours of free time, and gangs of neighborhood kids meeting up after school—was possible partly because each block contained houses in which women were busy but close by, all too willing to push open a window and yell at the neighbor boy to get his fool bike out of the street.

But an at-home mother feels little obligation to the house

itself; in fact, she is keenly aware that the house can be a vehicle of oppression. She is "at home" only because that is where her children happen to be. She does not define herself through her housekeeping; if she is in any way solvent (and many at-home mothers are), she has, at the very least, a once-a-month cleaning woman to do the most onerous tasks. (That some of the most significant achievements of the women's movement—specifically liberation from housework and child care—have been bought at the expense of poor women, often of poor brown-skinned women, is a bitter irony that very few feminists will discuss directly, other than to murmur something vague about "universal day care" and then, on reflex, blame the Republicans.) The at-home mother defines herself by her relationship to her children. She is making sacrifices on their behalf, giving up a career to give them something only she can. Her No. 1 complaint concerns the issue of respect: She demands it! Can't get enough of it! She isn't like a fifties housewife: ironing curtains, shampooing the carpets, stuck. She knows all about those women. She has seen *Pleasantville* and watched *Leave It to Beaver*; she's made more June Cleaver jokes than she can count. (In fact, June Cleaver—a character on a television show that went off the air in 1963—looms over her to a surprising extent, a sickening, terrifying specter: *Is that how people think I spend my time?*) If she has seen Todd Haynes's sumptuously beautiful recent movie, *Far From Heaven,* she understands and agrees wholeheartedly with the film's implication: that being a moneyed white housewife—with full-time help—in pre–Betty Friedan Hartford, Connecticut, was just as oppressive and soulwithering as being a black man in pre–civil rights Hartford. The at-home mother's attitude toward housewives of the fifties and sixties is a mixture of pity, outrage on their behalf, and gently mocking humor. (I recently received a birthday card that featured a perfectly coiffed fifties housewife standing in a gleaming kitchen. "The smart woman knows her way around the kitchen," the front of the card said. Inside: "Around the kitchen, out the back door, and to a decent restaurant.")

The at-home mother has a lot on her mind; to a significant extent she has herself on her mind. She must not allow herself to shrivel up with boredom. She must do things *for herself*. She must get to the gym, the spa, the yoga studio. To the book group. (She wouldn't be caught dead setting up tables and filling nut cups for a bridge party—June Cleaver! June Cleaver!—but a book group, which blends an agreeable seriousness of purpose with the kind of busy chitchat that women the world over adore, is irresistible.) She must go to lunch with like-minded friends, and to the movies. She needs to feed herself intellectually and emotionally; she needs to be on guard against exhaustion. She must find a way to combine the traditional women's work of childrearing with the kind of shared housework arrangements and domestic liberation that working mothers enjoy. Most important, she must somehow draw a line in the sand between the valuable, important work she is doing and the pathetic imprisonment, the *Doll's House* existence, of the housewife of old. It's a tall order.

•   •   •

In a recent *Los Angeles Times* article the Hollywood producer Lynda Obst decries the tendency of upper-level female studio executives to quit their jobs once they become mothers; she implores, "Doesn't anyone remember how painfully poignant it was to grow up with a brilliant mother stuck in the suburbs with nothing to do?" This, of course, is the politically correct attitude about such women. The general idea, implied in countless nitwit books and articles and in a variety of popular movies, is that shortly after President Truman dropped the big one on Nagasaki, an entire generation of brave, brilliant women—many of them enjoying the deep satisfaction of doing shift work in munitions factories (the extent to which the riveters' lot is glorified by professional-class feminists who never set foot on a factory floor is shameful)—was kidnapped by a bunch of rat-bastard men, deposited in Levittown, and told to mop. That women in large numbers were eagerly, joyfully complicit in this life plan, that women helped to create the plan, is rarely considered. To be a young woman during the war years was to know that many of the boys from your high school class were overseas and, perhaps, that several of them had died there. It was to have a steady, often unspoken fear that a future including children and a husband and a household—women used to be unconflicted and unashamed about wanting these things— might not be in the cards. For it all to change on a dime—for the men to come home in vast, apparently unscathed numbers, and for there to be the GI Bill and GI mortgages and plenty of good jobs for returning servicemen (remember, these were women who had experienced childhoods in which there were not enough jobs, in which it was highly possible for a family to be ruined)—must have been a relief beyond measure. That women, en masse, reconsidered their plan in fairly short order—*The Feminine Mystique* was published within twenty years of VJ Day—also gets scant mention. The postwar housewife era, whether one views it with horror or nostalgia, was short-lived.

Hollywood has a curious double obsession these days: lionizing the World War II serviceman and demonizing the fifties husband; what the brain trust fails to grasp is that he is the same man. The central heartbreaker of *Saving Private Ryan* is that Tom Hanks never makes it home to his adored wife; but if he'd gotten back to Pennsylvania in one piece, he would have been just another pot-roast-demanding, afternoon-newspaper-reading monster like Ward Cleaver (who was an engineer with the Seabees before dragging poor June off to his lair). Husbands lurk menacingly in the backgrounds of so many contemporary works set during the housewife period, emanating a threatening maleness (just the ticket at Normandy, but oh well), tramping their dirty feet across freshly scrubbed linoleum, demanding sex and clean laundry and subservience. In Michael Cunningham's spare and excellent novel *The Hours*, Laura Brown, a postwar California housewife so stultified by her lot that she ends up going cuckoo, kissing a neighbor lady, and eventually abandoning her children, must endure a day in which the responsibilities to her war-hero husband include not only the hellish complexity of baking a cake from scratch but also marital relations, an activity that forces her to make the ultimate sacrifice: putting a bookmark in *Mrs. Dalloway*. "There will be no reading tonight," the narrator informs us ominously. (Was Laura too oppressed to switch on the bedside lamp after the brute had been satisfied? Apparently so.)

•   •   •

Most curious about all of these representations is that they run so completely counter to my experience of housewives. I was raised by a housewife; my friends' mothers were housewives. Many of them, in retrospect, seemed mildly depressed; perhaps fulltime employment would have alleviated that depression quickly and completely (although the number of working mothers I know who are at sheer wits' end makes me question that central assumption of the women's movement). But what I remember most clearly about those housewives is not their ennui but, rather, their competence. They never served takeout for dinner; they cooked dinner—a protein, a starch, two vegetables, and dessert. They knew how to iron and mend and how to cope with the endless series of domestic crises that unseat me on a daily basis: the unraveled sweater sleeve, the chocolate stain on the tiny button-down shirt, the expensive set of sheets with the torn hem, the child who turns up with a raging fever two minutes before the Christmas pageant, the husband who announces that he'd like to invite someone from work to dinner that night. I would like to be the kind of woman who can cope—easily, effortlessly, while gabbing away about something else altogether—with all those things; I'm not. I'm an at-home mother, far too educated and uppity to have knuckled down and learned anything about stain removal or knitting or stretching recipes. My mother tried to teach me, and God knows I was a rapt student (like most adult obsessions, mine has its roots in childhood experience), but my attention kept attaching itself to the least important part of the lesson. "Now I'm ironing the placket," she would say, and I would stand beside her, thinking, *"Placket." Good word*. Perhaps I didn't have a great enough sense of urgency. I knew there were college and perhaps graduate school to contend with before I'd need to know how to line a baking sheet with rice paper. And as it turned out, by the time I had a household of my own, the world had changed. I have been married a total of fourteen years to a total of two men, and never once have I been asked to iron a single item of either man's clothing or to replace even one popped button, for which I suppose I have the women's movement to thank. But I realize now, late in the game, that we'd be much better off if I had a few of those skills.

Housewives, however, were not concerned solely with housework. Once I asked my mother why she didn't go to PTA meetings; she said, "That's for women who don't have anything better to do with their time." She was a housewife through and through, yet she had a sense of herself—highly accurate—as a purposefully busy woman. One reason that the women's movement took off in this country the way it did was that its organizers eventually realized that housewives were capable not only of weeping into their teacups and trying to name their unnameable problem but also of political action. In fact, they had a long history of political action. Consider the League of Women Voters, which during the period in question was mostly made up of non-employed, college-educated mothers married to professional men. These were women who cooked the family breakfast and sent the children off to school with packed lunch boxes, and then vacuumed their lovely living rooms and used them to host not book groups but, rather, meetings on civil-rights initiatives and opposition to the Vietnam War. These meetings tended to be somewhat proper and highly ladylike. They were run by women who had learned the finer points of parliamentary procedure in their college sororities; they were attended by women who had a firm belief in the civilizing power of combed hair and fresh lipstick and not talking out of turn. These were women, one might argue, badly in need of a consciousness-raising session. But if a truly raised consciousness includes an awareness of the injustice done to others and a willingness to try to stop it, then these women were at least halfway there.

Housewives were the people who put Trick or Treat for UNICEF boxes in millions of small hands. They were, of course, thrifty (thrift is the signal virtue of the housewife), but many of them were also high-minded, convinced that people ought to help one another out. George Harrison may have held a Concert for Bangladesh, but it was the mothers on my block who sat down and wrote little checks—ten dollars, fifteen dollars—to CARE. Many housewives shared a belief in the power of boycotts, which could so easily be conducted while grocery shopping. I remember hearing my mother's half of a long, complicated telephone discussion about whether it would or would not undermine the housewives' beef strike of 1973 if the caller defrosted and cooked meat bought prior to the strike. Tucked into the aforementioned copy of *The Settlement Cook Book,* along with handwritten recipes for Chocolate Diamonds and Oma's German Cheesecake, is a small card that reads FREEDOM AND JUSTICE FOR J.P. STEVENS WORKERS. The organizers of that long-ago boycott understood two things: first, that if you were going to cripple a supplier of household goods (J. P. Stevens manufactured table linens and hosiery and blankets), you had to enlist housewives; and second, that you stood a better chance of catching their attention if you printed your slogan on the reverse of a card that contained a table of common metric equivalents, a handy, useful reminder that 1 liter = 1 quart and also that the makers of Finesse hosiery exploited their workers.

·   ·   ·

The success of the women's movement depended on imposing a certain narrative—of boredom, of oppression, of despairing uselessness—on an entire generation of women, a narrative that has only gained strength as the years have passed, leaving people with a skewed and rather offensive view of those women. Consider the case of the most famous housewife of the era: Erma Bombeck. To think about her life in any depth is to realize that even the most "typical" housewife of them all—*Erma Bombeck*—led a life of infinitely greater complexity, worth, and dignity than any of the modern mythologizers, with their subdued and shrinking heroines, could imagine.

Like many housewives of her day, Bombeck had a rough Depression childhood, in Dayton, Ohio. Her father was a crane operator who died suddenly when she was nine; her mother—who had left school after sixth grade, married at fourteen, and given birth to her only child at sixteen—lost their house and their furniture. Together they moved into a front bedroom in her grandparents' house, and Erma Senior got a factory job. "One day you were a family," Bombeck recalled, "living in a little house at the bottom of a hill. The next day it was all gone." Erma Senior, a frustrated stage mother, sent her daughter to tap-dancing lessons, and pushed her into contests and radio appearances (the tap-dancing craze of the thirties was so powerful that a few minutes of frantic dancing by a girl Shirley Temple's age was the stuff even of a successful radio spot). But young Erma's inclinations ran in a different direction. She was clever and bookish; she loved James

Thurber and Robert Benchley and H. Allen Smith. When Erma was fourteen, the famous newspaper correspondent Dorothy Thompson came to Dayton, and Erma—even though she was coming down with measles—persuaded her mother to let her attend Thompson's lecture ("I infected the entire hall that night," she remembered). For Christmas she asked for and received an expensive book by Thompson. Not surprisingly, given the times and her station in life, she attended a vocational high school, which required students to spend two weeks a month pursuing a "commercial alternate." She must not have been particularly interested in the kind of department-store and telephone-company jobs usually recommended for girls, because in a burst of chutz-pah and innocence she wangled an interview with the managing editor of the *Dayton Journal-Herald*. She impressed him (one doesn't like to trade in clichés, but it's impossible to imagine the scene without the word "spunk" coming into play), but he said he had only one job opening, and it was a full-time position. On the spot she talked him into hiring a friend for the other two weeks a month, and so—at age fifteen, and with the title "copy girl" (hardly sexist, considering its opposite)—she began her newspa-per career.

Let us pause for a moment to consider how the story already diverges from the standard cant. Apparently it was possible, long before Rosie tied on her kerchief and flexed her fetching bicep, for a woman to get factory work when she needed to support her family. It was also possible for a young girl to nurture dreams of a professional career, and for her to find—decades before Take Our Daughters to Work Day—a female role model already pur-suing that work. It was possible for a bright, quick-thinking girl to storm as emphatically male an environment as a city newspa-per and to create the exact kind of job-sharing arrangement that contemporary working mothers think they invented. Most important, it was possible in those days for a girl to overcome a considerable amount of adversity—poverty, and the early loss of a father, and a tight net of employment law clearly intended to favor men—to make something of herself.

It was also possible to do all these things and still dream of children and of staying home to raise them. Erma had met a young reporter, Bill Bombeck, and after he returned from the service, in 1948, they married. Erma by then had a college degree and had been promoted at the *Journal-Herald,* from part-time to full-time copy girl and then to full-fledged newspaperwoman. She became friends with the reporter Phyllis Battelle, who remembered "a bouncy kid in bobbysocks, knife-pleated skirts and baggy sweaters." But what Erma really wanted was children: "Putting on panty hose every morning is just not whoopee time. My dream was to putter around the house, learn how to snap beans, put up curtains and bake bread." Finally—through the adoption of the Bombecks' first child, their purchase of a house in a subdivision outside Dayton, and Erma's resignation from the newspaper—those dreams came true. And she began to go absolutely bonkers.

In her best book, the memoir *A Marriage Made in Heaven . . . Or Too Tired for an Affair* (1993), she reports that the women of the suburbs were all "bored out of their skulls." In driveways and supermarket parking lots they "commiserated among ourselves as to what we had gotten ourselves into." What she needed, she soon realized—without benefit of *Working Mother* magazine or even a single book about achieving "work/life balance"—was a job. And with no fuss or fanfare (much the way my own mother did, when she realized she couldn't spend another afternoon washing the kitchen walls and climbed off the stepladder to take a curious look at the Help Wanted: Female section of the *San Francisco Chronicle*) she got one: editing the local shopping circular. In 1964, not long after her youngest child boarded the school bus bound for kindergarten, she combed her hair, braced herself, and asked the editor of her community's weekly newspaper for a job as a housewife columnist. Success came quickly, and it never left. She was soon back at the *Journal-Herald,* where, within three weeks of her return, her columns were syndicated nationally. A sensation.

· · ·

The idea of a housewife confessional was not new. Jean Kerr had achieved extraordinary success with *Please Don't Eat the Daisies* (1957) almost a decade before Bombeck began writing her columns. Shirley Jackson trod similar ground in *Raising Demons* (1957), a book whose jacket cover—happy children surrounding a pull-toy ducky—is as far from the spirit of "The Lottery" as it is possible to get. Jackson was also the author of *Special Delivery* (1960), the title page of which describes it as "A useful book for brand-new mothers in which Shirley Jackson as chief resident provides a sane and sage approach to the hilarious and homey situations which accompany the advent of motherhood." And any serious study of housewife writers must include Peg Bracken, who wrote her best-known books during the early sixties, when the women's movement was still a sleeping giantess; her attitude toward the housewife's lot, however, is not unconflicted: the titles of her two most famous books are *The I Hate to Cook Book* (1960) and *The I Hate to Housekeep Book* (1962). Her writing reveals her to be a cheerful sort, possessed of a winsome prose style; she is, she confesses, "but destiny's plaything," and her approach to housewifery combines whimsy and practicality (the accompanying Hilary Knight illustrations capture the spirit of the text with a precision not seen since the great days of the nineteenth-century illustrated novel). Her jolliness may well have had something to do with the fact that she clearly liked her hooch: *The I Hate to Cook Book* was written, she tells us, "for those of us who want to fold our big dishwater hands around a dry Martini instead of a wet flounder, come the end of a long day"; powdered milk, she once observed, is preferable to the real McCoy not only because it is cheaper but also because it can be a component of "a good frothy punch," one consisting of "milk, egg, sugar, whisky, beaten with an electric mixer." Bracken's feelings about her domestic work take the form of good-hearted acquiescence, although some of her books' most offhand humor reveals the edge of genuine despair: the recipe for Skid Row Stroganoff includes the instruction "Add the flour, salt, paprika, and mushrooms, stir, and let it cook five minutes while you light a cigarette and stare sullenly at the sink." (One hesitates to wander into the minefield of literary biography, but I find it impossible to read *The I Hate to Cook Book* without dwelling on the fact that while Bracken was writing it her husband told her it was the stupidest idea for a book he'd ever heard of; they divorced four years later.) Although her collected works are slightly less explicitly political than those of Beatrix Potter, anyone taking the historical long view can easily discover within them the seeds of the revolution that would soon be upon this country. How else to account for the fact that a book on housekeeping contains a chapter on coping with depression? "Every girl owes it to herself to hang onto her mind as long as she can," we learn in that chapter, which is called "How to Be Happy When You're Miserable." "If the fulfillment of your own purposes seems to be flickering," she writes, one ought to remember that many high achievers—Daumier, say, or Ogilby, who translated Homer and Virgil—got a late start. Women frustrated by the demands of motherhood ought to remember that "there is world enough and time," a bit of counsel as useful to the full-time mothers of today as to those of forty years ago. In fact, I found several bits of sound advice in *The I Hate to Housekeep Book*, among them "Each time you give the house a good going-over, start with a different room" and "Act immediately on whatever housewifely impulses come your way" (and, if I might add my own two cents on matters domestic: if you substitute the word "sexual" for the word "housewifely," you also end up with the best approach to conjugal relations I have hit upon thus far).

What is refreshing about the housewife writers is their candor about the tedium of raising children; although the at-home mother must think of the work as exalted (otherwise why isn't she back at the law firm, bringing home the big bucks?), housewives were willing to admit that the enterprise was often an emotional bust. And no one was more willing than Erma Bombeck, who—to be at once current and crass—"branded" the form. Why she was the one to have such out-of-the-park success with the subject has less to do with her prose than with the sheer force of her personality, her eye for the precise and homey detail, and her matchless way with a gag. I had expected to reread her work with a gentle, reminiscing smile, and was amazed by how often I found myself laughing. I do not want, however, to misrepresent her writing; she was, to a certain extent, a hack. How could she not have been? To write that frequently (she had written well in excess of 4,000 columns when she died, in 1996), on such tight deadlines and with such a tightly circumscribed length, is almost by definition to rely on formulas, to repeat oneself, to tread a few good one-liners almost to death. Even a true-blue fan will be shocked by Bombeck's almost shameless willingness to trot out the same jokes and observations over and over again. Certainly, her work achieved maximal effect in its original context: meted out regularly but sparingly, in 700-word doses on the women's page—snappy, chin-up reminders that everyone hates doing the laundry, and that even the most adored children can run you ragged with frustration and boredom. In those days no matter where you lived or what your local newspaper was, the women's page was firmly in the hands of a group of stalwart midwesterners. I grew up in Berkeley, where the front page often informed me of unsettling events close to home, of riots on Telegraph Avenue and of the Black Panthers (Huey Newton was once an honored guest speaker at a public school I attended) and, later, the Symbionese Liberation Army. But the back of the newspaper—a respite—gave me Erma and also the Iowans Abby and Ann, and the Minnesotan Charles Schulz. (Bil Keane, the creator of *Family*

Circus, was from the East, but he and Erma became neighbors and great pals.) They all seemed connected to the fabric of an America that I didn't live in but believed in passionately, a place in which "student unrest" was rarely mentioned, in which the central elements of the national consciousness weren't up for complete reassessment and rejection, in which most of life's difficulties could be handled with a combination of good humor and endurance, and in which graver matters were quickly dispatched by scheduling an appointment with one's "pastor or clergyman."

Read collectively, Bombeck's pieces offer a startlingly precise chronicle of her time. Anyone in search of a good topic for a women's-studies dissertation would do well to take a look at Bombeck's columns; it would be difficult to find a more comprehensive overview of the way middle-class women lived their lives—and of the way their lives changed—during the 1970s and 1980s. "Lady, you *are* the problem," a member of the women's liberation movement once wrote her. In fact she was not. She was a talented woman who had once dreamed of working for *The New York Times* and who ended up as one of the best-known figures in American journalism; she was a woman who combined work and motherhood as gracefully as it is possible to do, who championed working and at-home mothers with equal ardor, who campaigned tirelessly for the Equal Rights Amendment (her close friend Liz Carpenter, a press secretary for Lady Bird Johnson, recalls that the two were "the Thelma and Louise of the ERA").

There is no one my mother would less want to be compared to than Erma Bombeck, whose work—as far as I know—she never read. My mother was an accomplished hostess, a flirt, a reader. Her sensibilities were in no way midwestern. Yet in the two years since her death I have rarely remembered her more vividly—or missed her more keenly—than when I read all that Bombeck a few months back. In part this has to do with the simple household economies of the time, which I had forgotten about but of which Bombeck was a faithful recorder. To read

Bombeck is to find a constantly updated economic index of her day: the problem with a bathtub faucet left on the "shower" position is that it ruins an eight-dollar hairdo; the problem with a bored child's deciding to put lime wedges in glasses of soda pop is that limes cost $1.49 a pound. I don't think I ever spent a day with my mother—even late in her life, when her fortunes had improved considerably—when she didn't mention the price of something. Like Bombeck, like a lot of housewives of her generation, she grew up poor in a hard time, which she never discussed but never forgot. Like Bombeck, she kept the household accounts, and she was careful about them. I grew up in the most solidly middle-class academic family you can imagine, but every couple of months my mother would borrow a bottle-capping contraption so that she could put up her own root beer—made from Hires elixir, absolutely delicious, and roundly complimented by my father for its pennies-a-glass economy. As for me, child of my time, I could not tell you the price of a single item in my refrigerator; all I know—from long, unpleasant precedent—is that much of it is going bad and headed for the trash can.

But what reminds me most of my mother is harder to pinpoint. It has to do with the way both women dealt with motherhood, which is for me an exquisitely overwrought enterprise, full of guilt-wracked, sleepless nights and over-worried-about children and the never-ending sense that I'm doing too little or too much or the wrong thing, or missing the crucial moments, or somehow warping these perfect creatures that my body—that witless dud—had sense enough to knit together but my heart and mind can't seem to figure out how to raise with my mother's unworried ease. Housewives didn't trot after their children the way I trot after mine—Junior All-Stars! Karate! Art for Tots! Their children trotted after them. I whiled a childhood away leaning on the counters of dry cleaners and shoe repairmen, and I was happy to do it. I liked being with my mother. To me, she never seemed diminished or unimportant because of those endless domestic errands; on the contrary, the work she did was wholly connected to the life we were living. The notes my father took on the flyleaf of *Howards End* apparently got translated into words spoken in a lecture hall I could hardly imagine; but the steak my mother spent five minutes choosing showed up on my plate that night.

.   .   .

If you asked any of the mothers in my set how motherhood has changed us, we would tell you—in one way or another—that it has introduced into our lives an almost unbearably powerful form of love and also a ceaseless, grinding anxiety, one that often propels us to absurd activities. (I know a working mother who FedExed breast milk home from a business trip; I recently hosted a birthday party for thirty-two children because I couldn't arrive at any sensible way to compose a guest list.) For many of us this transformation has included a helpless sense of repeated failures, both large and small. For the women of an earlier generation, however, motherhood brought a clear and compelling awareness of human vulnerability, and a sense of having somehow been charged with the care of others. I can remember my mother faithfully cutting the wrappers off cans of dog food because if she sent in enough of them, the manufacturer would make a contribution to Guide Dogs for the Blind; I myself have compassion fatigue, and have limited my "charitable giving" to a certain few circumscribed causes. At the back of Erma Bombeck's last book, published after her death from complications following a kidney transplant, is an organ-donor card that the reader can fill out, along with information on the Erma Bombeck Organ Donor Awareness Project. I keep meaning to fill that card out; my mother would have done it in an instant, without thinking twice about it. But I've been busy—I'm a busy woman; my children are two-sport athletes at age five—and I haven't gotten around to it yet.

The New Yorker

WINNER, PUBLIC INTEREST

The Stovepipe

In this pithy article Seymour Hersh exposed the "selective intelligence" used by the Bush administration to justify the Iraq war. Detailing clandestine meetings and unraveling the complex business and political ties of the president's chosen advisers, Hersh gave New Yorker readers an early sense of the intelligence-gathering miscues so widely debated in recent months.

Seymour M. Hersh

The Stovepipe

How conflicts between the Bush Administration and the intelligence community marred the reporting on Iraq's weapons.

Since midsummer, the Senate Intelligence Committee has been attempting to solve the biggest mystery of the Iraq war: the disparity between the Bush Administration's prewar assessment of Iraq's weapons of mass destruction and what has actually been discovered.

The committee is concentrating on the last ten years' worth of reports by the C.I.A. Preliminary findings, one intelligence official told me, are disquieting. "The intelligence community made all kinds of errors and handled things sloppily," he said. The problems range from a lack of quality control to different agencies' reporting contradictory assessments at the same time. One finding, the official went on, was that the intelligence reports about Iraq provided by the United Nations inspection teams and the International Atomic Energy Agency, which monitored Iraq's nuclear-weapons programs, were far more accurate than the C.I.A. estimates. "Some of the old-timers in the community are appalled by how bad the analysis was," the official said. "If you look at them side by side, C.I.A. versus United Nations, the U.N. agencies come out ahead across the board."

There were, of course, good reasons to worry about Saddam Hussein's possession of W.M.D.s. He had manufactured and used chemical weapons in the past, and had experimented with biological weapons; before the first Gulf War, he maintained a multibillion-dollar nuclear-weapons program. In addition, there were widespread doubts about the efficacy of the U.N. inspection teams, whose operations in Iraq were repeatedly challenged and disrupted by Saddam Hussein. Iraq was thought to have manufactured at least six thousand more chemical weapons than the U.N. could account for. And yet, as some former U.N. inspectors often predicted, the tons of chemical and biological weapons that the American public was led to expect have thus far proved illusory. As long as that remains the case, one question will be asked more and more insistently: How did the American intelligence community get it so wrong?

Part of the answer lies in decisions made early in the Bush Administration, before the events of September 11, 2001. In interviews with present and former intelligence officials, I was told that some senior Administration people, soon after coming to power, had bypassed the government's customary procedures for vetting intelligence.

A retired C.I.A. officer described for me some of the questions that would normally arise in vetting: "Does dramatic information turned up by an overseas spy square with his access, or does it exceed his plausible reach? How does the agent behave? Is he on time for meetings?" The vetting process is especially important when one is dealing with foreign-agent reports—sensitive intelligence that can trigger profound policy decisions. In theory, no request for action should be taken directly to higher authorities— a process known as "stovepiping"—without the information on which it is based having been subjected to rigorous scrutiny.

The point is not that the President and his senior aides were consciously lying. What was taking place was much more systematic—and potentially just as troublesome. Kenneth Pollack, a former National Security Council expert on Iraq, whose book "The Threatening Storm" generally supported the use of force to remove Saddam Hussein, told me that what the Bush people did was "dismantle the existing filtering process that for fifty years had been preventing the policymakers from getting bad information. They created stovepipes to get the information they wanted directly to the top leadership. Their position is that the professional bureaucracy is deliberately and maliciously keeping information from them.

"They always had information to back up their public claims, but it was often very bad information," Pollack continued. "They were forcing the intelligence community to defend its good information and good analysis so aggressively that the intelligence analysts didn't have the time or the energy to go after the bad information."

The Administration eventually got its way, a former C.I.A. official said. "The analysts at the C.I.A. were beaten down defending their assessments. And they blame George Tenet"—the C.I.A. director— "for not protecting them. I've never seen a government like this."

• • •

A few months after George Bush took office, Greg Thielmann, an expert on disarmament with the State Department's Bureau of Intelligence and Research, or INR, was assigned to be the daily intelligence liaison to John Bolton, the Under-Secretary of State for Arms Control, who is a prominent conservative. Thielmann understood that his posting had been mandated by Secretary of State Colin Powell, who thought that every important State Department bureau should be assigned a daily intelligence officer. "Bolton was the guy with whom I had to do business," Thielmann said. "We were going to provide him with all the information he was entitled to see. That's what being a professional intelligence officer is all about."

But, Thielmann told me, "Bolton seemed to be troubled because INR was not telling him what he wanted to hear." Thielmann soon found himself shut out of Bolton's early-morning staff meetings. "I was intercepted at the door of his office and told, 'The Under-Secretary doesn't need you to attend this meeting anymore.'" When Thielmann protested that he was there to provide intelligence input, the aide said, "The Under-Secretary wants to keep this in the family."

Eventually, Thielmann said, Bolton demanded that he and his staff have direct electronic access to sensitive intelligence, such as foreign-agent reports and electronic intercepts. In previous Administrations, such data had been made available to under-secretaries only after it was analyzed, usually in the specially secured offices of INR. The whole point of the intelligence system in place, according to Thielmann, was "to prevent raw intelligence from getting to people who would be misled." Bolton, however, wanted his aides to receive and assign intelligence analyses and assessments using the raw data. In essence, the under-secretary would be running his own intelligence operation, without any guidance or support. "He surrounded himself with a hand-chosen group of loyalists, and found a way to get C.I.A. information directly," Thielmann said.

In a subsequent interview, Bolton acknowledged that he had changed the procedures for handling intelligence, in an effort to extend the scope of the classified materials available to his office. "I found that there was lots of stuff that I wasn't getting and that the INR analysts weren't including," he told me. "I didn't want it filtered. I wanted to see everything—to be fully informed. If that puts someone's nose out of joint, sorry about that." Bolton told me that he wanted to reach out to the intelligence community but that Thielmann had "invited himself" to his daily staff meetings. "This was my meeting with the four assistant secretaries who report to me, in preparation for the Secretary's 8:30 A.M. staff meeting," Bolton said. "This was within my family of bureaus. There was no place for INR or anyone else—the Human Resources Bureau or the Office of Foreign Buildings."

There was also a change in procedure at the Pentagon under Paul Wolfowitz, the Deputy Secretary of Defense, and Douglas Feith, the Under-Secretary for Policy. In the early summer of 2001, a career official assigned to a Pentagon planning office undertook a routine evaluation of the assumption, adopted by Wolfowitz and Feith, that the Iraqi National Congress, an exile group headed by Ahmad Chalabi, could play a major role in a coup d'état to oust Saddam Hussein. They also assumed that Chalabi, after the coup, would be welcomed by Iraqis as a hero.

An official familiar with the evaluation described how it subjected that scenario to the principle of what planners call "branches and sequels"—that is, "plan for what you expect not to happen." The official said, "It was a 'what could go wrong' study. What if it turns out that Ahmad Chalabi is not so popular? What's Plan B if you discover that Chalabi and his boys don't have it in them to accomplish the overthrow?"

The people in the policy offices didn't seem to care. When the official asked about the analysis, he was told by a colleague that the new Pentagon leadership wanted to focus not on what could go wrong but on what could go right. He was told that the study's exploration of option amounted to planning for failure. "Their methodology was analogous to tossing a coin five times and assuming that it would always come up heads," the official told me. "You need to think about what would happen if it comes up tails."

•   •   •

Getting rid of Saddam Hussein and his regime had been a priority for Wolfowitz and others in and around the Administration since the end of the first Gulf War. For years, Iraq hawks had seen a coup led by Chalabi as the best means of achieving that goal. After September 11th, however, and the military's quick victory in Afghanistan, the notion of a coup gave way to the idea of an American invasion.

In a speech on November 14, 2001, as the Taliban were being routed in Afghanistan, Richard Perle, a Pentagon consultant with long-standing ties to Wolfowitz, Feith, and Chalabi, articulated what would become the Bush Administration's most compelling argument for going to war with Iraq: the possibility that, with enough time, Saddam Hussein would be capable of attacking the United States with a nuclear weapon. Perle cited testimony from Dr. Khidhir Hamza, an Iraqi defector, who declared that Saddam Hussein, in response to the 1981 Israeli bombing of the Osiraq nuclear reactor, near Baghdad, had ordered future nuclear facilities to be dispersed at four hundred sites across the nation. "Every day," Perle said, these sites "turn out a little bit of nuclear materials." He told his audience, "Do we wait for Saddam and hope for the best, do we wait and hope he doesn't do what we know he is capable of . . . or do we take some preemptive action?"

In fact, the best case for the success of the U.N. inspection process in Iraq was in the area of nuclear arms. In October, 1997, the International Atomic Energy Agency issued a definitive report declaring Iraq to be essentially free of nuclear weapons. The I.A.E.A.'s inspectors said, "There are no indications that there remains in Iraq any physical capability for the production of amounts of weapon-usable nuclear material of any practical significance." The report noted that Iraq's nuclear facilities had been destroyed by American bombs in the 1991 Gulf War.

The study's main author, Garry Dillon, a British nuclear-safety engineer who spent twenty-three years working for the I.A.E.A. and retired as its chief of inspection, told me that it was "highly unlikely" that Iraq had been able to maintain a secret or hidden program to produce significant amounts of weapons-usable material, given the enormous progress in the past decade in the technical ability of

I.A.E.A. inspectors to detect radioactivity in ground locations and in waterways. "This is not kitchen chemistry," Dillon said. "You're talking factory scale, and in any operation there are leaks."

The Administration could offer little or no recent firsthand intelligence to contradict the I.A.E.A.'s 1997 conclusions. During the Clinton years, there had been a constant flow of troubling intelligence reports on Iraqi weapons of mass destruction, but most were in the context of worst-case analyses—what Iraq could do without adequate United Nations inspections—and included few, if any, reliable reports from agents inside the country. The inspectors left in 1998. Many of the new reports that the Bush people were receiving came from defectors who had managed to flee Iraq with help from the Iraqi National Congress. The defectors gave dramatic accounts of Iraq's efforts to reconstitute its nuclear-weapons program, and of its alleged production of chemical and biological weapons—but the accounts could not be corroborated by the available intelligence.

Greg Thielmann, after being turned away from Bolton's office, worked with the INR staff on a major review of Iraq's progress in developing W.M.D.s. The review, presented to Secretary of State Powell in December, 2001, echoed the earlier I.A.E.A. findings. According to Thielmann, "It basically said that there is no persuasive evidence that the Iraqi nuclear program is being reconstituted."

The defectors, however, had an audience prepared to believe the worst. Secretary of Defense Donald Rumsfeld had long complained about the limits of American intelligence. In the late nineteen-nineties, for example, he had chaired a commission on ballistic-missile programs that criticized the unwillingness of intelligence analysts "to make estimates that extended beyond the hard evidence they had in hand." After he became Secretary of Defense, a separate intelligence unit was set up in the Pentagon's policy office, under the control of William Luti, a senior aide to Feith. This office, which circumvented the usual procedures of vetting and transparency, stovepiped many of its findings to the highest-ranking officials.

.   .   .

In the fall of 2001, soon after the September 11th attacks, the C.I.A. received an intelligence report from Italy's Military Intelligence and Security Service, or SISMI, about a public visit that Wissam al-Zahawie, then the Iraqi Ambassador to the Vatican, had made to Niger and three other African nations two and a half years earlier, in February, 1999. The visit had been covered at the time by the local press in Niger and by a French press agency. The American Ambassador, Charles O. Cecil, filed a routine report to Washington on the visit, as did British intelligence. There was nothing untoward about the Zahawie visit. "We reported it because his picture appeared in the paper with the President," Cecil, who is now retired, told me. There was no article accompanying the photograph, only the caption, and nothing significant to report. At the time, Niger, which had sent hundreds of troops in support of the American-led Gulf War in 1991, was actively seeking economic assistance from the United States.

None of the contemporaneous reports, as far as is known, made any mention of uranium. But now, apparently as part of a larger search for any pertinent information about terrorism, SISMI dug the Zahawie-trip report out of its files and passed it along, with a suggestion that Zahawie's real mission was to arrange the purchase of a form of uranium ore known as "yellowcake." (Yellowcake, which has been a major Niger export for decades, can be used to make fuel for nuclear reactors. It can also be converted, if processed differently, into weapons-grade uranium.)

What made the two-and-a-half-year-old report stand out in Washington was its relative freshness. A 1999 attempt by Iraq to buy uranium ore, if verified, would seem to prove that Saddam had been working to reconstitute his nuclear program—and give the lie to the I.A.E.A. and to intelligence reports inside the American government that claimed otherwise.

The SISMI report, however, was unpersuasive. Inside the

American intelligence community, it was dismissed as amateurish and unsubstantiated. One former senior C.I.A. official told me that the initial report from Italy contained no documents but only a written summary of allegations. "I can fully believe that SISMI would put out a piece of intelligence like that," a C.I.A. consultant told me, "but why anybody would put credibility in it is beyond me." No credible documents have emerged since to corroborate it.

The intelligence report was quickly stovepiped to those officials who had an intense interest in building the case against Iraq, including Vice-President Dick Cheney. "The Vice-President saw a piece of intelligence reporting that Niger was attempting to buy uranium," Cathie Martin, the spokeswoman for Cheney, told me. Sometime after he first saw it, Cheney brought it up at his regularly scheduled daily briefing from the C.I.A., Martin said. "He asked the briefer a question. The briefer came back a day or two later and said, 'We do have a report, but there's a lack of details.'" The Vice-President was further told that it was known that Iraq had acquired uranium ore from Niger in the early nineteen-eighties but that that material had been placed in secure storage by the I.A.E.A., which was monitoring it. "End of story," Martin added. "That's all we know." According to a former high-level C.I.A. official, however, Cheney was dissatisfied with the initial response, and asked the agency to review the matter once again. It was the beginning of what turned out to be a year-long tug-of-war between the C.I.A. and the Vice-President's office.

As the campaign against Iraq intensified, a former aide to Cheney told me, the Vice-President's office, run by his chief of staff, Lewis (Scooter) Libby, became increasingly secretive when it came to intelligence about Iraq's W.M.D.s. As with Wolfowitz and Bolton, there was a reluctance to let the military and civilian analysts on the staff vet intelligence.

"It was an unbelievably closed and small group," the former aide told me. Intelligence procedures were far more open during the

Clinton Administration, he said, and professional staff members had been far more involved in assessing and evaluating the most sensitive data. "There's so much intelligence out there that it's easy to pick and choose your case," the former aide told me. "It opens things up to cherry-picking." ("Some reporting is sufficiently sensitive that it is restricted only to the very top officials of the government—as it should be," Cathie Martin said. And any restrictions, she added, emanate from C.I.A. security requirements.)

By early 2002, the SISMI intelligence—still unverified—had begun to play a role in the Administration's warnings about the Iraqi nuclear threat. On January 30th, the C.I.A. published an unclassified report to Congress that stated, "Baghdad may be attempting to acquire materials that could aid in reconstituting its nuclear-weapons program." A week later, Colin Powell told the House International Relations Committee, "With respect to the nuclear program, there is no doubt that the Iraqis are pursuing it."

The C.I.A. assessment reflected both deep divisions within the agency and the position of its director, George Tenet, which was far from secure. (The agency had been sharply criticized, after all, for failing to provide any effective warning of the September 11th attacks.) In the view of many C.I.A. analysts and operatives, the director was too eager to endear himself to the Administration hawks and improve his standing with the President and the Vice-President. Senior C.I.A. analysts dealing with Iraq were constantly being urged by the Vice-President's office to provide worst-case assessments on Iraqi weapons issues. "They got pounded on, day after day," one senior Bush Administration official told me, and received no consistent backup from Tenet and his senior staff. "Pretty soon you say 'Fuck it.'" And they began to provide the intelligence that was wanted.

· · · ·

In late February, the C.I.A. persuaded retired Ambassador Joseph Wilson to fly to Niger to discreetly check out the story of the uranium sale. Wilson, who is now a business consultant, had excellent credentials: he had been deputy chief of mission in Baghdad, had served as a diplomat in Africa, and had worked in the White House for the National Security Council. He was known as an independent diplomat who had put himself in harm's way to help American citizens abroad.

Wilson told me he was informed at the time that the mission had come about because the Vice-President's office was interested in the Italian intelligence report. Before his departure, he was summoned to a meeting at the C.I.A. with a group of government experts on Iraq, Niger, and uranium. He was shown no documents but was told, he said, that the C.I.A. "was responding to a report that was recently received of a purported memorandum of agreement"—between Iraq and Niger—"that our boys had gotten." He added, "It was never clear to me, or to the people who were briefing me, whether our guys had actually seen the agreement, or the purported text of an agreement." Wilson's trip to Niger, which lasted eight days, produced nothing. He learned that any memorandum of understanding to sell yellowcake would have required the signatures of Niger's Prime Minister, Foreign Minister, and Minister of Mines. "I saw everybody out there," Wilson said, and no one had signed such a document. "If a document purporting to be about the sale contained those signatures, it would not be authentic." Wilson also learned that there was no uranium available to sell: it had all been pre-sold to Niger's Japanese and European consortium partners.

Wilson returned to Washington and made his report. It was circulated, he said, but "I heard nothing about what the Vice-President's office thought about it." (In response, Cathie Martin said, "The Vice-President doesn't know Joe Wilson and did not know about his trip until he read about it in the press." The first press accounts appeared fifteen months after Wilson's trip.)

●　　　●　　　●

By early March, 2002, a former White House official told me, it was understood by many in the White House that the President had decided, in his own mind, to go to war. The undeclared decision had a devastating impact on the continuing struggle against terrorism. The Bush Administration took many intelligence operations that had been aimed at Al Qaeda and other terrorist groups around the world and redirected them to the Persian Gulf. Linguists and special operatives were abruptly reassigned, and several ongoing anti-terrorism intelligence programs were curtailed.

Chalabi's defector reports were now flowing from the Pentagon directly to the Vice-President's office, and then on to the President, with little prior evaluation by intelligence professionals. When INR analysts did get a look at the reports, they were troubled by what they found. "They'd pick apart a report and find out that the source had been wrong before, or had no access to the information provided," Greg Thielmann told me. "There was considerable skepticism throughout the intelligence community about the reliability of Chalabi's sources, but the defector reports were coming all the time. Knock one down and another comes along. Meanwhile, the garbage was being shoved straight to the President."

A routine settled in: the Pentagon's defector reports, classified "secret," would be funnelled to newspapers, but subsequent C.I.A. and INR analyses of the reports—invariably scathing but also classified—would remain secret.

"It became a personality issue," a Pentagon consultant said of the Bush Administration's handling of intelligence. "My fact is better than your fact. The whole thing is a failure of process. Nobody goes to primary sources." The intelligence community was in full retreat.

In the spring of 2002, the former White House official told me, Rumsfeld and Wolfowitz began urging the President to release more than ninety million dollars in federal funds to Chalabi. The 1998 Iraq Liberation Act had authorized ninety-seven million dollars for the Iraqi opposition, but most of the funds had not been expended. The State Department opposed releasing the rest of the money, arguing that Chalabi had failed to account properly for the funds he had already received. "The Vice-President came into a meeting furious that we hadn't given the money to Chalabi," the former official recalled. Cheney said, "Here we are, denying him money, when they"—the Iraqi National Congress—"are providing us with unique intelligence on Iraqi W.M.D.s."

In late summer, the White House sharply escalated the nuclear rhetoric. There were at least two immediate targets: the midterm congressional elections and the pending vote on a congressional resolution authorizing the President to take any action he deemed necessary in Iraq, to protect America's national security.

On August 7th, Vice-President Cheney, speaking in California, said of Saddam Hussein, "What we know now, from various sources, is that he . . . continues to pursue a nuclear weapon." On August 26th, Cheney suggested that Saddam had a nuclear capability that could directly threaten "anyone he chooses, in his own region or beyond." He added that the Iraqis were continuing "to pursue the nuclear program they began so many years ago." On September 8th, he told a television interviewer, "We do know, with absolute certainty, that he is using his procurement system to acquire the equipment he needs in order to enrich uranium to build a nuclear weapon." The President himself, in his weekly radio address on September 14th, stated, "Saddam Hussein has the scientists and infrastructure for a nuclear-weapons program, and has illicitly sought to purchase the equipment needed to enrich uranium for a nuclear weapon." There was no confirmed intelligence for the President's assertion.

The government of the British Prime Minister, Tony Blair, President Bush's closest ally, was also brought in. As Blair later told a British government inquiry, he and Bush had talked by telephone that summer about the need "to disclose what we knew or as much as we could of what we knew." Blair loyally took the lead: on September 24th, the British government issued a dossier dramatizing the W.M.D. threat posed by Iraq. In a foreword, Blair proclaimed that "the assessed intelligence has established beyond doubt that Saddam . . . continues in his efforts to develop nuclear weapons." The dossier noted that intelligence—based, again, largely on the SISMI report—showed that Iraq had "sought significant quantities of uranium from Africa." A subsequent parliamentary inquiry determined that the published statement had been significantly toned down after the C.I.A. warned its British counterpart not to include the claim in the dossier, and in the final version Niger was not named, nor was SISMI.

The White House, meanwhile, had been escalating its rhetoric. In a television interview on September 8th, Condoleezza Rice, the national-security adviser, addressing questions about the strength of the Administration's case against Iraq, said, "We don't want the smoking gun to be a mushroom cloud"—a formulation that was taken up by hawks in the Administration. And, in a speech on October 7th, President Bush said, "Facing clear evidence of peril, we cannot wait for the final proof—the smoking gun—that could come in the form of a mushroom cloud."

·   ·   ·

At that moment, in early October, 2002, a set of documents suddenly appeared that promised to provide solid evidence that Iraq was attempting to reconstitute its nuclear program. The first notice of the documents' existence came when Elisabetta Burba, a reporter for *Panorama,* a glossy Italian weekly owned by the publishing empire of Prime Minister Silvio Berlusconi, received a telephone call from an Italian businessman and security consultant whom she believed to have once been connected to Italian intelligence. He told her that he had information connecting

Saddam Hussein to the purchase of uranium in Africa. She considered the informant credible. In 1995, when she worked for the magazine *Epoca*, he had provided her with detailed information, apparently from Western intelligence sources, for articles she published dealing with the peace process in Bosnia and with an Islamic charity that was linked to international terrorism. The information, some of it in English, proved to be accurate. *Epoca* had authorized her to pay around four thousand dollars for the documents—a common journalistic practice in Italy.

Now, years later, "he comes to me again," Burba told me. "I knew he was an informed person, and that he had contacts all over the world, including in the Middle East. He deals with investment and security issues." When Burba met with the man, he showed her the Niger documents and offered to sell them to her for about ten thousand dollars.

The documents he gave her were photocopies. There were twenty-two pages, mostly in French, some with the letterhead of the Niger government or Embassy, and two on the stationery of the Iraqi Embassy to the Holy See. There were also telexes. When Burba asked how the documents could be authenticated, the man produced what appeared to be a photocopy of the code-book from the Niger Embassy, along with other items. "What I was sure of was that he had access," Burba said. "He didn't receive the documents from the moon."

The documents dealt primarily with the alleged sale of uranium, Burba said. She informed her editors, and shared the photocopies with them. She wanted to arrange a visit to Niger to verify what seemed to be an astonishing story. At that point, however, *Panorama*'s editor-in-chief, Carlo Rossella, who is known for his ties to the Berlusconi government, told Burba to turn the documents over to the American Embassy for authentication. Burba dutifully took a copy of the papers to the Embassy on October 9th.

A week later, Burba travelled to Niger. She visited mines and the ports that any exports would pass through, spoke to European businessmen and officials informed about Niger's uranium industry, and found no trace of a sale. She also learned that the transport company and the bank mentioned in the papers were too small and too ill-equipped to handle such a transaction. As Ambassador Wilson had done eight months earlier, she concluded that there was no evidence of a recent sale of yellowcake to Iraq. The *Panorama* story was dead, and Burba and her editors said that no money was paid. The documents, however, were now in American hands.

Two former C.I.A. officials provided slightly different accounts of what happened next. "The Embassy was alerted that the papers were coming," the first former official told me, "and it passed them directly to Washington without even vetting them inside the Embassy." Once the documents were in Washington, they were forwarded by the C.I.A. to the Pentagon, he said. "Everybody knew at every step of the way that they were false— until they got to the Pentagon, where they were believed."

The documents were just what Administration hawks had been waiting for. The second former official, Vincent Cannistraro, who served as chief of counter-terrorism operations and analysis, told me that copies of the Burba documents were given to the American Embassy, which passed them on to the C.I.A.'s chief of station in Rome, who forwarded them to Washington. Months later, he said, he telephoned a contact at C.I.A. headquarters and was told that "the jury was still out on this"—that is, on the authenticity of the documents.

George Tenet clearly was ambivalent about the information: in early October, he intervened to prevent the President from referring to Niger in a speech in Cincinnati. But Tenet then seemed to give up the fight, and Saddam's desire for uranium from Niger soon became part of the Administration's public case for going to war.

On December 7th, the Iraqi regime provided the U.N. Security

Council with a twelve-thousand-page series of documents in which it denied having a W.M.D. arsenal. Very few in the press, the public, or the White House believed it, and a State Department rebuttal, on December 19th, asked, "Why is the Iraqi regime hiding their Niger procurement?" It was the first time that Niger had been publicly identified. In a January 23rd Op-Ed column in the *Times*, entitled "Why We Know Iraq Is Lying," Condoleezza Rice wrote that the "false declaration . . . fails to account for or explain Iraq's efforts to get uranium from abroad." On January 26th, Secretary Powell, speaking at the World Economic Forum in Davos, Switzerland, asked, "Why is Iraq still trying to procure uranium?" Two days later, President Bush described the alleged sale in his State of the Union address, saying, "The British government has learned that Saddam Hussein recently sought significant quantities of uranium from Africa."

·　　·　　·

Who produced the fake Niger papers? There is nothing approaching a consensus on this question within the intelligence community. There has been published speculation about the intelligence services of several different countries. One theory, favored by some journalists in Rome, is that SISMI produced the false documents and passed them to *Panorama* for publication.

Another explanation was provided by a former senior C.I.A. officer. He had begun talking to me about the Niger papers in March, when I first wrote about the forgery, and said, "Somebody deliberately let something false get in there." He became more forthcoming in subsequent months, eventually saying that a small group of disgruntled retired C.I.A. clandestine operators had banded together in the late summer of last year and drafted the fraudulent documents themselves.

"The agency guys were so pissed at Cheney," the former officer said. "They said, 'O.K, we're going to put the bite on these guys.'"

My source said that he was first told of the fabrication late last year, at one of the many holiday gatherings in the Washington area of past and present C.I.A. officials. "Everyone was bragging about it—'Here's what we did. It was cool, cool, cool.'" These retirees, he said, had superb contacts among current officers in the agency and were informed in detail of the SISMI intelligence.

"They thought that, with this crowd, it was the only way to go—to nail these guys who were not practicing good tradecraft and vetting intelligence," my source said. "They thought it'd be bought at lower levels—a big bluff." The thinking, he said, was that the documents would be endorsed by Iraq hawks at the top of the Bush Administration, who would be unable to resist flaunting them at a press conference or an interagency government meeting. They would then look foolish when intelligence officials pointed out that they were obvious fakes. But the tactic backfired, he said, when the papers won widespread acceptance within the Administration. "It got out of control."

Like all large institutions, C.I.A. headquarters, in Langley, Virginia, is full of water-cooler gossip, and a retired clandestine officer told me this summer that the story about a former operations officer faking the documents is making the rounds. "What's telling," he added, "is that the story, whether it's true or not, is believed"—an extraordinary commentary on the level of mistrust, bitterness, and demoralization within the C.I.A. under the Bush Administration. (William Harlow, the C.I.A. spokesman, said that the agency had no more evidence that former members of the C.I.A. had forged the documents "than we have that they were forged by Mr. Hersh.")

The F.B.I. has been investigating the forgery at the request of the Senate Intelligence Committee. A senior F.B.I. official told me that the possibility that the documents were falsified by someone inside the American intelligence community had not been ruled out. "This story could go several directions," he said. "We haven't gotten anything solid, and we've looked." He said that the F.B.I. agents assigned to the case are putting a great deal of effort into the investigation. But "somebody's hiding something, and they're hiding it pretty well."

.   .   .

President Bush's State of the Union speech had startled Elisabetta Burba, the Italian reporter. She had been handed documents and had personally taken them to the American Embassy, and she now knew from her trip to Niger that they were false. Later, Burba revisited her source. "I wanted to know what happened," she said. "He told me that he didn't know the documents were false, and said he'd also been fooled."

Burba, convinced that she had the story of the year, wanted to publish her account immediately after the President's speech, but Carlo Rossella, *Panorama's* editor-in-chief, decided against it. Rossella explained to me, "When I heard the State of the Union statement, I thought to myself that perhaps the United States government has other information. I didn't think the documents were that important—they weren't trustable." Eventually, in July, after her name appeared in the press, Burba published an account of her role. She told me that she was interviewed at the American consulate in Milan by three agents for the F.B.I. in early September.

The State of the Union speech was confounding to many members of the intelligence community, who could not understand how such intelligence could have got to the President without vetting. The former intelligence official who gave me the account of the forging of the documents told me that his colleagues were also startled by the speech. "They said, 'Holy shit, all of a sudden the President is talking about it in the State of the Union address!' They began to panic. Who the hell was going to expose it? They had to build a backfire. The solution was to leak the documents to the I.A.E.A."

I subsequently met with a group of senior I.A.E.A. officials in

Vienna, where the organization has its headquarters. In an interview over dinner, they told me that they did not even know the papers existed until early February of this year, a few days after the President's speech. The I.A.E.A. had been asking Washington and London for their evidence of Iraq's pursuit of African uranium, without receiving any response, ever since the previous September, when word of it turned up in the British dossier. After Niger was specified in the State Department's fact sheet of December 19, 2002, the I.A.E.A. became more insistent. "I started to harass the United States," recalled Jacques Baute, a Frenchman who, as director of the I.A.E.A.'s Iraq Nuclear Verification Office, often harassed Washington. Mark Gwozdecky, the I.A.E.A.'s spokesman, added, "We were asking for actionable evidence, and Jacques was getting almost nothing."

On February 4, 2003, while Baute was on a plane bound for New York to attend a United Nations Security Council meeting on the Iraqi weapons dispute, the U.S. Mission in Vienna suddenly briefed members of Baute's team on the Niger papers, but still declined to hand over the documents. "I insisted on seeing the documents myself," Baute said, "and was provided with them upon my arrival in New York." The next day, Secretary Powell made his case for going to war against Iraq before the U.N. Security Council. The presentation did not mention Niger—a fact that did not escape Baute. I.A.E.A. officials told me that they were puzzled by the timing of the American decision to provide the documents. Baute quickly concluded that they were fake.

Over the next few weeks, I.A.E.A. officials conducted further investigations, which confirmed the fraud. They also got in touch with American and British officials to inform them of the findings, and give them a chance to respond. Nothing was forthcoming, and so the I.A.E.A.'s director-general, Mohamed El Baradei, publicly described the fraud at his next scheduled briefing to the U.N. Security Council, in New York on March 7th. The story slowly began to unravel.

Vice-President Cheney responded to ElBaradei's report mainly by attacking the messenger. On March 16th, Cheney, appearing on "Meet the Press," stated emphatically that the United States had reason to believe that Saddam Hussein had reconstituted his nuclear-weapons program. He went on, "I think Mr. ElBaradei frankly is wrong. And I think if you look at the track record of the International Atomic Energy Agency on this kind of issue, especially where Iraq's concerned, they have consistently underestimated or missed what it was Saddam Hussein was doing. I don't have any reason to believe they're any more valid this time than they've been in the past." Three days later, the war in Iraq got under way, and the tale of the African-uranium-connection forgery sank from view.

• • •

Joseph Wilson, the diplomat who had travelled to Africa to investigate the allegation more than a year earlier, revived the Niger story. He was angered by what he saw as the White House's dishonesty about Niger, and in early May he casually mentioned his mission to Niger, and his findings, during a brief talk about Iraq at a political conference in suburban Washington sponsored by the Senate Democratic Policy Committee (Wilson is a Democrat). Another speaker at the conference was the *Times* columnist Nicholas Kristof, who got Wilson's permission to mention the Niger trip in a column. A few months later, on July 6th, Wilson wrote about the trip himself on the *Times* Op-Ed page. "I gave them months to correct the record," he told me, speaking of the White House, "but they kept on lying."

The White House responded by blaming the intelligence community for the Niger reference in the State of the Union address. Condoleezza Rice, the national-security adviser, told a television interviewer on July 13th, "Had there been even a peep that the agency did not want that sentence in or that George Tenet did not want that sentence . . . it would have been gone." Five days later, a senior White House official went a step further, telling reporters at a background briefing that they had the wrong impression about Joseph Wilson's trip to Niger and the information it had yielded. "You can't draw a conclusion that we were warned by Ambassador Wilson that this was all dubious," the unnamed official said, according to a White House transcript. "It's just not accurate."

But Wilson's account of his trip forced a rattled White House to acknowledge, for the first time, that "this information should not have risen to the level of a Presidential speech." It also triggered retaliatory leaks to the press by White House officials that exposed Wilson's wife as a C.I.A. operative—and led to an F.B.I. investigation.

·　　·　　·

Among the best potential witnesses on the subject of Iraq's actual nuclear capabilities are the men and women who worked in the Iraqi weapons industry and for the National Monitoring Directorate, the agency set up by Saddam to work with the United Nations and I.A.E.A. inspectors. Many of the most senior weapons-industry officials, even those who voluntarily surrendered to U.S. forces, are being held in captivity at the Baghdad airport and other places, away from reporters. Their families have been told little by American authorities. Desperate for information, they have been calling friends and other contacts in America for help.

One Iraqi émigré who has heard from the scientists' families is Shakir al Kha Fagi, who left Iraq as a young man and runs a successful business in the Detroit area. "The people in intelligence and in the W.M.D. business are in jail," he said. "The Americans are hunting them down one by one. Nobody speaks for them, and there's no American lawyer who will take the case."

Not all the senior scientists are in captivity, however. Jafar

Dhia Jafar, a British-educated physicist who co-ordinated Iraq's efforts to make the bomb in the nineteen-eighties, and who had direct access to Saddam Hussein, fled Iraq in early April, before Baghdad fell, and, with the help of his brother, Hamid, the managing director of a large energy company, made his way to the United Arab Emirates. Jafar has refused to return to Baghdad, but he agreed to be debriefed by C.I.A. and British intelligence agents. There were some twenty meetings, involving as many as fifteen American and British experts. The first meeting, on April 11th, began with an urgent question from a C.I.A. officer: "Does Iraq have a nuclear device? The military really want to know. They are extremely worried." Jafar's response, according to the notes of an eyewitness, was to laugh. The notes continued:

> Jafar insisted that there was not only no bomb, but no W.M.D., period. "The answer was none." . . . Jafar explained that the Iraqi leadership had set up a new committee after the 91 Gulf war, and after the UNSCOM [United Nations] inspection process was set up. . . and the following instructions [were sent] from the Top Man [Saddam]—"give them everything."

The notes said that Jafar was then asked, "But this doesn't mean all W.M.D.? How can you be certain?" His answer was clear: "I know all the scientists involved, and they chat. There is no W.M.D."

Jafar explained why Saddam had decided to give up his valued weapons:

> Up until the 91 Gulf war, our adversaries were regional. . . . But after the war, when it was clear that we were up against the United States, Saddam understood that these weapons were redundant. "No way we could escape the United States." Therefore, the W.M.D. warheads did Iraq little strategic good.

Jafar had his own explanation, according to the notes, for one of the enduring mysteries of the U.N. inspection process—the six-thousand-warhead discrepancy between the number of chemical weapons thought to have been manufactured by Iraq before 1991 and the number that were accounted for by the U.N. inspection teams. It was this discrepancy which led Western intelligence officials and military planners to make the worst-case assumptions. Jafar told his interrogators that the Iraqi government had simply lied to the United Nations about the number of chemical weapons used against Iran during the brutal Iran-Iraq war in the nineteen-eighties. Iraq, he said, dropped thousands more warheads on the Iranians than it acknowledged. For that reason, Saddam preferred not to account for the weapons at all.

There are always credibility problems with witnesses from a defeated regime, and anyone involved in the creation or conceal-ment of W.M.D.s would have a motive to deny it. But a strong endorsement of Jafar's integrity came from an unusual source—Jacques Baute, of the I.A.E.A., who spent much of the past decade locked in a struggle with Jafar and the other W.M.D. scientists and technicians of Iraq. "I don't believe anybody," Baute told me, "but, by and large, what he told us after 1995 was pretty accurate."

·   ·   ·

In early October, David Kay, the former U.N. inspector who is the head of the Administration's Iraq Survey Group, made his interim report to Congress on the status of the search for Iraq's W.M.D.s "We have not yet found stocks of weapons," Kay reported, "but we are not yet at the point where we can say definitively either that such weapon stocks do not exist or that they existed before the war." In the area of nuclear weapons, Kay said, "Despite evidence of Saddam's continued ambition to acquire nuclear weapons, to date we have not uncovered evidence that Iraq undertook significant post-1998 steps to actually build nuclear weapons or produce fissile material." Kay was widely seen as having made the best case possible for President Bush's prewar claims of an imminent W.M.D. threat. But what he found fell far short of those claims, and the report was regarded as a blow to the Administration. President Bush, however, saw it differently. He told reporters that he felt vindicated by the report, in that it showed that "Saddam Hussein was a threat, a serious danger."

The President's response raises the question of what, if anything, the Administration learned from the failure, so far, to find significant quantities of W.M.D.s in Iraq. Any President depends heavily on his staff for the vetting of intelligence and a reasonable summary and analysis of the world's day-to-day events. The ultimate authority in the White House for such issues lies with the President's national-security adviser—in this case, Condoleezza Rice. The former White House official told me, "Maybe the Secretary of Defense and his people are short-circuiting the process, and creating a separate channel to the Vice-President. Still, at the end of the day all the policies have to be hashed out in the interagency process, led by the national-security adviser." What happened instead, he said, "was a real abdication of responsibility by Condi."

Vice-President Cheney remains unabashed about the Administration's reliance on the Niger documents, despite the revelation of their forgery. In a September interview on "Meet the Press," Cheney claimed that the British dossier's charge that "Saddam was, in fact, trying to acquire uranium in Africa" had been "revalidated." Cheney went on, "So there may be a difference of opinion there. I don't know what the truth is on the ground. . . . I don't know Mr. Wilson. I probably shouldn't judge him."

The Vice-President also defended the way in which he had involved himself in intelligence matters: "This is a very important area. It's one that the President has asked me to work on. . . . In terms of asking questions, I plead guilty. I ask a hell of a lot of questions. That's my job."

The Atlantic Monthly

FINALIST, REPORTING

Columbia's Last Flight

Many news organizations reported on the accident that destroyed the shuttle Columbia. But it took William Langewiesche to come up with the definitive story of both the shuttle's last mission and the investigation into the cause of the disaster. Exhibiting Langewiesche's keen eye for detail and uncanny ability to portray people vividly in very few words, "Columbia's Last Flight" is a painfully evocative narrative of the various technical, political and bureaucratic issues that led to the tragedy.

William Langewiesche

Columbia's Last Flight

The inside story of the investigation—and the catastrophe it laid bare

S pace flight is known to be a risky business, but during the minutes before dawn last February 1, as the doomed shuttle *Columbia* began to descend into the upper atmosphere over the Pacific Ocean, only a handful of people—a few engineers deep inside of NASA—worried that the vehicle and its seven souls might actually come to grief. It was the responsibility of NASA's managers to hear those suspicions, and from top to bottom they failed. After the fact, that's easy to see. But in fairness to those whose reputations have now been sacrificed, seventeen years and eighty-nine shuttle flights had passed since the *Challenger* explosion, and within the agency a new generation had risen that was smart, perhaps, but also unwise—confined by NASA's walls and routines, and vulnerable to the self-satisfaction that inevitably had set in.

Moreover, this mission was a yawn—a low-priority "science" flight forced onto NASA by Congress and postponed for two years because of a more pressing schedule of construction deliveries to the International Space Station. The truth is, it had finally been launched as much to clear the books as to add to human knowledge, and it had gone nowhere except into low Earth orbit, around the globe every ninety minutes for sixteen days, carrying the first Israeli astronaut, and performing a string of experiments, many of which, like the shuttle program itself, seemed to suffer from something of a make-work character—the examination of dust in the Middle East (by the Israeli, of course); the ever popular ozone study; experiments designed by schoolchildren in six countries to observe the effect of weightlessness on spiders, silkworms, and other creatures; an exercise in "astroculture" involving the extraction of essential oils from rose and rice flowers, which was said to hold promise for new perfumes; and so forth. No doubt some good science was done too—particularly pertaining to space flight itself—though none of it was so urgent that it could not have been performed later, under better circumstances, in the under-booked International Space Station. The astronauts aboard the shuttle were smart and accomplished people, and they were deeply committed to human space flight and exploration. They were also team players, by intense selection, and nothing if not wise to the game. From orbit one of them had radioed, "The science we're doing here is great, and it's fantastic. It's leading-edge." Others had dutifully reported that the planet seems beautiful, fragile, and borderless when seen from such altitudes, and they had expressed their hopes in English and Hebrew for world peace. It was Miracle Whip on Wonder Bread, standard NASA fare. On the ground so little attention was being paid that even the radars that could have been directed upward to track the *Columbia*'s re-entry into the atmosphere—from Vandenberg Air Force Base, or White Sands Missile Range—were sleeping. As a result, no radar record of the breakup exists—only of the metal rain that drifted down over East Texas, and eventually came into the view of air-traffic control.

Along the route, however, stood small numbers of shuttle enthusiasts, who had gotten up early with their video cameras and had arrayed themselves on hills or away from city lights to record the spectacle of what promised to be a beautiful display. The shuttle came into view, on track and on schedule, just after 5:53 Pacific time, crossing the California coast at about 15,000 mph in the superthin air 230,000 feet above the Russian River, northwest of San Francisco. It was first picked up on video by a Lockheed engineer in suburban Fairfield, who recorded a bright meteor passing almost directly overhead, not the shuttle itself but the sheath of hot gases around it, and the long, luminous tail of ionized air known as plasma. Only later, after the engineer heard about the accident on television, did he check his tape and realize that he had recorded what appeared to be two pieces coming off the *Columbia* in quick succession, like little flares in its wake. Those pieces were recorded by others as well, along with the third, fourth, and fifth "debris events" that are known to have occurred during the sixty seconds that it took the shuttle to cross California. From the top of Mount Hamilton, southeast of San Francisco, another engineer, the former president of the Peninsula Astronomical Society, caught all five events on tape but, again, did not realize it until afterward. He later said, "I'd seen four re-entries before this one. When we saw it, we did note that it was a little brighter and a little bit whiter in color than it normally is. It's normally a pink-magenta color. But you know, it wasn't so different that it really flagged us as something wrong. With the naked eye we didn't see the particles coming off."

One minute after the *Columbia* left California, as it neared southwestern Utah, the trouble was becoming more obvious to observers on the ground. There had been a bright flash earlier over Nevada, and now debris came off that was large enough to cause multiple secondary plasma trails. North of the Grand

Canyon, in Saint George, Utah, a man and his grown son climbed onto a ridge above the county hospital, hoping for the sort of view they had seen several years before, of a fireball going by. It was a sight they remembered as "really neat." This time was different, though. The son, who was videotaping, started yelling, "Jesus, Dad, there's stuff falling off!" and the father saw it too, with his naked eyes.

The *Columbia* was flying on autopilot, as is usual, and though it continued to lay flares in its wake, the astronauts aboard remained blissfully unaware of the trouble they were in. They passed smoothly into dawn above the Arizona border, and sailed across the Navajo reservation and on over Albuquerque, before coming to the Texas Panhandle on a perfect descent profile, slowing through 13,400 mph at 210,000 feet five minutes after having crossed the California coastline. Nineteen seconds later, at 7:58:38 central time, they got the first sign of something being a little out of the ordinary: it was a cockpit indication of low tire pressures on the left main landing gear. This was not quite a trivial matter. A blown or deflated main tire would pose serious risks during the rollout after landing, including loss of lateral control and the possibility that the nose would slam down, conceivably leading to a catastrophic breakup on the ground. These scenarios were known, and had been simulated and debated in the inner world of NASA, leading some to believe that the best of the imperfect choices in such a case might be for the crew to bail out—an alternative available only below 30,000 feet and 220 mph of dynamic airspeed.

Nonetheless, for *Columbia*'s pilots it was reasonable to assume for the moment that the indication of low pressure was due to a problem with the sensors rather than with the tires themselves, and that the teams of Mission Control engineers at NASA's Johnson Space Center, in Houston, would be able to sort through the mass of automatically transmitted data—the so-called telemetry, which was far more complete than what was available in the cockpit—and to draw the correct conclusion. The reverse side of failures in a machine as complex as the shuttle is that most of them can be worked around, or turn out to be small. In other words, there was no reason for alarm. After a short delay the *Columbia*'s commander, Rick Husband, calmly radioed to Mission Control, "And, ah, Houston . . ." Sheathed in hot atmospheric gases, the shuttle was slowing through 13,100 mph at 205,000 feet.

Houston did not clearly hear the call.

With the scheduled touchdown now only about fifteen minutes ahead, it was a busy time at Mission Control. Weather reports were coming in from the landing site at the Kennedy Space Center, in Florida. Radar tracking of the shuttle, like the final accurate ground-based navigation, had not yet begun. Sitting at their specialized positions, and monitoring the numbers displayed on the consoles, a few of the flight controllers had begun to sense, just barely, that something was going seriously wrong. The worry was not quite coherent yet. One of the controllers later told me that it amounted to an inexplicable bad feeling in his gut. But it was undeniable nonetheless. For the previous few minutes, since about the time when the shuttle had passed from California to Nevada, Jeff Kling, an engineer who was working the mechanical-systems position known as MMACS (pronounced *Macs*), had witnessed a swarm of erratic indications and sensor failures. The pattern was disconcerting because of the lack of common circuitry that could easily explain the pattern of such failures—a single box that could be blamed.

Kling had been bantering good-naturedly on an intercom with one of his team, a technician sitting in one of the adjoining back rooms and monitoring the telemetry, when the technician noted a strange failure of temperature transducers on a hydraulic return line. The technician said, "We've had some hydraulic 'ducers go off-scale low."

Kling had seen the same indications. He said, "Well, I guess!"

The technician said, "What in the world?"

Kling said, "This is not funny. On the left side."

The technician confirmed, "On the left side . . ."

Now Kling got onto the main control-room intercom to the lead controller on duty, known as the flight director, a man named Leroy Cain. In the jargon-laced language of the control room Kling said, "Flight, Macs."

Cain said, "Go ahead, Macs."

"FYI, I've just lost four separate temperature transducers on the left side of the vehicle, hydraulic return temperatures. Two of them on system one, and one in each of systems two and three."

Cain said, "Four hyd return temps?"

Kling answered, "To the left outboard and left inboard elevon."

"Okay, is there anything common to them? DSC or MDM or anything? I mean, you're telling me you lost them all at exactly the same time?"

"No, not exactly. They were within probably four or five seconds of each other."

Cain struggled to assess the meaning. "Okay, where are those . . . where is that instrumentation located?"

Kling continued to hear from his back-room team. He said, "All four of them are located in the aft part of the left wing, right in front of the elevons . . . elevon *actuators*. And there is no commonality."

Cain repeated, "No commonality."

But all the failing instruments were in the left wing. The possible significance of this was not lost on Cain: during the launch a piece of solid foam had broken off from the shuttle's external fuel tank, and at high speed had smashed into the left wing; after minimal consideration the shuttle program managers (who stood above Mission Control in the NASA hierarchy) had dismissed the incident as essentially unthreatening. Like almost everyone else at NASA, Cain had taken the managers at their word—and he still did. Nonetheless, the strange cluster of left-wing failures was an ominous development. Kling had more-specific reasons for concern. In a wonkish, engineering way he had discussed with his team the telemetry they might observe if a hole allowed hot gases into the wing during re-entry, and had come up with a profile eerily close to what was happening now. Still, he maintained the expected detachment.

Cain continued to worry the problem. He asked for reassurance from his "guidance, navigation, and control" man, Mike Sarafin. "Everything look good to you, control and rates and everything is nominal, right?"

Sarafin said, "Control's been stable through the rolls that we've done so far, Flight. We have good trims. I don't see anything out of the ordinary."

Cain directed his attention back to Kling: "All other indications for your hydraulic systems indications are good?"

"They're all good. We've had good quantities all the way across."

Cain said, "And the other temps are normal?"

"The other temps are normal, yes, sir." He meant only those that the telemetry allowed him to see.

Cain said, "And when you say you lost these, are you saying they went to zero . . ."

"All four of them are off-scale low."

" . . . or off-scale low?"

Kling said, "And they were all staggered. They were, like I said, within several seconds of each other."

Cain said, "Okay."

But it wasn't okay. Within seconds the *Columbia* had crossed into Texas and the left-tire-pressure indications were dropping, as observed also by the cockpit crew. Kling's informal model of catastrophe had predicted just such indications, whether from blown tires or wire breaks. The end was now coming very fast.

Kling said, "Flight, Macs."

Cain said, "Go."

"We just lost tire pressure on the left outboard and left inboard, both tires."

Cain said, "Copy."

At that moment, twenty-three seconds after 7:59 local time, the Mission Control consoles stopped receiving telemetry updates, for reasons unknown. The astronaut sitting beside Cain, and serving as the Mission Control communicator, radioed, "And *Columbia*, Houston, we see your tire-pressure messages, and we did not copy your last call."

At the same time, on the control-room intercom, Cain was talking again to Kling. He said, "Is it instrumentation, Macs? Gotta be."

Kling said, "Flight, Macs, those are also off-scale low."

From the speeding shuttle Rick Husband—Air Force test pilot, religious, good family man, always wanted to be an astronaut—began to answer the communicator. He said, "Roger, ah," and was cut off on a word that began with "buh . . ."

It turned out to be the *Columbia*'s last voice transmission. Brief communication breaks, however, are not abnormal during re-entries, and this one raised no immediate concern in Houston.

People on the ground in Dallas suddenly knew more than the flight controllers in Houston. Four seconds after eight they saw a large piece leave the orbiter and fall away. The shuttle was starting to come apart. It continued intermittently to send telemetry, which though not immediately displayed at Mission Control was captured by NASA computers and later discovered; the story it told was that multiple systems were failing. In quick succession two additional chunks fell off.

Down in the control room Cain said, "And there's no commonality between all these tire-pressure instrumentations and the hydraulic return instrumentations?"

High in the sky near Dallas the *Columbia*'s main body began to break up. It crackled and boomed, and made a loud rumble.

Kling said, "No, sir, there's not. We've also lost the nose-gear down talkback, and right-main-gear down talkback."

"Nose-gear and right-main-gear down talkbacks?"

"Yes, sir."

At Fort Hood, Texas, two Dutch military pilots who were training in an Apache attack helicopter locked on to the breakup with their optics and videotaped three bright objects—the main rocket engines—flying eastward in formation, among other, smaller pieces and their contrails.

Referring to the loss of communications, one minute after the main-body breakup, Laura Hoppe, the flight controller responsible for the communications systems, said to Cain, "I didn't expect, uh, this bad of a hit on comm."

Cain asked another controller about a planned switchover to a ground-based radio ahead, "How far are we from UHF? Is that two-minute clock good?"

Kling, also, was hanging on to hope. He said, "Flight, Macs."

Cain said, "Macs?"

Kling said, "On the tire pressures, we did see them go erratic for a little bit before they went away, so I do believe it's instrumentation."

"Okay."

At about that time the debris began to hit the ground. It fell in thousands of pieces along a swath ten miles wide and 300 miles long, across East Texas and into Louisiana. There were many stories later. Some of the debris whistled down through the leaves of trees and smacked into a pond where a man was fishing. Another piece went right through a backyard trampoline, evoking a mother's lament: "Those damned kids . . ." Still another piece hit the window of a moving car, startling the driver. The heaviest parts flew the farthest. An 800-pound piece of engine hit the ground in Fort Polk, Louisiana, doing 1,400 mph. A 600-pound piece landed nearby. Thousands of people began to call in, swamping the 911 dispatchers with reports of sonic booms and metal falling out of the sky. No one, however, was hit. This would be surprising were it not for the fact, so visible from above, that the world is still a sparsely populated place.

In Houston the controllers maintained discipline, and continued preparing for the landing, even as they received word that the Merritt Island radar, in Florida, which should by now have started tracking the inbound craft, was picking up only false targets. Shuttles arrive on time or they don't arrive at all. But, repeatedly, the communicator radioed, "*Columbia*, Houston, UHF comm check," as if he might still hear a reply. Then, at thirteen minutes past the hour, precisely when the *Columbia* should have been passing overhead the runway before circling down for a landing at the Kennedy Space Center, a phone call came in from an off-duty controller who had just seen a video broadcast by a Dallas television station of multiple contrails in the sky. When Cain heard the news, he paused, and then put the contingency plan into effect. To the ground-control officer he said, "GC, Flight."

"Flight, GC."

"Lock the doors."

"Copy."

The controllers were stunned, but lacked the time to contemplate the horror of what had just happened. Under Cain's direction they set about collecting numbers, writing notes, and closing out their logs, for the investigation that was certain to follow. The mood in the room was somber and focused. Only the most basic facts were known: the *Columbia* had broken up at 200,000 feet doing 12,738 mph, and the crew could not possibly have survived. Ron Dittemore, the shuttle program manager, would be talking to reporters later that day, and he needed numbers and information. At some point sandwiches were brought in and consumed. Like the priests who harvest faith at the bedsides of the dying, grief counselors showed up too, but they were not much used.

Cain insisted on control-room discipline. He said, "No phone calls off site outside of this room. Our discussions are on these loops—the recorded DVIS loops only. No data, no phone calls, no transmissions anywhere, into or out."

Later this was taken by some critics to be a typical NASA reaction—insular, furtive, overcontrolling. And it may indeed have reflected certain aspects of what had become of the agency's culture. But it was also, more simply, a rule-book procedure meant to stabilize and preserve the crucial last data. The room was being frozen as a crime scene might be. Somewhere inside NASA something had obviously gone very wrong—and it made sense to start looking for the evidence here and now.

· · ·

Less than an hour later, at 10:00 A.M. eastern time, a retired four-star admiral named Hal Gehman met his brother at a lawyer's office in Williamsburg, Virginia. At the age of sixty, Gehman was a tall, slim, silver-haired man with an unlined face and soft eyes. Dressed in civilian clothes, standing straight but not stiffly so, he had an accessible, unassuming manner that contrasted with the rank and power he had achieved. After an inauspicious start as a mediocre engineering student in the Penn State Naval ROTC program ("Top four fifths of the class," he liked to say), he had skippered a patrol boat through the thick of the Vietnam War and gone on to become an experienced sea captain, the commander of a carrier battle group, vice-chief of the Navy, and finally NATO Atlantic commander and head of the U.S. Joint Forces Command. Upon his retirement, in 2000, from the sixth-ranked position in the U.S. military, he had given all that up with apparent ease. He had enjoyed a good career in the Navy, but he enjoyed his civilian life now too. He was a rare sort of man—startlingly intelligent beneath his guileless exterior, personally satisfied, and quite genuinely untroubled. He lived in

Norfolk in a pleasant house that he had recently remodeled; he loved his wife, his grown children, his mother and father, and all his siblings. He had an old Volkswagen bug convertible, robin's-egg blue, that he had bought from another admiral. He had a modest thirty-four-foot sloop, which he enjoyed sailing in the Chesapeake, though its sails were worn out and he wanted to replace its icebox with a twelve-volt refrigeration unit. He was a patriot, of course, but not a reactionary. He called himself a fiscal conservative and a social moderate. His life as he described it was the product of convention. It was also the product of a strict personal code. He chose not to work with any company doing business with the Department of Defense. He liked power, but understood its limitations. He did not care to be famous or rich. He represented the American establishment at its best.

In the lawyer's office in Williamsburg his brother told him that the *Columbia* had been lost. Gehman had driven there with his radio off and so he had not heard. He asked a few questions, and absorbed the information without much reaction. He did not follow the space program and, like most Americans, had not been aware that a mission was under way. He spent an hour with the lawyer on routine family business. When he emerged, he saw that messages had been left on his cell phone, but because the coverage was poor, he could not retrieve them; only later, while driving home on the interstate, was he finally able to connect. To his surprise, among mundane messages he found an urgent request to call the deputy administrator of NASA, a man he had not heard of before, named Fred Gregory. Like a good American, Gehman made the call while speeding down the highway. Gregory, a former shuttle commander, said, "Have you heard the news?"

Gehman said, "Only secondhand."

Gregory filled him in on what little was known, and explained that part of NASA's contingency plan, instituted after the *Challenger* disaster of 1986, was the activation of a standing "interagency" investigation board. By original design the board consisted of seven high-ranking civilian and military officials who were pre-selected mechanically on the basis of job titles—the institutional slots that they filled. For the *Columbia*, the names were now known: the board would consist of three Air Force generals, John Barry, Kenneth Hess, and Duane Deal; a Navy admiral, Stephen Turcotte; a NASA research director, G. Scott Hubbard; and two senior civil-aviation officials, James Hallock and Steven Wallace. Though only two of these men knew much about NASA or the space shuttle, in various ways each of them was familiar with the complexities of large-scale, high-risk activities. Most of them also had strong personalities. To be effective they would require even stronger management. Gregory said that it was NASA's administrator, Sean O'Keefe, who wanted Gehman to come in as chairman to lead the work. Gehman was not immune to the compliment, but he was cautious. He had met O'Keefe briefly years before, but did not know him. He wanted to make sure he wasn't being suckered into a NASA sideshow.

O'Keefe was an able member of Washington's revolving-door caste, a former congressional staffer and budget specialist—and a longtime protégé of Vice President Dick Cheney—who through the force of his competence and Republican connections had briefly landed the position of Secretary of the Navy in the early 1990s. He had suffered academic banishment through the Clinton era, but under the current administration had re-emerged as a deputy at the Office of Management and Budget, where he had been assigned to tackle the difficult problem of NASA's cost overruns and lack of delivery, particularly in the Space Station program. It is hard to know what he thought when he was handed the treacherous position of NASA administrator. Inside Washington, NASA's reputation had sunk so low that some of O'Keefe's former congressional colleagues snickered that Cheney was trying to kill his own man off. But O'Keefe was not a space crusader, as some earlier NASA administrators had been, and he was not about to pick up the fallen banners of the visionaries and try to lead the way forward; he was a tough, level-headed money man, grounded in the realities of Washington, D.C., and sent in on a mission to bring discipline to NASA's budget and performance before moving on. NASA's true believers called him a carpetbagger and resented the schedule pressures that he brought to bear, but in fairness he was a professional manager, and NASA needed one.

O'Keefe had been at NASA for just over a year when the *Columbia* self-destructed. He was in Florida standing at the landing site beside one of his deputies, a former shuttle commander named William Readdy. At 9:05 eastern time, ten minutes before the scheduled landing, Readdy got word that communications with the shuttle, which had been lost, had not been re-established; O'Keefe noticed that Readdy's face went blank. At 9:10 Readdy opened a book to check a time sequence. He said, "We should have heard the sonic booms by now. There's something really wrong." By 9:29 O'Keefe had activated the full-blown contingency plan. When word got to the White House, the executive staff ducked quickly into defensive positions: President Bush would grieve alongside the families and say the right things about carrying on, but rather than involving himself by appointing an independent presidential commission, as Ronald Reagan had in response to the *Challenger* accident, he would keep his distance by expressing faith in NASA's ability to find the cause. In other words, this baby was going to be dropped squarely onto O'Keefe's lap. The White House approved Gehman's appointment to lead what would essentially be NASA's investigation—but O'Keefe could expect little further communication. There was a chance that the President would not even want to receive the final report directly but would ask that it be deposited more discreetly in the White House in-box. He had problems bigger than space on his mind.

Nonetheless, that morning in his car Gehman realized that even with a lukewarm White House endorsement, the position that NASA was offering, if handled correctly, would allow for a significant inquiry into the accident. Gregory made it clear that Gehman would have the full support of NASA's engineers and technical resources in unraveling the physical mysteries of the accident—what actually had happened to the *Columbia* out there in its sheath of fire at 200,000 feet. Moreover, Gehman was confident that if the investigation had to go further, into *why* this accident had occurred, he had the experience necessary to sort through the human complexities of NASA and emerge with useful answers that might result in reform. This may have been over-confident of him, and to some extent utopian, but it was not entirely blind: he had been through big investigations before, most recently two years earlier, just after leaving the Navy, when he and a retired Army general named William Crouch had led an inquiry into the loss of seventeen sailors aboard the USS *Cole*, the destroyer that was attacked and nearly sunk by suicide terrorists in Yemen in October of 2000. Their report found fundamental errors in the functioning of the military command structure, and issued recommendations (largely classified) that are in effect today. The success of the *Cole* investigation was one of the arguments that Gregory used on him now. Gehman did not disagree, but he wanted to be very clear. He said, "I know you've got a piece of paper in front of you. Does it say that I'm not an aviator?"

Gregory said, "We don't need an aviator here. We need an investigator."

And so, driving down the highway to Norfolk, Gehman accepted the job. When he got home, he told his wife that he was a federal employee again and that there wouldn't be much sailing in the spring. That afternoon and evening, as the faxes and phone calls came in, he began to exercise control of the process, if only in his own mind, concluding that the board's charter as originally written by NASA would have to be strengthened and expanded, and that its name should immediately be changed from the absurd International Space Station and Space Shuttle Mishap Interagency Investigations Board (the ISSSSMIIB) to the more workable *Columbia* Accident Investigation Board, or CAIB, which could be pronounced in one syllable, as *Cabe*.

NASA initially did not resist any of his suggestions. Gregory advised Gehman to head to Barksdale Air Force Base, in Shreveport, Louisiana, where the wreckage was being collected. As Gehman began to explore airline connections, word came that a NASA executive jet, a Gulfstream, would be dispatched to carry him, along with several other board members, directly to Barksdale. The jet arrived in Norfolk on Sunday afternoon, the day after the accident. One of the members already aboard was Steven Wallace, the head of accident investigations for the FAA. Wallace is a second-generation pilot, an athletic, tightly wound man with wide experience in government and a skeptical view of the powerful. He later told me that when Gehman got on the airplane, he was dressed in a business suit, and that, having introduced himself, he explained that they might run into the press, and if they did, he would handle things. This raised some questions about Gehman's motivations (and indeed Gehman turned out to enjoy the limelight), but as Wallace soon discovered, grandstanding was not what Gehman was about. As the Gulfstream proceeded toward Louisiana, Gehman rolled up his sleeves and, sitting at the table in the back of the airplane, began to ask for the thoughts and perspectives of the board members there—not about what might have happened to the *Columbia* but about how best to find out. It was the start of what would become an intense seven-month relationship. It was obvious that Gehman was truly listening to the ideas, and that he was capable of integrating them quickly and productively into his own thoughts. By the end of the flight even Wallace was growing impressed.

But Gehman was in some ways also naive, formed as he had been by investigative experience within the military, in which much of the work proceeds behind closed doors, and conflict of interest is not a big concern. The *Columbia* investigation, he discovered, was going to be a very different thing. Attacks against the CAIB began on the second day, and by midweek, as the board moved from Shreveport to Houston to set up shop, they showed no signs of easing. Congress in particular was thundering that Gehman was a captive investigator, that his report would be a whitewash, and that the White House should replace the CAIB with a *Challenger*-style presidential commission. This came as a surprise to Gehman, who had assumed that he could just go about his business but who now realized that he would have to accommodate these concerns if the final report was to have any credibility at all. Later he said to me, "I didn't go in thinking about it, but as I began to hear the *independence* thing—'You can't have a panel appointed by NASA investigating itself!'—I realized I'd better deal with Congress." He did this at first mainly by listening on the phone. "They told me what I had to do to build my credibility. I didn't invent it—they *told* me. They also said, 'We hate NASA. We don't trust them. Their culture is no good. And their cost accounting is no good.' And I said, 'Okay.'"

More than that, Gehman came to realize that it was the elected representatives in Congress—and neither O'Keefe nor NASA—who constituted the CAIB's real constituency, and that their concerns were legitimate. As a result of this, along with a growing understanding of the depth and complexity of the work at hand, he forced through a series of changes, establishing a congressional-liaison office, gaining an independent budget (ultimately of about $20 million), wresting the report from O'Keefe's control, rewriting the stated mission to include the finding of "root causes and circumstances," and hiring an additional five board members, all civilians of unimpeachable reputation: the retired Electric Boat boss Roger Tetrault, the former astronaut Sally Ride, the Nobel-laureate physicist Douglas Osheroff, the aerodynamicist and former Air Force Secretary Sheila Widnall, and the historian and space-policy expert John Logsdon. Afterward, the loudest criticism faded away. Still, Gehman's political judgment was not perfect. He allowed the new civilian members to be brought on through the NASA payroll (at prorated annual salaries of $134,000)—a strange lapse under the circumstances, and one that led to superficial accusations that the CAIB remained captive. *The Orlando Sentinel* ran a story about the lack of public access to the CAIB's interviews under the ambiguous headline "BOARD PAID TO ENSURE SECRECY." The idea evoked laughter among some of the investigators, who knew the inquiry's direction. But unnecessary damage was done.

Equally unnecessary was Gehman's habit of referring to O'Keefe as "Sean," a clubbish mannerism that led people to conclude, erroneously, that the two men were friends. In fact their relationship was strained, if polite. Gehman told me that he had never asked for the full story behind his selection on the morning of the accident—maybe because it would have been impossible to know the unvarnished truth. Certainly, though, O'Keefe had had little opportunity to contemplate his choice. By quick view Gehman was a steady hand and a good establishment man who could lend the gravitas of his four stars to this occasion; he was also, of course, one of the men behind the *Cole* investigation. O'Keefe later told me that he had read the *Cole* report during his stint as a professor, but that he remembered it best as the subject of a case study presented by one of his academic colleagues as an example of a narrowly focused investigation that, correctly, had not widened beyond its original mandate. This was true, but a poor predictor of Gehman as a man. His *Cole* investigation had not widened (for instance, into assigning individual blame) for the simple reason that other investigations, by the Navy and the FBI, were already covering that ground. Instead, Gehman and Crouch had gone deep, and relentlessly so. The result was a document that bluntly questioned current American dogma, identified arrogance in the command structure, and critiqued U.S. military assumptions about the terrorist threat. The tone was frank. For example, while expressing understanding of the diplomatic utility of labeling terrorists as "criminals," the report warned against buying into that language, or into the parallel idea that these terrorists were "cowards." When, later, I expressed my surprise at his freedom of expression, Gehman did not deny that people have recently been decried as traitors for less. But freedom of expression was clearly his habit: he spoke to me just as openly about the failures of his cherished Navy, of Congress, and increasingly of NASA.

When I mentioned this character trait to one of the new board members, Sheila Widnall, she laughed and said she'd seen it before inside the Pentagon, and that people just didn't understand the highest level of the U.S. military. These officers are indeed the establishment, she said, but they are so convinced of the greatness of the American construct that they will willingly tear at its components in the belief that its failures can be squarely addressed. Almost all of the current generation of senior leaders have also been through the soul-searching that followed the defeat in Vietnam.

O'Keefe had his own understanding of the establishment, and it was probably sophisticated, but he clearly did not anticipate Gehman's rebellion. By the end of the second week, as Gehman established an independent relationship with Congress and began to break through the boundaries initially drawn by NASA, it became clear that O'Keefe was losing control. He maintained a brave front of wanting a thorough inquiry, but it was said that privately he was angry. The tensions came to the surface toward the end of February, at about the same time that Gehman insisted, over O'Keefe's resistance, that the full report ultimately be made available to the public. The CAIB was expanding to a staff of about 120 people, many of them professional accident investigators and technical experts who could support the core board members. They were working seven days a week out of temporary office space in the sprawling wasteland of South Houston, just off the property of the Johnson Space Center. One morning several of the board members came in to see Gehman, and warned him that the CAIB was headed for a "shipwreck."

Gehman knew what they meant. In the days following the accident O'Keefe had established an internal Mishap Investigation Team, whose job was to work closely with the CAIB, essentially as staff, and whose members—bizarrely—included some of the decision-makers most closely involved with the *Columbia*'s final flight. The team was led by Linda Ham, a razor-sharp manager in the shuttle program, whose actions during the flight would eventually be singled out as an egregious example of NASA's failings. Gehman did not know that yet, but it dawned on him that Ham was in a position to filter the inbound NASA reports, and he remembered a recent three-hour briefing that she had run with an iron hand, allowing little room for spontaneous exploration. He realized that she and the others would have to leave the CAIB, and he wrote a careful letter to O'Keefe in Washington, requesting their immediate removal. It is a measure of the insularity at the Johnson Space Center that NASA did not gracefully acquiesce. Ham and another manager, Ralph Roe, in particular reacted badly. In Gehman's office, alternately in anger and tears, they refused to leave, accusing Gehman of impugning their integrity and asking him how they were supposed to explain their dismissal to others. Gehman suggested to them what Congress had insisted to him—that people simply cannot investigate themselves. Civics 101. Once stated, it seems like an obvious principle.

O'Keefe had a master's degree in public administration, but he disagreed. It was odd. He had not been with the agency long enough to be infected by its insularity, and as he later promised Congress, he was willing—no, eager—to identify and punish any of his NASA subordinates who could be held responsible for the accident. Nonetheless, he decided to defy Gehman, and he announced that his people would remain in place. It was an ill-considered move. Gehman simply went public with his letter, posting it on the CAIB Web site. Gehman understood that O'Keefe felt betrayed—"stabbed in the back" was the word going around—but NASA had left him no choice. O'Keefe surrendered. Ham and the others were reassigned, and the Mishap Investigation Team was disbanded, replaced by NASA staffers who had not been involved in the *Columbia*'s flight and would be more likely to cooperate with the CAIB's investigators. The board was never able to overcome completely the whiff of collusion that had accompanied its birth, but Gehman had won a significant fight, even if it meant that he and "Sean" would not be friends.

. . . .

The space shuttle is the most audacious flying machine ever built, an engineering fantasy made real. Before each flight it stands vertically on the launch pad at the Kennedy Space Center, as the core component of a rocket assembly 184 feet tall. The shuttle itself, which is also known as the orbiter, is a winged vehicle roughly the size of a DC-9, with three main rocket engines in the tail, a large unpressurized cargo bay in the midsection, and a cramped two-level crew compartment in the nose. It is attached to a huge external tank containing liquid fuel for the three main engines. That tank in turn is attached to two solid-fuel rockets, known as boosters, which flank the assembly and bear its full weight on the launch pad. Just before the launch, the weight is about 4.5 million pounds, 90 percent of which is fuel. It is a dramatic time, ripe with anticipation; the shuttle vents vapors like a breathing thing; the ground crews pull away until finally no one is left; the air seems unusually quiet.

Typically there are seven astronauts aboard. Four of them sit in the cockpit, and three on the lower level, in the living quarters known as the mid-deck. Because of the shuttle's vertical position, their seats are effectively rotated backward 90 degrees, so they are sitting on their backs, feeling their own weight in a way that tends to emphasize gravity's pull. At the front of the cockpit, positioned closer to the instrument panel than is necessary for the typical astronaut's six-foot frame, the commander and the pilot can look straight ahead into space. They are highly trained. They know exactly what they are getting into. Sometimes they have waited years for this moment to arrive.

The launch window may be just a few minutes wide. It is ruled by orbital mechanics, and defined by the track and position of the destination—usually now the unfinished International Space Station. Six seconds before liftoff the three main engines are ignited and throttled up to 100 percent power, producing more than a million pounds of thrust. The shuttle responds with what is known as "the twang," swaying several feet in the direction of the external tank and then swaying back. This is felt in the cockpit. The noise inside is not very loud. If the computers show that the main engines are operating correctly, the solid rocket boosters ignite. The boosters are ferocious devices—the same sort of monsters that upon failure blew the *Challenger* apart. Each of them produces three million pounds of thrust. Once ignited, they cannot be shut off or throttled back. The shuttle lifts off. It accelerates fast enough to clear the launch tower doing about 100 mph, though it is so large that seen from the outside, it appears to be climbing slowly.

The flying is done entirely by autopilot unless something goes wrong. Within seconds the assembly rotates and aims on course, tilting slightly off the vertical and rolling so that the orbiter is inverted beneath the external tank. Although the vibrations are heavy enough to blur the instruments, the acceleration amounts to only about 2.5 Gs—a mild sensation of heaviness pressing the astronauts back into their seats. After about forty seconds the shuttle accelerates through Mach 1, 760 mph, at about 17,000 feet, climbing nearly straight up. Eighty seconds later, with the shuttle doing about 3,400 mph and approaching 150,000 feet, the crew can feel the thrust from the solid rocket boosters begin to tail off. Just afterward, with a bright flash and a loud explosion heard inside the orbiter, the rocket boosters separate from the main tank; they continue to travel upward on a ballistic path to 220,000 feet before falling back and parachuting into the sea. Now powered by the main engines alone, the ride turns smooth, and the forces settle down to about 1 G.

One pilot described the sensations to me on the simplest level. He said, "First it's like, 'Hey, this is a rough ride!' and then, 'Hey, I'm on an electric train!' and then, 'Hey, this train's starting to go pretty darned fast!'" Speed is the ultimate goal of the launch sequence. Having climbed steeply into ultra-thin air, the shuttle gently pitches over until it is flying nearly parallel to Earth, inverted under the external tank, and thrusting at full power. Six minutes after launch, at about 356,000 feet, the shuttle is doing around 9,200 mph, which is fast, but only about half the speed required to sustain an orbit. It therefore begins a shallow dive, during which it gains speed at the rate of 1,000 mph every twenty seconds—an acceleration so fast that it presses the shuttle against its 3 G limit, and the engines have to be briefly throttled back. At 10,300 mph the shuttle rolls to a head-up position. Passing through 15,000 mph, it begins to climb again, still accelerating at 3 Gs, until, seconds later, in the near vacuum of space, it achieves orbital velocity, or 17,500 mph. The plumes from the main engines wrap forward and dance across the cockpit windows, making light at night like that of Saint Elmo's fire. Only eight and a half minutes have passed since the launch. The main engines are extinguished, and the external tank is jettisoned. The shuttle is in orbit. After further maneuvering it assumes its standard attitude, flying inverted in relation to Earth and tail first as it proceeds around the globe.

For the astronauts aboard, the uphill flight would amount to little more than an interesting ride were it not for the possibility of failures. That possibility, however, is very real, and as a result the launch is a critical and complicated operation, demanding close teamwork, tight coordination with Mission Control, and above all extreme concentration—a quality often confused with coolness under fire. I was given a taste of this by an active shuttle commander named Michael Bloomfield, who had me strap in beside him in NASA's full-motion simulator in Houston, and take a realistic run from the launch pad into space. Bloomfield is a former Air Force test pilot who has flown three shuttle missions. He had been assigned to assist the CAIB, and had been watching the investigation with mixed emotions—hopeful that some effects might be positive, but concerned as well that the inquiry might veer into formalism without sufficiently taking into account the radical nature of space flight, or the basic truth that every layer of procedure and equipment comes at a cost, often unpredictable. Bloomfield called this the "risk versus risk" tradeoff, and made it real not by defending NASA against specific criticisms but by immersing me, a pilot myself, in the challenges of normal operations.

Much of what he showed me was of the what-if variety, the essence not only of simulator work but also of the crew's real-world thinking. For instance, during the launch, as the shuttle rockets upward on autopilot, the pilots and flight controllers pass through a succession of mental gates, related to various combinations of main-engine failures, at various altitudes and speeds. The options and resulting maneuvers are complicated, ranging from a quick return to the launch site, to a series of tight arrivals at select runways up the eastern seaboard, to transatlantic glides, and finally even an "abort into orbit"—an escape route used by a *Challenger* crew in 1985 after a single main-engine failure. Such failures allow little time to make the right decision. As Bloomfield and I climbed away from Earth, tilted onto our backs, he occasionally asked the operators to freeze the simulation so that he could unfold his thoughts to me. Though the choices were clear, the relative risks were rarely so obvious. It was a deep view into the most intense sort of flying.

After we arrived in space, we continued to talk. One of the gates for engine failure during the climb to the Space Station stands at Mach 21.8 (14,900 mph), the last point allowed for a "high energy" arrival into Gander, Newfoundland, and the start of the emergency transatlantic track for Shannon, Ireland. An abort at that point provides no easy solution. The problem with Gander is how to bleed off excess energy before the landing (Bloomfield called this "a take-all-your-brain-cells type of flying"), whereas the problem with Shannon is just the opposite—how to stretch the glide. Bloomfield told me that immediately before his last space flight, in the spring of 2002, his crew and a Mission Control team had gone through a full-dress simulation during which the orbiter had lost all three engines by Mach 21.7 (less than 100 mph from the decision speed). Confident in his ability to fly the more difficult Canadian arrival, Bloomfield, from the cockpit of the simulator, radioed, "We're going high-energy into Gander."

Mission Control answered, "Negative," and called for Shannon instead.

Bloomfield looked over at his right-seat pilot and said, "I think we oughta go to Gander. What do you think?"

"Yeah."

Bloomfield radioed back: "No, we think we oughta go to Gander."

Mission Control was emphatic. "Negative. We see you having enough energy to make Shannon."

As commander, Bloomfield had formal authority for the decision, but Mission Control, with its expert teams and wealth of data, was expressing a strong opinion, so he acquiesced. Acquiescence is standard in such cases, and usually it works out for the best. Bloomfield had enormous respect for the expertise and competence of Mission Control. He was also well aware of errors he had made in the past, despite superior advice or instructions from the flight controllers. This time, however, it turned out that two of the flight controllers had not communicated correctly with each other, and that the judgment of Mission Control therefore was wrong. Lacking the energy to reach Shannon, the simulator went into the ocean well short of the airport. The incident caused a disturbance inside the Johnson Space Center, particularly because of the long-standing struggle for the possession of data (and ultimately control) between the pilots in flight and the engineers at their consoles. Nevertheless, the two groups worked together, hammered out the problems, and the next day flew the same simulator profile successfully. But that was not the point of Bloomfield's story. Rather, it was that these calls are hard to make, and that mistakes—whether his or the controllers'—may become obvious only after it is too late.

For all its realism, the simulator cannot duplicate the gravity load of the climb, or the lack of it at the top. The transition to weightlessness is abrupt, and all the more dramatic because it occurs at the end of the 3 G acceleration: when the main engines cut off, the crew gets the impression of going over an edge and suddenly dropping into a free fall. That impression is completely accurate. In fact the term zero gravity (0 G), which is loosely used to describe the orbital environment, refers to physical acceleration, and does not mean that Earth's gravitational pull has somehow gone away. Far from it: the diminution of gravitational pull that comes with distance is small at these low-orbit altitudes (perhaps 200 miles above the surface), and the shuttle is indeed now falling—about like a stone dropped off a cliff. The fall does not, of course, diminish the shuttle's mass (if it bumps the Space Station, it does so with tremendous force), but it does make the vehicle and everything inside it very nearly weightless. The orbital part of the trick is that though the shuttle is dropping like a stone, it is also progressing across Earth's surface so fast (17,500 mph) that its path matches (roughly) the curvature of the globe. In other words, as it plummets toward the ground, the ground keeps getting out of its way. Like the orbits of all other satellites, and of the

Space Station, and of the Moon as well, its flight is nothing but an unrestricted free fall around and around the world.

To help the astronauts adapt to weightlessness, the quarters are designed with a conventional floor-down orientation. This isn't quite so obvious as it might seem, since the shuttle flies inverted in orbit. "Down" therefore is toward outer space—and the view from the cockpit windows just happens to be of Earth sliding by from behind and overhead. The crews are encouraged to live and work with their heads "up" nonetheless. It is even recommended that they use the ladder while passing through the hatch between the two levels, and that they "descend" from the cockpit to the mid-deck feet first. Those sorts of cautions rarely prevail against the temptations of weightlessness. After Bloomfield's last flight one of his crew commented that they had all been swimming around "like eels in a can." Or like superhumans, as the case may be. It's true that there are frustrations: if you try to throw a switch without first anchoring your body, the switch will throw you. On the other hand, once you are anchored, you can shift multi-ton masses with your fingertips. You can also fly without wings, perform unlimited flips, or simply float for a while, resting in midair. Weightlessness is bad for the bones, but good for the soul. I asked Bloomfield how it had felt to experience gravity again. He said he remembered the first time, after coming to a stop on the runway in Florida, when he picked up a small plastic checklist in the cockpit and thought, "Man, this is so *heavy*!" He looked at me and said, "Gravity sucks."

And orbital flight clearly does not. The ride is smooth. When the cabin ventilation is turned off, as it must be once a day to exchange the carbon dioxide scrubbers, the silence is absolute. The smell inside the shuttle is distinctly metallic, unless someone has just come in from a spacewalk, after which the quarters are permeated for a while with "the smell of space," a pungent burned odor that some compare to that of seared meat, and that Bloomfield describes as closer to the smell of a torch on steel.

The dominant sensation, other than weightlessness, is of the speed across the ground. Bloomfield said, "From California to New York in ten minutes, around the world once in ninety minutes—I mean, we're *moving*." He told me that he took to loitering in the cockpit at the end of the workdays, just for the view. By floating forward above the instrument panel and wrapping his legs around one of the pilot seats, he could position his face so close to the front windshield that the structure of the shuttle would seem to disappear.

The view from there was etched into his memory as a continuous loop. In brief, he said: It's night and you're coming up on California, with that clearly defined coastline, and you can see all the lights all the way from Tijuana to San Francisco, and then it's behind you, and you spot Las Vegas and its neon-lit Strip, which you barely have time to identify before you move across the Rockies, with their helter-skelter of towns, and then across the Plains, with its monotony of look-alike wheels and spokes of light, until you come to Chicago and its lakefront, from which point you can see past Detroit and Cleveland all the way to New York. These are big cities, you think. And because you grew up on a farm in Michigan, played football there in high school, and still know it like a home, you pick out Ann Arbor and Flint, and the place where I-75 joins U.S. Highway 23, and you get down to within a couple of miles of your house before zip, you're gone. Zip goes Cleveland, and zip New York, and then you're out over the Atlantic beyond Maine, looking back down the eastern seaboard all the way past Washington, D.C. Ten minutes later you come up on Europe, and you hardly have time to think that London is a sprawl, France is an orderly display, the Alps are the Rockies again, and Italy is indeed a boot. Over Sicily you peer down into Etna's crater, into the glow of molten rock on Earth's inside, and then you are crossing Africa, where the few lights you see are not yellow but orange, like open flames. Past the Equator and beyond Madagascar you come to a zone of gray between the blackness of the night and the bright blue of the day. At the center of that zone is a narrow pink slice, which is the atmospheric dawn as seen from above. Daylight is for the oceans—first the Indian and then the Pacific, which is very, very large. Atolls appear with coral reefs and turquoise lagoons, but mostly what you see is cloud and open water. Then the pink slice of sunset passes below, and the night, and soon afterward you come again to California, though at another point on the coast, because ninety minutes have passed since you were last here, and during that time the world has revolved beneath you.

Ultimately the shuttle must return to Earth and land. The problem then is what to do with the vast amount of physical energy that has been invested in it—almost all the calories once contained in the nearly four million pounds of rocket fuel that was used to shove the shuttle into orbit. Some of that energy now resides in the vehicle's altitude, but most resides in its speed. The re-entry is a descent to a landing, yes, but primarily it is a giant deceleration, during which atmospheric resistance is used to convert velocity into heat, and to slow the shuttle by roughly 17,000 mph, so that it finally passes overhead the runway in Florida at airline speeds, and circles down to touch the ground at a well tamed 224 mph or less. Once the shuttle is on the runway, the drag chute and brakes take care of the rest.

The re-entry is a one-way ride that cannot be stopped once it has begun. The opening move occurs while the shuttle is still proceeding tail first and inverted, halfway around the world from the runway, high above the Indian Ocean. It is a simple thing, a brief burn by the twin orbital maneuvering rockets against the direction of flight, which slows the shuttle by perhaps 200 mph. That reduction is enough. The shuttle continues to free-fall as it has in orbit, but it now lacks the speed to match the curvature of Earth, so the ground no longer gets out of its way. By the time it reaches the start of the atmosphere, the "entry interface" at 400,000 feet, it has gently flipped itself around so that it is right-side up and pointed for Florida, but with its nose held 40 degrees higher than the angle of the descent path. The effect of this so-called angle of attack (which technically refers to the wings, not the nose) is to create drag, and to shield the shuttle's internal structures from the intense re-entry heat by cocking the vehicle up to greet the atmosphere with leading edges made of heat-resistant carbon-composite panels, and with 24,305 insulating surface tiles, each one unique, which are glued primarily to the vehicle's underside. To regulate the sink and drag (and to control the heating), the shuttle goes through a program of sweeping S-turns, banking as steeply as 80 degrees to one side and then the other, tilting its lift vector and digging into the atmosphere. The thinking is done by redundant computers, which use onboard inertial sensing systems to gauge the shuttle's position, altitude, descent rate, and speed. The flying is done by autopilot. The cockpit crews and mission controllers play the role of observers, albeit extremely interested ones who are ready to intervene should something go wrong. In a basic sense, therefore, the re-entry is a mirror image of the launch and climb, decompressed to forty-five minutes instead of eight, but with the added complication that it will finish with the need for a landing.

Bloomfield took me through it in simulation, the two of us sitting in the cockpit to watch while an experienced flight crew and full Mission Control team brought the shuttle in from the de-orbit burn to the touchdown, dealing with a complexity of cascading system failures. Of course, in reality the automation usually performs faultlessly, and the shuttle proceeds to Florida right on track, and down the center of the desired descent profile. Bloomfield expressed surprise at how well the magic had worked on his own flights. Because he had launched on high-inclination orbits to the Russian station Mir and the International Space Station, he had not flown a *Columbia*-style re-entry over the United States, but had descended across Central America instead. He said, "You look down over Central America, and you're so low that you can see the forests! You think, 'There's no *way* we're going to make it to Florida!' Then you cross the west coast of Florida, and you look inside, and you're still doing Mach 5, and you think, 'There's no way we're going to slow in time!'" But you do. Mach 5 is 3,500 mph. At that point the shuttle is at 117,000 feet, about 140 miles out. At Mach 2.5, or 1,650 mph, it is at 81,000 feet, about sixty miles out. At that point the crew activates the head-up displays, which project see-through flight guidance into the field of vision through the windshield. When the shuttle slows below the speed of sound, it shudders as the shock waves shift. By tradition if not necessity, the commander then takes over from the autopilot, and flies the rest of the arrival manually, using the control stick.

Bloomfield invited me to fly some simulated arrivals myself, and prompted me while I staggered around for a few landings—overhead the Kennedy Space Center at 30,000 feet with the runway and the coastal estuaries in sight below, banking left into a tight, plunging energy-management turn, rolling out onto final approach at 11,000 feet, following an extraordinarily steep, 18-degree glide slope at 345 mph, speed brakes on, pitching up through a "pre-flare" at 2,000 feet to flatten the descent, landing gear out at 300 feet, touching down on the main wheels with some skips and bumps, then drag chute out, nose gear gently down, and brakes on. My efforts were crude, and greatly assisted by Bloomfield, but they gave me an impression of the shuttle as a solid, beautifully balanced flying machine that in thick air, at the end, is responsive and not difficult to handle—if everything goes just right. Bloomfield agreed. Moreover, years have passed in which everything did go just right—leaving the pilots to work on the finesse of their touchdowns, whether they were two knots fast, or 100 feet long. Bloomfield said, "When you come back and you land, the engineers will pull out their charts and they'll say things like 'The boundary layer tripped on the left wing before the right one. Did you feel anything?' And the answer is always

'Well . . . no. It was an incredibly smooth ride all the way down.'"
But then, on the morning of February 1, something went really
wrong—something too radical for simulation, that offered the
pilots no chance to fly—and the *Columbia* lay scattered for 300
miles across the ground.

.   .   .

The foam did it. That much was suspected from the start, and
all the evidence converged on it as the CAIB's investigation proceeded through the months that followed. The foam was dense
and dry; it was the brownish-orange coating applied to the outside of the shuttle's large external tank to insulate the extreme
cold of the rocket fuels inside from the warmth and moisture of
the air. Eighty-two seconds after liftoff, as the *Columbia* was
accelerating through 1,500 mph, a piece of that foam—about
nineteen inches long by eleven inches wide, weighing about 1.7
pounds—broke off from the external tank and collided with the
left wing at about 545 mph. Cameras near the launch site
recorded the event—though the images when viewed the following day provided insufficient detail to know the exact impact
point, or the consequences. The CAIB's investigation ultimately
found that a gaping hole about ten inches across had been
punched into the wing's leading edge, and that sixteen days later
the hole allowed the hot gases of the re-entry to penetrate the
wing and consume it from the inside. Through enormous effort
this would be discovered and verified beyond doubt. It was
important nonetheless to explore the alternatives. In an effort
closely supervised by the CAIB, groups of NASA engineers created
several thousand flow charts, one for each scenario that could
conceivably have led to the re-entry breakup. The thinking was
rigorous. For a scenario to be "closed," meaning set aside,
absolute proof had to be found (usually physical or mathemati-
cal) that this particular explanation did not apply: there was no

cockpit fire, no flight-control malfunction, no act of terrorism or sabotage that had taken the shuttle down. Unexpected vulnerabilities were found during this process, and even after the investigation was formally concluded, in late August, more than a hundred scenarios remained technically open, because they could not positively be closed. For lack of evidence to the contrary, for instance, neither bird strikes nor micrometeorite impacts could be completely ruled out.

But for all their willingness to explore less likely alternatives, many of NASA's managers remained stubbornly closed-minded on the subject of foam. From the earliest telemetric data it was known that intense heat inside the left wing had destroyed the *Columbia*, and that such heat could have gotten there only through a hole. The connection between the hole and the foam strike was loosely circumstantial at first, but it required serious consideration nonetheless. NASA balked at going down that road. Its reasons were not rational and scientific but, rather, complex and cultural, and they turned out to be closely related to the errors that had led to the accident in the first place: simply put, it had become a matter of faith within NASA that foam strikes—which were a known problem—could not cause mortal damage to the shuttle. Sean O'Keefe, who was badly advised by his NASA lieutenants, made unwise public statements deriding the "foamologists"; and even Ron Dittemore, NASA's technically expert shuttle program manager, joined in with categorical denials.

At the CAIB, Gehman, who was not unsympathetic to NASA, watched these reactions with growing skepticism and a sense of déjà vu. Over his years in the Navy, and as a result of the *Cole* inquiry, he had become something of a student of large organizations under stress. To me he said, "It has been scorched into my mind that bureaucracies will do anything to defend themselves. It's not evil—it's just a natural reaction of bureaucracies, and since NASA is a bureaucracy, I expect the same out of them. As we go through the investigation, I've been looking for signs where the system is trying to defend itself." Of those signs the most obvious was this display of blind faith by an organization dependent on its engineering cool; NASA, in its absolute certainty, was unintentionally signaling the very problem that it had. Gehman had seen such certainty proved wrong too many times, and he told me that he was not about to get "rolled by the system," as he had been rolled before. He said, "Now when I hear NASA telling me things like '*Gotta* be true!' or 'We *know* this to be true!' all my alarm bells go off . . . Without hurting anybody's feelings, or squashing people's egos, we're having to say, 'We're sorry, but we're not accepting that answer.'"

That was the form that the physical investigation took on, with hundreds of NASA engineers and technicians doing most of the detailed work, and the CAIB watching closely and increasingly stepping in. Despite what Gehman said, it was inevitable that feelings got hurt and egos squashed—and indeed that serious damage to people's lives and careers was inflicted. At the NASA facilities dedicated to shuttle operations (Alabama for rockets, Florida for launch and landing, Texas for management and mission control) the CAIB investigators were seen as invaders of sorts, unwelcome strangers arriving to pass judgment on people's good-faith efforts. On the ground level, where the detailed analysis was being done, there was active resistance at first, with some NASA engineers openly refusing to cooperate, or to allow access to records and technical documents that had not been pre-approved for release. Gehman had to intervene. One of the toughest and most experienced of the CAIB investigators later told me he had a gut sense that NASA continued to hide relevant information, and that it does so to this day. But cooperation between the two groups gradually improved as friendships were made, and the intellectual challenges posed by the inquiry began to predominate over fears about what had happened or what might follow. As so often occurs, it was on an informal basis that information flowed best, and that much of the truth was discovered.

Board member Steven Wallace described the investigation not as a linear path but as a picture that gradually filled in. Or as a jigsaw puzzle. The search for debris began the first day, and soon swelled to include more than 25,000 people, at a cost of well over $300 million. NASA received 1,459 debris reports, including some from nearly every state in the union, and also from Canada, Jamaica, and the Bahamas. Discounting the geographic extremes, there was still a lot to follow up on. Though the amateur videos showed pieces separating from the shuttle along the entire path over the United States, and though search parties backtracked all the way to the Pacific coast in the hope of finding evidence of the breakup's triggering mechanism, the westernmost piece found on the ground was a left-wing tile that landed near a town called Littlefield, in the Texas Panhandle. Not surprisingly, the bulk of the wreckage lay under the main breakup, from south of Dallas eastward across the rugged, snake-infested brushland of East Texas and into Louisiana; and that is where most of the search took place. The best work was done on foot, by tough and dedicated crews who walked in tight lines across several thousand square miles. Their effort became something of a close sampling of the American landscape, turning up all sorts of odds and ends, including a few apparent murder victims, plenty of junked cars, and the occasional clandestine meth lab. More to the point, it also turned up crew remains and more than 84,000 pieces of the *Columbia*, which, at 84,900 pounds, accounted for 38 percent of the vehicle's dry weight. Certain pieces that had splashed into the murky waters of lakes and reservoirs were never found. It was presumed that most if not all the remaining pieces had been vaporized by the heat of re-entry, either before or after the breakup.

Some of the shuttle's contents survived intact. For instance, a vacuum cleaner still worked, as did some computers and printers and a Medtronic Tono-Pen, used to measure ocular pressure. A group of worms from one of the science experiments not only survived but continued to multiply. Most of the debris, however, was a twisted mess. The recovered pieces were meticulously plotted and tagged, and transported to a hangar at the Kennedy Space Center, where the wing remnants were laid out in correct position on the floor, and what had been found of the left wing's reinforced carbon-carbon (RCC) leading edge was reconstructed in a transparent Plexiglas mold—though with large gaps where pieces were missing. The hangar was a quiet, poignant, intensely focused place, with many of the same NASA technicians who had prepared the *Columbia* for flight now involved in the sad task of handling its ruins. The assembly and analysis went on through the spring. One of the principal CAIB agents there was an affable Air Force pilot named Patrick Goodman, an experienced accident investigator who had made both friends and enemies at NASA for the directness of his approach. When I first met him, outside the hangar on a typically warm and sunny Florida day, he explained some of the details that I had just seen on the inside—heat-eroded tiles, burned skin and structure, and aluminum slag that had emerged in molten form from inside the left wing, and had been deposited onto the aft rocket pods. The evidence was complicated because it resulted from combinations of heat, physical forces, and wildly varying airflows that had occurred before, during, and after the main-body breakup, but for Goodman it was beginning to read like a map. He had faith. He said, "We know what we have on the ground. It's the truth. The debris is the truth, if we can only figure out what it's saying. It's not a theoretical model. It exists." Equally important was the debris that did not exist, most significantly large parts of the left wing, including the lower part of a section of the RCC leading edge, a point known as Panel Eight, which was approximately where the launch cameras showed that the foam had hit. Goodman said, "We look at what we don't have. What we do have. What's *on* what we have. We start from there, and try to work backwards up the timeline, always trying to see the previous significant event." He called this "looking uphill." It was like a movie run in reverse, with the found pieces springing off the ground and flying upward to a point of reassembly above Dallas, and then the *Columbia*, looking nearly whole, flying tail-first toward California, picking up the Littlefield tile as it goes, and then higher again, through entry interface over the Pacific, through orbits flown in reverse, inverted but nose first, and then back down toward Earth, picking up the external tank and the solid rocket boosters during the descent, and settling tail-first with rockets roaring, until just before a vertical touchdown a spray of pulverized foam appears below, pulls together at the left-wing leading edge, and rises to lodge itself firmly on the side of the external tank.

The foam did it.

There was plenty of other evidence, too. After the accident the Air Force dug up routine radar surveillance tapes that upon close inspection showed a small object floating alongside the *Columbia* on the second day of its mission. The object slowly drifted away and disappeared from view. Subsequent testing of radar profiles and ballistic coefficients for a multitude of objects found a match for only one—a fragment of RCC panel of at least 140 square inches. The match never quite passed muster as proof, but investigators presumed that the object was a piece of the leading edge, that it had been shoved into the inside of the wing by the impact of the foam, and that during maneuvering in orbit it had floated free. The picture by now was rapidly filling in.

But the best evidence was numerical. It so happened that because the *Columbia* was the first of the operational shuttles, it was equipped with hundreds of additional engineering sensors that fed into an onboard data-collection device, a box known as a modular auxiliary data system, or MADS recorder, that was normally used for postflight analysis of the vehicle's performance. During the initial debris search this box was not found, but such was its potential importance that after careful calculation of its likely ballistic path, another search was mounted, and on March 19 it was discovered—lying in full view on ground that had been gone over before. The really surprising thing was its condition. Though the recorder was not designed to be crash-proof, and used Mylar tape that was vulnerable to heat, it had survived the breakup and fall completely intact, as had the data that it contained, the most interesting of which pertained to heat rises and sequential sensor failures inside the left wing. When combined with the telemetric data that already existed, and with calculations of the size and location of the sort of hole that might have been punched through the leading edge by the foam, the new data allowed for a good fit with computational models of the theoretical airflow and heat propagation inside the left wing, and it steered the investigation to an inevitable conclusion that the breach must have been in the RCC at Panel Eight.

By early summer the picture was clear. Though strictly speaking the case was circumstantial, the evidence against the foam was so persuasive that there remained no reasonable doubt about the physical cause of the accident. As a result, Gehman gave serious consideration to NASA's request to call off a planned test of the launch incident, during which a piece of foam would be carefully fired at a fully rigged RCC Panel Eight. NASA's argument against the test had some merit: the leading-edge panels (forty-four per shuttle) are custom-made, $700,000 components, each one different from the others, and the testing would require the use of the last spare Panel Eight in the entire fleet. NASA said that it couldn't afford the waste, and Gehman was inclined to agree, precisely because he felt that breaking the panel would prove nothing that hadn't already been amply proved. By a twist of fate it was the sole NASA member of the CAIB, the quiet, cerebral, earnestly scientific Scott Hubbard, who insisted that the test proceed. Hubbard was one of the original seven board members. At the time of the accident he had just become the director of NASA's Ames Research Center, in California. Months later now, in the wake of Gehman's rebellion, and with the CAIB aggressively moving beyond the physical causes and into the organizational ones, he found himself in the tricky position of collaborating with a group that many of his own people at NASA saw as the enemy. Hubbard, however, had an almost childlike belief in doing the right thing, and having been given this unfortunate job, he was determined to see it through correctly. Owing to the closeness of his ties to NASA, he understood an aspect of the situation that others might have overlooked: despite overwhelming evidence to the contrary, many people at NASA continued stubbornly to believe that the foam strike on launch could *not* have caused the *Columbia*'s destruction. Hubbard argued that if NASA was to have any chance of self-reform, these people would have to be confronted with reality, not in abstraction but in the most tangible way possible. Gehman found the argument convincing, and so the foam shot proceeded.

The work was done in San Antonio, using a compressed-nitrogen gun with a thirty-five-foot barrel, normally used to fire dead chickens—real and artificial—against aircraft structures in bird-strike certification tests. NASA approached the test kicking and screaming all the way, insisting, for instance, that the shot be used primarily to validate an earlier debris-strike model (the so-called Crater model of strikes against the underside tiles) that had been used for decision-making during the flight, and was now known to be irrelevant. Indeed, it was because of NASA obstructionism—and specifically the illogical insistence by some of the NASA rocket engineers that the chunk of foam that had hit the wing was significantly smaller (and therefore lighter) than the video and film record showed it to be—that the CAIB and Scott Hubbard finally took direct control of the testing. There was in fact a series of foam shots, increasingly realistic according to the evolving analysis of the actual strike, that raised the stakes from a glancing blow against the underside tiles to steeper-angle hits directly against leading-edge panels.

The second to last shot was a 22-degree hit against the bottom of Panel Six: it produced some cracks and other damage deemed too small to explain the shuttle's loss. Afterward there was some smugness at NASA, and even Sean O'Keefe, who again was badly advised, weighed in on the matter, belittling the damage. But the shot against Panel Six was not yet the real thing. That was saved for the precious Panel Eight, in a test that was painstakingly designed to duplicate (conservatively) the actual impact against the *Columbia*'s left wing, assuming a rotational "clocking angle" 30 degrees off vertical for the piece of foam. Among the engineers who gathered to watch were many of those still living in denial. The gun fired, and the foam hit the panel at a 25-degree relative angle at about 500 mph. Immediately afterward an audible gasp went through the crowd. The foam had knocked a hole in the RCC large enough to allow people to put their heads through. Hubbard told me that some of the NASA people were close to tears. Gehman had stayed away in order to avoid the appearance of gloating. He could not keep the satisfaction out of his voice, however, when later he said to me, "Their whole house of cards came falling down."

· · ·

NASA's house was by then what this investigation was really all about. The CAIB discovered that on the morning of January 17, the day after the launch, the low-level engineers at the Kennedy Space Center whose job was to review the launch videos and film were immediately concerned by the size and speed of the foam that had struck the shuttle. As expected of them, they compiled the imagery and disseminated it by e-mail to various shuttle engineers and managers—most significantly those in charge of the shuttle program at the Johnson Space Center. Realizing that their blurred or otherwise inadequate pictures showed nothing of the damage that might have been inflicted, and anticipating the need for such information by others, the engineers at Kennedy then went outside normal channels and on their own initiative approached the Department of Defense with a request that secret military satellites or ground-based high-resolution cameras be used to photograph the shuttle in orbit. After a delay of several days for the back-channel request to get through, the Air Force proved glad to oblige, and made the first moves to honor the request. Such images would probably have shown a large hole in the left wing—but they were never taken.

When news of the foam strike arrived in Houston, it did not seem to be crucially important. Though foam was not supposed to shed from the external tank, and the shuttle was not designed to withstand its impacts, falling foam had plagued the shuttle from the start, and indeed had caused damage on most missions. The falling foam was usually popcorn sized, too small to cause more than superficial dents in the thermal protection tiles. The CAIB, however, discovered a history of more-serious cases. For example, in 1988 the shuttle *Atlantis* took a heavy hit, seen by the launch cameras eighty-five seconds into the climb, nearly the same point at which the *Columbia* strike occurred. On the second day of the *Atlantis* flight Houston asked the crew to inspect the vehicle's underside with a video camera on a robotic arm (which the *Columbia* did not have). The commander, Robert "Hoot" Gibson, told the CAIB that the belly looked as if it had been blasted with shotgun fire. The *Atlantis* returned safely anyway, but afterward was found to have lost an entire tile, exposing its bare metal belly to the re-entry heat. It was lucky that the damage had happened in a place where a heavy aluminum plate covered the skin, Gibson said, because otherwise the belly might have been burned through.

Nonetheless, over the years foam strikes had come to be seen within NASA as an "in-family" problem, so familiar that even the most serious episodes seemed unthreatening and mundane.

Douglas Osheroff, a normally good-humored Stanford physicist and Nobel laureate who joined the CAIB late, went around for months in a state of incredulity and dismay at what he was learning about NASA's operational logic. He told me that the shuttle managers acted as if they thought the frequency of the foam strikes had somehow reduced the danger that the impacts posed. His point was not that the managers really believed this but that after more than a hundred successful flights they had come blithely to accept the risk. He said, "The excitement that only exists when there is danger was kind of gone—even though the danger was not gone." And frankly, organizational and bureaucratic concerns weighed more heavily on the managers' minds. The most pressing of those concerns were the new performance goals imposed by Sean O'Keefe, and a tight sequence of flights leading up to a drop-dead date of February 19, 2004, for the completion of the International Space Station's "core." O'Keefe had made it clear that meeting this deadline was a test, and that the very future of NASA's human space-flight program was on the line.

From Osheroff's scientific perspective, deadlines based on completion of the International Space Station were inherently absurd. To me he said, "And what would the next goal be after that? Maybe we should bring our pets up there! 'I wonder how a Saint Bernard urinates in zero gravity!' NASA sold the International Space Station to Congress as a great science center—but most scientists just don't agree with that. We're thirty years from being able to go to Mars. Meanwhile, the only reason to have man in space is to study man in space. You can do that stuff—okay—and there are also some biology experiments that are kind of fun. I think we *are* learning things. But I would question any statement that you can come up with better drugs in orbit than you can on the ground, or that sort of thing. The truth is, the International Space Station has become a huge liability for NASA"—expensive to build, expensive to fly, expensive to resupply. "Now members of Congress are talking about letting its orbit decay—just letting it fall into the ocean. And it does turn out that orbital decay is a very good thing, because it means that near space is a self-cleaning place. I mean, garbage does not stay up there forever."

In other words, completion of the Space Station could provide a measure of NASA's performance only in the most immediate and superficial manner, and it was therefore an inherently poor reason for shuttle managers to be ignoring the foam strikes and proceeding at full speed. It was here that you could see the limitations of leadership without vision, and the consequences of putting an executive like O'Keefe in charge of an organization that needed more than mere discipline. This, however, was hardly an argument that the managers could use, or even in private allow themselves to articulate. If the Space Station was unimportant—and perhaps even a mistake—then one had to question the reason for the shuttle's existence in the first place. Like O'Keefe and the astronauts and NASA itself, the managers were trapped by a circular space policy thirty years in the making, and they had no choice but to strive to meet the timelines directly ahead. As a result, after the most recent *Atlantis* launch, in October of 2002, during which a chunk of foam from a particularly troublesome part of the external tank, known as the "bipod ramp," had dented one of the solid rocket boosters, shuttle managers formally decided during the post-flight review not to classify the incident as an "in-flight anomaly." This was the first time that a serious bipod-ramp incident had escaped such a classification. The decision allowed the following two launches to proceed on schedule. The second of those launches was the *Columbia*'s, on January 16.

The videos of the foam strike reached Houston the next day, January 17. They made it clear that again the offending material had come from the area of the bipod ramp, that this time the foam was larger than ever before, that the impact had occurred later in the climb (meaning at higher speed), and that the wing had been hit, though exactly where was not clear. The astronauts were happily in orbit now, and had apparently not felt the impact, or been able to distinguish it from the heavy vibrations of the solid rocket boosters. In other words, they were unaware of any trouble. Responsibility for disposing of the incident lay with engineers on the ground, and specifically with the Mission Management Team, or MMT, whose purpose was to make decisions about the problems and unscripted events that inevitably arose during any flight. The MMT was a high-level group. In the Houston hierarchy it operated above the flight controllers in the Mission Control room, and just below the shuttle program manager, Ron Dittemore. Dittemore was traveling at the time, and has since retired. The MMT meetings were chaired by his protégé, the once rising Linda Ham, who has come to embody NASA's arrogance and insularity in many observers' minds. Ham is the same hard-charging manager who, with a colleague, later had to be forcefully separated from the CAIB's investigation. Within the strangely neutered engineering world of the Johnson Space Center, she was an intimidating figure, a youngish, attractive woman given to wearing revealing clothes, yet also known for a tough and domineering management style. Among the lower ranks she had a reputation for brooking no nonsense and being a little hard to talk to. She was not smooth. She was a woman struggling upward in a man's world. She was said to have a difficult personality.

As the head of the MMT, Ham responded to news of the foam strike as if it were just another item to be efficiently handled and then checked off the list: a water leak in the science lab, a radio communication failure, a foam strike on the left wing, okay, no safety-of-flight issues here—right? What's next? There was a trace of vanity in the way she ran her shows. She seemed to revel in her own briskness, in her knowledge of the shuttle systems, in her use of acronyms and the strange, stilted syntax of aerospace engineers. She was decisive, and very sure of her sense for what was important and what was not. Her style got the best of her on day six of the mission, January 21, when at a recorded MMT meeting she spoke just a few words too many, much to her later regret.

It was at the end of a report given by a mid-ranking engineer named Don McCormack, who summarized the progress of an ad hoc engineering group, called the Debris Assessment Team, that had been formed at a still lower level to analyze the foam strike. The analysis was being done primarily by Boeing engineers, who had dusted off the soon to be notorious Crater model, primarily to predict damage to the underwing tile. McCormack reported that little was yet resolved, that the quality of the Crater as a predictor was being judged against the known damage on earlier flights, and that some work was being done to explore the options should the analysis conclude that the *Columbia* had been badly wounded. After a brief exchange Ham cut him short, saying, "And I'm really . . . I don't think there is much we can do, so it's not really a factor during the flight, since there is not much we can do about it." She was making assumptions, of course, and they were later proved to be completely wrong, but primarily she was just being efficient, and moving the meeting along. After the accident, when the transcript and audiotapes emerged, those words were taken out of context, and used to portray Ham as a villainous and almost inhumanly callous person, which she certainly was not. In fact, she was married to an astronaut, and was as concerned as anyone about the safety of the shuttle crews. This was a dangerous business, and she knew it all too well. But like her boss, Ron Dittemore, with whom she discussed the *Columbia* foam strike several times, she was so immersed in the closed world of shuttle management that she simply did not elevate the event—this "in-family" thing—to the level of concerns requiring action. She was intellectually arrogant, perhaps, and as a manager she failed abysmally. But neither she nor the others of her rank had the slightest suspicion that the *Columbia* might actually go down.

.   .   .

The frustration is that some people on lower levels were actively worried about that possibility, and they understood clearly that not enough was known about the effects of the foam strike on the wing, but they expressed their concerns mostly to one another, and for good reason, because on the few occasions when they tried to alert the decision-makers, NASA's management system overwhelmed them and allowed none of them to be heard. The question now, of course, is why.

The CAIB's search for answers began long before the technical details were resolved, and it ultimately involved hundreds of interviews and 50,000 pages of transcripts. The manner in which those interviews were conducted became a contentious issue, and it was arguably Gehman's biggest mistake. As a military man, advised by military men on the board, he decided to conduct the interviews according to a military model of safety probes, in which individual fault is not formally assigned, and the interviews themselves are "privileged," meaning forever sealed off from public view. It was understood that identities and deeds would not be protected from view, only individual testimonies to the CAIB, but serious critics cried foul nonetheless, and pointed out correctly that Gehman was using loopholes to escape sunshine laws that otherwise would have applied. Gehman believed that treating the testimony as privileged was necessary to encourage witnesses to talk, and to get to the bottom of the story, but the long-term effect of the investigation will be diminished as a result (for instance, by lack of access to the raw material by outside analysts), and there was widespread consensus among the experienced (largely civilian) investigators actually conducting the interviews that the promise of privacy was having little effect on what people were willing to say. These were not criminals they were talking to, or careful lawyers. For the most part they were sincere engineering types who were concerned about what had gone wrong, and would have been willing even without privacy to speak their minds. The truth, in other words, would have come out even in the brightest of sunshine.

The story that emerged was a sad and unnecessary one, involving arrogance, insularity, and bad luck allowed to run unchecked. On the seventh day of the flight, January 22, just as the Air Force began to move on the Kennedy engineers' back-channel request for photographs, Linda Ham heard to her surprise that this approach (which according to front-channel procedures would have required her approval) had been made. She immediately telephoned other high-level managers in Houston to see if any of them wanted to issue a formal "requirement" for imagery, and when they informed her that they did not, rather than exploring the question with the Kennedy engineers she simply terminated their request with the Department of Defense. This appears to have been a purely bureaucratic reaction. A NASA liaison officer then e-mailed an apology to Air Force personnel, assuring them that the shuttle was in "excellent shape," and explaining that a foam strike was "something that has happened before and is not considered to be a major problem." The officer continued, "The one problem that this has identified is the need for some additional coordination within NASA to assure that when a request is made it is done through the official channels." Months later one of the CAIB investigators who had followed this trail was still seething with anger at what had occurred. He said, "Because the problem was not identified in the traditional way—'Houston, we have a problem!'—well, then, 'Houston, we *don't* have a problem!' Because *Houston* didn't *identify* the problem."

But another part of Houston was doing just that. Unbeknownst to Ham and the shuttle management, the low-level engineers of the Debris Assessment Team had concluded that the launch films were not clear enough to indicate where the foam had hit, and particularly whether it had hit the underside tile or a leading-edge RCC panel. Rather than trying to run their calculations in the blind, they had decided that they should do the simple thing and have someone take a look for damage. They had already e-mailed one query to the engineering department, about the possibility of getting the astronauts themselves to take a short spacewalk and inspect the wing. It later turned out that this would have been safe and easy to do. That e-mail, however, was never answered. This time the Debris Assessment engineers decided on a still simpler solution—to ask the Department of Defense to take some high-resolution pictures. Ignorant of the fact that the Kennedy group had already made such a request, and that it had just been peevishly canceled, they sent out two requests of their own, directed, appropriately, to Ron Dittemore and Linda Ham, but through channels that were a little off-center, and happened to fail. Those channels were ones they had used in their regular work as engineers, outside the formal shuttle-management structure. By unfortunate circumstance, the request that came closest to getting through was intercepted by a mid-level employee (the assistant to an intended recipient, who was on vacation) who responded by informing the Debris Assessment engineers, more or less correctly, that Linda Ham had decided against Air Force imagery.

The confusion was now total, yet also nearly invisible—and within the suppressive culture of the human space-flight program, it had very little chance of making itself known. At the top of the tangle, neither Ron Dittemore nor Linda Ham ever learned that the Debris Assessment Team wanted pictures; at the bottom, the Debris Assessment engineers heard the "no" without suspecting that it was not an answer to their request. They were told to go back to the Crater model and numerical analysis, and as earnest, hardworking engineers (hardly rebels, these), they dutifully complied, all the while regretting the blind assumptions that they would have to make. Given the obvious potential for a catastrophe, one might expect that they would have gone directly to Linda Ham, on foot if necessary, to make the argument in person for a spacewalk or high-resolution photos. However, such were the constraints within the Johnson Space Center that they never dared. They later said that had they made a fuss about the shuttle, they might have been singled out for ridicule. They feared for their standing, and their careers.

The CAIB investigator who asked the engineers what conclusion they had drawn at the time from management's refusal later said to me, "They all thought, 'Well, none of us have a security clearance high enough to view any of this imagery.' They talked about this openly among themselves, and they figured one of three things:

"'One: The "no" means that management's already got photos, and the damage isn't too bad. They can't show us the photos, because we don't have the security clearance, and they can't *tell* us they have the photos, or *tell* us the damage isn't bad, because that tells us how accurate the photos are—and we don't have the security clearance. But wait a minute, if that's the case, then what're we doing here? Why are we doing the analysis? So no, that can't be right.

"'Okay, then, two: They already took the photos, and the damage is so severe that there's no hope for recovery. Well . . . that can't be right either, because in that case, why are we doing the analysis?

"'Okay, then, three: They took the photos. They can't tell us they took the photos, and the photos don't give us clear definition. So we need to do the analysis. That's gotta be it!'"

What the Debris Assessment engineers could not imagine is that no photos had been taken, or ever would be—and essentially for lack of curiosity by NASA's imperious, self-convinced managers. What those managers in turn could not imagine was that people in their own house might really be concerned. The communication gap had nothing to do with security clearances, and it was complete.

Gehman explained the underlying realities to me. He said, "They claim that the culture in Houston is a 'badgeless society,' meaning it doesn't matter what you have on your badge—you're concerned about shuttle safety together. Well, that's all nice, but the truth is that it *does* matter what badge you're wearing. Look, if you really do have an organization that has free communication and open doors and all that kind of stuff, it takes a special kind of management to make it work. And we just don't see that management here. Oh, they *say* all the right things. 'We have open doors and e-mails, and anybody who sees a problem can raise his hand, blow a whistle, and stop the whole process.' But then when you look at how it really works, it's an incestuous, hierarchical system, with invisible rankings and a very strict informal chain of command. They all know that. So even though they've got all the trappings of communication, you don't actually *find* communication. It's very complex. But if a person brings an issue up, what caste he's in makes all the difference. Now, again, NASA will deny this, but if you talk to people, if you really listen to people, all the time you hear 'Well, I was afraid to speak up.' Boy, it comes across loud and clear. You listen to the meetings: 'Anybody got anything to say?' There are thirty people in the room, and *slam!* There's nothing. We have plenty of witness statements saying, 'If I had spoken up, it would have been at the cost of my job.' And if you're in the engineering department, you're a nobody."

One of the CAIB investigators told me that he asked Linda Ham, "As a manager, how do you seek out dissenting opinions?"

According to him, she answered, "Well, when I hear about them . . ."

He interrupted. "Linda, by their very nature you may not hear about them."

"Well, when somebody comes forward and tells me about them."

"But Linda, what techniques do you use to *get* them?"

He told me she had no answer.

This was certainly not the sort of risk-versus-risk decision-making that Michael Bloomfield had in mind when he described the thinking behind his own shuttle flights.

•   •   •

At 7:00 A.M. on the ninth day, January 24, which was one week before the *Columbia*'s scheduled re-entry, the engineers from the Debris Assessment Team formally presented the results of their numerical analysis to Linda Ham's intermediary, Don McCormack. The room was so crowded with concerned observers that some people stood in the hall, peering in. The fundamental purpose of the meeting would have been better served had the engineers been able to project a photograph of a damaged wing onto the screen, but, tragically, that was not to be. Instead they projected a typically crude PowerPoint summary, based on the results from the Crater model, with which they attempted to explain a nuanced position: first, that if the tile had been damaged, it had probably endured well enough to allow the *Columbia* to come home; and second, that for lack of information they had needed to make assumptions to reach that conclusion, and that troubling unknowns therefore limited the meaning of the results. The latter message seems to have been lost. Indeed, this particular PowerPoint presentation became a case study for Edward Tufte, the brilliant communications specialist from Yale, who in a subsequent booklet, *The Cognitive Style of PowerPoint*, tore into it for its dampening effect on clear expression and thought. The CAIB later joined in, describing the widespread use of PowerPoint within NASA as one of the obstacles to internal communication, and criticizing the Debris Assessment presentation for mechanically underplaying the uncertainties that remained.

Had the uncertainties been more strongly expressed as the *central* factor in question, the need to inspect the wing by spacewalk or photograph might have become obvious even to the shuttle managers. Still, the Mission Management Team seemed unprepared to hear nuance. Fixated on potential tile damage as the relevant question, assuming without good evidence that the RCC panels were strong enough to withstand a foam strike, subtly skewing the discussion away from catastrophic burn-through and toward the potential effects on turnaround times on the ground and how that might affect the all-important launch schedule, the shuttle managers were convinced that they had the situation as they defined it firmly under control.

At a regularly scheduled MMT meeting later that morning McCormack summarized the PowerPoint presentation for Linda Ham. He said, "The analysis is not complete. There is one case yet that they wish to run, but kind of just jumping to the conclusion of all that, they do show that [there is], obviously, a potential for significant tile damage here, but thermal analysis does not indicate that there is potential for a burn-through. I mean, there could be localized heating damage. There is . . . obviously there is a lot of uncertainty in all this in terms of the size of the debris and where it hit and the angle of incidence."

Ham answered, "No burn-through means no catastrophic damage. And the localized heating damage would mean a tile replacement?"

"Right, it would mean possible impacts to turnaround repairs and that sort of thing, but we do not see any kind of safety-of-flight issue here yet in anything that we've looked at."

This was all too accurate in itself. Ham said, "And no safety of flight, no issue for this mission, nothing that we're going to do different. There may be a turnaround [delay]."

McCormack said, "Right. It could potentially [have] hit the RCC . . . We don't see any issue if it hit the RCC . . ."

The discussion returned to the tiles. Ham consulted with a tile specialist named Calvin Schomburg, who for days had been energetically making a case independent of the Debris Assessment analysis that a damaged tile would endure re-entry—and thereby adding, unintentionally, to the distractions and false assumptions of the management team. After a brief exchange Ham cut off further discussion with a quick summary for some people participating in the meeting by conference call, who were having trouble hearing the speakerphone. She said, "So, no safety-of-flight kind of issue. It's more of a turnaround issue similar to what we've had on other flights. That's it? All right, any questions on that?"

And there were not.

For reasons unexplained, when the official minutes of the meeting were written up and distributed (having been signed off on by Ham), all mention of the foam strike was omitted. This was days before the *Columbia*'s re-entry, and seems to indicate sheer lack of attention to this subject, rather than any sort of cover-up.

The truth is that Linda Ham was as much a victim of NASA as were *Columbia*'s astronauts, who were still doing their science experiments then, and free-falling in splendor around the planet. Her predicament had roots that went way back, nearly to the time of Ham's birth, and it involved not only the culture of the human space-flight program but also the White House, Congress, and NASA leadership over the past thirty years. Gehman understood this fully, and as the investigation drew to a close, he vowed to avoid merely going after the people who had been standing close to the accident when it occurred. The person standing closest was, of course, Linda Ham, and she will bear a burden for her mismanagement. But by the time spring turned to summer, and the CAIB moved its operation from Houston to Washington, D.C., Gehman had taken to saying, "Complex systems fail in complex ways," and he was determined that the CAIB's report would document the full range of NASA's mistakes. It did, and in clean, frank prose, using linked sentences and no Power-Point displays.

As the report was released, on August 26, Mars came closer to Earth than it had in 60,000 years. Gehman told me that he continued to believe in the importance of America's human space-flight effort, and even of the return of the shuttle to flight—at least until a replacement with a clearer mission can be built and put into service. It was a quiet day in Washington, with Congress in recess and the President on vacation. Aides were coming from Capitol Hill to pick up several hundred copies of the report and begin planning hearings for the fall. The White House was receiving the report too, though keeping a cautious distance, as had been expected; it was said that the President might read an executive summary. Down in Houston, board members were handing copies to the astronauts, the managers, and the families of the dead.

Gehman was dressed in a suit, as he had been at the start of all this, seven months before. It was up to him now to drive over to NASA headquarters, in the southwest corner of the city, and deliver the report personally to Sean O'Keefe. I went along for the ride, as did the board member Sheila Widnall, who was there to lend Gehman some moral support. The car was driven by a Navy officer in whites. At no point since the accident had anyone at NASA stepped forward to accept personal responsibility for contributing to this accident—not Linda Ham, not Ron Dittemore, and certainly not Sean O'Keefe. However, the report in Gehman's hands (248 pages, full color, well bound) made responsibility very clear. This was not going to be a social visit. Indeed, it turned out to be extraordinarily tense. Gehman and Widnall strode up the carpeted hallways in a phalanx of anxious, dark-suited NASA staffers, who swung open the doors in advance and followed close on their heels. O'Keefe's office suite was practically imperial in its expense and splendor. High officials stood in small, nervous groups, murmuring. After a short delay O'Keefe appeared—a tall, balding, gray-haired man with stooped shoulders. He shook hands and ushered Gehman and Widnall into the privacy of his inner office. Ten minutes later they emerged. There was a short ceremony for NASA cameras, during which O'Keefe thanked Gehman for his important contribution, and then it was time to leave. As we drove away, I asked Gehman how it had been in there with O'Keefe.

He said "Stiff. Very stiff."

We talked about the future. The report had made a series of recommendations for getting the shuttle back into flight, and beyond that for beginning NASA's long and necessary process of reform. I knew that Gehman, along with much of the board, had volunteered to Congress to return in a year, to peer in deeply again, and to try to judge if progress had been made. I asked him how genuine he thought such progress could be, and he managed somehow to express hope, though skeptically.

•   •   •

By January 23, the *Columbia*'s eighth day in orbit, the crew had solved a couple of minor system problems, and after a half day off, during which no doubt some of the astronauts took the opportunity for some global sightseeing, they were proceeding on schedule with their laboratory duties, and were in good spirits and health. They had been told nothing of the foam strike. Down in Houston, the flight controllers at Mission Control were aware of it, and they knew that the previous day Linda Ham had canceled the request for Air Force photographs. Confident that the issue would be satisfactorily resolved by the shuttle managers, they decided nonetheless to inform the flight crew by e-mail—if only because certain reporters at the Florida launch site had heard of it, and might ask questions at an upcoming press conference, a Public Affairs Office, or PAO, event. The e-mail was written by one of the lead flight controllers, in the standard, overly upbeat style. It was addressed to the pilots, Rick Husband and William McCool.

Under the subject line "info: Possible PAO Event Question," it read,

> Rick and Willie,
>
> You guys are doing a fantastic job staying on the timeline and accomplishing great science. Keep up the good work and let us know if there is anything that we can do better from an MCC/POCC standpoint.
>
> There is one item that I would like to make you aware of for the upcoming PAO event . . . This item is not even worth mentioning other than wanting to make sure that you are not surprised by it in a question from a reporter.

The e-mail then briefly explained what the launch pictures had shown—a hit from the bipod-ramp foam. A video clip was attached. The e-mail concluded,

> Experts have reviewed the high speed photography and there is no concern for RCC or tile damage. We have seen this same phenomenon on several other flights and there is absolutely no concern for entry. That is all for now. It's a pleasure working with you every day.

The e-mail's content honestly reflected what was believed on the ground, though in a repackaged and highly simplified form. There was no mention of the inadequate quality of the pictures, of the large size of the foam, of the ongoing analysis, or of Linda Ham's decision against Air Force imagery. This was typical for Mission Control communications, a small example of a long-standing pattern of something like information-hoarding that was instinctive and a matter as much of style as of intent: the astronauts had been told of the strike, but almost as if they were children who didn't need to be involved in the grown-up conversation. Two days later, when Rick Husband answered the e-mail, he wrote, "Thanks a million!" and "Thanks for the great work!" and after making a little joke, that "Main Wing" could sound like a Chinese name, he signed off with an e-mail smile—:). He made no mention of the foam strike at all. And with that, as we now know, the crew's last chance for survival faded away.

Linda Ham was wrong. Had the hole in the leading edge been seen, actions could have been taken to try to save the astronauts' lives. The first would have been simply to buy some time. Assuming a starting point on the fifth day of the flight, NASA engineers subsequently calculated that by requiring the crew to rest and sleep, the mission could have been extended to a full month, to February 15. During that time the *Atlantis*, which was already being prepared for a scheduled March 1 launch, could have been processed more quickly by ground crews working around the clock, and made ready to go by February 10. If all had proceeded perfectly, there would have been a five-day window in which to blast off, join up with the *Columbia*, and transfer the stranded astronauts one by one to safety, by means of tethered spacewalks. Such a rescue would not have been easy, and it would have involved the possibility of another fatal foam strike and the loss of two shuttles instead of one; but in the risk-versus-risk world of space flight, veterans like Mike Bloomfield would immediately have volunteered, and NASA would have bet the farm.

The fallback would have been a desperate measure—a jury-rigged repair performed by the *Columbia* astronauts themselves. It would have required two spacewalkers to fill the hole with a combination of heavy tools and metal scraps scavenged from the crew compartment, and to supplement that mass with an ice bag shaped to the wing's leading edge. In theory, if much of the payload had been jettisoned, and luck was with the crew, such a repair might perhaps have endured a modified re-entry and allowed the astronauts to bail out at the standard 30,000 feet. The engineers who came up with this plan realized that in reality it would have been extremely dangerous, and might well have led to a high-speed burn-through and the loss of the crew. But anything would have been better than attempting a normal re-entry as it was actually flown.

The blessing, if one can be found, is that the astronauts remained unaware until nearly the end. A home video shot on board and found in the wreckage documented the relaxed mood in the cockpit as the shuttle descended through the entry interface at 400,000 feet, at 7:44:09 Houston time, northwest of Hawaii. The astronauts were drinking water in anticipation of gravity's redistributive effect on their bodies. The *Columbia* was flying at the standard 40-degree nose-up angle, with its wings level, and still doing nearly 17,000 mph; outside, though the air was ultra-thin and dynamic pressures were very low, the aerodynamic surfaces were beginning to move in conjunction with the array of control jets, which were doing the main work of maintaining the shuttle's attitude, and would throughout the re-entry. The astronauts commented like sightseers as sheets of fiery plasma began to pass by the windows.

The pilot, McCool, said, "Do you see it over my shoulder now, Laurel?"

Sitting behind him, the mission specialist Laurel Clark said, "I was filming. It doesn't show up nearly as much as the back."

McCool said to the Israeli payload specialist, Ilan Ramon, "It's going pretty good now. Ilan, it's really neat—it's a bright orange-yellow out over the nose, all around the nose."

The commander, Husband, said, "Wait until you start seeing the swirl patterns out your left or right windows."

McCool said, "Wow."

Husband said, "Looks like a blast furnace."

A few seconds later they began to feel gravity. Husband said, "Let's see here . . . look at that."

McCool answered, "Yup, we're getting some Gs." As if it were unusual, he said, "I let go of the card, and it falls." Their instruments showed that they were experiencing one hundredth of a G. McCool looked out the window again. He said, "This is amazing. It's really getting, uh, fairly bright out there."

Husband said, "Yup. Yeah, you definitely don't want to be outside now."

The flight engineer, Kalpana Chawla, answered sardonically, "What—like we did before?" The crew laughed.

Outside, the situation was worse than they imagined. Normally, as a shuttle streaks through the upper atmosphere it heats the air immediately around it to temperatures as high as 10,000°, but largely because of the boundary layer—a sort of air cushion created by the leading edges—the actual surface temperatures are significantly lower, generally around 3,000°, which the vehicle is designed to withstand, if barely. The hole in the *Columbia*'s leading edge, however, had locally undermined the boundary layer, and was now letting in a plume of superheated air that was cutting through insulation and working its way toward the inner recesses of the left wing. It is estimated that the plume may have been as hot as 8,000° near the RCC breach. The aluminum support structures inside the wing had a melting point of 1,200°, and they began to burn and give way.

The details of the left wing's failure are complex and technical, but the essentials are not difficult to understand. The wing was attacked by a snaking plume of hot gas, and eaten up from the inside. The consumption began when the shuttle was over the Pacific, and it grew worse over the United States. It included wire bundles leading from the sensors, which caused the data going into the MADS recorder and the telemetry going to Houston to fail in ways that only later made sense. At some point the plume blew right through the top of the left wing, and began to throw molten metal from the insides all over the aft rocket pods. At some point it burned its way into the left main gear well, but it did not explode the tires.

As drag increased on the left wing, the autopilot and combined flight-control systems at first easily compensated for the resulting tendency to roll and yaw to the left. By external appearance, therefore, the shuttle was doing its normal thing, banking first to the right and then to the left for the scheduled energy-management turns, and tracking perfectly down the descent profile for Florida. The speeds were good, the altitudes were good, and all systems were functioning correctly. From within the cockpit the ride appeared to be right.

By the time it got to Texas the *Columbia* had already proved itself a heroic flying machine, having endured for so long at hypersonic speeds with little left of the midsection inside its left wing, and the plume of hot gas still in there, alive, and eating it away. By now, however, the flight-control systems were nearing their limits. The breakup was associated with that. At 7:59:15 Mission Control noticed the sudden loss of tire pressure on the left gear as the damage rapidly progressed. This was followed by Houston's call "And *Columbia*, Houston, we see your tire-pressure messages, and we did not copy your last call," and at 7:59:32 by *Columbia*'s final transmission, "Roger, ah, buh ..."

The *Columbia* was traveling at 12,738 mph, at 200,000 feet, and the dynamic pressures were building, with the wings "feeling" the air at about 170 mph. Now, suddenly, the bottom surface of the left wing began to cave upward into the interior void of melted and burned-through bracing and structure. As the curvature of the wing changed, the lift increased, causing the *Columbia* to want to roll violently to the right; at the same time, because of an increase in asymmetrical drag, it yawed violently to the left. The control systems went to their limits to maintain order, and all four right yaw jets on the tail fired simultaneously, but to no avail. At 8:00:19 the *Columbia* rolled over the top and went out of control.

The gyrations it followed were complex combinations of roll, yaw, and pitch, and looked something like an oscillating flat spin.

They seem to have resulted in the vehicle's flying backwards. At one point the autopilot appears to have been switched off and then switched on again, as if Husband, an experienced test pilot, was trying to sort things out. The breakup lasted more than a minute. Not surprisingly, the left wing separated first. Afterward the tail, the right wing, and the main body came apart in what investigators later called a controlled sequence "right down the track." As had happened with the *Challenger* in 1986, the crew cabin broke off intact. It assumed a stable flying position, apparently nose high, and later disintegrated like a falling star across the East Texas sky.

The New Yorker

FINALIST, REPORTING

The David Kelly Affair

In "The David Kelly Affair," John Cassidy painstakingly unravels the political scandal surrounding the suicide of a British weapons scientist in minute, well-sourced detail. Both a haunting portrait of a mysterious man unwittingly caught in the spotlight and a searing indictment of the British government's reckless hunger for war in Iraq, the story underscores the dangers of sensationalistic journalism.

John Cassidy

The David Kelly Affair

A scientist's death, a reporter's credibility, and the unravelling of Tony Blair's case for war

Shortly after 3 P.M. on Thursday, July 17, 2003, David Kelly, a fifty-nine-year-old scientist employed by the British government, walked out of his house in Southmoor, a small village ten miles southwest of Oxford. Kelly, a slight, wiry man, with thinning gray hair, glasses, and a beard, lived with his wife, Janice, in a handsome stone cottage that sits on about half an acre of land at the western edge of the village, opposite the Wagon & Horses pub. He crossed the road and headed up a bridle path that goes by the pub's car park. It was a warm day, but he was wearing a thick blue jacket, hiking boots, and jeans. The path leads north, past some fields where, a couple of months previously, Kelly and one of his three daughters, Rachel, had spotted a newborn foal. They had arranged to go and see how the foal was doing that evening.

Kelly had a lot on his mind. Two days before, he had been questioned at a televised hearing of the House of Commons Foreign Affairs Committee about an unauthorized interview he had given to a BBC journalist in May. His employer, the Ministry of Defence, had told him that it wouldn't take any disciplinary action, but Kelly, a deeply private man, had found the publicity excruciating. He was also getting ready to join the Iraq Survey Group, a team of American, Australian, and British experts who are searching for Saddam Hussein's weapons of mass destruction. He was due to depart for Baghdad in eight days.

After crossing the A420, the main road between Oxford and Swindon, Kelly carried on to the neighboring village of Longworth, where he ran into a neighbor, Ruth Absalom, who was walking her dog, Buster. Absalom, an elderly woman with white hair and a thick rural accent, asked Kelly how he was. "Not too bad," he replied. They chatted for a few minutes. Buster was pulling on his leash, and Kelly told Absalom he had to be getting along. "Cheerio, Ruth," he said.

Kelly and his wife were well liked locally, but most of his neighbors weren't fully aware of what he did for a living. For almost twenty years, he had been one of the British government's leading experts in chemical and biological warfare. During the nineteen-nineties, he had served as a United Nations weapons inspector in Iraq, and in 1996 the Queen had made him a Companion of the Order of St. Michael and St. George, an official honor that ranks just below a knighthood.

Kelly kept walking. On the northern side of Longworth, a tree-lined lane runs through a pretty valley to Harrowdown Hill, a local landmark that affords magnificent views of Oxfordshire. Kelly sometimes walked well beyond the hill, but his wife was expecting him home soon. Janice Kelly suffers from arthritis, and when Kelly left she was lying down, because she wasn't feeling well. Reaching a dense wood at the top of the hill, Kelly headed into the trees. After about fifty or sixty yards, the way was blocked by thick bramble bushes and other undergrowth. In a small clearing, he sat down with his back against a tree. In the pocket of his jacket he was carrying a cell phone, some of his wife's painkillers, and a lock knife that he usually kept in his desk drawer. He had almost complete privacy. The area attracts ramblers, but it was a weekday afternoon, and few people were about.

Between 5 P.M. and 6 P.M., two of his colleagues at the Ministry of Defence called his cell phone. Kelly didn't answer. At some point, he removed his spectacles and put them in his pocket. He got out the painkillers, swallowed more than twenty of them, and washed them down with some Evian water he was carrying. After waiting for them to take effect, he held the knife, which had a three- or four-inch-long blade, and slashed at his left wrist. The first incisions were shallow—the kind of cuts that pathologists refer to as "hesitation marks." With blood running down his arm, Kelly took off his watch and laid it on the ground, then cut deeper, severing the ulnar artery, which runs along the left side of the wrist. Within minutes, he was dead.

•   •   •

In early September last year, Prime Minister Tony Blair made a visit to his parliamentary constituency, Sedgefield, a small town in northeast England. During the flight from London, Blair talked with Alastair Campbell, his longtime press secretary and strategist, about the need to persuade a skeptical British public that Saddam Hussein represented a serious danger, and that he had to be confronted. The previous week, Vice-President Dick Cheney had called Saddam a "mortal threat." Blair was scheduled to visit President George Bush at Camp David later in the month, a meeting that the British papers were already billing as a war summit.

Campbell, a talented but controversial former journalist, shared Blair's concerns. For more than ten years, the British government had supported a policy of containing Iraq, but it had recently adopted the Bush doctrine of regime change. In order to help explain its change of policy, Downing Street had previously considered publishing an intelligence dossier detailing the menace from Iraq's chemical-, biological-, and nuclear-weapons programs, but nothing had appeared. Blair told Campbell he wanted to revive the idea. When he reached Sedgefield, he announced publicly that the government would soon release a dossier on Iraq's weapons of mass destruction. He charged Campbell with overseeing the production and presentation of the document.

Campbell grew up in Keighley, a gritty town in West Yorkshire. After graduating from Cambridge University and training on provincial papers, he worked at *Today*, a tabloid that is now defunct, and the *Daily Mirror*, the paper of the northern workingman. In the nineteen-eighties, he drank himself into a nervous breakdown. As he was lying in a hospital bed, a close friend and fellow Fleet Street hack came in and handed him some marbles, saying, "Don't lose them again." Campbell gave up drinking. After he returned to work, he became a close adviser to Neil Kinnock, the leftist Welshman who was then the leader of the Labour Party, which had been out of office since 1979. When Blair took over as Party leader, in 1994, Campbell became his press spokesman and confidant. After the Labour Party won power, in May, 1997, Campbell set up a Downing Street media operation of unprecedented scale and efficiency, which he presided over with a blend of sarcasm, intense work, and belligerence. "Tony needs a hard man, and that's what I am," he told David Yelland, then the editor of the *Sun*, Britain's best-selling newspaper. "Alastair was brilliant," Yelland recalled. "He could intimidate anybody."

On Thursday, September 5, 2002, Campbell chaired a meeting about the dossier in his office at 10 Downing Street. Among those attending were three of Britain's top civil servants, nonpartisan public employees who are supposed to avoid political entanglements: Sir David Manning, Blair's senior foreign-policy adviser, who is now Britain's Ambassador to the United States; Julian Miller, the head of the assessment staff at the Cabinet Office, an élite bureaucracy that provides administrative support to the government; and Sir John Scarlett, the head of the Joint Intelligence Committee, a secretive body that supplies intelligence assessments to the Prime Minister.

Thanks to evidence presented to Lord Hutton, a senior judge who is carrying out an inquiry into David Kelly's death, we know that the officials had in front of them a draft of a dossier on Iraq's W.M.D. that the British intelligence services and the Foreign Office, the British equivalent of the State Department, had produced in the spring and summer of 2002. It said that "Iraq has a capability to produce chemical and biological weapons," but did not say that Saddam had actually produced any such weapons in recent years. It also said, "Iraq has a nuclear weapons program," but added that Iraq "will find it difficult to produce fissile material while sanctions remain in place," and went on to say that even if sanctions were lifted "Iraq would need at least five years to produce a weapon."

Downing Street hadn't given any reason for not publishing this dossier, but inside the government it was widely believed that Blair was disappointed with it. "We all knew why it wasn't put out," one of Kelly's former colleagues told me. "Because it didn't make the case strongly enough." The dossier's ambivalent tone reflected the fact that there had been little reliable intelligence since 1998, when United Nations weapons inspectors left Iraq. "The Americans had incredible aerial reconnaissance, but everything that mattered was hidden under a roof or underground," the former colleague went on. "We were left with human intelligence, especially from defectors. But defectors have an incentive to provide interesting material."

Campbell didn't think much of the existing dossier. Writing in his diary, he expressed the hope that its replacement would be "revelatory," and "part of a bigger case." Scarlett, who took charge of revising the text in co-operation with Miller and his staff in the Cabinet Office, agreed that it did not contain enough "detail and information." After the meeting, Campbell sent an e-mail to

Blair's chief of staff, Jonathan Powell, which read, "Re dossier, substantial rewrite, with JS and Julian M in charge. . . . Structure as per TB's discussion. Agreement that there has to be real intelligence material in their presentation as such."

A few days later, Campbell and Scarlett met again, along with several others. The *Financial Times* and the *Daily Telegraph* had reported that some people in the intelligence services were uneasy about revising the dossier. (Britain has four intelligence agencies, all of which are represented on the Joint Intelligence Committee.) Scarlett, a former spy, whom the Russians expelled from Moscow in 1994, asked Campbell to confirm that Scarlett would be in charge of the dossier's contents. Campbell agreed. In a two-page memo, he noted, "It goes without saying that there should be nothing published that you and they"—the intelligence agencies—"are not 100% happy with." However, Campbell did not fully abdicate responsibility for the dossier. In the final paragraph of his memo, he wrote, "I will chair a team that will go through the document from a presentational point of view, and make recommendations to you."

The next day, September 10th, Scarlett circulated a new draft of the dossier, which drew on intelligence that MI6, the spying agency that Ian Fleming and John le Carré immortalized, had picked up the previous month from a confidential source inside Iraq. The Joint Intelligence Committee had incorporated this intelligence in a secret draft assessment on September 5th, which read, "Iraq has probably dispersed its special weapons, including its CBW"—chemical and biological weapons. "Intelligence also indicates that from forward-deployed storage sites, chemical and biological munitions could be with military units and ready for firing within 45 minutes." This statement referred to battlefield weapons, such as mortar rounds and artillery shells, not longer-range weapons, such as ground- and air-launched missiles. But this crucial qualification was not included in the revised dossier, which suggested that Iraq's W.M.D. constituted a regional threat. Iraq "envisages the use of weapons of mass destruction in its current military planning," the dossier said, "and could deploy such weapons within 45 minutes of the order being given for their use."

The new draft also alleged that Iraq "has purchased large quantities of uranium ore" and "has acquired mobile laboratories for military use, corroborating earlier reports about the mobile production of biological warfare agents." Despite the new material, the revision didn't impress some members of the Downing Street press office. "Think we're in a lot of trouble with it as it stands now," Philip Bassett, a former *Financial Times* reporter, wrote in an e-mail to his press-office colleagues on September 11th. Another member of the press office, Daniel Pruce, added, "Our aim should also be to convey the impression that things have not been static in Iraq but that over the past decade he"—Saddam—"has been aggressively and relentlessly pursuing WMD while brutally repressing his own people."

It isn't clear if these comments were passed on to Scarlett and Miller—Campbell later claimed that Daniel Pruce was offering suggestions "above his pay grade"—but on the afternoon of September 11th a Cabinet Office official sent an e-mail to the intelligence agencies entitled "Iraqi dossier—Questions from No. 10." Among other things, it asked the agencies to supply the exact number, and type, of chemical and biological weapons that Iraq possessed. "I appreciate everyone, us included, has been around at least some of these buoys before," the official wrote. "But No. 10 through the Chairman want the document to be as strong as possible within the bounds of available intelligence. This is therefore a last (!) call for any items of intelligence that agencies think can and should be included."

On Monday, September 16th, Scarlett circulated another updated dossier. The text had been reorganized to highlight the most recent intelligence, and some of the language had been strengthened. The dossier now said that Iraq's misbehavior "has included recent production of chemical and biological agents," but it didn't contain any evidence to support the charges.

Campbell remained intimately involved in the dossier's progress.

On September 17th, he sent a memo to Scarlett in which he relayed the Prime Minister's reaction to the latest version: "He said he thought you'd done a very good job and it was convincing (though I pointed out he is hardly a 'don't know' on the issue)."

Campbell also offered Scarlett detailed comments of his own. For example:

8. On page 15, can we list quantities of e.g. shells, sprays, etc.
9. On page 16, bottom line, "might" reads very weakly.
10. On page 17, 2 lines from the bottom, "may" is weaker than in summary.

These drafting points went well beyond matters of presentation. In No. 9, the word "might" referred to a claim that Iraq "might already have" started producing VX gas. No. 10 referred to the sentence "The Iraq military *may* be able to deploy chemical or biological weapons within forty five minutes of an order to do so." (Italics added.) Less than twenty-four hours later, Scarlett replied to Campbell, saying, "We have been able to amend the text in most cases as you proposed." Among other changes Scarlett had made, the sentence referred to in No. 10 now read, "Intelligence indicates that the Iraqi military *are* able to deploy chemical or biological weapons within forty five minutes of an order to do so."

Campbell wasn't satisfied yet. "Sorry to bombard on this point," he wrote to Scarlett, "but I do worry that the nuclear section will become the main focus and as currently drafted is not in great shape." An earlier draft had suggested that if Saddam somehow obtained fissile material and other components from abroad he could build a nuclear weapon within a year or two. The September 16th version had left out this claim, and Campbell suggested reinstating it in the next round. Scarlett agreed.

Campbell had also been working on a foreword that Blair was

planning to contribute to the published version of the dossier. On September 17th, he sent Scarlett a draft that read:

> Alone among leaders, Saddam has used chemical weapons. Intelligence reports make clear that he sees the possession of WMD, and the belief overseas that he would use them, as vital to his strategic interests, and in particular his goal of regional domination. And the document discloses that his military planning allows for some of the WMD to be ready within 45 minutes of an order to use them.

· · ·

The dossier was a joint effort. MI6 provided most of the raw intelligence that went into it; the Defence Intelligence Staff, which is part of the Ministry of Defence, reviewed it; the Cabinet Office collated it; and the Joint Intelligence Committee made the final decision about what to include. Some analysts at the Defence Intelligence Staff were uneasy about the new material that had been inserted into the dossier—especially the forty-five-minutes claim, which MI6's source said originated with a senior Iraqi military officer. "The way in which the information was reported did not give us any confidence that the primary source knew very much about the subject," Brian Jones, a former senior official in the Defence Intelligence Staff's assessments section, told Lord Hutton. "And so we were left wondering, Well, did the secondary source know these sorts of things?"

Jones, who worked for the Ministry of Defence from 1973 until earlier this year, when he retired, was on vacation in the first half of September, 2002. When he got back, he discovered that members of his staff had been trying to qualify some of the language in the dossier. In a note forwarded to the Cabinet Office, one analyst pointed out that the forty-five-minutes claim was "rather strong since it is based on a single source" and proposed amending the dossier to say "intelligence suggests" it was true. Jones's expert on chemical weapons had expressed concern about the assertion that Iraq had continued to produce chemical and biological agents. Jones explained to Lord Hutton, "He did not dismiss that it may have happened, and there was certain evidence that suggested it could have happened, but he did not have good evidence that it had happened."

Jones took these matters up with his supervisor, but he didn't get far. At an interagency meeting, senior officials from MI6 had already reiterated their faith in the intelligence behind the forty-five-minutes claim, saying that it came from an "established and reliable" source, and their assurances had been accepted. Jones wasn't prepared to let things rest. On September 18th, he talked with David Kelly, who sometimes acted as a consultant to the Defence Intelligence Staff.

A biologist by training, Kelly was officially the head of microbiology at the Defence Science and Technology Laboratory at Porton Down, a government chemical- and biological-weapons research center, where he had worked since 1984. But his actual duties extended well beyond Porton Down. Between 1991 and 1996, he spent much of his time as a weapons inspector with UNSCOM, the United Nations mission charged with verifying that Iraq destroyed its unconventional-weapons programs. Kelly had proved to be an indefatigable sleuth, and he played a key role in forcing the Iraqi government to admit that it had a biological-weapons program. "The reason he was so effective with the Iraqis is that he was tough, very tough, and they respected that," somebody who knew Kelly well told me. "He was always very polite, but he wouldn't let them get away with anything. He was absolutely relentless." After Kelly returned from Iraq, he was still attached to Porton Down, but he now also acted as a scientific adviser to the Ministry of Defence, the Foreign Office, and MI6. Earlier in 2002, the Foreign Office had asked him to contribute an account of Iraq's biological-weapons program to the historical section of the W.M.D. dossier.

Kelly told Jones he thought that the dossier was a good idea, and he agreed with its over-all thrust. His years in Iraq had convinced him that Saddam did have active W.M.D. programs, which he wouldn't give up unless forced to do so. But Kelly, like many other British experts, also believed that the Iraqi programs were modest, partly because of the U.N. inspections.

The following day, September 19th, Kelly went through the dossier with Jones and some of his analysts. They agreed that some of the new information in the dossier appeared questionable. Kelly suggested a number of specific changes, which were forwarded to the Cabinet Office. For example, the latest draft of the dossier stated, "UNSCOM established that Iraq was planning to conceal from the inspectors the capability to produce biological warfare agents by developing mobile facilities." Kelly proposed amending this to read, "UNSCOM established that in 1987 Iraq considered the use of mobile BW production facilities." He added, "Rationale: UNSCOM did not establish that Iraq was planning to conceal from the inspectors the capability to produce BW agents by developing mobile facilities."

Downing Street wanted to publish the dossier on Tuesday, September 24th, when Parliament was due to convene for a special session. Jones felt as though "the shutters were coming down." On September 20th, Scarlett circulated the final version of the dossier, which didn't include the changes that Jones's staff had suggested. Ignoring bureaucratic protocol, one of them wrote a protest letter to a top official in the Ministry of Defence. It began:

The 20th September draft still includes a number of statements which are not supported by evidence available to me.

Prime Minister's Foreword, 5th paragraph states: "What I believe the assessed intelligence has established beyond doubt is that Saddam has continued to produce chemical (and biological) weapons. . . ." I acknowledge that in this statement the Prime Minister will be expressing his own "belief" about what the assessed intelligence has established. What I wish to record is that based on the intelligence available to me it has NOT established beyond doubt that Saddam has continued to produce chemical (and biological) weapons.

Turning to the dossier's executive summary, which contained a bald assertion of the forty-five-minutes claim, the analyst went on:

This is based on a single source. It is not clear what is meant by "weapons are deployable within 45 minutes." The judgement is too strong considering the intelligence on which it is based.

• • •

In the Downing Street press office, the dossier's reviews were much more positive. "V good script—particularly page 2 on nukes," Godric Smith, one of the Prime Minister's two official spokesmen, wrote in an e-mail that circulated on September 19th. Tom Kelly, the other spokesman, agreed. "I think the key point in our favour is the systematic nature of what Saddam is up to," Kelly wrote. "The weakness, obviously, is our inability to say that he could pull the nuclear trigger any time soon. But the basic message of by then it would be too late does deal with that I think."

Campbell, ever vigilant, had some final changes. In addition to the foreword and the executive summary, the dossier contained three chapters of text and a conclusion. Campbell didn't see any need for the conclusion, which reiterated many of the points in the foreword and the executive summary. He wrote to Scarlett and suggested dropping it. A couple of hours later, Jonathan Powell, Blair's chief of staff, sent an e-mail to Scarlett and Campbell. "I agree with Alastair you should drop the conclusion," he wrote. Then, referring to the London *Evening Standard*, Powell added, "Alastair—what will be the headline in the *Standard* on the day of publication? What do we want it to be?"

Once again, Scarlett acceded to Campbell's wishes, omitting the conclusion from the final version of the dossier. In a cover note, he wrote, "I am content that the text now reflects as fully and accurately as possible the intelligence picture on Saddam's mass destruction weapons." On Tuesday, September 24th, Blair stood up in the House of Commons and raised the dossier aloft. "The threat of Saddam and weapons of mass destruction is not American or British propaganda," he declared. "The history and present threat are real."

When the early edition of the *Evening Standard* hit the streets, a front-page banner headline answered Powell's question: "45 MINUTES FROM ATTACK." The next day, the national newspapers all devoted extensive coverage to the dossier, with the *Sun* leading the way. Its front page blared, "HE'S GOT 'EM . . . LET'S GET HIM."

．　　　　．　　　　．

The Charing Cross Hotel sits atop the railway station of the same name, just off Trafalgar Square. Here, on the afternoon of Thursday, May 22, 2003, David Kelly met with Andrew Gilligan, a thirty-five-year-old defense and diplomatic correspondent for BBC Radio 4's "Today" program. Gilligan, a stout, pasty-faced fellow, had recently returned from Baghdad, where he had covered the war and its aftermath. He wasn't on close terms with Kelly—they had met a couple of times—but he knew that Kelly was familiar with the September dossier. Kelly later said that he met with Gilligan because he wanted to hear about the reporter's experiences in Baghdad. After leaving Iraq in 1998, Kelly continued to monitor developments there, but he had to rely on secondhand information. He had clearance to talk to the media about the scientific details of chemical and biological warfare, and he had co-operated with many reporters, including Judith Miller, of the New York *Times;* Tom Mangold, formerly of the BBC; and James Bone, a New York correspondent of the London *Times,* who profiled him at length. "He was sophisticated with the press, but he wasn't slavishly party line," Bone told me. "In my experience, he didn't initiate leaks, but he gave candid answers to honest questions."

What Kelly and Gilligan said to each other remains contentious. Gilligan said that they talked for an hour and a half; Kelly claimed that the conversation lasted forty-five minutes. A receipt Gilligan retained for his expenses shows that they ordered an apple juice and a Coke. Gilligan—a rarity among British journalists—seldom touches alcohol. Kelly used to drink moderately, but after joining the Baha'i faith, in 1999, he took a vow of abstinence.

There is no dispute that Gilligan described his experiences in Baghdad, including his dealings with Iraqi government minders and his impression of the coalition attacks. Eventually, the conversation turned to the September dossier and the failure to find any W.M.D. Gilligan took out a personal organizer and jotted down what Kelly had to say. His notes began:

> Transformed week before publication to make it sexier. The classic was the 45 minutes. Most things in dossier were double sourced but that was single sourced. One source said it took 45 minutes to set up a missile assembly. That was misinterpreted. Most people in intelligence weren't happy with it because it didn't reflect the considered view they were putting forward.

At the *Sunday Telegraph*, where Gilligan worked before joining the BBC, he was known as an enterprising story-getter, whose ability to break news persuaded his editors to put up with his nocturnal hours and his frequent absences from the office. "Gilligan was clearly a maverick, but he was highly regarded in his field, and he had very good contacts," Matthew d'Ancona, the deputy editor of the *Sunday Telegraph*, says. "He lived for his work, and he spent most of his time pursuing his work. He was, and is, an implacably determined reporter."

Traditionally, the BBC trained its own reporters and took pride in its reputation as a reliable source of information. In recent years, parts of the corporation, including the "Today" program, have adopted a more aggressive approach to newsgathering, a trend reflected in Gilligan's hiring. As Gilligan listened to Kelly, he knew, he said later, that he had the makings of a good story. According to his account, he asked how the dossier had been transformed, and Kelly replied with one word: "Campbell." Gilligan then followed up: "What, Campbell made it up?" Kelly said, "No, it was real information. But it was unreliable, and it was in the dossier against our wishes."

This version of events has been challenged. Olivia Bosch, a friend of Kelly's who works at the Royal Institute of International Affairs, said to Lord Hutton that Kelly had told her that Gilligan brought up Campbell's name, saying he wanted to "play a name game" in order to guess who was responsible for inserting information into the dossier. Bosch said that Kelly was taken aback by this attempt to elicit information. He told her that he initially refused to confirm or deny Campbell's involvement, but eventually, under pressure from Gilligan, he said, "Maybe."

      •   •   •

In the days after he met Kelly, Gilligan called a couple of his government contacts and put it to them that the dossier had been transformed at Campbell's urging. One refused to comment; the other said, "Keep digging." Gilligan also spoke with an American expert on W.M.D., Gary Samore, who told him that similar charges were being made in Washington about the Bush Administration. These were the only people Gilligan approached. Despite having no independent confirmation for his story, he decided to broadcast it. He didn't check it out with Downing Street, and he didn't call Kelly to confirm what he had said.

The "Today" program is a venerable British institution. It begins at 6 A.M. every weekday and runs for three hours. One of its hosts is John Humphrys, a fractious character whose idea of a good question when interviewing, say, the Health Minister might be: "So, Minister, glossing over the fact that you are having an affair with your secretary and taking her for dirty weekends in Paris at the taxpayers' expense, what have you got to say about the alarming rise in breast cancer?" At 6:07 A.M. on Thursday, May 29th, Humphrys introduced Gilligan by saying that the government was facing more tough questions over its prewar claims about Iraqi weapons of mass destruction, particularly the Prime Minister's statement that they would be ready to go in forty-five minutes. Gilligan was speaking live, and without a script, from his home, in Greenwich:

> That's right. That was the central claim in his dossier, which he published in September, the main, erm, case, if you like, against, er, against Iraq, and the main statement of the British government's belief of what it thought Iraq was up to. And what we've been told by one of the senior officials in charge of drawing up that dossier was that, actually, the government probably, erm, knew that the forty-five-minute figure was wrong, even before it decided to put it in. What this person says is that a week before the publication date of the dossier, it was actually rather, erm, a bland production. It didn't, the draft prepared for Mr Blair by the intelligence agencies actually didn't say very much more than was public knowledge already, and, erm, Downing Street, our source says, ordered a week before publication, ordered it to be sexed up, to be made more exciting, and ordered more facts to be, er, to be discovered.

Humphrys interrupted Gilligan and asked him what he meant by "ordered more facts to be discovered." He didn't seem terribly impressed by the stuttering reporter. "Does any of this matter now, all these months later?" he demanded. "The war's been fought and won." Gilligan seemed to be shocked into coherence. "Well, the forty-five minutes isn't just a detail," he replied. "It did go to the heart of the government's case that Saddam was an imminent threat, and it was repeated four times in the dossier, including by the Prime Minister himself, in the foreword. So I think it probably does matter."

Shortly after seven-thirty, Humphrys reintroduced Gilligan. The Downing Street press office had already issued a strenuous denial of his first report, claiming that the entire dossier was the work of the intelligence services. Humphrys put this denial to Gilligan and asked, "Are you suggesting, let's be very clear about this, that it was not the work of the intelligence agencies?" Gilligan replied, "No. The information which I'm told was dubious did come from the agencies, but they were unhappy about it, because they didn't think it should have been in there. They thought it was—it was not corroborated sufficiently, and they actually thought it was wrong."

•　　•　　•

Gilligan was hardly the first reporter to question the government's pre-war claims. Ever since President Bush declared Iraq to be part of an "axis of evil," much of the British media, including the BBC, had adopted a critical approach to Blair's pro-U.S. line. Military victory and Saddam's removal hadn't silenced the doubters, liberal or conservative. By late May, hardly a day went by when the left-leaning *Independent, Guardian,* and *Daily Mirror* and the right-leaning *Daily Mail* and *Daily Telegraph* did not devote at least part of their front pages to the missing Iraqi weapons.

Still, Gilligan's story carried the BBC's imprimatur, and it was timed to do maximum damage. On May 29th, Blair and Campbell were in Kuwait on their way to a morale-boosting appearance with British troops in Basra. Somebody in Downing Street called Tom Kelly, the Prime Minister's spokesman, to tell him about the "Today" story. Campbell, who was standing next to Kelly when the call came, divides stories he doesn't like into three categories: "bollocks," "complete bollocks," and "bollocks on stilts." His first reaction was that nobody would take this one seriously, but by the time he reached Basra he realized that he had miscalculated. The travelling press corps was less interested in reporting on Blair's speech than in pursuing Gilligan's allegation that the government had "sexed up" the September dossier. Back in London, the early editions of the *Evening Standard* featured the headline "BLAIR FLIES INTO GROWING ROW OVER REASON FOR WAR."

From Iraq, the British party travelled to Poland, for a meeting with Leszek Miller, the Polish prime minister. At a press conference, Blair, visibly angry, insisted, "The idea that we authorized or made our intelligence agencies invent some piece of evidence is completely absurd." Gilligan's story had already been picked up around the world, partly because of its distribution on the BBC World Service. After leaving Poland, Blair went on to St. Petersburg, to attend the city's three-hundredth-anniversary celebrations. There Joschka Fischer, the German foreign minister, attacked him, saying that if no Iraqi W.M.D. were found Blair should "admit he has misused intelligence reports and misled world opinion."

On Sunday, June 1st, there was still no sign of the story's dying down. "WHEN SPIES MEET SPIN" was the headline in the *Observer*. "LIE ANOTHER DAY," trumpeted the *Sunday Times*. The *Mail on Sunday,* one of Campbell's least favorite newspapers, contained two articles guaranteed to give him a headache: an opinion poll showing that two-thirds of the British public believed that Blair had misled them on Iraqi W.M.D., and a full-page piece by none other than Andrew Gilligan, which, for the first time, identified the person who had ordered the dossier to be "sexed up." The headline read, "I asked my intelligence source why Blair misled us all over Saddam's weapons. His reply? One word . . . CAMPBELL."

Later that day, Campbell confided to his diary, "It is grim for me, and it is grim for TB. And there is this huge stuff about trust." On Tuesday, June 3rd, he wrote Blair a lengthy memo, advising him on how to respond at his weekly Prime Minister's Question Time. "The current frenzy flows from the fact that apart from the 2 mobile labs nothing new has been found," Campbell noted. "Everything stems from that, so tomorrow is in part about saying as much as you can about the process towards discovery—who is involved, what sort of numbers, where are they searching, who are they interviewing, how are we verifying."

At this stage, nobody in the government knew that Gilligan's source was David Kelly. Gilligan had reported that his information came from an official in charge of drawing up the dossier, which pointed to a very senior person. Campbell spoke to John Scarlett, who insisted that reports about unhappiness within the intelligence agencies weren't coming from the top. Campbell accepted Scarlett's assurances, but others in Blair's circle were not so sure. John Reid, who was then the leader of the House of Commons, suggested that "rogue elements" in the security services might be trying to undermine the government.

·   ·   ·

The BBC—or the Beeb, as it is often referred to—was founded in 1922 by a group of radio manufacturers, and has since developed into the world's leading public-service media company, employing around twenty-five thousand people and providing news and entertainment through four mediums: television, radio, the Internet, and print. It is an independent organization, but it operates under a state charter and is financed by a mandatory license fee. When Margaret Thatcher and the Tories were in power, serious consideration was given to breaking up, or even privatizing, the BBC, but that threat vanished with Blair's election. One of his historic missions, as he saw it, was to demonstrate that big public-sector organizations, such as the BBC and the National Health Service, could thrive in a market-driven economy. In 2001, Blair appointed Gavyn Davies, a former partner at Goldman Sachs, to the chairmanship of the corporation. Davies's wife works for Gordon Brown, the Chancellor of the Exchequer. Conservative critics accused Blair of hiring a crony, but fears that the BBC would pander to the government turned out to be misplaced.

In the run-up to the 2001 election, which Labour won easily, many observers thought that the BBC did a better job of criticizing the government than the Conservative Party did. During the war in Afghanistan, Downing Street complained furiously that the BBC exaggerated civilian casualties. An essential component of Alastair Campbell's media-management strategy was to respond immediately to anything he perceived as slanted or inaccurate. One "Today" producer received so many letters of complaint that he used them to decorate his office.

When the invasion of Iraq began, Campbell peppered Richard Sambrook, the head of BBC News, with letters, including several about Andrew Gilligan's reporting from Baghdad. "Can you tell me who told him the Republican Guard hasn't been damaged—the Iraqi Ministry of Information?" Campbell asked in one missive. He mocked a suggestion by Gilligan that Uday Hussein had been "reined in a bit" by the regime, commenting, "Uday *is* in large part the regime. Has Mr Gilligan ever met or seen him?"

Undoubtedly, the BBC covered the war more critically than the American networks did. Before the fighting began, BBC reporters repeatedly warned of heavy civilian casualties. When these failed to materialize, they switched their attention to chaos and looting. On April 11th, in a live report that prompted yet another complaint from Campbell, Gilligan said, "People here may be free, but they're passing their first days of freedom in more fear than they've ever known before." He went on, "Fear that their property's going to be invaded, their daughters will be raped, and they'll be killed."

One of the BBC's own defense correspondents complained about its reporting from Iraq, but his comments didn't have much impact. The BBC had a dozen reporters on the ground, and its editors argued that they were merely reporting what they were witnessing. After the war ended, Greg Dyke, the BBC's chief executive, forcefully defended its coverage, comparing the BBC favorably with Fox News, which he accused of "gung-ho patriotism."

Such arguments didn't impress Campbell. On June 6th, he wrote a private letter to Sambrook, in which he demanded to know whether Gilligan's story about the dossier had breached the BBC's producer guidelines, which say that program-makers should be reluctant to rely on only one source. The BBC's coverage of the W.M.D. issue "has been driven for days now by the false claim of a single uncorroborated source that Gilligan claims to be reliable," Campbell asserted. He concluded, "You will, I imagine, seek to defend your reporting, as you always do. In this case, you would be defending the indefensible."

Sambrook's reply to Campbell was somewhat disingenuous. "We have not suggested that the forty-five-minute point was invented by anyone in Downing Street against the wishes of anyone in the intelligence community," he wrote. "We have suggested that there are pertinent and serious questions to be asked about the presentation of the intelligence material." On June 16th, after Campbell had written to Sambrook again and asked whether the BBC was going to launch an internal inquiry into how Gilligan's story got on the air, Sambrook suggested that Campbell should take his grievance to the BBC's Programme Complaints Unit, which deals with complaints from ordinary viewers and listeners. For the moment, Campbell couldn't do much about this snub. Gilligan's source still hadn't emerged. Until he did, there was no way for independent observers to judge who was telling the truth.

·　　·　　·

David Kelly didn't listen to Gilligan's broadcasts. On May 29th, he was at the United Nations headquarters visiting the offices of UNMOVIC, the United Nations weapons-inspection agency that succeeded UNSCOM. At midmorning, East Coast time, Gavin Hewitt, a correspondent for BBC television's "Ten o'Clock News," called him from London to follow up the "Today" story. Hewitt had no idea that Kelly was Gilligan's source; he had obtained his cell-phone number from a former colleague who recommended him as an expert on Iraq's W.M.D. Kelly showed no sign of being nervous, and, once Hewitt had assured him that the conversation would be on a non-attributable basis, he talked openly. When Hewitt asked for his over-all opinion of the September dossier, Kelly replied, "No. 10 spin came into play." The material that the intelligence services provided was "fundamentally reasonable," he went on, but it had been presented "in a very black-and-white way."

The following day, when Kelly arrived back in England, he received a call from another BBC television journalist, Susan Watts, the science editor of "Newsnight," a current-affairs show that appears five nights a week. Watts had interviewed Kelly many times before, on stories ranging from the training of U.N. inspectors to the anthrax attacks in the United States. As recently as early May, they had been talking about the September dossier and Kelly had mentioned Alastair Campbell in conjunction with the forty-five-minutes claim. Watts didn't report Kelly's remarks at the time—she later described them as a "gossipy aside"—but when she heard about the "Today" story she suspected that Kelly was its source.

This time, Watts recorded her conversation with Kelly. The tape, which didn't emerge until August, when Lord Hutton started holding hearings, begins with Kelly discussing his trip to New York. Watts then brings up the "Today" program, the forty-five-minutes claim, and their previous conversation, saying, "I may have missed a trick on that one"—meaning that she might have missed a story. Kelly laughs. He tells Watts that he has also spoken with Gavin Hewitt, but he doesn't mention Gilligan and he doesn't appear concerned about being identified as the source of any damaging stories. "I mean, they wouldn't think it was me, I don't think," he says. "Maybe they would, maybe they wouldn't. I don't know."

Watts asks Kelly whether it is true that the government was advised not to include the forty-five-minutes claim in the September dossier. Kelly replies, "There were lots of people saying that. I mean, it was an interesting week before the dossier was put out because there were so many things in there that people were saying: Well, we're not so sure about that. Or, in fact, they were happy with it being in, but not expressed the way that it was. Because, you know, the wordsmithing is actually quite important; and the intelligence community are a pretty cautious lot, on the whole."

The main problem with the dossier, Kelly goes on, is its implication that Iraq possessed a "vast arsenal," which wasn't what the experts believed. "The real concern that everyone had, it was not so much what they"—the Iraqis—"have now but what they would have in the future," Kelly says. "But that, unfortunately, wasn't expressed strongly in the dossier, because that takes away the case for war, to a certain extent."

Toward the end of the tape, Watts presses Kelly on who transformed the dossier. Referring to their previous conversation, she asks Kelly if he can confirm that Alastair Campbell was responsible for the inclusion of the forty-five-minutes claim. "No, I can't," Kelly says. "All I can say is the No. 10 press office. I've never met Alastair Campbell." Then he goes on, "But I think Alastair Campbell is synonymous with that press office, because he is responsible for it."

· · ·

It is not clear from Watts's tape whether Kelly knew that he was the source of the "Today" story. As the dispute between the government and the BBC escalated, he visited the Middle East on a reconnaissance mission, which included several days at Baghdad International Airport, where the Iraq Survey Group was establishing a forward base. He bunked down in a vermin-infested bungalow with three walls, half a roof, and no running water. An American officer showed him a couple of mobile laboratories that the coalition forces had discovered, but Kelly quickly dismissed the possibility that these were designed to manufacture biological weapons. He later told his daughter Rachel that he was disappointed not to have spoken to any "real Iraqis."

On Tuesday, June 17th, Martin Howard, the Deputy Chief of Defence Intelligence at the Ministry of Defence, attended a cocktail party at the headquarters of MI5, the domestic security service, where he ran into Patrick Lamb, a friend of Kelly's at the Foreign Office. Lamb remarked that Kelly had told him a couple of weeks previously that he had spoken to Andrew Gilligan and Susan Watts. Hitherto, Kelly's colleagues hadn't suspected him of being involved in the "Today" story, assuming, like most people, that the source was a senior official at one of the intelligence agencies. Howard reported his conversation with Lamb to Sir Kevin Tebbit, the permanent under-secretary at the Ministry of Defence. In normal circumstances, Kelly would probably have been hauled in immediately. However, the ministry was already investigating who in the department had given Gilligan access to a top-secret report casting doubt on the links between Iraq and Al Qaeda. Kelly, it turned out, was also a suspect in that investigation. (He was later cleared.) The ministry decided to hold off on any further action in case it prejudiced the ongoing inquiry.

While the government was trying to discover the origin of Gilligan's story, the House of Commons Foreign Affairs Committee was holding televised hearings about the decision to go to war. On June 19th, Gilligan, who had steadfastly defended his reporting, appeared before the committee. He described his source as an official "quite closely connected with the question of Iraq's weapons of mass destruction." A few days later, Olivia Bosch, Kelly's friend at the Royal Institute of International Affairs, told him to look at Gilligan's testimony, because some of it seemed familiar to her. On the evening of June 25th, Kelly and Bosch spoke by telephone, and Kelly agreed that some of the things Gilligan had attributed to his source, such as the fact that

Iraq's W.M.D. programs were modest, sounded like things he might have said. At this stage, Kelly either was misleading his friend or still hadn't realized that he was the source of Gilligan's story. He told Bosch that in order to clear his own mind he was thinking of telling his superiors he had met Gilligan.

Kelly's family had started to notice that something was preying on him. Janice Kelly thought that he seemed preoccupied and withdrawn. One evening, he said he was going to the Hind's Head pub, at the other end of the village, where he sometimes played cribbage. About forty minutes later, he returned and said he had gone for a walk instead, "to think something through." Janice thought he might be worrying about her health. "It is not you," Kelly assured her. "It is a professional thing."

At least one of Kelly's former colleagues believes that Kelly knew all along that he was the source of the "Today" story. "He was no fool," the person told me. "He knew this was a politically charged subject. He knew he wasn't supposed to speak to Gilligan in those terms, but he believed the dossier was exaggerated. Then, when Gilligan embellished what he had said, he found himself trapped."

On Monday, June 30th, Kelly sent a letter to his immediate superior at the Ministry of Defence, Bryan Wells, in which he admitted meeting Gilligan "to privately discuss his Iraq experiences and definitely not to discuss the dossier." Kelly went on:

> The issue of 45 minutes arose in terms of the threat (aerial versus land launch) and I stated that I did not know what it refers to (which I do not). He asked why it should be in the dossier and I replied probably for impact. He raised the issue of Alastair Campbell and since I was not involved in the process (not stated by me) I was unable to comment. This issue was not discussed at any length and was essentially an aside. I made no allegations or accusations about any issue related to the dossier or the government's case for war.

Turning to the "Today" story, Kelly continued:

I can only conclude one of three things: Gilligan has considerably embellished my meeting with him; he has met with other individuals who truly were intimately associated with the dossier; or he has assembled comments from both multiple direct and indirect sources for his articles.

Kelly's letter arrived at the ministry on July 1st. On Friday, July 4th, Wells and Richard Hatfield, the director of personnel at the Ministry of Defence, interviewed Kelly. As Hatfield went through Gilligan's testimony to the Foreign Affairs Committee, Kelly conceded that some of the things the BBC reporter attributed to his source sounded like him, but he strenuously denied being the source of the "sexing up" allegations. He failed to mention that he had also talked to Gilligan's BBC colleagues Gavin Hewitt and Susan Watts. At the end of the interview, Hatfield said that barring further revelations he was satisfied Kelly was not Gilligan's primary source, and he would not pursue any disciplinary action. As far as Wells was concerned, the Gilligan matter had now been dealt with.

Kelly apparently knew better. The following day, he went to Oxford, where his daughter Rachel lives, and met her for lunch. He was so quiet that when Rachel got home she told her fiancé she was worried. Kelly had plenty to be concerned about. Throughout his professional life, he had been known as a rigorous scientist who chose his words carefully and valued the truth above all. As a weapons inspector, he had earned an international reputation by catching the Iraqis out in their lies and deceptions. Now he was the one prevaricating.

·   ·   ·

One of the notable things about the Kelly saga is how each of its three main characters unwittingly unleashed forces that ultimately proved devastating to them all. When Kelly went to the Charing Cross Hotel, he had no reason to believe that the meeting was anything other than a routine background talk with a reporter. When Gilligan put out his story, he can't have imagined that it would cause such a stir. And when Campbell tore into Gilligan and the BBC he had no conception of how his attack would rebound.

On June 25th, Campbell appeared at a televised hearing of the Foreign Affairs Committee. After delivering a lengthy if not very persuasive defense of the September dossier, he launched an impassioned assault on the BBC's reporting, declaring, "I simply say, in relation to the BBC story: It is a lie, it was a lie. It is a lie that is continually repeated, and until we get a public apology for it I will keep making sure that Parliament, people like yourselves, and the public know that it was a lie."

Even by Campbell's standards, this was an incendiary statement. Some critics suggested that it was intended to divert attention from the fact that still no Iraqi W.M.D. had been found. Perhaps it was, but Campbell was also displaying his obsessive streak. After his appearance, he recorded in his diary that he felt a lot better, because he had "opened a flank on the BBC." A couple of days later, he renewed his offensive, agreeing to a rare television interview, with Jon Snow, the presenter of "Channel 4 News," a competitor of the BBC. When Snow asked about the "sexing up" charges, Campbell reacted furiously, repeatedly jabbing his fingers in the journalist's face. People who had known Campbell for years had rarely seen him so angry. Some of them worried that he might be losing his perspective.

Even Blair, who until now had seemed untroubled by Campbell's aggressive tactics, was concerned. Like Campbell, the Prime Minister believed the only thing that would correct the impression that he had misled the public about Iraq was an unequivocal statement from the BBC that Gilligan's story was wrong. But Blair had now come to the conclusion that the dispute with the BBC was interfering with his efforts to shift the political agenda to home affairs, and that it was time to move on. The day after Campbell's television interview, Blair told him to leave the fight with the BBC for the Foreign Affairs Committee to resolve.

On Thursday, July 3rd, Blair travelled to northwest England, where he had arranged to deliver a major speech setting out his domestic agenda, which included reforming public education and the National Health Service. But he couldn't leave the BBC controversy behind. Jonathan Powell, his chief of staff, called from London to inform him of Kelly's letter, which Geoff Hoon, the Minister of Defence, had just learned about. The Prime Minister advised caution, saying that the Ministry of Defence should deal with the matter according to its usual personnel procedures.

Campbell and Hoon displayed a greater sense of urgency. Contrary to Gilligan's report, Kelly was not "one of the senior officials in charge of drawing up that dossier." His involvement with the dossier had been limited. If these discrepancies were made public, the BBC reports would be at least partly discredited. On Friday, July 4th, the same day Kelly was questioned, Campbell and Hoon spoke at length. "GH said that his initial instinct was to throw the book at him"—Kelly—"but in fact there was a case for trying to get some kind of plea bargain," Campbell recorded in his diary. "Says that he'd come forward and he was saying yes to speak to AG, yes he said intel went in late, but he never said the other stuff. It was double-edged, but GH and I agreed it would fuck Gilligan if that was his source." (Hoon later claimed he didn't recall making some of the comments Campbell attributed to him.)

The BBC's governing board, which is supposed to monitor the corporation's activities, was scheduled to meet over the weekend to discuss Gilligan's story, and on the following Monday the Foreign Affairs Committee was due to publish its report about the decision to go to war. Campbell noted in his diary that he and Hoon wanted to approach both of these bodies immediately and let them know about Kelly's letter. On Saturday, July 5th, Campbell called Powell, who was mountain climbing in Wales, and said he was worried that the government would be accused of a coverup if it didn't tell the Foreign Affairs Committee that a possible source had emerged. The following day, Hoon repeated the message.

Powell called the Prime Minister, who was at Chequers, his country retreat. He had already been talking with Sir David Omand, the government's intelligence and security co-ordinator, who had received a memo about Kelly's interview from the Ministry of Defence, which said it was unclear whether Kelly was Gilligan's main source. The Prime Minister's political instincts are second to none. He didn't want to be accused of a coverup, but he also didn't want to lay himself open to the charge that he had overruled his most senior civil servants and leaked confidential information for political advantage. He decided that nothing further should be done until Kelly had been interviewed a second time and more was known about his dealings with Gilligan.

Campbell was increasingly frustrated. For weeks, he had been firing verbal fusillades at the BBC, to no avail. Now he finally had some live ammunition, but his boss had effectively ordered him not to use it. "GH"—Hoon—"said he was almost as steamed up as I was," he wrote in his diary. "TB said he didn't want to push the system too far. But my worry was that I wanted a clear win not a messy draw and if they presented it as a draw that was not good enough for us."

The BBC was standing by Gilligan and refusing to admit any errors. Its chairman, Gavyn Davies, was determined to assert the Beeb's independence. When the governors met, he kept them focussed on whether proper editorial procedures had been followed, rather than on the substance of Gilligan's allegations. After the meeting, the governors issued a resounding defense of the BBC, claiming that its coverage of the Iraq war had been impartial, and that "Today" had acted in the public interest in running Gilligan's story about the dossier.

It subsequently emerged that the governors' statement masked growing concern within the BBC about Gilligan's reporting. "This story was a good piece of investigative journalism marred by flawed reporting," Kevin Marsh, the editor of "Today," wrote to a colleague on June 27th. "Our biggest mill-stone has been his"—Gilligan's—"loose use of language and lack of judgement in some of his phraseology. It was also marred by the quantity of writing for other outlets that varied what was said or was loose with the terms of the story."

· · · ·

Blair knew nothing of these internal communications. To Down-ing Street, the public statement from the BBC governors was just another display of defiance. On Monday, July 7th, the Prime Minis-ter spoke with Davies, who again refused to consider withdrawing Gilligan's allegations. Then he met with his senior advisers in his "den"—a small office at the back of 10 Downing Street. The Foreign Affairs Committee had just issued a report concluding that "minis-ters did not mislead Parliament" in publishing the September dossier, and that Alastair Campbell did not "exert or seek to exert improper influence" on the dossier. However, the fact that the com-mittee had split along party lines, with the Labour majority insuring a favorable report for the government, meant that the media and the public were unlikely to accept its judgment as final.

One possibility that was discussed at the meeting was to have Kelly testify before a parliamentary committee and contradict Gilligan's report. Blair asked what was known about Kelly's views. Sir Kevin Tebbit, the permanent under-secretary at the Ministry of Defence, said that Kelly supported the war and believed Saddam had concealed some W.M.D., but he might have some discomforting things to say about parts of the dossier. Tebbit also pointed out that Kelly had come forward voluntarily and that there was no suggestion that he had breached the Offi-cial Secrets Act. As the meeting ended, Tebbit said he would arrange for Kelly to be re-interviewed at the first opportunity.

What to do about Kelly had somehow turned into the most

pressing issue facing the British government. The next morning, Tuesday, July 8th, Blair gave a typically accomplished performance when he appeared before the House of Commons Liaison Committee, a bipartisan body that questions him at length on all aspects of government policy. On returning to Downing Street, he met with Campbell, Powell, Tom Kelly, and three senior civil servants: David Manning, David Omand, and John Scarlett. Once again, the topic was Kelly.

Kelly's second interview, which had taken place the previous afternoon, had proved inconclusive, but Martin Howard, of the Defence Intelligence staff, who was there, received the impression that Kelly probably was Gilligan's source, even if he had been misrepresented. This information was passed along to the Prime Minister. With the agreement of his advisers, Blair decided it was time to announce that an official had come forward. He later defended the decision by saying that the news would almost certainly have leaked anyway, and the government would have been accused of a coverup. This explanation is hardly convincing. Under his leadership, Downing Street has proved remarkably adept at preventing leaks. Blair could have simply accepted Kelly's protestations that he wasn't Gilligan's source and declared the matter closed, but in that case the government would have missed its chance to discredit Gilligan's story, which Blair considered an indefensible attack on his personal integrity.

The Prime Minister and his colleagues didn't appear to know much about Kelly, beyond the fact that he was a government scientist who had contributed to the historical section of the dossier. There was some talk at the meeting about how he would handle the publicity, but, according to Blair's testimony before Lord Hutton, there was "nothing in the discussion that we had that would have alerted us to him being anything other than someone, you know, of a certain robustness, who was used to dealing with the interchange between politics and the media."

Once Blair and his colleagues had made their decision, the

question was how to release the news. Campbell favored issuing a statement naming Kelly and explaining that he had contradicted Gilligan's report, but he wasn't in charge. Omand suggested sending an open letter about Kelly to Ann Taylor, the chairman of the parliamentary Intelligence and Security Committee, thereby putting the onus on her to deal with the media, but when, during a break in the meeting, this idea was put to Taylor she balked. Blair then authorized the Ministry of Defence, which wasn't even represented at the meeting, to issue a press release.

Powell, Scarlett, and Campbell were among a group of officials who went into another office to draw up a draft. Kevin Tebbit, who was late for the meeting, took the draft back to the Ministry of Defence and worked on it further with officials there. When the statement was released, later that afternoon, it said, "An individual working in the MOD has come forward to volunteer that he met Andrew Gilligan of the BBC on May 22." It didn't name Kelly directly, but it provided enough information for anybody who knew him well to recognize the description: "The individual is an expert on WMD who has advised ministers on WMD and whose contribution to the Dossier of September 2002 was to contribute towards drafts of historical accounts of UN inspections. . . . He is not a member of the Intelligence Services or the Defence Intelligence Staff." The Ministry of Defence press office also told reporters that it would confirm the official's identity if the correct name was put to it. Despite subsequent denials from all concerned, this maneuver appears to have been designed to get Kelly's identity into the public domain without the government officially releasing it.

Kelly was driving from R.A.F. Honington, in East Anglia, where he had been training for his return to Iraq, when Richard Hatfield, the director of personnel at the Ministry of Defence, called to read him the press release. Hatfield told Lord Hutton that Kelly reacted with calm resignation, but Janice Kelly gave a very different story. When Kelly got home, at about 7 P.M., she was interviewing some people for the local historical society. After she finished, she and

Kelly ate dinner and switched on the evening news. The fact that a possible source had come forward in the Andrew Gilligan row was one of the top stories. Kelly turned to Janice and said, "It's me."

According to Janice, Kelly said that his name was sure to emerge, as the press would quickly "put two and two together." He was "really, really unhappy about it," she told Lord Hutton. "Totally dismayed. He mentioned he had had a reprimand at that stage from the MOD but they had not been unsupportive, were his words. We talked a little bit generally about it and what it would mean for him in real terms. He was a bit backward in coming forward, may I say, in saying what he meant. I deliberately at that point said, 'Would it mean a pension problem, would it mean you having to leave your job?' He said it could be if it got worse, yes."

The next morning, the newspapers reported the Ministry of Defence statement and set about discovering the anonymous official's name. James Blitz, the political editor of the *Financial Times*, went to the daily press briefing at No. 10, where Tom Kelly described the official as a technical expert who worked for one department but was paid by another. (For obscure bureaucratic reasons, the Foreign Office paid Kelly, even though he worked primarily for the Ministry of Defence.) Armed with these clues, Blitz called a Whitehall source, who said that the official was being paid by the Foreign Office. Blitz rang the Foreign Office's press office, but it refused to help him. Eventually, he enlisted a colleague, Christopher Adams, who searched the Internet for government consultants with expertise in unconventional weapons. Among the search results, Adams found a list of participants in an international conference on chemical weapons. One of them was David Kelly, who was identified as a senior adviser to the Ministry of Defence. At about five-thirty, Adams called Pam Teare, the ministry's director of news, and asked if David Kelly was the right name. She said it was.

·　　·　　·

Kelly spent the afternoon in his vegetable garden. He told Janice he felt let down and betrayed. At three minutes past seven, Kelly's supervisor, Bryan Wells, called him on his cell phone and said the Ministry of Defence had released his name to reporters. Kelly didn't tell Janice immediately. He went to put his garden tools in the tool shed, which was next to the driveway. While he was at the front of the house, Nick Rufford, a reporter from the *Sunday Times*, pulled into the car park of the Wagon & Horses and walked across the road to speak to him.

According to Rufford, who had long suspected that Kelly was Gilligan's source, Kelly said he had just received a call alerting him to the fact that his identity had been made public. Kelly added that he was shocked that his name was coming out, saying, "I was told it would all be confidential." Rufford advised him to leave his house before he was besieged by journalists, telling him the *Sunday Times* would pick up his hotel bills. He also asked Kelly if he would write a story for the *Sunday Times*. Kelly said he would have to check with the Ministry of Defence press office. According to Rufford, the conversation was amicable and lasted about fifteen minutes.

Janice Kelly, however, who witnessed the encounter from the other end of the garden, told Lord Hutton that it lasted four or five minutes, at the end of which an angry Kelly said, "Please leave now." After Rufford departed, Kelly told her, his voice almost breaking, that he was to be named publicly that night. Rupert Murdoch, the owner of the *Sunday Times*, was offering to put them up in a hotel in return for his writing an article, he went on, but he had refused the offer, at which point Rufford had told him that the gloves were off.

Right after Rufford left, the Ministry of Defence press office called Kelly. By this time, journalists from the *Guardian* and the *Times* had obtained his name by a process of trial and error. (The defense correspondent of the *Times* put twenty names to the ministry before he got the right one.) After hanging up, Kelly told Janice they would have to leave immediately. They packed quickly, and within ten minutes or so were driving south toward the M4, a highway that goes from London to southwest England. A friend of Janice's owned a vacation home in Cornwall that was empty. During the drive, Kelly took a call from Olivia Bosch. He said to her, "I have cut and run."

. . .

After a sleepless night at a hotel in Weston-super-Mare, Kelly got up, ate breakfast, and read a story in the *Times* that described him as a middle-ranking official. Strictly speaking, this was true: Kelly had never been admitted to the top grades of the civil service. But he had advised ministers, represented his country abroad, and received the Order of St. Michael and St. George. In a filing cabinet in his study, he had an official letter telling him that he was being considered for another official honor.

The Kellys reached Cornwall around noon, and Kelly got upset again. Janice was unable to comfort him, she later recounted, and she decided that the best she could do was to keep him busy and well fed. Perhaps they could convert their enforced trip into a kind of holiday, she thought. After all, they hadn't been away together in a long time.

The Kellys' marriage, like many others, is hard to fathom. He didn't discuss his work with Janice; he rarely mentioned his conversion to Baha'i to her; and he was away a lot, sometimes in the company of female friends, such as Mai Pederson, an Arab-American military linguist, whom he had met in Iraq. One of Pederson's ex-husbands told a British newspaper that she was a spy working for American military intelligence, a charge she refutes. It was Pederson who introduced Kelly to the Baha'i faith, an offshoot of Islam that preaches the value of spirituality, truth, and universal peace. He spent time in Monterey, California, where she was attached to the Defense Language Institute, and it was there, in 1999, that he became a Baha'i. The *Mail on Sunday* uncovered evidence that Kelly had received mail at her homes in Alabama and West Virginia. After

Kelly's death, the Thames Valley Police interviewed Pederson, but the conversation added "nothing that was of relevance" to their inquiry, according to Michael Page, the Assistant Chief Constable. Mark Zaid, a Washington lawyer, issued a statement on Pederson's behalf denying that she and Kelly had a romantic attachment.

Kelly kept pieces of his life in different compartments, and, clearly, he was unable to unburden himself to his wife. The next morning, Friday, July 11th, they went to see the Lost Gardens of Heligan, a popular tourist attraction, but, according to Janice, Kelly was so withdrawn that he hardly seemed to notice the plants and flowers. He took several calls, including one from Bryan Wells, who told him that he had been asked to appear the following week before both the Intelligence and Security Committee and the Foreign Affairs Committee, with the latter hearing to be televised. According to Wells, Kelly took the news stoically, saying, "If I am asked, I will do it." His wife remembers things differently. She said Kelly went "ballistic" after learning that he would have to appear on television. "He just did not like that idea at all," she told Lord Hutton. "He felt it— he did not say this in so many words, but he felt it would be a continuation of a kind of reprimand in the public domain."

The decision to have Kelly testify before the Foreign Affairs Committee had been taken at the highest levels. On July 10th, Jonathan Powell, Blair's chief of staff, sent an e-mail to Alastair Campbell and other senior officials saying, "Tried PM out on Kelly before FAC and ISC next Tuesday. He thought he probably had to do both but need to be properly prepared beforehand. I passed this on to MOD." Tom Kelly replied, "This is now a game of chicken with the Beeb—the only way they will shift is if they see the screw tightening." The one obstacle to Kelly's appearing before the committees was Sir Kevin Tebbit, who pointed out that the Foreign Affairs Committee had already completed its report. "A further reason for avoiding two hearings, back to back, is to show some regard for the man himself," Tebbit wrote to Geoff Hoon. "He has come forward voluntarily, is not used to being thrust into the public eye, and is not on trial." Tebbit's objections were overruled, and Kelly was dispatched to appear before both committees.

On Sunday, July 13th, Kelly travelled from Cornwall to Oxford, where he had arranged to stay for a few nights with his daughter Rachel, away from the media. When he arrived, his appearance shocked Rachel. "There was a lot of distress and anxiety, perhaps a bit of humiliation," she said at the Hutton inquiry. "He was seeing his daughter for the first time since all this news about his work had broken, and I was just very surprised. He almost—he did not seem quite like a broken man, that is probably too strong a term, but he was certainly very distressed."

Tuesday, July 15th, the date of the Foreign Affairs Committee hearing, was Kelly's thirty-sixth wedding anniversary, but Janice had remained behind in Cornwall. Kelly took the nine-fifteen train to London. A bomb scare in Parliament Square meant that he had to walk part of the way to the House of Commons and fight his way through a media scrum. The hearing room was warm and stuffy, but Kelly kept his jacket on as he sat before the television cameras. The previous day, he had met with Bryan Wells and Martin Howard, of Defence Intelligence, to discuss what he would say. Kelly had said he would stick to the line that the government's over-all Iraq policy was a matter for ministers. He had asked whether he could also say that he didn't believe he was Gilligan's primary source, to which Howard had replied that he should follow his conscience.

Kelly was a highly intelligent man who took pride in his powers of analysis. He must have known that the main reason he had been sent to Westminster was to discredit Gilligan and provide support for an embattled government. But if he criticized Gilligan's reporting too sharply Gavin Hewitt or Susan Watts might well come forward and defend a BBC colleague. Watts, in particular, could have pointed out that Kelly had twice told her that the September dossier was transformed at the behest of the Downing Street press office.

Understandably, Kelly was cautious. In a voice so soft that he was asked three times to speak up, he described the dossier as a fair representation of the available evidence, and said Gilligan's broadcast was "not a factual account of my interactions with him." Asked whether he was the source of the allegation that Alastair Campbell was responsible for "sexing up" the dossier, he replied, "I cannot recall using the name Campbell in that context. It does not sound like a thing that I would say."

Several M.P.s said Kelly's testimony did not convince them that Gilligan's story had originated with him. Kelly agreed, saying, "I do not believe I am the source." This wasn't what Downing Street wanted to hear, but it won Kelly the sympathy of some members of the committee. Sir John Stanley suggested that Kelly had been thrown to the wolves. Andrew Mackinlay said, "I reckon you are chaff. You have been thrown up to divert our probing. Have you ever felt like a fall guy? You have been set up, have you not?" Kelly refused to be drawn by these provocateurs. "I accept the process that is going on," he told Mackinlay.

The first time Kelly appeared unnerved was when David Chidgey, a Liberal Democrat M.P., asked him about his dealings with Susan Watts. Kelly replied that he had met her on one occasion. Chidgey then read out a lengthy quote:

> In the run-up to the dossier the government was obsessed with finding intelligence to justify an immediate Iraqi threat. While we were agreed on the potential Iraqi threat in the future there was less agreement about the threat the Iraqis posed at the moment. That was the real concern, not so much what they had now but what they would have in the future, but that unfortunately was not expressed strongly in the dossier, because that takes the case away for war, to a certain extent.

Chidgey paused, and then read out another quote:

> The 45 minutes was a statement that was made and it got out of all proportion. They were desperate for information.

They were pushing hard for information that could be released. That was one that popped up and it was seized on and it was unfortunate that it was.

When Chidgey had finished, he turned to Kelly and said, "I understand from Ms. Watts that this is the record of a meeting you had with her. Do you still agree with those comments?" Kelly hesitated. "I do not recognize those comments, I have to say," he said awkwardly. Later in the hearing, Richard Ottaway, a Conservative M.P., read parts of the same quote, pointing out that Watts had used it in a report on "Newsnight." Again, Kelly seemed taken aback. "It does not sound like my expression of words," he said. Ottaway pressed him further, saying, "You deny that those are your words?" Kelly replied, "Yes."

Some British journalists believe that these exchanges contain the key to Kelly's death. When he heard his own words read back to him, they argue, he must have realized that his double game—the practice of saying one thing to reporters and another to his superiors—was over. Chidgey had stated live on television that Susan Watts had identified Kelly as the source of her "Newsnight" report. Once Kelly's bosses realized that he had misled them about his contacts with Watts, he would be exposed as a leaker and a liar.

It is a plausible theory, but the evidence supporting it isn't overwhelming. When the hearing ended, Bryan Wells, who had escorted Kelly, congratulated him on his performance. Kelly seemed greatly relieved that his public ordeal was over. Although he had to testify the following day before the Intelligence and Security Committee, the hearing would be held in private. That evening, he spoke with Olivia Bosch. He told her that the questions about the Susan Watts quote had thrown him, but his tone seemed curious rather than alarmed. "Is that the kind of thing I could have said all in one long go?" Bosch recalls him asking.

Kelly also mentioned the Susan Watts quote to his sister, Sarah Pape, who called to find out how he was doing. He added that he had been heartened that a number of friends and colleagues had offered their support. Pape, who is a plastic surgeon, often deals with car-crash victims and other injured people who have suicidal thoughts. In the weeks following this conversation with her brother, she anguished over whether she had missed anything. But she doesn't think she did. "He certainly did not convey to me that he was feeling depressed; and absolutely nothing that would have alerted me to the fact that he might have been considering suicide," she told Lord Hutton.

The next day, Kelly answered questions before the Intelligence and Security Committee with no reporters or cameras present. After the session ended, he seemed to have regained some peace of mind. He told a colleague that the pressure associated with the hearings had been worse than his Ph.D. orals. He also spoke with Bryan Wells about his upcoming trip to Iraq, and they agreed to a tentative departure date of Friday, July 25th, which was just nine days away. In the evening, when Rachel met him at Oxford station, he seemed much more talkative than he had been. He said he was eager to return to Southmoor, so he could do some work on his computer. Rachel persuaded him to stay for dinner. Janice Kelly arrived in Oxford from Cornwall at about eight-thirty. After having dinner with Rachel and her fiancé, Kelly and Janice loaded their bags into his car. Rachel promised to visit Kelly the following evening. During the journey to Southmoor, Kelly didn't say much. When he got home, he went into his study and downloaded some e-mails. Then he went to bed.

.　　.　　.

On Thursday, July 17th, Kelly got up at about eight-thirty, had breakfast, and went into his study. Andrew Mackinlay, from the Foreign Affairs Committee, had asked the Ministry of Defence to list all the journalists Kelly had met during the previous two years, including Andrew Gilligan, and to supply the dates and purposes of these meetings. In addition, the clerk of the committee had asked Kelly to catalogue all his contacts with journalists, not just meetings. At 9:22 A.M., Kelly sent an e-mail to a colleague, Wing Commander John Clark, who had agreed to collate his replies and pass them on to Bryan Wells for approval. In response to Mackinlay, Kelly named five journalists besides Gilligan that he had met: Jane Corbin and Tom Mangold, of the BBC; Nick Rufford, of the *Sunday Times;* Alex Nicoll, of the *Financial Times;* and Philip Sen, of *The Engineer.* In reply to the clerk of the Foreign Affairs Committee, Kelly provided a list of twenty-four reporters, noting it was "essentially a list of those journalists that I have business cards for or have recorded in my electronic contacts list." The names included "Susan Wells, BBC," an apparent typo, but they didn't include Gavin Hewitt.

At about ten o'clock, Kelly spoke with Clark. He said that he was holding up all right, although his wife had taken things badly and was upset. They talked about Kelly's return to Iraq and confirmed the departure date. "Dr Kelly was very keen to get back to Iraq to support the ISG," Clark told Lord Hutton. After the conversation, he booked Kelly a flight. Kelly also spoke with Olivia Bosch, whom he called to ask for a reporter's name. Bosch got the impression that Kelly was considering adding more contacts with journalists to his lists. "I think I am just going to mention all of them," he told her.

Shortly before noon, Janice went into the study to show Kelly some photographs. He hadn't quite finished. Some senior officials at the Ministry of Defence had suggested restructuring his contacts list to distinguish one-on-one interviews from casual encounters and phone calls. Kelly made the changes, and sent them to Clark. He also spent some time replying to friends and colleagues who had sent him supportive e-mails. Judith Miller, of the New York *Times,* had written to him the previous evening, "David, I heard from another member of your fan club that things went well for you today. Hope it's true. J." Kelly wrote back, "I will wait until the end of the week before judging. Many dark actors playing games. Thanks for your support. I appreciate your friendship at this time. Best, David."

The phrase "dark actors playing games" has attracted a lot of attention, but there is no way of telling what Kelly was referring to. After his death, some of his friends initially refused to believe that he had committed suicide, but the physical evidence seems incontrovertible. Still, most of the e-mails Kelly sent suggest that he was looking forward to the coming weeks. "Many thanks for your thoughts," he wrote to one colleague. "It has been difficult. Hopefully it will all blow over by the end of the week and I can travel to Baghdad and get on with the real work." In all, Kelly sent eight e-mails, six of which referred to his upcoming departure for Iraq. At the Hutton inquiry, Keith Hawton, a professor of psychiatry at Oxford University who is one of Britain's leading experts on suicide, was asked about Kelly's state of mind when he wrote these messages. "A logical conclusion would be that he was not thinking of suicide at that time," Hawton replied.

Of course, Kelly may have been keeping his innermost thoughts to himself. He must have known that, even if he returned to Iraq, he wouldn't necessarily be able to put the Gilligan affair behind him. Earlier that morning, the Ministry of Defence had forwarded Kelly copies of four more parliamentary questions, in which Bernard Jenkin, who was then the Conservative spokesman on defense, had demanded to know if his dealings with Gilligan had breached government regulations, and if the Ministry of Defence would be taking disciplinary action against him. The deadline for answering these questions was not until September 8th.

At about twelve-thirty, Janice saw Kelly sitting alone in the living room, something he rarely did. She made some sandwiches, but when they sat down to eat Kelly said hardly anything. In Janice's testimony to Lord Hutton, she said that he looked like a man with a broken heart, but added that she had no idea that he might be considering doing himself harm. She wasn't feeling well herself, and she decided to go upstairs and lie down. Kelly said that he would probably go out for his afternoon walk, and returned to his study.

Wells had by then authorized a final version of Kelly's answers to the first set of parliamentary questions. However, shortly after two, Peter Watkins, the private secretary to the Minister of Defence, called Wing Commander Clark and requested some last-minute changes, including more details about Kelly's contacts with Susan Watts. Just before three, Janice came downstairs and saw Kelly talking on the phone. Clark had called him to discuss what to include about Watts. The news that the Minister of Defence's private office had zeroed in on his contacts with Watts can hardly have been reassuring news to Kelly. He and Clark agreed to say, "He met with Susan Watts (BBC) following his presentation at the Foreign Office Open Day on the 5 November 2002. Other than those noted above, Dr Kelly does not have records of contacts with journalists." No mention was made of Kelly's lengthy conversations with Watts in May. Minutes after hanging up with Clark, Kelly put on his jacket and walked out the door. Janice, who had gone back upstairs, didn't hear him leave.

·   ·   ·

The summer of 2003 in Britain was one of the hottest and driest on record. Hyde Park turned brown, and the temperature at Heathrow Airport reached a hundred degrees for the first time in a century. On Monday, August 11th, in this strangely tropical atmosphere, Lord Hutton started taking evidence about the circumstances surrounding Kelly's death. When Tony Blair's motorcade arrived at the Royal Courts of Justice on the morning of Thursday, August 28th, the protesters were waiting for him with posters—"WANTED: Bush and Blair for War Crimes," "Bliar, Bliar, Iraq's on Fire"—and chants: "Tony, Tony, Tony: Out! Out! Out!" Nick Buxton, a thirty-one-year-old Web-site manager, was wearing a Pinocchio nose.

"The problem is the Hutton inquiry looks at only part of the picture," he told me. "It's turned into a row between the BBC and the government. That's not the point. The point is, was the war justified and has it led to the things they said it would?"

For more than two hours, Blair answered questions put to him by James Dingemans, Q.C., Lord Hutton's senior counsel, a strapping former rugby player. "I do not think we need an introduction," Dingemans began. "May I start with the dossiers?" After six and a half years in power, Blair, at fifty, has gray hair above his ears and deep lines on his forehead. (In October, he was briefly hospitalized for an irregular heartbeat.) He said that the September dossier described the available evidence "in a way that was perfectly justified," and insisted that he had been unaware of any unhappiness in the intelligence agencies about its contents. He also stressed how seriously he had taken Andrew Gilligan's claim that the government had deliberately misled the public, saying, "Had the allegation been true, it would have merited my resignation." He denied deliberately leaking Kelly's identity, although on this he was uncharacteristically vague, averring, "It was an extremely difficult and unusual set of circumstances."

After the Prime Minister left the witness stand, Andrew Grice, the political editor of the *Independent*, commented to me that he had "got off easy." That may be true, but Kelly's death concentrated public anger about the war in Iraq and gave it a human focus. As Blair's motorcade departed, the early edition of the *Evening Standard* was reporting, "50th British Soldier Killed in Iraq as Mob Opens Fire with Guns and Grenades." Twenty-four hours later, Alastair Campbell announced his resignation, saying that he had been planning to leave for some time. Downing Street promptly unveiled an overhaul of its media operation, which was clearly designed to project the image that it was putting spin behind it.

More than seventy witnesses testified at the inquiry. They included former colleagues of Kelly's, family members, journalists, police officers, pathologists, medics, intelligence experts, Downing

Street officials, Cabinet ministers, and an expert on the Baha'i faith. Every so often, Lord Hutton, who spent twenty years locking up suspected terrorists in Northern Ireland, would interrupt and, in his aristocratic accent, ask a question. If he liked the answer, he would nod. If he didn't, he would stare at the witness over his half-moon spectacles and emit a long and strangulated "Yeeee-es."

Gilligan was among the first witnesses. Under questioning from Dingemans, he conceded that some of the language in his May 29th broadcasts, especially the earlier one, "was not perfect." Gilligan also admitted that it was he, and not Kelly, who first uttered the phrase "sexed up"; Kelly merely repeated back to him the phrase that launched a thousand headlines. The reporter's standing was further tarnished when it emerged that it was also he, and not Susan Watts, who alerted David Chidgey to Watts's "Newsnight" report and suggested that Kelly must be the source. "That's it!" an excited BBC reporter, who doesn't work for "Today," exclaimed to me when this snippet emerged. "Gilligan killed Kelly by shopping him to the Foreign Affairs Committee."

Gavyn Davies, the BBC's chairman, didn't fare much better. Try as he might, the doleful former investment banker couldn't explain why the BBC had failed to retract at least some of Gilligan's claims. However, the BBC's discomfort was small consolation to the government, which suffered one embarrassment after another as it struggled to justify its treatment of Kelly. On the last day of the hearings, in the middle of October, Sir Kevin Tebbit confirmed that the trail led all the way to Blair, pointing out that the Prime Minister had presided over the crucial meeting, in Downing Street on July 8th, where the decision to identify Kelly was made.

Two of the most dramatic moments came when Sir John Scarlett and Sir Richard Dearlove, the head of MI6, who is officially known only as "C," emerged from secrecy to answer Dingemans's questions. Both of them insisted that the compilation of the September dossier had been perfectly proper, but they also revealed some damning information. Dingemans asked Dearlove, who gave his testimony from a remote location, with only an audio feed into the courtroom, whether the dossier had given undue prominence to the forty-five-minutes claim:

DEARLOVE: Well, I think given the misinterpretation that was placed on the forty-five-minutes intelligence, with the benefit of hindsight you can say that is a valid criticism. But I am confident that the intelligence was accurate and that the use made of it was entirely consistent with the original report.

LORD HUTTON: Would you just elaborate what you mean by the misinterpretation placed on the forty-five-minutes claim?

DEARLOVE: Well, I think the original report referred to chemical and biological munitions, and that was taken to refer to battlefield weapons. I think what subsequently happened in the reporting was that it was taken that the forty-five minutes applied, let us say, to weapons of a longer range.

This exchange surely demonstrates that Gilligan was right when he reported that the dossier had been "sexed up," and that Kelly was right when he told Gavin Hewitt, "No. 10 spin came into play." Iraqi battlefield weapons loaded with chemical and biological warheads, even if they did exist—and none have been found—presented no threat to the stability of the Middle East, still less to Britain and the United States. Documentary evidence provided to the inquiry demonstrated that senior people inside Downing Street knew the evidence about Iraqi W.M.D. was weak. Shortly before the dossier was published, Jonathan Powell, Blair's chief of staff, sent an e-mail to John Scarlett saying, "The document does nothing to demonstrate a threat, let alone an imminent threat, from Saddam. . . . We will need to make it clear in launching the document that we do not claim that we have evidence that he is an imminent threat." This warning had been ignored.

Where Gilligan and Kelly went wrong was in asserting that the dossier was transformed against the wishes of the intelligence agencies. In fact, the people in charge of the agencies went along with Downing Street's deception. Kelly, whose intelligence contacts were fairly low-level, had no way of knowing this. Unfortunately, he had to die for the full truth to emerge.

Lord Hutton's report is expected next month. If it blames Blair for Kelly's death, the Prime Minister might well be forced to resign, but such an assignation of responsibility seems unlikely. Ultimately, Kelly took his own life, for reasons that may never be entirely clear. "I still can't understand it, because he was so excited about going back to Iraq," one of his friends told me. "This was the culmination of ten years of hard labor. This was his life's work." Some people who knew Kelly think that the whole story of his death has yet to be told. "This was a man who reduced Dr. Germ, the Iraqi anthrax expert, to tears in an interrogation," James Bone, the London *Times* journalist who broke the story of Kelly's friendship with Mai Pederson, told me. "He was not somebody to buckle under media pressure, unless there was something else going on. There must be some other explanation." It recently emerged that Kelly's mother also killed herself, in 1964, following a stroke, a fact that may or may not be significant.

Blair is still trying, without much success, to persuade the British public that he and President Bush, who visited London last month, did the right thing. Despite the unpopularity of his Iraq policy, he isn't in any immediate peril. The next election doesn't have to be held until the spring of 2006, and the opposition Conservative Party, which recently changed its leader, is in poor shape. But the Prime Minister may never regain his reputation as an honest and straightforward man. A man lining up to get into the Hutton inquiry said of Blair, "If he told you the time, you'd check your watch."

GQ

FINALIST, ESSAYS

The Vulgarian in the Choir Loft

"The Vulgarian in the Choir Loft," by Andrew Corsello, begins with an amusing autobiographical history by a self-described boor, then evolves into a beautifully written and hilarious piece on the physical pleasure and redemptive power of singing in a church choir. Corsello is not, he insists, religious, but finds spiritual nourishment in singing without really repudiating his inner lout. It's as if a bear had danced a gorgeous pas de deux.

Andrew Corsello

The Vulgarian in the Choir Loft

The strange but true tale of one man's pilgrimage from jerkdom to choirboy. Proof once again that music soothes the foul beast? Well, let's not go too far.

I was an unpleasant child, not well liked. Bitter, odd, quick to coldcock. On the playground I hit hard and hit first. In church I pocketed change from the collection plate. On the soccer field, my bag of dirty tricks inspired parents (opponents', teammates', and, once, even my own mother) to yell for my ejection. When it came to my peers, two refrains—"You're so immature" and "You have a *dirty mind*"—soundtracked my childhood.

When it came to my elders, I didn't so much seek to question their authority as to terrorize it, and on more than one occasion employed my own poop in this cause.

Once, after pounding another third grader after she mucked up the simple right-hand piano part of "The Entertainer," I was sent to a counselor. I liked this woman. She understood that for whatever reasons, I was a person who could make sense of things and people only by placing myself in opposition to them, a person whose unerring default mode was: "*Pfthwehh!*" She was one of the few adults I didn't enjoy lying to. "What do you want to be when you grow up?" she once asked, and I actually told her: a military dictator, known and feared throughout the world, who spends his days ordering smarter, more attractive, more popular people to perform humiliating monkey tricks for his amusement. All of it televised, of course.

She pondered this. "Better to be known for something, even if that something is bad, than not to be known at all, hmmmm?"

"Yes, ma'am."

"Oh, Andy," she sighed, "you'll never be a choirboy, will you?"

.   .   .

Picture a choirboy in your mind's eye, if you will: the little white smock and the beaming upturned face and the mouth opened obediently into pretty little *ooooooos* and *ahhhhhs*. A haloed, ineffectual figure. Sugary. Does what he's told. Exists not for himself but for the group. Strains his voice of idiosyncrasy, makes of it a clean light-filled beam, then offers it up to somebody else, says in effect, "Use me, I'm yours." In my youth, choirboys of all stripes struck me as somehow . . . Soviet, creepily self-abnegating. The uncut descendants of castrati—those boys who in centuries past had their very vitality hacked off for the sake of harmonizing with others.

Become a choirboy? Please. Instead, I took the foul clay of my immaturity and my dirty mind and molded it into a self. After a number of decades I grew, somewhat, to like this self. It is disarming and alarming and it gravitates toward the graphic, all of which has made and maintained me as a magazine writer—a profession for loners and poop-flingers if ever there was one. Ninety-nine percent of the time the poop sticks to what it hits, most often with amusing results. When it doesn't and the results are not amusing, it is still useful, because it signifies the presence of something holy.

I married a priest, by the way.

·   ·   ·

An episcopalian. I found her irresistible because she was the most peaceful and certain, the most *called* person—and thus the most incomprehensible—I had ever met. (And because she was hot.)

When Dana was 10, her cousin ran away for two weeks. Several days into the search, Dana underwent a clarifying moment. As she sat with her aunt and uncle, beholding their terror and grief, words suddenly appeared in her brain, sure as Scripture.

I will never cause such pain. I will be . . .good.

Not just to act, but to *be* good, from within. An astonishing ambition, because merely "acting" good is not good at all, but goody, a justification by works rather than faith. And this girl—who came from an unchurched family, and who quarterbacked her school's football team (in *Texas*) until the seventh grade, at which point officials decided this was an unholy thing—was no goody. Yet from age 10 on, Dana did it: inhabited a childhood, then a teenhood, then an adulthood, that were the photographic negatives of the 'hoods in which I'd chosen to grow up. A real choirgirl, Dana.

During our first few years together, a presumption emerged to explain how a skank such as myself could sustain a commitment to a woman of the cloth. My contradictory needs to be good enough for her on the one hand, and to corrupt her on the other, created a tension, the story went—a tension from which a strong and sustaining current flowed. ("Baby, you put the ho' in holy!" I told her on the day of her ordination; "I will pray for you now," she responded with a kind smile.) According to this story, my loogie-hawking ways were not only permissible but imperative—our relationship would wither without them—and I found a certain spiritual affirmation in the frequent observation of friends that "he married a priest, yes, but he's still a pig."

But then one day, the choirmaster of her church, a trim, sharp-eyed man with a shaved head and a look of intense bemusement, put a hand in the small of my back and spoke in a confidential tone.

"Andrew," he said, "I would like you to sing in the parish choir from now on. I feel it will . . . enhance your worship."

A shrill reflexive thought: *My worship—ha!*

Another: *Don't get sucked in, dude.*

Then this: "Sure. Tell me what to do."

Where did these words come from? I had no ambition to sing. In fact, I've always loathed the sound of my own voice, both singing and speaking. No character, no muscle. Whenever I hear it on tape, or played back over an answering machine, the timbre sounds clotted and froggy, as if a gremlin has distilled all my existential discomfort and tightness to a gluey sediment, then painted it onto my tonsils. I feel I'm listening to somebody trying to pass himself off as smarter than he is. Such a tight-jawed voice. A pre-infarction voice.

And when, by way of my wife, I'd duly begun attending church, I'd discovered a truly peculiar something: The incantations of the liturgy (Nicene and Apostles' Creeds, Lord's Prayer, psalms, etc.) sounded both more sincere and more meaningful if I delivered them in somebody else's voice. Out of "my own" mouth, "And on the third day he rose again" bore a damp fatigue. I might as well have been reciting the ingredients off the back of a shampoo bottle. But out of, say, Christopher Walken's mouth, with his odd emphases on conjunctions and articles (with an extortionist's irritability: "*And* forgive us our trespasses"), they became electric and new. How odd: I could attain sincerity—could overcome my journalist's refusal to take anything at face value; to approach anything with straight-ahead, earnest *belief*—only with somebody else's voice. Even the old prayer for faith inspired by the Book of Mark ("Lord, cure me of my unbelief . . ."), which I began invoking before going to bed at night, passed more meaningfully through my soul when uttered in the voice of a goitrous plumber.

And now I had agreed to take this voice and amplify it, publicly, into singing.

· · ·

What is singing? Voice coaches often try to demystify it, call it a mere vibration of vocal cords due to a movement of air. But that is a lie. Singing is nakedness. And it is a far more fathomless form of nakedness than that achieved by the removal of clothes. Anyone who watched the early tryout-phase episodes of *American Idol* knows this—knows, in fact, that those episodes featured some of the most graphic violence ever seen on network television. Not physical violence, of course, but psychological, which scars more deeply. For every two talented candidates, the show's producers would throw a freakishly tin-eared aspirant before the judges. To juice the spectacle, they'd air interview footage of the contestant bearing their witness—"Singing is my destiny, my soul . . ."—before cutting to the audition, in which he or she would stand unaccompanied before the panel and, in essence, cough up a turd. Inevitably, the most pornographic moment—and it *did* register like pornography; one found it irresistible at the same time one knew that it was probably bad for humanity—occurred in the dead space between the end of the "performance" and the beginning of the judging. The contestant would stand beaming, expectant, innocent; the more tin-eared the performance, the greater the innocence. And then it would begin: "You are *ghastly*. You have *no talent*. There *cannot possibly* be a worse singer in all of New York . . ." As the camera zeroed in—the smile losing tensile strength, the dawning awareness that this wasn't a joke, that millions were watching—I kept thinking, *I have never seen such human nakedness. People shouldn't be so naked.* I kept thinking, too, of the Christians in the Colosseum. A bit melodramatic, but the analogy holds: their hymn singing— the pure expression of what they considered their destiny, their souls—as the animals tore the meat from their bones, followed by the mocking laughter of the spectators.

To be honest, my reaction to *American Idol* wasn't so Christian. Or rather, it passed through several stages before arriving at sympathy. I think this has to do with a certain cultural presumption, or demand, that applies to singing as to no other field of endeavor except, perhaps, writing. As a friend of mine now taking voice lessons puts it, "If you tell somebody you're going off to learn to play the guitar or the piano, they say, 'That's nice, it must be hard.' But with singing, it's, 'Can you sing?' They think you must be on an ego trip, that the only reason you're doing it is that you think you're 'good.'" Indeed, before I found *Idol* horrifying, I found it *satisfying*. Heartbreaking as those deluded kids were, their public evisceration aroused in me, and, I'm sure, in other viewers, a deep predatory instinct to expose and destroy true believers, pretenders—anyone who would dare to rise above the rest of us lumpen. There *is* in each of us a bit of that feudal lord from *Monty Python and the Holy Grail* who shrieks *"STOP THAT!"* whenever his ebulliently gay son attempts to sing. Or as my friend studying voice puts it, "The point of that show isn't singing. It's silence."

When I asked Mark Whitmire, my choirmaster and the director of music at St. James's Episcopal Church in Richmond, Virginia, about the violent nudity of *Idol,* he responded with a question: "Do you get nervous when you play the piano in church?" (I am a recreational pianist who sometimes does the 'ludes—preludes and postludes—at church services.) Yes, I said, I get nervous—but not nearly so nervous as when I sing. Which is odd, since the piano work is solo and the singing work is choral. Odder still, given that I've got a lot of ego tied up in being known as a good piano player, and none in being known as a singer of any merit.

"If a person plays a piano badly, you think there's something wrong with their piano playing," he said. "If a person sings badly, there's something wrong with *them*. There's not that divorce between what they are and what they are doing."

When I explained the fear singing instills in me to Deborah Lapidus, who teaches singing to actors at both Juilliard and New York University's Tisch School of the Arts, she explained it further. "Your Steinway sounds like your Steinway regardless of whether you're sad or happy, or whether or not you stayed up all night smoking. But when you are your own instrument, it gets very emotional. There's nowhere to run and nowhere to hide. That's why the things [*Idol* panelist Simon Cowell] says seem so violating. He's not telling these kids they're poor musicians or that they selected a bad song. He's saying, '*You* are ugly. Your *soul* is ugly.'" And then she added something truly provocative: "To do singing right, you have to get in touch with something deeply personal about yourself. It is almost impossible . . . to *lie* when you sing."

· · ·

The St. James's Parish Choir, in which I have spent the past year as a bass, rehearses every Thursday night for two hours. On Sunday we bring it. Of the five choirs run by Mark Whitmire and his wife, Virginia, who serves as St. James's organist, ours is the most "sober"—a strict diet of Bach, Britten and Barber. (Another adult choir handles the Beatles, Dave Matthews and Ziggy Marley oeuvres.) It's difficult music, requiring time at the piano with my scores during the week, and a crystalline efficiency on the part of the Whitmires come Thursday.

Virginia, who sits at the piano, often functions as a spiritual guide. "You sound as if you don't believe a word you're singing," she'll say. (Or if she feels compelled to drop a bomb: "You're singing like the *congregation*.") Her approach is lyric, impressionistic, and I have found that when replaying in my mind the things she has said about a piece of music, her words have the properties more of singing than of talking. Mark, on the other hand, is the Don Corleone of choirmasters, a man who does not ask but—gently, always gently—tells; a man so calmly confident in his own mastery that a person to whom he makes his wishes known always feels beseeched, never instructed. He is imbued, spookily willful. There is within and about him a strange and glorious motion, a kind of ongoing fugue, which one never quite knows how to prepare for or guard against. After not seeing you for a week, he will wheel around a corner, take your arm and say not "hello" but "As a fellow head-shaving man, Andrew, I know you understand that . . ." The ellipsis beginning the conversation unnerves. *What did I forget? Did we speak of this before? Are we speaking of it now? I'd . . . better do what he wants.*

Mark thinks anatomically. (He studied biology and physiology before becoming a music major.) He almost always introduces us to music in a strategic, rather than linear, way—starting off the altos on page 11 of a magnificat because "that is where the musical DNA of this piece lies." He is a creature of exactitude whose mind I visualize as a series of excellent knives: a scalpel when paring the twang from our southern vowels; a putty knife when caressing our long notes into pleasing, pregnant shapes. He is the kind of guy who can get away with saying things like "That was good, tenors, but now you need to make it more elfin and fey."

Though Mark meticulously plans days in advance how long he will rehearse a given passage, the deliciousness of the music often causes him to linger.

"Hold the second beat of measure 59!" he'll command, to emphasize the fleeting sand-grit frisson of a D sounding against a D-sharp. Once we're out of breath, he'll smile knowingly. "Now tell me who has the coolest note."

The altos?

"The altos indeed! Now do it again!"

And again, and again, and again, we'll give him what he wants, until the angry chromatic buzz of D fighting D-sharp alters the barometric pressure of the room—seemingly generates an *aroma* he can savor—and he declares, "That's as much fun as I can afford to have there. Let's move on!"

Needless to say, I find the Whitmires to be terribly contagious people. They are consumed. They make no bones about the fact that they regard their work as not only important but urgent, yet nothing about them seems the least bit self-important.

"It basically comes down to *essences,* our carnal and spiritual selves, and trying to touch what is outside the fleshly realm," Mark says when I ask why we sing what we sing. "I can't tell you exactly what that is, but I know it when we do it, as surely and clearly as I can see the slate gray sky or smell fresh-brewed coffee." When I ask the more elemental question—"Why does the human animal sing?"—he just smiles and says, "Because it can't stop."

These sentiments, their loveliness and intensity, are a bit startling and alien to a person such as myself, whose adult aesthetic—whose job requirement, even—largely involves cultivating the inability to take anything, including himself, seriously. (I am, in the end, a fat boy whose vanity plate reads 6 PK ABS.) My brain has long been dipped in the deconstructionist's notion that everything a person feels, says or does is received, unoriginal. This mental template is not without value. I can suss out fakers and fops as reflexively as I blink. But it often makes me more smart than thoughtful, and it leaves me dumb and abashed in the presence of belief that is absolute, and absolutely good. The Whitmires'. My wife's. And its limitations are never more obvious than when my college buddies ask me, as they inevitably do, "So do you believe in 'God' now, choirboy?" and I quip, meaninglessly and inanely, "Dude, that is a *stupid* question."

·　　　·　　　·

So yes, dude, it's true: I revere my choir. Of course, it freaked me out at first. I felt like the sausage-fingered vulgarian at a formal dinner who has no idea what all those forks are for; to compensate, I sat up very straight, sang very quietly and spoke to nobody. Eventually, though, I came to learn what a curious collection of individuals I was harmonizing with. Among the tenors and baritones are a pharmacist, an alternative rock musician and a conservative lawyer. Across from them in the alto section is a woman who married a death-row inmate (now, after retrial, a lifer); another is a multilingual Jewish auto mechanic. Laced throughout the basses and sopranos are a hairstylist, a state-budget analyst, an architect (another Jew!) and a collegiate music student we refer to as the Bird, as well as a smattering of housewives, retirees and FFVs.[1] Were it not for the choir, my encounters with this lot would in all likelihood be of a passing nature; there would be no argot, no human traction. (In fact, many of these people, had I met them thirty years ago, I surely would have beaten up.) Instead, I'll be spending ten days of my hard-earned vacation time with them this summer, singing in residence at Gloucester Cathedral in England.

Even so, many of us remain largely unknown to one another. The only reason I'm aware of so-and-so's conservatism or so-and-so's feminism is that my wife has told me. To a degree that might seem odd given current events, nobody talks politics in the choir room. There's no explicit taboo. It's more that upon entering the singing space, one clicks into a mental gear in which it simply never occurs to a person to engage in everyday polemics. Everything but the music, and the fellowship intrinsic to its making, is irrelevant.

So it is that my choir has trained me in ways I could never have anticipated. It has underlined for me, by way of contrast, the fact that I have spent the past three decades dedicating myself almost exclusively to solo pursuits (exhibit A: the byline on this piece) and,

---

[1]An acronym for First Families of Virginia.

in turn, have regarded these pursuits not as *essences,* not as intrinsically worthy things, but as means. Means of competing. Means of acquiring recognition. Means of kicking ass. The ambition has always been for *voice*—not just to acquire it, but to impose it. In a way, my job is but a refined and slightly less violent version of my childhood fantasy of one-man dictatorship; a license to subvert whatever and whoever comes before me, including myself.

But this indulgent, soloing voice of mine, which seeks to spread its scent onto everything it touches, is an instantly and entirely mute one in the choir room. Thankfully and blessedly so. I did not know how much I was longing to lose my voice until church singing systematically stripped me of it. Such an odd notion: losing one's voice in order to sing; singing in order to lose one's voice.[2] But there is simply something therapeutic about resolving to be a lamb, surrendering to the Whitmire brain and then disappearing into it—and into the furling sound produced by twenty-five other men and women. At times, when everyone is not only nailing the centers of his and her notes but listening to everyone else nail theirs, one is able to both hear and see the structure of a piece. There is a contradictory sense of existing in two places at one time, of being both unearthly and rooted, *in one's place.* The feeling this brings—humble, guileless, supplicating—leads me to believe that the prayer Mark Whitmire leads before each rehearsal is not only a spiritual necessity but a musical one. In it, I feel I am finally and willingly heeding the admonition, issued on every report card I ever received as a child, that "Andy must learn to get along with other children."

.   .   .

There is a physical component to this. I hesitate to say so, because it somehow feels a bit breathless, a bit unmanly, a bit . . .

---

[2] "For those who want to save their life will lose it, and those who lose their life for my sake, and for the sake of the Gospel, will save it."—Mark 8:35.

elfin and fey, to maintain that singing makes you feel good. But dammit, *singing makes you feel good.* It *is* revivifying.

Sometimes when I sing (surely the most elfin and fey word combination in the English language), I can slip through the skin of the music I'm making and into a pocket on the other side, a numb space in which I can observe in real time the mechanical workings of my own body. (You can also attain this state in a bath if you lie very still with your ears below water level; once the water ceases to ripple, your hearing will slowly penetrate your innards; first you will hear your heart and then, beneath its thumpings, the mad careening of blood through the pipes.) Specific notes have specific locations in the hollows and solids of the torso, and if I pay attention, I can feel my own sound leaping from one place to another as it rises and falls. The low F vibrates at my gravitational center. The E-flat below it hovers at the forward edge of the spine. D and D-flat rattle the hardened glue of the sternum. And C and B, on those rare occasions I can hit them, reside all the way down; B is an angry taloned thing that grips what oughtn't be gripped in public. One should have the decency not to hit a B in church.

Which is all to say that frequent singing tunes you to your physical aspect in a way that makes you think, strangely, *My body was present all along and I never even knew it.* There is an awareness of some essential, long-forgotten organ roused from dormancy—a sense of how physically *unnatural* one's life was prior to singing. Mark Whitmire tells me that from a singing point of view, babies and young children breathe perfectly: from the diaphragm, and with the correct carriage of throat, nose and mouth. (Which is why they can scream at the top of their lungs for an hour without ravaging their throats.) "If you line up a bunch of 4-year olds and tell them to breathe deep, they breathe low, and fully—like singers should," he says. "Do it with a bunch of 7-year-olds and they heave their chests into a kind of military posture and then breathe high and shallow; by that age, they've internalized our culture's discomfort with protruding bellies"—and forgotten what comes naturally. It's only a matter of time before they've bought into the corrosive *American Idol*–ish notion that singing is the stuff of, well, idols, rather than a birthright. "I have never met a person who I thought was born tone-deaf," adds Deborah Lapidus. "It is an acquired disability."

I know from my own profession that the same pattern exists in the realm of writing. Most people who claim they "can't write" don't suffer from a lack of talent; they suffer from a lack of license. Way back when, some tyrannical fifth-grade English teacher insisted that they couldn't possibly write a story until they'd mastered spelling and cursive. From then on they remained shackled to the notion that when it comes to writing there is, out there in the ether, a "correct answer," and that if one doesn't have the technical expertise to attune one's natural voice to that imaginary *thing,* one is simply "ungifted" and should give up. The truth is that when done right, the struggle to be a good writer—and a good singer—is a struggle not to be good but to be *free.* Which is why a number of fellow choir members I have interviewed claim the greatest gift the Whitmires give their singers is not musical know-how, but *permission.*

I am tempted to call the bodily self-awareness that singing brings—the conviction I have after choir practices that my lungs are robust and glowing ruby red, that my flesh has temporarily been made honest—an ushering into virtue. But then I remember that some of the greatest boobs of recent memory—Christina Aguilera, John Ashcroft—are singers. So I will hold my tongue.

Instead, I will mention the fact that as of this writing, Mark Whitmire—a man who claims his greatest talent is the ability to look into a person's eye and divine not only whether, but *what,* that person needs to sing—has scheduled me to lead the congregation in a Lenten psalm. The match of cantor and psalm—*Create in me a clean heart, O God*—is clearly no coincidence.

I pray it works.

Esquire

WINNER, FICTION

The Red Bow

This story, economical yet fully realized, is perfectly calibrated to the Esquire *audience. "The Red Bow" grippingly evokes a dark moment when hysteria takes hold of a small town.*

George Saunders

The Red Bow

Next night, walking out where it happened, I found her little red bow.

I brought it in, threw it down on the table, said: My God my God.

Take a good look at it and also I'm looking at it, said Uncle Matt. And we won't ever forget it, am I right?

First thing of course was to find the dogs. Which turns out, they were holed up back of the—the place where the little kids go, with the plastic balls in cages, they have birthday parties and so forth—holed up in this sort of nest of tree debris dragged there by the Village.

Well we lit up the debris and then shot the three of them as they ran out.

But that Mrs. Pearson, who'd seen the whole—well she said there'd been four, four dogs, and next night we found that the fourth had gotten into Mullins Run and bit the Elliotts' Sadie and that white Muskerdoo that belonged to Evan and Millie Bates next door.

Jim Elliott said he would put Sadie down himself and borrowed my gun to do it, and did it, then looked me in the eye and said he was sorry for our loss, and Evan Bates said he couldn't do it, and would I? But then finally he at least led Muskerdoo out into that sort of field they call the Concourse, where they do the barbecues and whatnot, giving it a sorrowful little kick (a gentle kick, there was nothing mean in Evan) whenever it snapped at him, saying Musker Jesus!—and then he said *okay, now* when he was ready for me to do it, and I did it, and afterwards he said he was sorry for our loss.

Around midnight we found the fourth one gnawing at itself back of Bourne's place, and Bourne came out and held the flashlight as we put it down and helped us load it into the wheelbarrow alongside Sadie and Muskerdoo, our plan being—Dr. Vincent had said this was best—to burn those we found, so no other animal would—you know, via feeding on the corpses—in any event, Dr. Vincent said it was best to burn them.

When we had the fourth in the wheelbarrow my Jason said: Mr. Bourne, what about Cookie?

Well no I don't believe so, said Bourne.

He was an old guy and had that old-guy tenderness for the dog, it being pretty much all he had left in the world, such as for example he always called it *friend-of-mine*, as in: How about a walk, friend-of-mine?

But she is mostly an outside dog? I said.

She is almost completely an outside dog, he said. But still, I don't believe so.

And Uncle Matt said: Well, Lawrence, I for one am out here tonight trying to be certain. I think you can understand that.

I can, Bourne said, I most certainly can.

And Bourne brought out Cookie and we had a look.

At first she seemed fine, but then we noticed she was doing this funny thing where a shudder would run through her and her eyes would all of a sudden go wet, and Uncle Matt said: Lawrence, is that something Cookie would normally do?

Well, ah . . . said Bourne.

And another shudder ran through Cookie.

Oh Jesus Christ, said Mr. Bourne, and went inside.

Uncle Matt told Seth and Jason to trot out whistling into the field and Cookie would follow, which she did, and Uncle Matt ran after, with his gun, and though he was, you know, not exactly a runner, still he kept up pretty good just via sheer effort, like he wanted to make sure this thing got done right.

Which I was grateful to have him there, because I was too tired in mind and my body to know what was right anymore, and sat down on the porch, and pretty soon heard this little pop.

Then Uncle Matt trotted back from the field and stuck his head inside and said: Lawrence do you know, did Cookie have contact with other dogs, was there another dog or dogs she might have played with, nipped, that sort of thing?

Oh get out, get away, said Bourne.

Lawrence my God, said Uncle Matt. Do you think I like this? Think of what we've been through. Do you think this is fun for me, for us?

There was a long silence and then Bourne said well all he could think of was that terrier at the Rectory, him and Cookie sometimes played when Cookie got off her lead.

.   .   .

When we got to the Rectory, Father Terry said he was sorry for our loss, and brought Merton out, and we watched a long time and Merton never shuddered and his eyes remained dry, you know, normal.

Looks fine, I said.

Is fine, said Father Terry. Watch this: Merton, genuflect.

And Merton did this dog stretchy thing where he sort of like bowed.

Could be fine, said Uncle Matt. But also could be he's sick but just at an early stage.

We'll have to be watchful, said Father Terry.

Yes, although, said Uncle Matt. Not knowing how it spreads and all, could it be we're in a better-safe-than-sorry type of situation? I don't know, I truly don't know. Ed, what do you think?

And I didn't know what I thought. In my mind I was all the time just going over it and over it, the before, the after, like her stepping up on that footstool to put that red bow in, saying these like lady phrases to herself, such as Well Who Will Be There, Will There Be Cakes?

I hope you are not suggesting putting down a perfectly healthy dog, said Father Terry.

And Uncle Matt produced from his shirt pocket a red bow and said: Father, do you have any idea what this is and where we found it?

But it was not the real bow, not Emily's bow, which I kept all the time in my pocket, it was a pinker shade of red and was a little bigger than the real bow, and I recognized it as having come from our Karen's little box on her dresser.

No I do not know what that is, said Father Terry. A hair bow.

I for one am never going to forget that night, said Uncle Matt. What we all felt. I for one am going to work to make sure that no one ever again has to endure what we had to endure that night.

I have no disagreement with that at all, said Father Terry.

It is true you don't know what this is, Uncle Matt said, and put the bow back in his pocket. You really really have no experience whatsoever of what this is.

Ed, Father Terry said to me. Killing a perfectly healthy dog has nothing to do with—

Possibly healthy but possibly not, said Uncle Matt. Was Cookie bitten? Cookie was not. Was Cookie infected? Yes she was. How was Cookie infected? We do not know. And there is your dog, who interacted with Cookie in exactly the same way that Cookie interacted with the known infected animal, namely through being in close physical proximity.

It was funny about Uncle Matt, I mean funny as in great, admirable, this sudden stepping up to the plate, because previously—I mean, yes, he of course loved the kids, but had never been particularly—I mean he rarely even spoke to them, least of all to Emily, her being the youngest. Mostly he just went very quietly around the house, especially since January when he'd lost his job, avoiding the kids really, a little ashamed almost, as if knowing that, when they grew up, they would never be the out-of-work slinking-around uncle, but instead would be the owners of the house where the out-of-work slinking uncle etc etc.

But losing her had, I suppose, made him realize for the first time how much he loved her, and this sudden strength—focus, certainty, whatever—was a comfort, because tell the truth I was not doing well at all—I had always loved autumn and now it was full autumn and you could smell woodsmoke and fallen apples but all of the world, to me, was just, you know, flat.

It is like your kid is this vessel that contains everything good. They look up at you so loving, trusting you to take care of them, and then one night—what gets me, what I can't get over, is that while she was being—while what happened was happening, I was—I had sort of snuck away downstairs to check my e-mail, see, so that while—while what happened was happening, out there in the schoolyard, a few hundred yards away, I was sitting there typing—typing!—which, okay, there is no sin in that, there was no way I could have known, and yet—do you see what I mean? Had I simply risen from my computer and walked upstairs and gone outside and for some reason, any reason, crossed the schoolyard, then, believe me, there is not a dog in the world, no matter how crazy—

And my wife felt the same way and had not come out of our bedroom since the tragedy.

So Father you are saying no? said Uncle Matt. You are refusing?

I pray for you people every day, Father Terry said. What you are going through, no one ever should have to go through.

Don't like that man, Uncle Matt said as we left the Rectory. Never have and never will.

And I knew that. They had gone to high school together and there had been something about a girl, some last-minute prom-date type of situation that had not gone in Uncle Matt's favor, and I think some shoving on a ball field, some name-calling, but all of this was years ago, during like say the Kennedy administration.

He will not observe that dog properly, said Uncle Matt. Believe me. And if he does notice something, he won't do what is necessary. Why? Because it is his dog. *His* dog. Everything that's his? It's special, above the law.

I don't know, I said. Truly I don't.

He doesn't get it, said Uncle Matt. He wasn't there that night, he didn't see you carrying her inside.

Which, tell the truth, Uncle Matt hadn't seen me carrying her inside either, having gone out to rent a video—but still, yes, I got his drift about Father Terry, who had always had a streak of ego, with that silver hair with the ripples in it, and also he had a weight set in the Rectory basement and worked out twice a day and had, actually, a very impressive physique, which he showed off, I felt, we all felt, by ordering his priest shirts perhaps a little too tight.

Next morning during breakfast Uncle Matt was very quiet and finally said well he might be just a fat little unemployed guy who hadn't had the education some had, but love was love, honoring somebody's memory was honoring somebody's memory, and since he had no big expectations for his day, would I let him borrow the truck, so he could park it in the Burger King lot and keep an eye on what was going on over at the Rectory, sort of in memory of Emily?

And the thing was, we didn't really use that truck anymore and so—it was a very uncertain time, you know, and I thought: Well, what if it turns out Merton really is sick, and somehow gets away and attacks someone else's—so I said yes, he could use the truck.

He sat all Tuesday morning and Tuesday night, I mean not leaving the truck once, which for him—he was not normally a real dedicated guy, if you know what I mean. And then Wednesday night he came charging in and threw a tape in the VCR and said watch, watch this.

And there on the TV was Merton, leaning against the Rectory fence, shuddering, arching his back, shuddering again.

So we took our guns and went over.

Look I know I know, said Father Terry. But I'm handling it here, in my own way. He's had enough trouble in his life, poor thing.

Say what? said Uncle Matt. Trouble in his life? You are saying to this man, this father, who has recently lost—the dog has had trouble in his life?

Well, however, I should say—I mean, that was true. We all knew about Merton, who had been brought to Father Terry from this bad area, one of his ears sliced nearly off, plus it had, as I understood it, this anxiety condition, where it would sometimes faint because dinner was being served, I mean, it would literally pass out due to its own anticipation, which, you know, that couldn't have been easy.

Ed, said Father Terry. I am not saying Merton's trouble is, I am not comparing Merton's trouble to your—

Christ let's hope not, Uncle Matt said.

All's I'm saying is I'm losing something too, said Father Terry.

Ho boy, said Uncle Matt. Ho boy ho boy.

Ed, my fence is high, said Father Terry. He's not going anywhere, I've also got him on a chain in there. I want him to—I want it to happen here, just him and me. Otherwise it's too sad.

You don't know from sad, said Uncle Matt.

Sadness is sadness, said Father Terry.

Bla bla bla, said Uncle Matt. I'll be watching.

·　　　·　　　·

Well later that week this dog Tweeter Deux brought down a deer in the woods between the TwelvePlex and the Episcopal Church, and that Tweeter Deux was not a big dog, just, you know, crazed, and how the DeFrancinis knew she had brought down a deer was, she showed up in their living room with a chewed-off foreleg.

And that night—well the DeFrancini cat began racing around the house, and its eyes took on this yellow color, and at one point while running it sort of locked up and skidded into the baseboard and gave itself a concussion.

Which is when we realized the problem was bigger than we had initially thought.

The thing was, we did not know and could not know how many animals had already been infected—the original four dogs had been at large for several days before we found them, and any animal they might have infected had been at large for nearly two weeks now, and we did not even know the precise method of infection—was it bites, spit, blood, was something leaping from coat to coat? We knew it could happen to dogs, it appeared it could happen to cats—what I'm saying is, it was just a very confusing and frightening time.

So Uncle Matt got on the iMac and made up these flyers, calling a Village Meeting, and at the top was a photo he'd taken of the red bow (not the real bow but Karen's pinkish-red bow, which he'd color-enhanced on the iMac to make it redder and also he had superimposed Emily's Communion photo) and along the bottom it said FIGHT THE OUTRAGE, and underneath in smaller letters it said something along the lines of, you know, why do we live in this world but to love what is ours, and when one of us has cruelly lost what we loved, it is the time to band together to stand up to that which threatens that which we love, so that no one else ever has to experience this outrage again. Now that we have known and witnessed this terrific pain, let us resolve together to fight against any and all circumstances which might cause or contribute to this or a similar outrage now or at any time in the future—and we had Seth and Jason run these around town, and on Friday night ended up with nearly four hundred people in the high school gym.

Coming in, each person got a rolled-up FIGHT THE OUTRAGE poster of the color-enhanced bow, and also on these Uncle Matt had put in—I objected to this at first, until I saw how people responded—well he had put in these tiny teeth marks, they were not meant to look real, they were just, you know, as he said, symbolic reminders, and down in one corner was Emily's Communion photo and in the opposite corner a photo of her as a baby, and Uncle Matt had hung a larger version of that poster (large as a closet) up over the speaker's podium.

And I was sort of astonished by Uncle Matt, I mean, he was showing so much—I'd never seen him so motivated. This was a guy whose idea of a big day was checking the mail and getting up a few times to waggle the TV antenna—and here he was, in a suit, his face all red and sort of proud and shiny—

Well Uncle Matt got up and thanked everyone for coming, and Mrs. DeFrancini, owner of Tweeter Deux, held up that chewed-up foreleg, and Dr. Vincent showed slides of cross sections of the brain of one of the original four dogs, and then at the end I talked, only I got choked up and couldn't say much except thanks to everybody, their support had meant the world to us, and I tried to say about how much we had all loved her but couldn't go on.

Uncle Matt and Dr. Vincent had, on the iMac, on their own (not wanting to bother me) drawn up what they called a Three-Point Emergency Plan, which the three points were: 1) All Village animals must immediately undergo an Evaluation, to determine was the animal Infected, and 2) all Infected or Suspected Infected animals must be destroyed at once, and 3) all Infected or Suspected Infected animals, once destroyed, must be burned at once to minimize the possibility of Second-Hand Infection.

Then someone asked could they please clarify the meaning of "suspected"?

Suspected, you know, said Uncle Matt. That means we suspect and have good reason to suspect that an animal is, or may be, Infected.

The exact methodology is currently under development, said Dr. Vincent.

How can we, how can you, ensure that this assessment will be fair and reasonable though? the guy asked.

Well that is a good question, said Uncle Matt. The key to that is, we will have the assessment done by fair-minded persons who will do the Evaluation in an objective way that seems reasonable to all.

Trust us, said Dr. Vincent. We know it is so very important.

Then Uncle Matt held up the bow—actually a new bow, very big, about the size of a ladies' hat, really, I don't know where he found that—and said: All of this may seem confusing but it is not confusing if we remember that it is all about *This*, simply *This*, about honoring *This*, preventing *This*.

Then it was time for the vote, and it was something like 393 for and none against, with a handful of people abstaining, which I found sort of hurtful, but then following the vote everyone rose to their feet and, regarding me and Uncle Matt with—well they were smiling these warm smiles, some even fighting back tears— it was just a very nice, very kind moment, and I will never forget it, and will be grateful for it until the day I die.

.   .   .

After the meeting Uncle Matt and Trooper Kelly and a few others went and did what had to be done in terms of Merton, over poor Father Terry's objections—I mean, he was upset about it, of course, so upset it took five men to hold him back, him being so fit and all—and then they brought Merton, Merton's body, back to our place and burned it, out at the tree line where we had burned the others, and someone asked should we give Father Terry the ashes, and Uncle Matt said why take the chance, we have not ruled out the possibility of airborne transmission, and, putting on the little white masks supplied by Dr. Vincent, we raked Merton's ashes into the swamp.

That night my wife came out of our bedroom for the first time since the tragedy, and we told her everything that had been happening.

And I watched her closely, to see what she thought, to see what I should think, her having always been my rock.

Kill every dog, every cat, she said very slowly. Kill every mouse, every bird. Kill every fish. Anyone objects, kill them too.

Then she went back to bed.

Well that was—I felt so bad for her, she was simply not herself—I mean, this was a woman who, finding a spider, used to make me take it outside in a cup. Although, as far as killing all dogs and cats—I mean, there was a certain—I mean, if you did that, say, killed every dog and cat, regardless of were they Infected or not, you could thereby guarantee, to 100 percent, that no other father in town would ever again have to carry in his— God there is so much I don't remember about that night but one thing I do remember is, as I brought her in, one of her little clogs thunked off onto the linoleum, and still holding her I bent down to—and she wasn't there anymore, she wasn't, you know, there, there inside her body. I had passed her thousands of times on the steps, in the kitchen, had heard her little voice from everywhere in the house and why, why had I not, every single time, rushed up to her and told her everything that I—but of course you can't do that, it would malform a child, and yet—

What I'm saying is, with no dogs and no cats, the chance that another father would have to carry his animal-murdered child into their home, where the child's mother sat, doing the bills, happy or something like happy for the last time in her life, happy until the instant she looked up and saw—what I guess I'm saying is, with no dogs and no cats, the chances of that happening to someone else (or to us again) went down to that very beautiful number of Zero.

Which is why we eventually did have to enact our policy of sacrificing all dogs and cats who had been in the vicinity of the Village at the time of the incident.

But as far as killing the mice, the birds, the fish, no, we had no evidence to support that, not at that time anyway, and had not yet added the Reasonable Suspicion Clause to the Plan, and as far as the people, well my wife wasn't herself, that's all there was to it, although soon what we found was—I mean, there was something prescient about what she'd said, because in time we did in fact have to enact some very specific rules regarding the physical process of extracting the dogs and/or cats from a home where the owner was being unreasonable—or the fish, birds, whatever—and also had to assign specific penalties should these people, for example, assault one of the Animal Removal Officers, as a few of them did, and finally also had to issue some guidelines on how to handle individuals who, for whatever reason, felt it useful to undercut our efforts by, you know, obsessively and publicly criticizing the Five- and Six-Point Plans, just very unhappy people.

But all of that was still months away.

I often think back to the end of that first Village Meeting, to that standing-ovation moment. Uncle Matt had also printed up T-shirts, and after the vote everyone pulled the T-shirt with Emily's smiling face on it over his or her own shirt, and Uncle Matt said that he wanted to say thank you from the bottom of his heart, and not just on behalf of his family, this family of his that had been so sadly and irreversibly malformed by this unimaginable and profound tragedy, but also, and perhaps more so, on behalf of all the families we had just saved, via our vote, from similar future profound unimaginable tragedies.

And as I looked out over the crowd, at all those T-shirts—I don't know, I found it deeply moving, that all of those good people would feel so fondly towards her, many of whom had not even known her, and it seemed to me that somehow they had come to understand how good she had been, how precious, and were trying, with their applause, to honor her.

The New Yorker

FINALIST, PROFILE WRITING

Newshound

"Newshound," Calvin Trillin's anecdotally rich profile of prolific journalist R. W. Apple unveils a Falstaffian figure, a marvelously entertaining and sometimes maddening force of nature who has left an enduring mark on American letters.

Calvin Trillin

Newshound

The triumphs, travels, and movable feasts of R. W. Apple, Jr.

There is a consensus in the trade, I am pleased to report, that Johnny Apple—R. W. Apple, Jr., of the New York Times—is a lot easier to take now than he once was. Even Apple believes that. When I asked him not long ago about the paragraph in Gay Talese's 1969 book on the Times, "The Kingdom and the Power," which presents him as a brash young eager beaver, he said it was, alas, "quite an accurate portrait," although he doesn't recall boasting in the newsroom that while covering the war in Vietnam he had personally killed a few Vietcong—the remark that, in Talese's account, led an older reporter to say, "Women and children, I presume." In speaking of those early days, Apple said, "I was desperate to prove myself." You could argue, I suppose, that, in the words of a longtime colleague, "he doesn't have to argue the case anymore." In a forty-year career with the newspaper, he has been a political reporter whose stories at times seemed to set the agenda for a Presidential campaign; a war reporter who led the Times coverage in Vietnam for two years in the late sixties, and its coverage of the Gulf War a quarter of a century later; a foreign correspondent who has been in a hundred and nine countries (yes, he keeps a tally); the newspaper's premier writer of analytical pieces from Washington; and, these days, a wide-ranging writer on culture and travel and, especially, food. Of course, it's always possible that Apple's accomplishments are not, in fact, the principal source of his mellowing. There are any number of other theories about what might account for descriptions of the mature Apple that actually employ the word "endearing"—theories that include the possibility that we've simply grown used to him. "It's like having a big old Labrador dog," Jim Wooten, of ABC, said recently of Apple. "He knocks over the lamp with his tail. He slobbers on everything. But you still love him."

It is certainly true that Apple, at sixty-eight, could hardly be described as having shyly withdrawn from the spotlight. In a trade whose flamboyant characters are increasingly in short supply, he is still so widely discussed among reporters that Apple stories constitute a subgenre of the journalistic anecdote. Apple stories often portray R. W. Apple, Jr., checking into a hotel so staggeringly expensive that no other reporter would dare mention it on his expense account, or confidently knocking out a complicated lead story at a political convention as the deadline or the dinner hour approaches, or telling a sommelier that the wine won't do (even if the sommelier has brought out the most distinguished bottle in that part of Alabama), or pontificating on architecture or history or opera or soccer or horticulture. He still travels grandly and eats prodigiously. In Apple stories that take place in restaurants or hotels or even newsrooms, the verb used to describe his manner of entry is normally "swept in." Although people often find him charming, he is still capable of reducing a news clerk or a waiter or a campaign travel co-ordinator to tears now and then—like an ogre past his scariest days who just wants to keep his hand in. All in all, I can imagine that people who meet R. W. Apple, Jr., for the first time in his maturity might assume that some time-travel production of "The Man Who Came to Dinner" had managed to land Sir John Falstaff for the role of Sheridan Whiteside.

Physically, Apple is more noticeable than ever. He has a round face and a pug nose that give him a rather youthful appearance; a former colleague once said that when Apple flashes his characteristic look of triumph he resembles "a very big four-year-old." His form reflects the eating habits of someone who has been called Three Lunches Apple, a nickname he likes. Andrew Rosenthal, now the deputy editorial-page editor of the *Times,* once said that Johnny Apple had the best mind and the worst body in American journalism. Apple famously sees to his early-morning tasks—sending off a flurry of e-mails, perusing his investments, absorbing the newspapers—while encased in one of the brightly striped nightshirts made for him by Harvie & Hudson, of Jermyn Street, the same firm that makes his dress shirts, so that a house guest not yet fully recovered from a late night at the Apple table can be startled by the impression that a particularly festive party tent has somehow found its way indoors.

Apple's method of locomotion—which he accomplishes in short, almost dainty steps—has some resemblance to a man carefully steering a large stomach down a narrow path that is being cleared at that very moment by native bearers; it is easily mistaken for a swagger. He speaks with as much authority as he ever did, whether the conversation is on the foreign policy of John Foster Dulles or on which three zinfandels are the zinfandels worth drinking. To characterize the great man's speaking style, collectors of Apple stories often use the phrase "holding forth," although he is also, truth be told, someone who takes in just about everything everyone else in the conversation says and files it away in what Morley Safer, of CBS, who has been a friend of Apple's since they were in Vietnam together, calls "that Palm Pilot of a brain he has." On the whole, what Apple says while holding forth is considered by his friends worth listening to. The way Ben Bradlee, the former editor of the Washington *Post,* puts it is "I'd like to hear Apple on almost any subject, reserving the right to tell him he's full of shit."

. . .

Although sometimes years have passed between our meetings, I have kept vague tabs on R. W. Apple, Jr., for long enough to consider my observation of him a sketchy version of what social scientists would call a longitudinal study. I first encountered him in the spring of 1956, my junior year in college. I was then the chairman of the Yale *Daily News,* and Apple walked into my office to introduce himself as the chairman of the *Daily Princetonian.* It turned out to be a position he didn't hold long. A couple of months after he began to spend every waking hour at the *Prince,* he was booted out of Princeton, for the second time. By his standards, I have occasionally acknowledged to him, I failed to throw myself wholeheartedly into the job of running a college newspaper: I graduated.

Looking back, I realize that Apple differed from most of our contemporaries from places like Princeton and Yale who ended up in the trade, in that he'd always known that he wanted to be a newspaper reporter. In the mid-fifties, a trickle of undergraduate journalists moved resolutely from the Harvard *Crimson* toward the New York *Times,* but most people I knew who became reporters in those pre-Watergate days sort of backed in. They couldn't face law school, or the novel just didn't pan out, or they happened to be working for a magazine around the time they realized they were incapable of making a career decision.

Apple had known since he was thirteen, growing up in Akron, Ohio, not simply that he wanted to be a reporter but that he wanted to be a reporter for the New York *Times.* Having found the Akron *Beacon Journal's* coverage of the 1948 Olympics insufficiently detailed, he'd gone to the library to look up results in the *Times,* and decided on the spot that being paid for going to places that weren't Akron and writing about them was precisely the life he'd had in mind. Coincidentally, his skills could well have been designed for the *Times*. Some of his contemporaries who stood out at the paper—Talese, for instance, and David Halberstam and the late J. Anthony Lukas—found newspaper work confining, and left fairly early on to write books. For Apple, newspapering was in no way transitional; the *Times* news story seemed to be his natural form. "At an early age, he had a strong idea of what he wanted to be—an outsized romantic idea—and he was able to fulfill it," Tom Brokaw told me. "It isn't just that he found the right trenchcoat."

Perhaps because his dream actually came true, Apple had at the start—and still has—an enthusiasm for journalism and for the *Times* that is rare among reporters, most of whom like to grouse about their calling and look upon the organization they work for through narrowed eyes, the way they might look upon a press release from the State Department. It's not that he is shy about expressing his opinion of a *Times* editor who has done damage to his copy. But, in the words of the novelist Ward Just, a Vietnam pal who finds his friend's institutional loyalty admirable if somewhat puzzling, "He really is a *Times* man. He believes in the *Times*. You can't separate the two."

Apple's cultural interests also set him apart from most of his contemporaries in the trade. If he's in a European city for a political story or a Midwestern city searching for superior bratwurst, he is unlikely to leave before visiting a museum or inspecting a notable new building—a custom not followed, I'm in a position to say, by most reporters of his era. He is a student of history. Recalling Apple's writings in the *Times*, friends often mention, say, a piece on the Eugene McCarthy campaign which began with a quote from "Henry V" or a piece on Germany after the fall of the Berlin Wall which tossed in an evaluation of Haydn's place in Middle European music. When Apple was Washington bureau chief and thus required to attend by audio hookup the noon and four-thirty meetings held every day by the top editors in New York, he was known to pass the less scintillating moments of the discussion leafing through auction catalogues relevant to the collection of Arts and Crafts vases he has in his weekend house in Pennsylvania. Apple has a wide range of accomplished friends outside the worlds of journalism and politics, and he is up to carrying on, say, a serious discussion of architecture with James Stewart Polshek or a serious discussion of music with William Bolcom. "Johnny is such a flamboyant personality that people sometimes don't get the fact that underneath the occasional oratorical overkill there's a deep, fundamental knowledge," I was told by Howell Raines, who, when he was Washington bureau chief and again when he was executive editor, would have been Apple's boss if Apple went in for that sort of thing.

Apple once told me that his interest in music began in the Lutheran Church, where he heard Bach every Sunday, and some of his interest in art and architecture began while he was at Princeton. ("I didn't do very well by Princeton's lights, but I did very well by my lights.") The writer Jane Kramer, who lived in the same Upper West Side apartment building as Apple in the early sixties, when she was a graduate student and he was working at NBC on the Huntley-Brinkley program, says that he was the only one of her friends in those days whose idea of a good time was dinner at Le Pavillon and whose hobbies included collecting Old Master drawings. A range of interests that includes fine wine and elegant buildings may fit more gracefully on a portly fellow of Apple's years than it did on a hustling cub reporter. Speaking of Apple's air of being a cultivated man of the world, Joseph Lelyveld, a contemporary of Apple's who became the executive editor of the *Times,* has said, "I used to say that Johnny grew into the person he was pretending to be when we were young. Now I wonder whether he actually *was* that person then and the rest of us didn't know enough to realize it."

. . .

During Apple's early days on the paper, he was resented by his colleagues for getting plum assignments without going through the seven levels of purgatory then expected of new boys at the *Times*. To some people in the newsroom, his enthusiasm seemed indistinguishable from buttering up superiors. It didn't help that Apple's contemporaries on the paper were under the impression that he was making more money than they were. "Apple bragged he was being paid fifty dollars more than he actually was, which would have made him the highest-salaried reporter in the city room, except for Homer Bigart," Arthur Gelb, then the deputy metropolitan editor, writes in his forthcoming memoir, "City Room." (As Apple remembers it, he did get paid more than the others, the *Times* having matched his salary when he came over from NBC, and word spread through an overheard telephone conversation.) It probably also didn't help that Apple seemed not to notice the effect that all of this was having on his colleagues. "A cape buffalo is what a cape buffalo is," Jim Wooten told me, at which point I limited him to two animal images in discussing Apple. "It rambles through the brush. It eats what it wants to eat. It does whatever it wants to do, without knowing how much other animals resent it."

Early on, Apple was jumped over more senior reporters to become the *Times* bureau chief in Albany. "John had developed skills that none of us yet had," I was told by Sydney Schanberg, who was in the bureau, but "he needed training in socialization issues." One of the other reporters in the bureau was Doug Robinson, who became the city editor of the Philadelphia *Inquirer*. Robinson, now retired, would not be thought of as someone who always took a completely respectful view of people he worked for, having got into the habit at one point in his *Times* career of calling the executive editor a "borderline psychotic" and describing the managing editor, the second-in-command, as "a man who couldn't find kitty litter in a cat box." In Albany, Robinson recalls, Johnny Apple was resented partly for an air of superiority that was galling to the other reporters, "particularly when they realized, upon sober reflection, that he *was* superior. That was the part that was the hardest to take—that he was so damn good."

Robinson was the protagonist of what I'm tempted to call the authorized version of the most often told Apple story: State-house reporters who hung out at a local bar, having decided that their conversation was overly dominated by complaints about Johnny Apple, agreed that anyone who mentioned Apple's name would have to put a quarter in a drink fund—an agreement that made cocktail hour more soothing until, as Robinson recalled recently, "I came in, and I said, 'That son of a bitch! He's done it again!' And I pulled out a whole fistful of quarters, laid them on the table, and excoriated Apple for fifteen minutes."

Apple stories often come in multiple versions, and a lot of tales that may not be true have attached themselves to him, in the way that a lot of quotes have attached themselves to, say, Dorothy Parker or Yogi Berra. Correcting some of them recently, Apple said that it's not true that he conspired on his first honeymoon to book a cabin on a ship to Naples next to the cabin of the then publisher, Arthur (Punch) Sulzberger (Apple insists that the booking was coinciden-tal). He says he never owned part of a British football team and never chartered a plane to catch up with a political campaign after oversleeping, although he has chartered some planes in his time. It is not true that he once put in for a fur coat on an expense account from Iceland, or maybe Greenland, and, having had that item rejected, filed expenses for the same total again without mentioning the coat and attached a note saying, "Find it." (That's an old chestnut told about any number of foreign correspondents; Apple's coat was down, was bought inFinland, and was paid for by the *Times*.) It is not true that in the most recent political convention in Los Angeles he stayed in a suite at the Bel-Air while just about everyone else from the *Times* was at a charmless commercial hotel; he says that the room he stayed in at the Bel-Air, being decently commodious, may simply have given the impression of being a suite.

Apple now tells Apple stories on himself. In a speech at the Century Club not long ago, he said that when he arrived at Princeton he decided it might be advantageous to claim a home town with a bit more cachet than Akron ("just till I got my feet on the ground"), and chose one he'd seen mentioned in the golf results as the home of the Winged Foot Golf Club. Unfortunately, he had never heard the name of the place pronounced, and was thus able to set off great hilarity among a group of Eastern-boarding-school graduates—the sort that some Midwestern high-school boys at Princeton then referred to as Tweedy Shitballs—by saying that he was from "Mamma-RONN-nick."

He knows Apple stories about his girth and Apple stories about his tendency to hold forth—a state that Tom Brokaw has referred to as being "in full Apple." He loves the story about a dinner-table conversation early in his experience as a stepfather. His first marriage had broken up in the seventies, in Washington, when he fell in love with Betsey Brown, a charming woman who speaks in the sort of plummy accent heard among Richmond débutantes discussing cocktail napkins but happens to be a Bryn Mawr graduate who reads more newspapers than Apple does. She was also married, and she had two children. ("Within a limited social circle in Washington," Apple now says, "I think it would be fair to say that it was a brief but fairly vivid scandal.") A trip to Europe had not completely melted the hearts of the children, John and Catherine Brown, who were unaccustomed to being herded through quite that many cathedrals that intently by someone with that much information at his fingertips and that many reference books in his satchel. Then, at dinner one evening, an American Indian design on Betsey's dress inspired the assigning of Indian names, until everyone had one but R. W. Apple, Jr. "That's easy," John Brown, who was then about nine, finally said. "You're Sitting Bullshit." As Catherine tells the story, there was a moment of shocked silence, and then "Johnny gave one of his full-body laughs." After that, the children felt free to name Apple's stomach—Eugene, and, eventually, Eugene Maximus.

In support of the notion that Apple is something like a lovable old Labrador, it should be said that many Apple stories portray him as enormously generous—generous with his hospitality and generous with the telephone numbers of his sources and generous with his good offices at the *Times* for someone he thinks should work there and generous with his restaurant recommendations ("The only place in Scotland to have Scottish beef is in Linlithgow, and here's the name of the owner . . ."). The political-campaign reporters who rode one bus or another with him—people like Richard Cohen, of the Washington *Post,* and Curtis Wilkie, of the Boston *Globe,* and Jack Germond and Jules Witcover, of the Baltimore *Sun*—liked to play jokes on him and liked to complain about him, but, as Germond said recently, "Most of us had an affection for John, even when he was at his most bumptious."

A *Times* contemporary of Apple's has pointed out that the Apple stories that "make you shudder" tend to date back to the sixties. A number of them were collected in "The Boys on the Bus," Timothy Crouse's book on the reporters covering the 1972 Presidential campaign—a book that served for years as the standard text on R. W. Apple, Jr. "Read one way, the book is immensely flattering to me," Apple told me. "Read another way, it basically says I'm an asshole." The book angered Apple—although one Apple-mellowing theory holds that it did him the favor of providing the cape buffalo a glimpse of how some of the other animals might view him.

What was flattering to Apple in "The Boys on the Bus" was, by and large, its discussion of his competence as a reporter. A McGovern worker was quoted describing his first glimpse of how the national press operates: "Johnny Apple of the New York *Times* sat in a corner and everyone peered over his shoulder to find out what he was writing." Apple's competitors give him mixed reviews on the 1972 campaign—some of them believe he became too attached to the string of endorsements that Edmund Muskie was accumulating—but virtually all of them say, without being asked, that his campaign coverage four years later was worthy of a Pulitzer, a prize he has never won. David Broder, of the Washington *Post,* told me that in 1976 Apple "damn near invented the Iowa caucuses" as a serious element of the Presidential campaign—it was Apple who first spotted the potential strength of Jimmy Carter—and after that, as Curtis Wilkie has put it, "he ran rings around everyone."

What Crouse referred to as Apple's "braggadocio, his grandstanding, his mammoth ego" dominated the portrait in "The Boys on the Bus." An account of Apple's first meeting with David Halberstam is fairly typical of Crouse's Apple stories. It describes Apple sauntering over to Halberstam's desk to inform him, at some length, that at a party the previous evening—a party that included some Sulzberger cousins and a *Times* vice-president—Halberstam's name had been mentioned quite favorably. Finally, Crouse wrote, "Halberstam said his first words to Johnny Apple: 'Fuck off, kid!'"

Looking back, Halberstam says of Apple's behavior in those early days, "When it was egregious, which was often, it was never out of malice." Halberstam believes that young reporters at the *Times*—most of them edgy and competitive and still not certain that they deserved to be where they seemed to have fetched up—found Apple hard to take partly because of "a fear that he symbolized your own lesser self." That's not far from the notion that Apple differed from his contemporaries at the *Times* not so much in what he was like as in the fact that he let it show—or, in Crouse's shrewd phrase, that he stuck out "in a business populated largely by *shy* egomaniacs." In Halberstam's view, "It would be interesting to know what went on in Akron to produce this fearful insecurity—the ego, the unfinished quality that made him even worse than the rest of us."

•　　　•　　　•

Johnny Apple's father—Raymond Walter Apple, Sr., also known as Johnny—was, the junior Apple finally concluded, a hard case. He was the son of a skilled worker who mixed chemicals for glass. The family name had been Apfel; it was presumably changed around the time of the First World War, when there was a lot of ill feeling toward people with names reminiscent of the Hun. R. W. Apple, Sr., was a football star at Wittenberg University, a small Lutheran school in Ohio, and, as the family story is told, he fell in love with the homecoming queen, Julia Albrecht, whose equally German but considerably more prosperous family owned a lot of grocery stores that were to make the transition into a substantial Akron supermarket chain called Acme.

According to Johnny, Jr., his father's dream was to be a football coach, but, the homecoming queen having said that she didn't want to be married to a football coach, he came into her family's business—eventually helping to run it, apparently with the zeal of the converted. He tried his best to hide his disappointment that his only son was not an athlete, Johnny, Jr., says, but was less successful at accepting that son's decision not to go to work for Acme Markets. Nor did R. W. Apple, Sr., have much respect for the trade his son had chosen over running a successful supermarket chain. "He didn't think it was a legit way to make a living," Johnny, Jr., says. Apparently, R. W. Apple, Sr., never quite got over the notion that R. W. Apple, Jr., was spending his life in something akin to typing.

Earlier this year, I had a talk with Apple about his father. We were speaking in a small Gloucestershire cottage that the Apples bought while he was based in London, where he served as the *Times* bureau chief from 1977 until 1985. Johnny and Betsey Apple had come to rest at the cottage after a trip to the Far East that I had characterized as an attempt to break the world's single-trip expense-account record, now held by R. W. Apple, Jr. His parents, Apple said, had come to see him while he was London bureau chief, a job he revelled in. Like a lot of *Times* bureau chiefs over the years, he acquired some English airs and some English clothing. He was enthralled with British politics and some of the multidimensional people in it. He entertained grand people grandly, and he was once quoted as saying that the *Times* might never transfer him back to the United States, because his bosses at the paper wouldn't want to pay for transporting all of the wine he had in his cellar.

"I was proud of being the London bureau chief of the New York *Times*," he told me, in discussing his parents' visit. "It's not shit. Betsey had made the flat very pretty, and we had some of our most interesting friends to dinner. David and Debbie Owen, among others. I think Margaret Drabble was there. People who had something to say. And I thought, you know, I hope he's proud of me. I hope he finds it nice that I have this job and that I have interesting friends. We had a round table and David Owen asked me a question about something that was happening in the Middle East, and before I could answer, my father said, 'How the hell would *he* know?' And it went downhill from there."

I asked Apple if R. W. Apple, Sr., had ever come to respect what his son had accomplished as a journalist. "When they had their sixtieth-wedding anniversary, I was the m.c.," he said. "They had the same dinner—lobster Newburg on toast points—that they had in the same place, the Portage Country Club, sixty years before. Many of the same people, because they had stayed put. It was really quite a wonderful evening, and I hope I was modestly funny. And he didn't say anything to me afterward. But after he died, which was a year or two later, my mother said to me, 'You know, when we came home from that party at the club, we were taking off our clothes and he said to me, "Well, maybe I'm wrong. Maybe he *does* amount to something." ' I said, 'Mother!' And she said, 'What can I tell you?'"

· · ·

Unable to match his father's athletic exploits, the younger Apple became a voracious consumer of information about sports and, eventually, the sports editor of the newspaper at Western Reserve Academy—an institution that reminds some people of a small New England boarding school in a small New England town, although the town, Hudson, is about halfway between Akron and Cleveland. By the time he got to Princeton and entered what was then called the "heeling competition" required of those who wanted to work on the *Princetonian,* his writing was already fluid enough to astonish his classmates—a fact he credits partly to the stern efforts of an English teacher at Reserve named Franklyn S. (Jiggs) Reardon, who, in class and on the student newspaper, demanded clear and concise prose. Young Apple had the nearly maniacal energy that eventually resulted in the back-to-back interviews and blizzard of telephone calls that characterized his political reporting. He was also displaying the sort of intense curiosity that can seem to suck all the information out of the room, although the focus of his curiosity was not always on the courses he had signed up to take.

At the time, the *Princetonian* had what amounted to a board of advisory grownups, and the managing editor of the *Wall Street Journal*—Barney Kilgore, who happened to live in Princeton—was among its members. Once Apple was informed that he would not be continuing at the university, Kilgore arranged for him to work at the *Journal,* and he eventually got his degree from the Columbia School of General Studies. The *Journal* employment lasted until there was a lengthy meeting to discuss why other bureaus were getting a certain type of piece in the paper so much more often than the New York bureau, and young Johnny Apple finally said, "Maybe they don't have to spend their time in chickenshit meetings like this."

At least that's Apple's story. I'm not sure I'd take it literally. Not that Apple is one of those reporters, much written about of late, whose copy has often been treated with some suspicion by their colleagues. (Some time before the revelations last spring that ended the editorship of Howell Raines and resulted in the departure of Jayson Blair and Rick Bragg, Apple says, he warned Raines that Bragg was such a reporter.) One foreign correspondent who often covered the same stories as Apple told me, "He's a very good and careful writer, but when he's talking there's some self-aggrandizement—a need to oversell and put the best coloration on his exploits." When Apple is talking about a decision at the *Times,* for instance, his first-person plural sometimes makes the decision sound like, in the words of one colleague, "what Arthur and I worked out." When I asked Apple the precise circumstances of his second expulsion from Princeton, he told me what he had once told Brian Lamb, of C-SPAN, during a television interview—that it came about because he'd criticized the university administration during a campaign the *Princetonian* was waging against anti-Semitism in the eating-club system. Many of his contemporaries on the *Princetonian* remember Apple fondly as a great character among the almost willfully bland undergraduates of the fifties Ivy League, but they're certain that nothing the newspaper wrote about the club system, a perennial target of the *Prince*, had anything whatever to do with his departure. Apple, when pressed, said that the dean, after citing papers unwritten and classes cut and chapel (then compulsory at Princeton) unattended, implied that some of these offenses might have been overlooked if Apple hadn't been such a troublemaker as chairman of the *Princetonian*. Although it's an oversimplification to say so, I think that people who have known Johnny Apple over the years tend to discount a bit whatever he says about himself and to trust whatever he writes in the New York *Times*.

· · ·

Journalism is sometimes thought of as a field for generalists—a kind word for those contemporaries of mine who couldn't make a career decision—but the needs of a newspaper are often quite specific. So are the skills of most reporters. Apple was never thought of by his editors as an investigative reporter, for instance, but he became known as someone who could be dispatched to cover a story in unfamiliar territory—what is sometimes called in the trade "parachuting in." Given his ability to synthesize information quickly, he also became particularly valued at the *Times* as a writer of the lead-all—a piece on the far-right-hand column of the front page which essentially tells readers what has happened in various aspects of an important story since the last time they picked up the paper. A lead-all writer often has to worry about not only knitting together half a dozen disparate developments but also fending off editors in New York who would like all of those developments mentioned before the story jumps from the front page to the inside of the paper. Allan Siegal, a longtime assistant managing editor at the *Times* who was widely thought of as the editor in charge of standards even before he was formally given that title this month, has said that for a lead-all "you need bold synthesis at the top of a story. There are only three people in my time that I can remember doing it consistently: Scotty Reston, Max Frankel, and Apple—people who would write some encompassing statement of what had happened that day and only then go into the procedural details."

One of Apple's other great specialties became the news-analysis piece that is known at the *Times* as a Q-head, a form invented some years ago for James Reston when he was Washington bureau chief. A Q-head, which is supposed to reflect reporting rather than the writer's own views, is the sort of piece that, for instance, outlines the options open to a President facing an important decision, often within the context of how similar Presidential decisions played out in the past. Apple's willingness to sound authoritative—some would say Olympian—is an asset in writing Q-heads. So is his historical perspective. So is the fact that he is, as he puts it, "a natural centrist." Writing a balanced analytical piece is much more difficult for a reporter who, consciously or unconsciously, has a political agenda or a deep contempt for one side or the other. Trying to give me some idea of his political beliefs, Apple said during our talk in England that when he was the London bureau chief he found himself somewhat attracted by the policies of the Tory Wets and of the Social Democratic Party. If I had to categorize his politics in American terms, I'd say that he might be a Rockefeller Republican, if there were still such a thing as a Rockefeller Republican—both in the views he holds and in the fact that he does not hold them with great intensity. Like a lot of people who have spent many years reporting politics, he is engaged by the game but not by the ideology.

A Q-head is not necessarily a profound or blindingly original piece of work. Two or three days after it's written, it can look dated or even wrong, particularly in a constantly changing situation like war. When the military campaign against the Taliban in Afghanistan seemed bogged down, for instance, Apple used some Vietnam analogies that were later criticized as not being predictive of how the war went. (John Leo's column in *U.S. News & World Report* was headlined "Quagmire, Schmagmire.") You could argue that some Q-heads, when all is said and done, amount to conventional wisdom, since they reflect the observations of people asked to assess the situation in terms of what happens, conventionally, when such situations occur.

All of that does not mean that there are any number of people on the *Times* who can consistently produce the sort of Q-heads the editors are looking for. According to the current executive editor, Bill Keller, the notion of running a Q-head often doesn't come up until the middle of the afternoon, making it "an intellectual wind sprint." Given the need for a twelve-hundred-word Q-head by six o'clock, someone who can actually file twelve hundred words of clean copy by six is immeasurably more valuable than someone who, although perhaps equally knowledgeable and equally thoughtful and equally conscientious about doing fresh reporting, is likely to turn in an eighteen-hundred-word piece with some tangled sentences in it sometime around six-thirty. Apple was once asked to give members of the Washington bureau what amounted to a master class in Q-head writing. The difficulty of replicating his touch with the form may be reflected in the fact that, long after he gave up the sort of daily Washington reporting that replenishes sources and stores up information for analytical pieces, the *Times'* coverage of a momentous event—the attack on the World Trade Center, for instance— tended to include a Q-head by R. W. Apple, Jr.

Andy Rosenthal, one of the people at the *Times* who tell Apple stories with good humor rather than clenched teeth, recalls that in 1999, a couple of years after Apple had turned his attention from government to the table, the Senate, in an unexpected vote, rejected the Comprehensive Test Ban Treaty. Rosenthal, who was then on the foreign desk, called Apple at six in the evening to say that the paper needed what he called a "not since Versailles" Q-head. Apple, pointing out that his stepdaughter's rehearsal dinner was to take place at seven-thirty, berated Rosenthal for making such a request at such a time, and, an hour later, filed a Q-head. It was written in clear English. It had historical references to SALT II and the Panama Canal treaties and the tension between Woodrow Wilson and Henry Cabot Lodge during the formation of the League of Nations. It was one thousand one hundred and seventy-one words long. Eleven of those words were, like a tip of the hat to Rosenthal, "Not since the Versailles Treaty was voted down in November 1919 . . ."

·   ·   ·

In discussions of Apple-mellowing, nobody much goes for my theory that Johnny Apple was saved by gluttony. I'm still attracted by the notion, though, that his outsized supply of energy and drive and competitiveness was drained off at table, in the savoring of a decent Burgundy or the perfect crab cake. (I was present when he found what he described in the *Times* as his "nominee for the single best crab dish in Baltimore, if not the Western Hemisphere"— the jumbo-lump crab cake at Faidley Seafood, in the Lexington Market—and I can testify that his look of triumph did give him some resemblance to a very big four-year-old.) Some of the people who don't go for my theory say that Apple was a glutton to start with, and some, of course, believe that he has not yet been saved. I developed the theory in the mid-seventies, when Apple arrived in London as bureau chief. At the time, I mentioned one piece of evidence in a book, giving Apple the *nom de table* of Charlie Plum, as I have done in print now and then: "In an effort to find the perfect dining spot he had eaten in sixty French restaurants in London within a few months. (When Plum's friends are asked to name his principal charms, they often mention relentlessness.)"

Even before then, Apple had a serious interest in good meals and good wine. When he was in the Washington bureau in the early seventies, before he went to London, colleagues found that a casual "Let's get a bite of lunch" could mean going across the street to what was then one of the fanciest French restaurants in town and having a three-course meal with appropriate wine. Given the fact that most reporters think a bite of lunch has something to do with a B.L.T., Apple's food and wine standards became an obvious target for pranks: sending a bottle of Lancer's rosé over to his table during a political convention in Kansas City; phoning him in the guise of a fawning reader to ask his advice on the proper wine for wild, as opposed to domestic, goose; concocting a scheme in Iran to refill bottles Apple had obtained from the Shah's cellar with what Horace Rumpole would call the local plonk.

The pranks had no effect at all on Apple's dining habits. At some point during his long stint in London, he began putting his eating adventures into print, taking advantage of the fact that, as he puts it, "Americans, or at least New York *Times* readers, care about a broader spectrum of British life than they do about French or German or Japanese life." He is not the sort of food writer who makes reservations in the name of Nero Wolfe characters or slips in quietly disguised as the Korean consul-general. In restaurants or anywhere else, Apple seems more comfortable once the people he's dealing with are aware of his rank and station. The simplest description I've heard of his customary reception at a restaurant is "Everybody falls to the ground when Johnny walks in."

The Apple-at-table stories that don't involve his three-lunch capacity involve his standards. When his dining companion at the Kansas City restaurant, B. Drummond Ayres, then also of the *Times,* refused to let him send the bottle of Lancer's away—after a long day talking to politicians and a long wait for service, Ayres was ready to start in on any tipple available—Apple hid it under the table. On a Presidential visit Bill Clinton made to Africa, Apple had dinner one night in Kampala, Uganda, whose restaurant possibilities he had, of course, researched in some depth before leaving Washington. "We go to what Johnny has found out is the best Indian restaurant in the country," Maureen Dowd, who was in Apple's party that evening, told me. "We're the only ones in the restaurant. That would worry some people, but Johnny knows it's the right place because he's there." After tucking in his napkin, she went on, Apple said, in stentorian tones that seemed to be addressed to no one in particular, "No prawns at this altitude!" That remains a phrase that Apple watchers occasionally use to greet each other—"No prawns at this altitude!"

"Oscar Wilde said that a man who could command a London dinner table can rule the world," I was told not long ago by the legal philosopher Ronald Dworkin, who became friendly with Apple when the Apples lived in London, "and Johnny always commanded the dinner table." Dworkin was one of the eight people gathered for Apple's fiftieth-birthday luncheon, held at Gidleigh Park—a Devon country inn and restaurant that had been celebrated by Apple in the *Times* and eventually won what was apparently the first Michelin star ever awarded to an establishment run by Americans. (As a Midwesterner, albeit a Midwesterner with made-to-order English shirts, Apple is particularly proud that Paul and Kay Henderson, who run the place, both graduated from Purdue.) In a private dining room, the celebrants, including the Hendersons, consumed Beluga caviar, sautéed foie gras with quince sauce, salad of red mullet and lettuce with olive-oil-and-coriander dressing, tagliatelle with white truffles, partridge mousse with morels and spinach, roasted saddle of hare, Muenster and single Gloucester cheeses, mango and eau-de-vie-de-poire sorbets, *gâteau marjolaine*, coffee, and six wines—all from 1934, the year of Apple's birth. "Around five or five-thirty, I was as close to death by eating as I've ever been," Dworkin told me. "We were about to break up and go up to the bedroom and have a nap. Then Apple was saying, 'We have to have a talk about dinner. Just a quick word. We've eaten rather well. So something simple. I have an idea. The truffles that came with the tagliatelle came boxed in rice. You could make us a risotto out of the rice the truffles came in. Let's have a Saint-Julien, a late-growth Saint-Julien. A '79 would be all right.'"

Much of this eating and travel is, of course, underwritten by the *Times*. When it comes to what Homer Bigart used to call "feeding at the Sulzberger trough," it is widely acknowledged that R. W. Apple, Jr., is without peer. Joe Lelyveld, who even as executive editor was not known for demanding a prime position at the trough, once stopped in London when he was the foreign editor and took his bureau chief to dinner—a lavish dinner, as it turned out, since his bureau chief was R. W. Apple, Jr. When the check arrived, Apple reached over to scoop it up. "You better let me take this," he said. "They'd never believe it coming from you."

I once suggested to Apple that he bequeath his expense accounts to the Smithsonian Institution. "But the *Times* has them," he said. "I turned them in." He sounded a bit regretful, it seemed to me, that he was not in a position to give posterity an opportunity to inspect some of his more stunning creations. At the *Times*, the various departments have what is called a cost center—what amounts to a budget line. The foreign desk has a cost center. The editorial board has a cost center. R. W. Apple, Jr., has a cost center. "It's been my fate and privilege over the years to sit next to various people who were approving Apple's expense accounts," Al Siegal says. "There were hoots, and once in a while you'd look up and the person—these were various assistant managing editors—was shaking his head and reading off 'Wine from my cellars . . .'" Siegal, who is a great admirer of R. W. Apple, Jr., thinks that, all in all, the *Times* has received good value.

Asked about having his own cost center, Apple is suddenly overcome with modesty. "It's because I write for all these different parts of the paper," he told me. Not long ago, Apple was appointed an associate editor of the *Times,* a position that is something of an honorific, and some acquaintances asked what difference the new title would make, since he already seemed to do whatever he wanted. Before being named associate editor, Apple said, there were two hotels he could not stay in on his expense account. Now, as he interprets company policy, he can.

．　　．　　．

In 1979, after covering the revolution in Iran, R. W. Apple, Jr., then the London bureau chief of the *Times,* and some other foreign correspondents had a long lunch in Paris at a tiny Lyonnaise restaurant called Cartet, near the Place de la République. In Iran, Apple had apparently been brilliant in organizing what amounted to a press pool to cover Ayatollah Khomeini's arrival in Tehran. By chance, the editor of the *International Herald Tribune,* whose editorial headquarters is in Paris, had just left the paper, and, after considerable wine had been consumed, a couple of those present decided that Apple should be the *Trib*'s new editor. Apple apparently began by dismissing the notion but eventually said—according to Jonathan Randal, an old friend of his who was then with the Washington *Post*—"Well, if you're so God-damned smart, make it happen."

It did not happen—memories vary on just why—but the conversation reflected a realization by Apple and his friends, even when he was only forty-five, that R. W. Apple, Jr., was unlikely to rise on the masthead of the *Times.* The London posting had been widely seen as a sort of consolation prize for not being named chief of the Washington bureau, a seventy-reporter operation whose management involves responsibilities that have something in common with those carried by the executive editor. One mellowing theory holds that Apple's own realization that he wasn't going to run the *Times* uncoupled him from one of the engines powering his competitiveness, but Apple himself has always said that he never had any desire to be executive editor of the *Times*. Some of his friends believe that under severe torture he might at least own up to having wanted to be managing editor.

Nearly fifteen years later, the *Times* did make Apple the Washington bureau chief. He held the job for five years, but it did not turn out to be among the high points in his career. Apple says he was conscious of trying not to be what's known in the trade as a big foot, a celebrated reporter who takes over major stories from the person on the beat—he was aware that a previous bureau chief had been presented at his going-away party with a size-18 sneaker—but at the end of the day, I was told by someone who spent years at the *Times*, "Johnny is a performer. You can't be a performer and manage the Washington bureau." Also, Apple was away a lot. People who were there say that Andy Rosenthal, who was what the *Times* calls the Washington editor, actually managed the bureau. "He would introduce me to people as his No. 2," Rosenthal told me cheerfully. "As if he were the lord of the admiralty." Rosenthal was involved in an Apple story treasured by people who worked in the bureau in those years. Apple, infuriated that another reporter's political story from the same region had made the front page while his hadn't, was heard to shout at his No. 2, "I will not be little-footed!"

Apple's tenure as bureau chief ended in 1997. "He could still make calls into the Clinton White House, often at a level or two higher than the beat reporters could," one of his editors told me, but, particularly after the congressional-election sweep engineered by Newt Gingrich in 1994, Apple was less in tune with legislators. During our talk in Gloucestershire, he said, "Different sorts of people began to be elected to Congress, and they behaved in a different ways. They didn't go to each other's houses. In many cases, they didn't even have houses. Many of them slept in their offices. And this was one of the elements that led to this constant nastiness rather than debate. Furthermore, you began to have fewer and fewer people around who were truly expert in any field, and few left around who are what I always thought of as the mud that holds the straw of the deeply partisan together. As it became much more adversarial and much less substantive, it slipped away from me. I don't mean that I didn't understand it, but I didn't want to live my life in the middle of it."

. . .

It was not the first time that Apple had lost his trademark enthusiasm for the task at hand. A decade earlier, just after he'd returned from London to be the *Times'* chief Washington correspondent, there had been a period when he seemed to have lost interest in pursuing the usual political stories or even in showing up regularly at the bureau. "That was a precursor of finally deciding I just don't want to do this again and again and again," he told me. "I loved doing it when there was a big story running and I could make a contribution. But just to write routine political and foreign stuff, I thought, Oh man!" Newspaper reporting of the sort that regularly results in front-page stories in the *Times*—that is, reporting that has to do with politics or government or foreign policy—is repetitious work. A lot of distinguished reporters eventually get the feeling that they've done what is essentially the same story one too many times. Some of them become columnists, but that was not in store for Apple. The absence of an ideological point of view may be an advantage in a Q-head writer but it is a disadvantage in a columnist. At the *Times,* Apple was regarded as someone with a nearly encyclopedic knowledge of politics, but not as a singular political thinker. Whether or not he ever yearned for a column, as some of his friends maintain, he now says that it wouldn't have been a good fit. "I'm not any good at writing columns in which I say what this country needs or what the world needs is the following," he told me. "I see two sides to too many things."

The path he did take had its origin in his days in the London bureau, when he had begun to write about food and travel. Toward the end of his stint as bureau chief, he'd written a series of travel pieces in Europe—pieces that were eventually collected in a book called "Apple's Europe." At the time, Apple's increasing interest in writing about bistros and cathedrals was causing some uneasiness among his masters in New York. But, looking back recently on the sort of writing he had done toward the end of his London stay, Apple said, "That was sort of the beginning of my reinventing myself."

Not long after he stepped down as Washington bureau chief, the *Times* made Apple something called chief correspondent—essentially a ticket to write about whatever interested him. Betsey Apple—who, together with her children, can be thought of as another theory of what mellowed R. W. Apple, Jr.—had suggested a travel series about American cities similar to the series Apple had done in Europe. As the trips evolved, she was usually at the wheel while her husband deconstructed the maps with an adroitness that presumably comes from having had to find his way around strange cities in a hundred and nine different countries. She continued in that role in the next series, on food, in which she is routinely mentioned once in each piece, more or less in the way Hitchcock put in a fleeting appearance in each movie. Last fall, at the Southern Foodways Alliance conference on barbecue, in Oxford, Mississippi, Betsey Apple introduced herself to one of the participants by saying, "I'm Betsey. I drive Mister Daisy."

Apple watchers have interpreted Apple's emergence as a food writer in a number of ways. Some of them see it as the *Times* rewarding so many years of extraordinary service by putting Apple out to a particularly luxuriant pasture. Some see it as Apple's response to having been deprived of the few rewards of the business that have not been bestowed on him—a column or a Pulitzer or an editorship—by following the maxim that living well is the best revenge. Bill Keller and his recent predecessors see it as extending into the so-called special sections of the paper—the sections that increasingly are becoming fundamental to the identity of the *Times* and to its commercial well-being—the work of a reporter who is, in Keller's words, "as much a marquee name in the food section as he is in the political pages." That's the way Apple sees it.

The change in portfolio has made Apple an unusual figure in Washington. He retains all the trappings associated with members of what is sometimes called the permanent government. He has a house in Georgetown. He has known most of the capital's principal players for years. (He met George Bush and Al Gore in 1970, when they were serving their fathers as drivers in unsuccessful Senate campaigns; the President, it almost goes without saying, calls him Juanito.) But what he normally writes about day to day is not, say, the future of the North Atlantic alliance but where to find herring that actually tastes like herring. Apple's friends like to tease him about the switch in subject matter. But they believe that he has emerged triumphant at a time in his career when a lot of reporters who never came in from the field are faced with a choice I used to think of as the Ottawa bureau or the bottle. The byline of R. W. Apple, Jr., still regularly appears in the *Times,* often on stories from places that make his colleagues muse on what the fanciest hotel there is really like. "He's got a second act," Ben Bradlee said of Apple not long ago, "and he probably has others up his sleeve, just in case he eats all the food in the world."

With R. W. Apple, Jr., triumph is a given. He approaches food writing the same way he approached political reporting or war reporting or parachuting in. In preparation for the Baltimore piece that uncovered the blissful crab cake, he told me, he had reread some Mencken and reread some of Russell Baker's memoir of growing up in Baltimore and spent a lot of time on the Internet and on the phone. When he wasn't indulging in one of his three lunches in Baltimore, he was in his room finishing up a piece on the early-twentieth-century East Bay architect Bernard Maybeck ("a precursor of the modern movement like Otto Wagner in Vienna, Charles Rennie Mackintosh in Glasgow, Victor

Horta in Brussels, and the brothers Charles and Henry Greene in Pasadena") and a travel piece on Bermuda that began, "When Claudio Vigilante was a waiter at Le Gavroche, the last redoubt of classic French haute cuisine in London . . ."

At the time I spoke to Apple in Gloucestershire, he had sixteen or seventeen notebooks filled with research from the Far East trip, but it seemed likely he'd be interrupted by war in Iraq before he transformed them all into *Times* stories. The *Times*' plans for war coverage included calling him from the table for Q-head duty. When the war started, Apple did return to writing Q-heads—which, as it turned out, drew some of the same sort of criticism that had been directed at him during the Afghanistan campaign. Keller believes that, as the *Times* allows more analytical writing in news stories, it is becoming less tied to the notion that "every big news event has to be accompanied by a story about what you were supposed to think about that news event." Still, at the time when war with Iraq seemed imminent, an old *Times* hand told me that it would probably constitute what the management considered "a Johnny Apple moment."

By late spring, Apple was mining the notebooks. The Asia trip had been designed to produce eight pieces for the *Times*, not to speak of a piece on the twenty-fifth anniversary of Gidleigh Park. He had already published a piece on eating dim sum in Hong Kong, but he had before him a piece on Vietnamese pho and a piece on mangosteens in Bangkok and a piece on pepper in Kerala and a piece on Keralan cuisine and a travel piece on Bangkok. A lengthy piece on Singapore street food appeared in the *Times* earlier this month. The reporting, if that's the word, had required eighteen eating stops in a single, sixteen-hour day. Cautioned by his guide to taste rather than eat, Apple wrote, "I tried, but I failed. More gourmand than gourmet, I finished much of what was put before me." Presumably, he will now be referred to by some—maybe even by me—as Eighteen Lunches Apple. Relentlessness remains one of Charlie Plum's principal charms.

The New Yorker

WINNER, ESSAYS

A Sudden Illness

In this essay about her long,

nearly unfathomable fight with

chronic fatigue syndrome, Laura

Hillenbrand delivers rich,

suspenseful, cinematic details and

imagery that transport the reader

deep into the heart of her

nightmare—until it seems you are

experiencing her claustrophobic

and horrific reality. "A Sudden

Illness" champions the

importance of respecting personal

experience as valid (despite an

army of "authorities" who work

to discredit it) and creates an

inspiring testament to the will to

live and create.

Laura Hillenbrand

A Sudden Illness

How my life changed.

We were in Linc's car, an aging yellow Mercedes sedan, big and steady, with slippery blond seats and a deep, strumming idle. Lincoln called it Dr. Diesel. It was a Sunday night, March 22, 1987, nine-thirty. Rural Ohio was a smooth continuity of silence and darkness, except for a faintly golden seam where land met sky ahead, promising light and people and sound just beyond the tree line.

We were on our way back to Kenyon College after spring break. Linc, my best friend, was driving, his arm easy over the wheel. My boyfriend, Borden, sat behind him. I rode shotgun, a rose from Borden on my lap. Slung over my arm was a nineteen-forties taffeta ball gown I had bought for twenty dollars at a thrift shop. I was nineteen.

The conversation had dropped off. I was making plans for the dress and for my coming junior year abroad at the University of Edinburgh. My eyes strayed along the right shoulder of the road: a white mailbox, the timid glint of an abandoned pickup's tail-light. The pavement racing under the car was gunmetal gray. We were doing fifty or so. A balled-up bag from a drive-through burger joint bumped against my ankle.

A *deer*.

At first, he was only a suggestion of an animal, emerging from the darkness by degrees: a muzzle, a sharp left eye. Then the headlights grasped him.

He was massive, a web of antlers over his head, a heavy barrel, round haunches lifting him from the downward slope of the highway apron. Briefly, his forehooves rested on the line between the shoulder and the highway. I saw his knee bending, the hoof lifting: he was stepping into the car's path.

In the instant that I spent waiting for the deer to roll up over the car's hood and crash through the windshield I was aware of my body warm in the seat, Linc's face lit by the dash, Borden breathing in the back, the cool sulfur glow of the car's interior, the salty smell of the burger bag. I watched the deer's knee and waited for it to straighten. I drew a sharp breath.

The bumper missed the deer's chest by an inch, maybe two. The animal's muzzle passed so close that I could see the swirl of hair around his nostrils. Then he was gone behind us.

I blinked at the road. My eyes caught something else. A brilliant light appeared through the top of the windshield and arced straight ahead of the car at terrific speed. It was a meteor. It burned through the rising light of the horizon and vanished in the black place above the road and below the sky.

My breath escaped in a rush. I turned toward Linc to share my amazement. He was as loose as he had been, his eyes slowly panning the road, his long body unfolding over the seat. I looked back at Borden and could just make out his face. They had seen nothing.

I was about to speak when an intense wave of nausea surged through me. The smell from the bag on the floor was suddenly sickening. I wrapped my arms over my stomach and slid down in my seat. By the time we reached campus, half an hour later, I was doubled over, burning hot, and racked with chills. Borden called the campus paramedics. They hovered in the doorway, pronounced it food poisoning, and left.

•   •   •

I fell asleep sitting up on my bed, leaning against Borden's shoulder. In the morning, my stomach seethed. I walked to the dining hall and sat with Linc, unable to eat. In my history seminar, I drank from a water bottle and tried to concentrate. After class, I walked to my apartment and heated some oatmeal. I swallowed a spoonful; nausea rose in my throat and I pushed the bowl away.

In the next few days, everything I ate made my abdomen balloon. I radiated heat, and my joints and muscles felt bruised. Every day on the way to classes, I struggled a little harder to make it up the hill behind my apartment. Eventually, I began stopping halfway to rest against the trunk of a tree.

One morning, I woke to find my limbs leaden. I tried to sit up but couldn't. I lay in bed, listening to my apartment-mates move through their morning routines. It was two hours before I could stand. On the walk to the bathroom, I had to drag my shoulder along the wall to stay upright. Linc drove me to the campus physician, who ran test after test but couldn't find the cause of my illness. After three weeks of being stranded in my room, I had no choice but to drop out of college. I called my sister and asked if she could drive me home to Maryland.

I sat in the doorway of the apartment while Borden and Linc packed my sister's car. As they pushed the last of my belongings into the back seat, a downpour broke over them. We pulled out, and Kenyon was lost in a falling grayness. I turned to wave to Borden and Linc, but I couldn't see them anymore.

•   •   •

My mother's house was a dignified Colonial that sat back from the road, behind a pine tree that had been mostly denuded by Hurricane Agnes and an anemic cherry tree that would soon collapse onto the den. In the back yard stood a hemlock that had been missing its upper third since my brother and I accidentally set it on fire. Inside, the house was a warren of small rooms that had suited our two-parent, four-kid, two-collie family when my parents bought it, in 1971. My father had walked out in 1977, the elder collie had died three days later, and the house had gradually emptied until my departure for Kenyon, which had left only my mother and my cat, Fangfoss.

The sun was setting as we pulled up to the back door. I walked upstairs and lay down in my childhood bedroom, which over-looked the back yard and the charred tree. The next morning, I stepped on a scale. I had lost twenty pounds. The lymph nodes on my neck and under my arms and collarbones were painfully swollen. During the day, I rattled with chills, but at night I soaked my clothes in sweat. I felt unsteady, as if the ground were swaying. My throat was inflamed and raw. A walk to the mailbox on the corner left me so tired that I had to lie down.

Sometimes I'd look at words or pictures but see only mean-ingless shapes. I'd stare at clocks and not understand what the positions of the hands meant. Words from different parts of a page appeared to be grouped together in bizarre sentences: "Endangered Condors Charged in Shotgun Killing." In conversa-tion, I'd think of one word but say something completely unre-lated: "hotel" became "plankton"; "cup" came out "elastic." I couldn't hang on to a thought long enough to carry it through a sentence. When I tried to cross the street, the motion of the cars became so disorienting that I couldn't move. I was at a sensory distance from the world, as if I were wrapped in clear plastic.

•   •   •

I had never been in poor health and didn't have an internist, so I went to my old pediatrician. I sat in a child's chair in a waiting room wallpapered with jungle scenes, watching a boy dismember an action figure. When my doctor drew the thermometer from my mouth, he asked me if I knew that my temperature was a hundred and one. He swabbed my throat, left for a few minutes, and returned with the news that I had strep throat. Puzzled by the other symptoms, he prescribed antibiotics and suggested that I see an internist.

The doctor I found waved me into a chair and began asking questions and making notes, pausing to rake his fingers through a hedge of dark hair that drifted onto his brow. He ran some tests and found nothing amiss. He told me to take antacids. A few weeks later, when I returned and told him that I was getting worse, he sat me down. My problem, he said gravely, was not in my body but in my mind; the test results proved it. He told me to see a psychiatrist.

I went to Dr. Charles Troshinsky, a respected psychiatrist whom I had seen when I was fifteen, after my high-school boyfriend had died suddenly. He was shocked at how thin I was. I was just under five feet five, but my weight had dropped to a hundred pounds. Dr. Troshinsky said that he had seen several people with the same constellation of symptoms, all referred by physicians who dismissed them as mentally ill. He wrote my internist a letter stating that he would stake his reputation on his conclusion that I was mentally healthy but suffering from a serious physical illness.

"Find another psychiatrist," my internist said over the phone, a smile in his voice. How did he explain the fevers, chills, exhaustion, swollen lymph nodes, dizziness? What I was going through, he suggested, was puberty. I had just turned twenty. "Laura, everyone goes through this," he said with the drizzly slowness one uses with a toddler. "It's a normal adjustment to adulthood. You'll grow out of it in a few years." He told me to come back in six months.

"But I'm not happy with my treatment," I said.

He laughed. "Well, I am."

I called his secretary and asked for my medical records. I sat on my bedroom floor and flipped through the doctor's notes. *Couldn't handle school,* he had written. *Dropped out.*

.   .   .

My next doctor was a plump, pink man with the indiscriminate gaiety of a golden retriever. He was halfway through a hair transplant, and clumps of hair were lined up in neat rows on his scalp, like spring seedlings.

I again tested positive for strep, and he renewed the antibiotics. He ran a blood test for a virus called Epstein-Barr and found a soaring titer, a measurement of the antibody in my system. I had, he said with pep-rally enthusiasm, something called Epstein-Barr virus syndrome. He had it, too, he said, but he had discovered nutritional-supplement pills that cured it. "Whenever I feel it coming on," he said, "I just take these." He talked about how much skiing he could do.

I took the supplements. They had no effect. Nor did the antibiotics; the strep raged on. The doctor changed my prescription repeatedly, to no avail.

At the end of one of my appointments, the doctor followed me into the waiting room and asked my mother to make an appointment so that he could test her for strep. She said she felt fine, but he insisted that she might be infected but asymptomatic.

Our appointments fell on the same day. I went in first and sat while a nurse swabbed my throat. A few minutes later, the doctor bounded in, waving the positive-test swab, and bent over to look at my throat. I'd had strep for nearly three months. I dropped my face into my hands. He straightened abruptly and backed out of the room, repeating that the pills would cure the Epstein-Barr. "I go skiing a lot!" he hollered from down the hall.

I was still crying as I paid the bill. The receptionist gave me a sympathetic smile. She understood how I felt, she said, because she had Epstein-Barr, too. "It's amazing," she said. "The doctor has found that everyone working here has it."

I sat down. Several other patients were sitting near me, and I asked if the doctor had given any of them a diagnosis of Epstein-Barr. Each one said yes. While we were talking, my mother emerged from the doctor's office. He had told her that she, too, had Epstein-Barr.

· · ·

That year, millions of cicadas boiled up from the ground, teemed over tree limbs, and carpeted lawns and roads. The TV news showed people eating them on skewers. Cicadas burrowed into the house, scaled the curtains, swung from our clothes. I sat in bed, watching them bounce off the windowpane and nosedive into the grass, where they flapped and floundered as if they were drowning. Newton, the Dalmatian puppy my mother had adopted, zigzagged around the yard and snapped them out of the air. We called them flying dog snacks.

My world narrowed down to my bed and my window. I could no longer walk the length of my street. My hair was starting to fall out. I hadn't had a period in four months. My mouth and throat were pocked with dozens of bleeding sores and my temperature was spiking to a hundred and one every twelve hours, attended by a ferocious sweat; in addition to the strep, I now had trench mouth, a rare infection of the gums. Sleeping on my side was uncomfortable because I had little body fat left and my bones pressed into the skin on my hips, knees, and shoulders.

In sleep, I dreamed of vigorous motion. I had swum competitively for ten years, from age seven to seventeen. I had been riding horses since childhood. Smitten with Thoroughbred racing, I had spent my mid-teens learning to ride short-stirrup at a gallop, and praying that I wouldn't grow too tall to become a jockey. At Kenyon, I had been a tennis junkie. Now, as I lost the capacity to move, sports took over my dream world. I won at swimming in the Olympics, out-pedalled the *peloton* in the Tour de France, skimmed over a racetrack on a Kentucky Derby winner. When I woke, I felt the weight of illness on me before I opened my eyes.

Most of the people around me stepped backward. Linc said my friends asked him how I was, but after one or two get-well cards I stopped hearing from them. Now and then, I called people I had known in high school. The conversations were awkward and halting, and I felt foolish. No one knew what to say. Everyone had heard rumors that I was sick. Someone had heard I had AIDS. Another heard I was pregnant.

I missed Borden. At Kenyon, I had often studied in a deli run by a groovy guy named Craig, who cruised around the place in fluorescent-yellow sunglasses. It was there, in September of 1986, that Borden had first smiled at me. He was a senior, with a gentle, handsome face and wavy black hair. He had torn up his knee running track, and to avoid walking he used a battered bike to get around campus. The bike had no chain, so he could really ride it only downhill, wiggling it to keep it going when the ground levelled out. On the uphills, he stabbed at the ground with his good leg, Fred Flintstone style. Eventually, some frat brothers kidnapped the bike and hung it from a tree over the Scrotum Pole, a stone marker that had earned its nickname during a legendary fraternity vaulting incident.

From the day we met in the deli, Borden and I had been inseparable. Since I left Kenyon, he had sent me off-color postcards and silly drawings, mailed between papers and finals and graduation. I wrote dirty limericks and mailed them back to him.

That summer, he showed up at my door. He got a job as an assistant editor at a foreign-policy quarterly, moved in with me and my mother, and took care of me, making plans for the things we'd do when I got better.

Of my friends, only Linc visited. Home for the summer in Chicago, he drove Dr. Diesel fifteen hours to my house, where he would sit in a dilapidated denim armchair at the foot of my bed. The seat on the chair had collapsed, but he sat there anyway, his long thighs pointing up at the ceiling. Each time he saw me after a long absence, a wide startled look would pass over his face. He once said that he could sense the disease on me. I knew what he meant. I was disappearing inside it.

· · ·

I saw my next physician only once. My jeans slid down my hips as I walked into the exam room, and he watched me tug them up. He asked how often I weighed myself. Often, I replied. You shouldn't weigh yourself, he said, and you have to eat. I'm not dieting, I replied. Girls shouldn't be so thin, he said. I know, I don't want to be this thin. Yes, yes, but girls *shouldn't* be so thin.

After the appointment, I went to the bathroom, and as I opened the door to leave the doctor nearly fell into me. I was halfway home when I realized that he had been trying to hear if I was vomiting.

The next doctor was a pretty, compact woman with a squirrelly brightness. She found that I still had strep and changed the antibiotics. She ran the same tests that everyone else had run, and, again, the results were normal. I fought off the strep, but the other symptoms remained. I kept returning to see this doctor, hoping she could find some way to make me feel better. She couldn't, and I could see that it was wearing on her.

In September, I was so weak that on a ride over to her office I had to drop my head to my knees to avoid passing out. When the nurse entered, I was lying down, holding my head, the room swimming around me. She took my blood pressure: 70/50. The doctor came in. She wouldn't look at me.

"I don't know why you keep coming here," she said, her lips tight.

I told her that I felt faint and asked about my blood pressure. She said that it was normal and left, saying nothing else. She then went to see my mother, who was in the waiting room. "When is she going to realize that her problems are all in her head?" the doctor said.

I returned home, lay down, and tried to figure out what to do. My psychiatrist had found me to be mentally healthy, but my physicians had concluded that if my symptoms and the results of a few conventional tests didn't fit a disease they knew of, my problem *had* to be psychological. Rather than admit that they didn't know what I had, they made a diagnosis they weren't qualified to make.

Without my physicians' support, it was almost impossible to find support from others. People told me I was lazy and selfish. Someone lamented how unfortunate Borden was to have a girlfriend who demanded coddling. Some of Borden's friends suggested that he was foolish and weak to stand by me. "The best thing my parents ever did for my deadbeat brother," a former professor of his told him, "was to throw him out." I was ashamed and angry and indescribably lonely.

.   .   .

For seven months I had remained hopeful that I would find a way out of my illness, but the relentless decline of my body, my isolation, and the dismissal and derision I was experiencing took their toll. In the fall of 1987, I sank into a profound depression. I stopped seeing my physician and didn't try to find a new one. One afternoon, I dug through my mother's drawer and found a bottle of Valium that had been prescribed for back spasms. I poured the pills onto the bed and fingered them for an hour, pushing them into lines along the patterns on the quilt. I thought about Borden and couldn't put the pills in my mouth.

I went back to Dr. Troshinsky. He told me to make an appointment with Dr. John G. Bartlett, the chief of the Division of Infectious Diseases at Johns Hopkins University School of Medicine. Bartlett was the foremost authority in his field, Dr. Troshinsky said. If there was an answer, he would have it.

At Johns Hopkins, after a lengthy exam and review of my records, Dr. Bartlett sat down with Borden and me. My internists, he said, were wrong. My disease was real.

"You have chronic fatigue syndrome," he said. He explained that it was one of the most frustrating illnesses he had encountered in his practice; presented with severely incapacitated patients, he could do very little to help them. He suspected that it was viral in origin, although he believed that the Epstein-Barr virus was not involved; early lab tests had linked the virus to C.F.S., but subsequent research had demonstrated that some patients had had no exposure to the virus. He could offer no treatment. Eventually, he said, some patients recovered on their own.

"Some don't?"

"Some don't."

That night, for the first time since March, I didn't dream of being an athlete. I dreamed of being ill. In my dreams, I was never healthy again.

.   .   .

In the ensuing months, I began to improve. I hitched Newton to a leash and she tugged me through the neighborhood, first one block, then two, then three. My feet, soft from months in bed, blistered. The fever remained, but I was less prone to chills.

In the fall of 1988, Borden began graduate studies in political philosophy at the University of Chicago, and I felt well enough to move there with him. From the airport, we took a cab to Hyde Park, where Borden had rented a one-room apartment. The front door appeared to have been crowbarred for criminal purposes at least once. Inside, there was a mattress splayed across plastic milk crates and a three-legged dresser propped up on a brick. Roaches skittered over the walls and across the floor. The bathtub was heaped with used kitty litter. A weeks-old hamburger sat on the stove, shrunken into a shape that resembled the head of a mummy. The roaches were in various attitudes of repose around it.

We gave the mummy head a proper burial, roachproofed our toothbrushes by storing them in the refrigerator, and tried to make ends meet on Borden's nine-thousand-dollar-a-year stipend and our savings. The apartment was four flights up, with no elevator, so most days I spent my time inside, reading about the French Revolution and listening to our neighbor throw things at her husband.

I wanted to be useful, but I wasn't strong enough for a conventional job. The one thing I could still do, however, was write. Shortly after arriving in Chicago, while watching a video of the 1988 Kentucky Derby, I had an idea for an article on the impact of overcrowded fields on the race. I researched and wrote the piece, then mailed it to an obscure racing magazine. I got a job offer: fifty dollars per story, no benefits. I took only assignments that I could do from home and wrote them in bed. The magazine never paid me, but my bylines drew assignments at better publications, ultimately earning me regular work covering equine medicine and horse-industry issues at *Equus*.

I was growing much stronger, but whenever I overextended myself my health disintegrated. One mistake could land me in bed for weeks, so the potential cost of even the most trivial activities, from showering to walking to the mailbox, had to be painstakingly considered. Sometimes I relapsed for no reason at all. Living in perpetual fear of collapse was stressful, but on my good days I was functioning much better. By 1990, I could walk all over Hyde Park, navigate the stairs of the apartment with ease, and, for half an hour on one blissful afternoon, ride a horse. Three years after becoming ill, I wrote to Linc about the curious sensation of growing younger.

· · ·

In the summer of 1991, while visiting my mother during Borden's summer break, he and I decided to drive to New York to see the racetrack at Saratoga. A ten-hour road trip was risky, but I had grown tired of living so confined a life.

As we set out, the skies darkened. By the time we reached the interstate, a ferocious thunderstorm was crashing around us. Rain and hail hammered the roof of the car and gusts of wind buffeted us across the lane. We were caught in speeding traffic, but because the sheets of rain sweeping down the windshield limited visibility to a blurry tinge of lights ahead and behind, we couldn't slow down or pull over. It was more than an hour before we were able to escape into a rest stop. I sat on the floor of the bathroom, looking out a high window and watching the trees sway. The rain tapered off. My hands were shaking.

We had planned to stop at the New Jersey farmhouse where our friends Bill and Sarah were staying, but we were very late. Borden called them on a pay phone while I waited in the car, watching him through the beads of rain on the windshield. He climbed back in, and we sat with the engine idling. I was frightened by the draining sensation in my body.

Should we turn around? I asked. Borden's brow furrowed. Sometimes you've gotten a second wind, he said gently, as if asking a question. I wanted to believe him, so I agreed. He put the car in gear and we drove in silence. I felt worse and worse. I think we should turn around, I said, struggling to push the words out. We're closer to Bill's than we are to home, he said. If we keep going, you can rest sooner. He was scared now, leaning forward, driving fast. We entered New Jersey. We have to turn around, I said. Please. My head was pressed against the window, and I was crying. We're almost there, he said. We turned into the farmhouse driveway. There were rows of melons in the field.

Bill took us to a guest room. Borden turned on the TV and left me to rest. By the time he returned to check on me, I was sweating profusely and chills were running over me in waves. He took my hand and was horrified: it was gray and cold, and the veins had vanished.

He spread blankets over me and tried to help me drink a glass of milk. I couldn't sit up, so he cupped my head in his hand and tipped the milk into my mouth sideways. It ran down my cheek and pooled on the pillow. My teeth chattered so much that I couldn't speak. Borden called an emergency room. The nurse thought that I was in shock and urged him to rush me in. But we were far from the hospital, and doctors had never been able to help. I was sure that being moved would kill me.

Borden lay down and held me. Wide awake, I slid into delirium. I was in a vast desert, looking down at a dead Indian. His body was desiccated and hardened, his skin shiny and black and taut over his sinews, his arms bent upward, hands grasping, clawlike. His shrivelled tongue was thrust into an empty eye socket. I lay there and trembled, whispering *I love you, I love you, I love you* to Borden through clenched teeth. *I'm sorry,* he said.

Hours passed. The sun rose over the melon field.

Borden drove me back to my mother's house. I lay exhausted for three days. When I opened my eyes on the morning of the fourth day, I had a black feeling. I couldn't get up.

· · ·

For as long as two months at a time, I couldn't get down the stairs. Bathing became nearly impossible. Once a week or so, I sat on the edge of the tub and rubbed a washcloth over myself. The smallest exertion plunged me into a "crash." First, my legs would weaken and I'd lose the strength to stand. Then I wouldn't be able to sit up. My arms would go next, and I'd be unable to lift them. I couldn't roll over. Soon, I would lose the strength to speak. Only my eyes were capable of movement. At the bottom of each breath, I would wonder if I'd be able to draw the next one.

The corpse of the Indian hung in my mind. Borden and I never spoke of it, or of the events of that night, and we never spoke of the future. To corral my thoughts, he made lists with me: candybars from A to Z, Kentucky Derby winners, Vice-Presidents in backward order, N.F.L. quarterbacks, Union Army commanders. Over and over, I asked him if I was going to survive. He always answered yes.

Late one night, as I walked down the hall, I heard a soft, low sound and looked down the stairway. I saw Borden, pacing the foyer and sobbing. I started to call to him, then stopped myself, realizing that he wished to be alone. The next morning, he was as cheerful and steady as ever. But sometimes when I looked out the window I'd see him walking around the yard in endless revolutions, head down, hands on his temples.

One afternoon in September, he came in, sat on my bed, and told me that classes were starting and he had to return to Chicago. Before he left, he gave me a silver ring engraved with the words "*Vous et nul autre.*" I slid it on my finger and pressed my face to his chest.

·   ·   ·

With Borden in Chicago and my mother at work, I needed assistance to get through the day. I went through several helpers hired from nanny services. The first one clattered in with stacks of crimson-beaded Moroccan shoes and harem pants. She dumped them on my bed. "Twenty for the shoes, thirty for the pants," she said. She prowled through the house, appraising the furniture. "How much do you want for your refrigerator?" she asked.

When I asked the woman who followed to take Newton into the back yard, she opened the front door and shooed the dog onto the street. Lying in bed upstairs, I heard the dog barking gleefully as she galloped westward. I called to the woman but got no response. I sat up and looked out the window. The woman was standing high in our apple tree, mouth open, gaping at the vacant sky. The dog returned; the woman did not.

The third helper sympathized and commiserated, then bustled around downstairs while I lay upstairs in bed. It wasn't until she abruptly vanished that I discovered she had been packing armloads of my belongings into her car each evening. I went to the closet and found only a hanger where my taffeta ball gown had been.

On a rainy afternoon in January of 1993, I was sitting on the bed reading a magazine when the room began whirling violently. I dropped the magazine and grabbed on to the dresser. I felt as though I were rolling and lurching, a ship on the high seas. I clung to the dresser and waited for the feeling to pass, but it didn't. At five the next morning, I woke with a screeching, metal-on-metal sound in my ears. My eyes were jerking to the left, and I couldn't stop them. My eyes, upper lip, and cheeks were markedly swollen.

I went to a neurologist for tests. A technician asked me to lie down on a table. He produced something that looked like a blowtorch and pushed it into my ear. A jet of hot air roared out, spinning the vestibular fluid in my inner ear. It triggered such a forceful sensation of spinning that I gripped the table with all my strength, certain that I was about to fly off and slam into the wall. The tests determined that my vertigo was neurological in origin and virtually untreatable. The doctor prescribed diuretics and an extremely low-sodium diet to control the facial edema, which seemed to be linked to the vertigo. He could do little else.

The vertigo wouldn't stop. I didn't lie on my bed so much as ride it as it swung and spun. There was a constant shrieking sound in my ears. The furniture flexed and skidded around the room, and the walls folded and unfolded. Every few days there was a sudden plunging sensation, and I would throw my arms out to catch myself. The leftward eye-rolling came and went. Sleep brought no respite; every dream took place on the deck of a tossing ship, a runaway rollercoaster, a plane caught in violent turbulence, a falling elevator. Looking at anything close-up left me reeling. I couldn't read or write. I rented audiobooks, but I couldn't follow the narratives.

Borden called several times a day. He told me about Xenophon and Thucydides, the wind off Lake Michigan, the athletic feats of the roaches. When I asked him about himself, he changed the subject.

On Valentine's Day, a package from Borden arrived in the mail. Inside was a gold pocket watch. I hung it from my window frame and stared at it as the room bent and arced around it. Weeks passed, and then months. The watch dial meted out each day, the light sliding across it: reddish in the morning, hard and colorless at midday, red again at dusk. In the dark, I could hear it ticking.

Outside, the world went on. Linc got married, my siblings had children, my friends got graduate degrees and jobs and mort-gages. None of it had any relation to me. The realm of possibility began and ended in that room, on that bed. I no longer imagined anything else. If I was asked what month it was, I had to think for a while before I could answer.

While I was lying there, I began to believe that we had struck the deer back in 1987, that he had come through the windshield and killed me, and that this was Hell.

.   .   .

Two years passed. In late 1994, Borden took his qualifying exams, and left Chicago. When I first saw him, lugging his green backpack, he was so thin that I gasped.

In 1995, by tiny increments, the vertigo began to abate. Eventually, I could read the back of a cornflakes box. My strength began to return. Instead of sitting on the edge of the tub with a washcloth, I could sit on the shower floor while the water ran over me. The first time I showered, dead skin peeled off in sheets. A hair stylist came and cut off eight inches of my hair, which had been growing like kudzu for several years and was now nearing my waist. In time, I could walk down the stairs almost every day. I sat on the patio looking at the trees.

Since my visit to Johns Hopkins, I had searched for an internist I could trust. In 1988, C.F.S. had been officially recognized and described by the Centers for Disease Control and Prevention. Subsequent research suggested endocrinologic, immunologic, and neurological abnormalities in many C.F.S. patients, though the causes remained elusive. Physicians were becoming aware of the disease, but many of them knew less about it than I did. Others hawked dubious treatments. For a while, I tried almost anything. A few treatments caused disastrous side effects. The rest did nothing.

Then a friend referred me to Dr. Fred Gill, a renowned infectious-disease specialist. He was an angular, elegant man with a neat, Amish-style beard rimming a sharp jawline. As Borden and I told him my story, I found my stomach tightening in anticipation of a dismissive verdict. But Dr. Gill listened for the better part of an hour. When we had finished, he nodded. He couldn't cure me, he said, but he would do everything he could to help me cope with the illness. In the following years, Dr. Gill managed my symptoms and coördinated my care with other specialists.

Eager to be productive, I called my *Equus* editor, Laurie Prinz, and asked if I could write something. She assigned a story on equine surgery and told me not to worry about a deadline. I did the interviews on the phone from bed. Because looking at the page made the room shimmy crazily around me, I could write only a paragraph or two a day. When I could no longer stand the spinning, I'd take a pillow into the yard and lie in the grass with Newton, fixing my eyes on the treetops while she dissected a bone. It took me six weeks to write fifteen hundred words, but, four years after the abortive trip to Saratoga, I was coming back.

In 1996, with Borden and Fangfoss the cat, I moved into a small apartment in northwest Washington, D.C. One block away stood a fire station, and if Washington has an arson district we were in the heart of it. At the Taiwanese consulate, which was next door, a group of protesters soon set up camp, hauled in a loudspeaker and blasted a Chinese rallying song, sung by shrieky children. They apparently had a loop tape, so the song never ended. It was like listening to a bone saw. After a few weeks, I started dreaming to it.

I turned up my radio and wrote as much as I could, mostly equine veterinary medical articles for *Equus*. On breaks, I took brief walks. I bought new shoes—I'd been lying around in socks for years—and discovered that my feet had shrunk two sizes. I had lived for so long in silence and isolation that the world was a sensory explosion. At the grocery store, I dragged my hands along the shelves, touching boxes and bags, smelling oranges and pears and apples. At the hardware store, I'd plunge my arm into the seed bins to feel the pleasing weight of the grain against my skin. I was a toddler again.

After years of seeing people almost exclusively on television, I found their three-dimensionality startling: the light playing off their faces, the complexity of their hands, the strange electric feel of their nearness. One afternoon, I spent fifteen minutes watching a shirtless man clip a hedge, enthralled by the glide of the muscles under his skin.

•   •   •

On a cool fall day in 1996, I was sifting through some documents on the great racehorse Seabiscuit when I discovered Red Pollard, the horse's jockey. I saw him first in a photograph, curled over Seabiscuit's neck. Looking out at me from the summer of 1938, he had wistful eyes and a face as rough as walnut bark.

I began looking into his life and found a story to go with the face. Born in 1909, Red was an exceptionally intelligent, bookish child with a shock of orange hair. At fifteen, he was abandoned by his guardian at a makeshift racetrack cut through a Montana hayfield. He wanted to be a jockey, but he was too tall and too powerfully built. That didn't stop him, though. He began race riding in the bush leagues and fared so badly that he took to part-time prizefighting in order to survive. He lived in horse stalls for twelve years, studying Emerson and the "Rubáiyát," piloting neurotic horses at "leaky roof" tracks, getting punched bloody in cowtown clubs, keeping painfully thin with near-starvation diets, and probably pills containing the eggs of tapeworms.

He was appallingly accident prone. Racehorses blinded his right eye, somersaulted onto his chest at forty miles per hour, trampled him, and rammed him into the corner of a barn, virtually severing his lower leg. He shattered his teeth and fractured his back, hip, legs, collarbone, shoulder, ribs. He was once so badly mauled that the newspapers announced his death. But he came back every time, struggling through pain and fear and the limitations of his body to do the only thing he had ever wanted to do. And in the one lucky moment of his unlucky life he found Seabiscuit, a horse as damaged and persistent as he was. I hung Red's picture above my desk and began to write.

What began as an article for *American Heritage* became an obsession, and in the next two years the obsession became a book. Borden and I moved to a cheap rental house farther downtown, and I arranged my life around the project. At the local library, I pored over documents and microfilm I requisitioned from the Library of Congress. If I looked down at my work, the room spun, so I perched my laptop on a stack of books in my office, and Borden jerry-rigged a device that held documents vertically. When I was too tired to sit at my desk, I set the laptop up on my bed. When I was too dizzy to read, I lay down and wrote with my eyes closed. Living in my subjects' bodies, I forgot about my own.

I mailed the manuscript off to Random House in September, 2000, then fell into bed. I was lying there the following day when the room began to gyrate. Reviewing the galleys brought me close to vomiting several times a day. Most of the gains I had made since 1995 were lost. I spent each afternoon sitting with Fangfoss on my back steps, watching the world undulate and sliding into despair.

·   ·   ·

In March of 2001, Random House released "Seabiscuit: An American Legend." Five days later, I was lying down, when the phone rang. "You are a best-selling writer," my editor said. I screamed. Two weeks later, I picked up the phone to hear him and my agent shout in tandem, "You're No. 1!" Borden threw a window open and yelled it to the neighborhood.

That spring, as I tried to cope with the dreamy unreality of success and the continuing failure of my health, something began to change in Borden. At meals, he sat in silence, his gaze disconnected, his jaw muscles working. His sentences trailed off in the middle. He couldn't sleep or eat. He was falling away from me, and I didn't know why.

He came into my office one night in June, sat down, and slid his chair up to me, touching his knees to mine. I looked at his face. He was still young and handsome, his hair black, his skin seamless. But the color was gone from his lips, the quickness from his eyes. He tried to smile, but the corners of his mouth wavered. He dropped his chin to his chest.

He began to speak, and fourteen years of unvoiced emotions spilled out: the torment of watching the woman he loved suffer;

his feelings of responsibility and helplessness and anger; his long-ing for children we probably couldn't have; the endless strain of living in obedience to an extraordinarily volatile disease.

We talked for much of the night. I found myself revealing all the grief that I had hidden from him. When I asked him why he hadn't said anything before, he said he thought I would shatter. I realized that I had feared the same of him. In protecting each other from the awful repercussions of our misfortune, we had become strangers.

When we were too tired to talk anymore, I went into the bed-room and sat down alone. I slid his ring from my finger and dropped it into a drawer.

We spent a long, painful summer talking, and for both of us there were surprises. I didn't shatter, and neither did he. I pre-pared myself for him to leave, but he didn't. We became, for the first time since our days at Kenyon, alive with each other.

·   ·   ·

One night that fall, I walked to the back of the yard. As Fang-foss hunted imaginary mice in the grass, I looked out at the hill behind the house. Beyond it, downtown Washington hummed like an idling engine, the city lights radiating over the ridge. I looked west, where a line of row-house chimneys filed down the hill until they became indistinguishable from the trunks of the walnut trees at the road's end. Borden came out and joined me briefly, draping his arms over my shoulders, then he went inside. I watched the screen door slap behind him.

As I turned back, I saw a slit of light arc over the houses and vanish behind the trees. It was the first meteor I had seen since that night in Linc's car. I thought, for the first time in a long time, of the deer.

In the depths of illness, I believed that the deer had crashed through the windshield and ushered me into an existence in which the only possibility was suffering. I was haunted by his form in front of the car, his bent knee, the seeming inevitability of catastrophe, and the ruin my life became.

I had forgotten the critical moment. The deer's knee didn't straighten. He didn't step into our path, we didn't strike him, and I didn't die. As sure as I was that he had taken everything from me, I was wrong.

The car passed him and moved on.

The Atlantic Monthly

FINALIST, PROFILE WRITING

Wynton's Blues

Written with depth and nuance, David Hajdu's "Wynton's Blues" tells the story of Wynton Marsalis, the man with the horn, as he turns forty. Displaying a thorough grasp of the history and current state of jazz, Hajdu presents a layered portrait of this one-time "young lion" poised at a crossroads.

David Hajdu

Wynton's Blues

For two decades Wynton Marsalis ruled the jazz universe, enjoying virtually unqualified admiration as a musician and unsurpassed influence as the music's leading promoter and definer. But after a series of sour notes—he parted from his record label, has been caught up in controversy at Jazz at Lincoln Center, and has been drawing increasing fire from critics and fellow musicians alike for his narrow neotraditionalism— perhaps the biggest name in jazz faces an uncertain future. Just like jazz itself.

Manhattan is empty during the last week of August, and the kind of emptiness it achieves is like that of the mind during meditation—a temporary, unnatural purity. On a Tuesday evening in late August of 2001 I was wandering around Greenwich Village and ended up at the Village Vanguard. After sixty-some years of business the illustrious little jazz haunt hasn't changed; it remains one of the inexplicable constants of the Manhattan landscape. Its midtown cousin, Birdland (named for the bebop saxophonist Charlie "Yardbird" Parker), closed down decades ago and was replaced by a strip joint, Flash Dancers, which has been in business longer than Birdland was; a theme nightclub near Times Square now uses the Birdland name. There's still a Cotton Club in Harlem, but not in the original location, and now it's a seedy disco. The Vanguard has somehow survived in its primordial basement and has retained all the bohemian eccentricities that have always helped make it cool: the fence-post marquee, with performers' names handwritten vertically; the treacherously angled stairwell; no food served; no credit cards accepted. Lorraine Gordon, the Vanguard's owner and the widow of the club's founder, is a Medici of the jazz world, a patron and kingmaker. Among jazz fans and musicians the Village Vanguard is clearly a paragon of the music's own kind of purity—one that's neither temporary nor unnatural.

I walked in on a set in progress and took the next-to-last seat on the burgundy-leather banquette that runs along the east wall. The end table, Lorraine Gordon's, was vacant, indicating that Gordon was probably in the kitchen, where she does the books and where musicians congregate between sets. (Although foodless, the Vanguard has one of the most venerable kitchens in New York.) A small combo was running through the bebop classic "Blue 'n' Boogie" at a duly vertiginous speed. There was no mistaking the bandleader: Charles McPherson, an alto saxophonist who was a protégé of the late bassist and composer Charles Mingus. McPherson is a venturesome musician who upends the jazz repertoire on the bandstand, and he composes pieces built on surprise, as Mingus did.

Although he is a superior talent, he's not a top jazz attraction, which is why he was scheduled for the last week in August. For his second tune after my arrival McPherson, in homage to his mentor, played Mingus's homage to Lester Young, "Goodbye Pork Pie Hat." The performance was languid, and my eyes drifted, settling eventually on the trumpet player, because he was turned away from the audience and even from the rest of the band, staring at the floor. Although I couldn't place him, he looked vaguely familiar, like an older version of Wynton Marsalis.

During the third song, Charlie Parker's "Chasin' the Bird," the trumpeter stepped to the center of the bandstand to take a solo. "Excuse me," I whispered to the fellow next to me (a jazz guitarist, I later learned). "Is that Wynton Marsalis?"

"I very seriously doubt that," he snapped back, as if I had asked if it was Parker himself.

Stylishly dressed in an Italian-cut gray suit, a dark-blue shirt, and a muted blue tie, the soloist had the burnished elegance that Wynton Marsalis and his musician brothers have been bringing to jazz for two decades. If this man was not Wynton, he looked like what "Marsalis" means—but older and heavier, and not just in appearance. There was a weight upon him; he didn't smile, and his eyes were small and affectless. I could barely reconcile the sight before me with the image of youthful élan that Wynton Marsalis has always called to mind.

The fourth song was a solo showcase for the trumpeter, who, I could now see, was indeed Marsalis, but who no more sounded than looked like what I expected. He played a ballad, "I Don't Stand a Ghost of a Chance With You," unaccompanied. Written by Victor Young, a film-score composer, for a 1930s romance, the piece can bring out the sadness in any scene, and Marsalis appeared deeply attuned to its melancholy. He performed the song in murmurs and sighs, at points nearly talking the words in notes. It was a wrenching act of creative expression. When he reached the climax, Marsalis played the final phrase, the title statement, in declarative tones, allowing each successive note to linger in the air a bit longer. "I don't stand ... a ghost ... of ... a ... chance ..." The room was silent until, at the most dramatic point, someone's cell phone went off, blaring a rapid singsong melody in electronic bleeps. People started giggling and picking up their drinks. The moment—the whole performance—unraveled.

Marsalis paused for a beat, motionless, and his eyebrows arched. I scrawled on a sheet of notepaper, MAGIC, RUINED. The cell-phone offender scooted into the hall as the chatter in the room grew louder. Still frozen at the microphone, Marsalis replayed the silly cell-phone melody note for note. Then he repeated it, and began improvising variations on the tune. The audience slowly came back to him. In a few minutes he resolved the improvisation—which had changed keys once or twice and throttled down to a ballad tempo—and ended up exactly where he had left off: "with ... you ..." The ovation was tremendous.

Lorraine Gordon had come in shortly before the final notes. Leaning over to me, she said, "What did I miss?"

. . .

That was a good question, and I had others. What was Wynton Marsalis, perhaps the most famous jazz musician alive, doing as a sideman in a band led by a little-known saxophonist in the slowest week of the year? Where were the scores of fans who used to line up on the sidewalk whenever Marsalis played, regardless of whether he was billed and promoted? Why did he look so downtrodden, so leaden ... so different that he was scarcely recognizable? How could his playing have been so perfunctory (as it was for most of that evening) and yet so transcendent on one bittersweet song about loss and self-doubt? What happened to Wynton Marsalis?

That may be like asking What happened to jazz? For twenty years the fates of Marsalis and jazz music have appeared inextricably intertwined. He was a young newcomer on the New York scene at a time when jazz seemed dominated and diminished by rock-oriented "fusion," marginalized by outré experimentation and electronics, and disconnected from the youth audience that has driven American popular culture since the postwar era. Extraordinarily gifted and fluent in both jazz and classical music, not to mention young, handsome, black, impassioned, and articulate, especially on the importance of jazz history and jazz masters, Marsalis was ideally equipped to lead a cultural-aesthetic movement suited to the time, a renaissance that raised public esteem for and the popular appeal of jazz through a return to the music's traditional values: jazz for the Reagan revolution. In 1990 *Time* magazine put him on the cover and announced the dawn of "The New Jazz Age." Record companies rediscovered the music and revived long-dormant jazz lines, signing countless young musicians inspired by Marsalis, along with three of his five brothers (first his older brother, Branford, a celebrated tenor saxophonist; later Delfeayo, a trombonist; and eventually the youngest, Jason, a percussionist) and his father, Ellis (a respected educator and pianist in the family's native New Orleans). By the 1990s Wynton Marsalis had become an omnipresent spokesperson for his music and also one of its most prolific and highly decorated practitioners (he was the first jazz composer to win a Pulitzer Prize, for *Blood on the Fields,* his oratorio about slavery)—something of a counterpart to Leonard Bernstein in the 1950s. He took jazz up and over the hierarchical divide that had long isolated the music from the fine-arts establishment; the modest summer jazz program he created won a full constituency at Lincoln Center. In 1999, to mark the end of the century, Marsalis issued a total of fifteen CDs—about one new title every month.

In the following two years he did not release a single CD of new music. In fact, after two decades with Columbia Records, the prestigious and high-powered label historically associated with Duke Ellington, Thelonious Monk, and Miles Davis, Marsalis has no record contract with any company. Nor does his brother Branford, who just a few years ago was not only one of Columbia's recording stars but an executive consultant overseeing the artists-and-repertory direction of the label's jazz division. (Branford recently formed an independent record company.) Over the past few years Columbia has drastically reduced its roster of active jazz musicians, shifting its emphasis to reissues of old recordings. Atlantic folded its jazz catalogue into the operations of its parent company, Warner, and essentially gave up on developing new artists. Verve is a fraction of the size it was a decade ago. In addition, jazz clubs around the country have been struggling, and the attacks of September 11 hurt night life everywhere; New York's venerable Sweet Basil closed in the spring of 2001, after twenty-five years in operation, and later reopened as a youth-oriented world-music place. In the institutional arena, Carnegie Hall discontinued its in-house jazz orchestra at the end of the 2001–2002 season.

For this grim state of affairs in jazz Marsalis, the public face of the music and the evident master of its destiny, has been declared at least partly culpable. By leading jazz into the realm of unbending classicism, by applying the Great Man template to establish an iconography (Armstrong, Ellington, Parker, Coltrane), and by sanctifying a canon of their own choosing (Armstrong's "Hot Fives," Ellington's Blanton-Webster period, Parker's Savoy sessions, Coltrane's *A Love Supreme*), Marsalis and his adherents are said to have codified the music in a stifling orthodoxy and inhibited the revolutionary impulses that have always advanced jazz.

"They've done a lot to take the essence of jazz and distort it," the composer and pianist George Russell told *The New York Times* in 1998. "They've put a damper on the main ingredient of jazz, which is innovation."

A former executive with Columbia Records who has worked intimately with five Marsalises says, "For many people, Wynton has come to embody some retro ideology that is not really of the moment, you know—it's more museumlike in nature, a look back. I think as each day passes, Wynton does lose relevance as a shaper of musical direction. He's not quite the leader of a musical movement any longer. That doesn't mean he's not remark-able, or without considerable clout, or that he's not the leader of a cultural movement. But within the record industry the Marsalises are no longer seen as the top guys."

Six weeks after he played in Charles McPherson's band at the Village Vanguard, Wynton Marsalis turned forty. (His publicists will have to come up with a nickname to replace "the young lion.") Marsalis has been struggling, clearly. In addition to the rest of his troubles, he and his fiancée broke off the engagement that might have brought stability to his notoriously mercurial romantic life (he has three sons by two single women, one on each coast), and Jazz at Lincoln Center suffered a setback shortly after Marsalis's birthday, when the chairman of its board of directors was murdered in his home. This February, Marsalis returned briefly to the spotlight, when he, his three musical brothers, and their father joined forces on their first CD together, *The Marsalis Family: A Jazz Celebration*— released on Branford's new label, Marsalis Music, and supported by a high-profile PBS special and a brief national tour starting a few days later. But this effort to celebrate the Marsalis legacy is seen by some in the jazz world as just another exercise in nostalgia. It's a criticism that familiarly echoes the one that has bedeviled jazz as a whole for some years. Yet if the lives of this man and America's great indigenous music are indeed entwined, their predicament calls for fuller scrutiny and better understanding. It's too easy to dismiss Marsalis's condition as a midlife crisis.

.   .   .

Every icon needs an origin myth. Born in the same city as jazz, Wynton Marsalis was blessed with a signifying provenance. "I'm from New Orleans," he has told an interviewer, as shorthand for his musical background. "We don't need a concert hall for jazz." In many ways Marsalis's story is so neatly connected to jazz history that it defies credulity. Had a screenwriter created Wynton

Marsalis, a cynical producer would have sent back the opening scenes for rewrite: too perfect. Not only did he come from the cradle of jazz but he plays the trumpet, the instrument that originally defined the music. "The first jazz musician was a trumpeter, Buddy Bolden," Marsalis once said, "and the last will be a trumpeter, the archangel Gabriel." Moreover, Marsalis rose to prominence in the mid-1980s, just as jazz was approaching its centennial. "There's a tremendous symbolic resonance that has always been a part of what Wynton's about," says Jeff Levenson, a veteran jazz writer who also worked as an executive at both Columbia and Warner Bros. Records. "This kid emerges who's a hotshot . . . and the whole thing has a kind of symmetry to it. Louis Armstrong starts things off—trumpet player, New Orleans, turn of the century. Wynton closes it out—a trumpet player from New Orleans."

Dolores and Ellis Marsalis still live in the house Wynton left when he moved to New York on a scholarship to Juilliard, in 1979. It is a nice, modest house of green-painted clapboard, in a neighborhood that used to be nicer. To enter the house one goes through an iron gate and past a patch of lawn with manicured shrubbery and a statue of a black madonna in the center. The interior looks large without six boys frolicking in it at once. (Only thirty-two-year-old Mboya, who is autistic, lives at home now.) Dolores Marsalis keeps the house, her husband tells me with a pride they obviously share: everything is just so, and communicates to the visitor in a gracious way. The chairs have pressed crocheted doilies pinned to their backs: they are not for horseplay. The walls are covered with paintings and graphics portraying African-American themes: they are not decorations but art. The table next to the front door holds a display of photographs of women in the family: everybody counts.

Ellis Marsalis is a sturdy man, sixty-eight, who moves with a deliberate bounce. A lifelong educator who has taught music on every level from elementary school to college, he held a chair in jazz studies endowed by Coca-Cola at the University of New Orleans until his retirement, in 2001. When he speaks, his words have the measured authority of a lesson. Wynton Marsalis is very much like his father in the way he holds himself (hunched a bit, as if he were reading from a music stand), sits (legs spread), gestures (forward and in tempo), and speaks (with a disarming touch of New Orleans patois).

To Ellis Marsalis, the work ethic his own father taught by example is primary to success, be it in commerce or in art. "When I was teaching [high school]," he says, "I used to see a lot of talent that didn't particularly go anywhere, and at first it was really mysterious to me. I couldn't really understand it—I mean, to see a seventeen-year-old kid who's a natural bass. Those are born. You don't learn to do that. And to hear coloratura sopranos who couldn't care less. I was forced to reappraise what my understanding of talent is. Then I eventually began to discover that talent is like the battery in a car. It'll get you started, but if the generator is bad, you don't go very far."

A musician by aspiration who took up teaching by necessity, Ellis Marsalis was ambivalent about his own decision to stay in New Orleans and raise his children, rather than to pursue a big-time career in New York. "At the time Wynton was growing up, I still had a lot of anxiety about going to New York," he recalls. I asked him if he thought Wynton had recognized his frustrations and had set out to aim higher by making New York his home base. Was he trying to fulfill his father's dream? "Could be," Ellis said, nodding slowly. "It could be."

In *The History of Jazz* (1997) Ted Gioia wrote, "[Wynton] Marsalis's rise to fame while barely out of his teens was an unprecedented event in the jazz world. No major jazz figure—not Ellington or Armstrong, Goodman or Gillespie—had become so famous, so fast." The facts are impressive even twenty years later: while still at Juilliard, Marsalis was invited to join another kind of conservatory, the Jazz Messengers, a band led by the drummer Art Blakey; soon after, he was appointed the group's musical director, at age nineteen. As Ellis Marsalis says, "He called up and said, 'Man, I have a chance to join Art Blakey's band. What do you think?' I said, 'Well, one thing about Juilliard, man,' I said, 'Juilliard's going to be there when they're shoveling dirt in your face. Art Blakey won't.'" By 1982, when he turned twenty-one, Wynton had toured with the jazz star Herbie Hancock and had played with distinction on half a dozen albums, leading "the jazz press to declare him a prodigy," Jon Pareles wrote in *The New York Times* in the mid-1980s. Columbia Records signed him in an extraordinary contract that called for Marsalis to make both classical and jazz recordings, and he started a collection of Grammys in both categories. No jazz musician has had such success since.

To a degree Marsalis's aesthetic, which draws reverentially on the African-American traditions of the blues and swing, seems to repudiate the style of the previous era. Swing was a rejection of traditional New Orleans jazz, bebop a rejection of swing, cool jazz a rejection of bop, free jazz a rejection of the cool, and fusion a rejection of free jazz. (Though reductive and Oedipal, this theory bears up well enough if one ignores the innumerable overlaps, inconsistencies, and contradictions, and also the entire career of Duke Ellington.) Wynton and his young peers were rejecting fusion, an amorphous mixture of jazz and pop-rock, which they saw as fatuous and vulgar, and which they thought pandered to commercialism.

As the composer and trumpeter Terence Blanchard, a childhood friend of Wynton's who followed him to New York and into Blakey's band, recalls, "In the early eighties we had to fight for our existence in the music war. The fusion thing was real big, and we were trying to get back to, like, just the fundamental elements in jazz."

But for all fusion's attributes as a target (it was slick, ostentatious, cold, and elementally white, much like the big-band "innovations in modern music" of Stan Kenton and the "third-stream" pretenses of the 1950s), the style scarcely dominated the New York jazz scene when the Marsalis brothers and Blanchard started out. In fact, when Wynton Marsalis played at the club Seventh Avenue South in the last week of January 1982, to promote his eponymous first solo album, nearly every jazz room in town featured bebop (or older styles of the music): Kai Winding was at the Vanguard, Anita O'Day at the Blue Note, Dizzy Gillespie at Fat Tuesday's, Archie Shepp at Sweet Basil, George Shearing at Michael's Pub.

"There was a whole lot of jazz in New York then, and it was straight-ahead [bebop], by and large," recalls the pianist and educator Barry Harris. "You had all the work you could do [as a bebop musician], and nobody was doing fusion but the kids. Now, they made the festivals and whatnot for the younger crowd. That was where that was at. It was no big thing. That was a good time for straight-ahead [music] in New York."

Although marginal to the core jazz constituency, centered in New York (as it had been for decades and continues to be), fusion had a voguish appeal to college audiences and other young people. The Marsalis revolution was especially radical, then, in rejecting a style popular among musicians of the revolutionary's own age, rather than the music established by his elders; it was subversive methodologically as well as aesthetically, and the ensuing polarization in jazz circles on the subject of Marsalis and his music was uniquely intra-generational.

The musical landscape Marsalis entered in full stride and soon dominated was far more complex than most accounts have suggested—as is the actual music he has made. Marsalis was never a nostalgist like the tuba player Vince Giordano, who re-creates jazz styles of the early twentieth century. The improvisations on the first few Wynton Marsalis albums employed elements of the blues and swing (along with other styles, including free jazz), but in the service of personal expression; and Marsalis's earliest compositions, with their harmonic surprises and their lightning shifts in time signature, were less homage than montage. In the image his detractors like to paint (over and over), Marsalis single-handedly halted jazz's progress. "Wynton has the car in reverse," the trombonist and composer Bob Brookmeyer has said, "and the pedal to the metal"; if so, the vehicle was already in gear. Over the course of the 1970s a movement to elevate esteem for jazz and protect the music's heritage was emerging in one sphere at the same time that fusion and the music of the living bebop masters coexisted in their own spheres. The Smithsonian Institution began an effort to preserve the musical archives of Duke Ellington and other jazz masters; the bandleader and trumpeter Herb Pomeroy was leading a repertory jazz program at the Berklee College of Music, in Boston; the saxophonist Loren Schoenberg was working with Benny Goodman to revive his big band; the bassist Chuck Israels formed the National Jazz Ensemble; the musicologist and conductor Gunther Schuller was conducting vintage jazz works and writing about them as if there were a canon; the impresario George Wein founded the New York Jazz Repertory Company. "I just felt like it was time," recalls Wein, who later produced the neo-traditional concerts of the Carnegie Hall Jazz Band. "There was a lot of that percolating at the time, and that's the atmosphere that Wynton and the others came into."

The revival movement itself was a revival. Back in the late 1930s, when the "From Spirituals to Swing" concerts at Carnegie Hall gave American jazz the imprimatur of the cultural establishment, the music had changed course and languished in a contemplative state. Writers and musicians of the period rediscovered the artists and styles of the music's (relatively recent) past—a respite, time has shown us, during which jazz began metamorphosing into bebop.

The debate over classicism that has swirled around Marsalis is nothing new either. The enduring issue is, of course, not which work is entitled to a place in the canon—Manet's *Déjeuner sur l'herbe*? Jelly Roll Morton's "Black Bottom Stomp"?—but who is empowered to confer that distinction. Marsalis has compounded things substantially, not only by making music that he expects will be taken seriously but also by defining the terms, and by challenging white critics and white-dominated institutions to yield authority over such matters.

The scholar and author Gerald Early, a professor at Washington University in St. Louis, says, "Wynton Marsalis is a target for criticism because, unlike a lot of artists, he's become a quite outspoken critic himself, and he has articulated a historical theory and an aesthetic theory about jazz music. I think that critics feel kind of threatened and rather uncomfortable when an artist comes along who's capable of doing that pretty well—well enough so that a critic has to respect it." Indeed, most of the early press about Marsalis was laudatory, until he dared to use his platform to advance ideas about jazz history and black identity. Ever since, jazz critics, most of whom are white, have tended to treat Marsalis more severely. "The fact that these critics are white, that a lot of the audience for jazz music is white," Early says, "I think is a source of tension for many of the artists who are black. White critics basically codified and structured the history of this music and made the judgments about who is significant in the music and so forth, and I think in this culture that can't help but be a real source of tension for many black jazz musicians."

Stanley Crouch, a critic and a long-standing influence on Marsalis, is quick to expand on the theme. "I think a lot of the criticism of Wynton's music is based upon a hostility toward him. Marsalis, any way the critics look at him, is superior to them. He's a greater musician than any of them are writers. He's a good-looking guy. He has access to and has had access to a far higher quality of female than any of them could ever imagine. He doesn't look up to them, and that's a problem."

· · ·

Wynton Marsalis lives in an airy eight-room apartment on the twenty-ninth floor of a high-rise tower a few dozen footsteps from the stage entrance to Alice Tully Hall, where Lincoln Center's jazz orchestra has been playing since it started, in 1987. His home is as conscientiously detailed as the house of his parents. On a visit a year ago I asked him if his mother had helped him decorate it, and he laughed. "Maybe she should have," he said. "She knows what she's doing." But he has his own taste, and it isn't his mother's. The living room, which is so spacious that at first I didn't notice the grand piano in the corner, is done in vivid colors; Marsalis says that he likes Matisse for the "positivity and affirmation" of his work, and that he picked up the artist's vibrant palette in his appointments. Patterns on the carpeting and the fabrics suggest crescents, the symbol of his home town. Sunlight floods the room from banks of windows at the room's outer corners. "I like the sun," Marsalis told me as we sat on sofas opposite each other. "The source of life. There's a lot of sun in New Orleans." An enormous lithograph of Duke Ellington hangs over one of the sofas, and other prints and photographs of Ellington, along with those of Armstrong and Blakey, line the hall leading to the other rooms.

Gerald Early has commented on Marsalis's sense of style: "Whether he is at the cutting edge of what's going on in jazz now is neither here nor there. He represents a certain kind of image, which I think is enormously important, of the jazz musician as this kind of well-dressed, extremely sophisticated person, and a person who lives well—a person who reads books, a person who, you know, enjoys a kind of *GQ* sort of life."

Until recently Wynton Marsalis seemed physically unaccountable to time. His good looks were the boyish kind. Full-cheeked and bright-eyed, he was adorable. At the same time, he always carried himself with a poised surety, a masculine grace, that tended to make women straighten up and men start poking their toes at things. The nickname "young lion" seemed appropriate, Marsalis being a creature of fearsome beauty who is also nocturnal, combative, and nomadic. But his body has begun its midlife thickening. He projects a quieter, softer, slower presence now, although he still plays a tough game of basketball.

For most of the past twenty years he has been on view in his natural state: working. Marsalis is living by the work ethic that his father passed on from his grandfather, with a determination that would seem pathological if it weren't utterly normal for him. He is not manic; he works at a moderate pace but never stops. Indeed, although Marsalis has not been recording much lately, he is constantly working with the Lincoln Center Jazz Orchestra. From his office in the headquarters of Jazz at Lincoln Center he oversees its creative and educational activities. He practices the trumpet for several hours every day. He plays with his sons when they are with him. And in the evening he goes out—leaving just a few hours a night for sleep. When we spoke at his home, I asked him what the man in the lithograph over his head, Duke Ellington, meant to him.

"Indefatigable worker. He loved music and people and playing. He played a lot, and he loved jazz, and he loved the Afro-American people."

"Do you have a performance philosophy?"

"I've always tried to be respectful of my audience. I always sign people's autographs, always acted like I was working for them. I try to play people's requests, try to come up with a way of playing that I thought people would want to listen to—never thought I was above them. I'm here to do a job. I always try to be professional, and many times, in halls across the country, I'm the last one to leave—all the crews are gone.

"For me to tell people who are spending their money and have worked their jobs and are going on a date with their husbands or their wives, tell them, 'I know you all are here, and you should be honored that I'm here'—that's just not my philosophy."

He keeps a dressing room full of elegant clothing—closets of dark suits and formal wear, and a rack of hats. The bedroom has a long cabinet with framed family photos and other memorabilia on display; when Marsalis sits up in his bed, they are what he sees.

He flopped onto his mattress and focused on the task of

cleaning and lubricating his trumpet. "I should properly do this all the time," he said, shaking his head at himself. "I keep playing till it's so filthy all you hear when I play it is the dirt." Marsalis pulled his instrument apart and began a consuming procedure that involved massaging a viscous fluid onto each of the parts. As he worked, he talked about music, which is what he seems most at home doing wherever he is.

"My daddy said to me, when I was leaving high school, you know, debating whether I would go to New York, should I go into music, and the whole thing was, 'Well, you don't want to go into music, because you'll end up being like your daddy.' He struggled his whole life. He said, 'Man, I can tell you one thing. Do it if you want to do it and if you love doin' it. But if you don't want to do it for that reason, don't do it. Because when it really, really gets hard, you have to tell yourself, This is what I want to do.' My father told me, 'Don't sit around waiting for publicity, money, people saying you're great. Son, that might never happen. If you want to do it and you love doin' it, do it. But if you don't . . .'" Marsalis shook his head.

For all his success and acclaim, Marsalis is vexed by his critics in the jazz establishment. "My relationship with the jazz critics has never been good," he said, pausing for some time, at least half a minute. "It's never been a great relationship. I've never been portrayed accurately—not at all. The whole thing was always, like, trying to water down your level of seriousness, always trying to make you seem like an angry young man and all this. Man, you know—that was just bullshit.

"When I hear that term, 'classicism,' it's hard for me to figure out what people are talking about. There are so many musicians playing today—like, the way Joe Lovano plays, the way Marcus Roberts plays, the way that Joshua Redman plays, the way that Danilo Pérez plays, the way Cyrus Chestnut plays. There are a lot of musicians playing a lot of different styles. In any period of any music a vast majority of the practitioners sought some common language, and then there are people who do variations on that language. I think we need to delve deeper into the tradition, not run away from it. See, musicians are always encouraged to run away from it. You know, if you're a musician, you want to run from it, for a basic reason—because you don't compare well against it."

.   .   .

A decade ago *The New Yorker* ran a cartoon depicting a middle-aged white man lying in bed. Two young children are bursting into the room. "Dad! Dad! Wake up!" one of the kids yells. "They just discovered another Marsalis!" As each of his musician brothers—and their father—followed Wynton onto the national jazz scene, the Marsalis era took a shape that began to seem dynastic. The family looked like musical Kennedys, from the strong-willed patriarch to the pair of handsome, charismatic sons who led their generation to the younger siblings struggling to fulfill impossible expectations. Eventually all five musicians ended up working at Columbia Records—back under the same roof but in a variety of roles.

Easily reduced to clichés of sibling contrast, Wynton and Branford have personified the duality Wynton sees in the world of the arts: purity versus corruption. In its cover story on Wynton and the young lions, *Time* emphasized the brothers' polar attributes.

> Wynton, extraordinarily disciplined and driven by an insatiable desire to excel, was a straight-A student who starred in Little League baseball, practiced his trumpet three hours a day and won every music competition he ever entered. Branford . . . was an average student, a self-described "spaz" in sports and a naturally talented musician who hated to practice.

Branford has played with rock and pop musicians such as Sting and the Grateful Dead; Wynton has derided pop-jazz players as "cult figures, talking-all-the-time heroes, who have these spur-of-the-moment, out-of-their-mind, left-bank, off-the-wall theories about music which make no sense at all to anybody who knows anything about music." Branford has performed and recorded funk music under the pseudonym Buckshot LeFonque (derived from a pseudonym that the saxophonist Cannonball Adderley used in the 1950s). Wynton told a Kennedy Center audience in 1998, "There's nothing sadder than a jazz musician playing funk."

They maintain a respectful distance, playing together on occasion and rarely explicitly criticizing each other in public. "I love my brother, man," Wynton told me emphatically. "That doesn't mean we talk every day. We might not get a chance to talk to each other at all for a long time, and we might not agree on everything when we do talk—or when we don't. But I love my brother Branford, man. I love all my brothers."

Branford toed the same line when I interviewed him last year, and yet he promptly drew a distinction between his work and Wynton's. "I love my brother," he said, "but we're totally different. I don't agree with some of the statements that he makes when he says jazz lost the world when it stopped being dance music. One of the things that attracted me to jazz was the fact that it wasn't dance music. I wouldn't want to play jazz and have people dance to it. That's not my thing."

Although at first praising Wynton's efforts to carry on the legacy of jazz, Branford couldn't seem to resist taking a thinly veiled shot. "I think it's something that should have been done a long time ago and has to be done," he said. "I use classical music as a role model. There are classical musicians who preserve music. There are people who play madrigals. There are people who only play in their Baroque chamber orchestras."

Some of those who know the two brothers well see sibling dynamics as an explanation for every step in their careers. "They have tremendous love and tremendous respect for each other, and they will fight to defend one another when speaking to outsiders," Jeff Levenson, the former Columbia executive, says. "But I really do believe that for Wynton and Branford, each of their achievements has been a competitive strike against the other. They've channeled all that rivalry stuff into their own motivational energy."

Branford's career has largely followed pop-culture convention—he's been a musical anti-hero. He exudes a lusty nonchalance, an Elvis quality, that also infuses his saxophone playing. His music is muscular and aggressive. Thoroughly aware of his bad-boy reputation and its market value, he has sustained it into his forties through practice. "They [writers] think I'm an arrogant cuss, which I am," he told me. When Wynton speaks of being mistaken for "an angry young man," the man might be his older brother. Branford's success, coursing through the turbulence of pop-music stardom, network television, and best-selling genres including funk, seems, if not inevitable, at least easy to understand.

Wynton, for his part, rose on a bubble made from an unprecedented mixture of seemingly incompatible ingredients: youth culture, history, the African-American experience, mass marketing, and the ideals of fine art. He was a young man who honored his elders, promoted higher standards in a cynical business, and played a black music thought to be in decline to become a national sensation. How long could he float like that?

• • •

When jazz musicians teach improvisation, they often start with a basic assignment: Go home and listen to a recording you like. Take one musical phrase that appeals to you, and use it to construct a composition of your own.

The record industry spent the 1990s on a similar project: the big labels heard what Wynton Marsalis was saying, took from it what appealed to them, and used it to build a new business of their own. In seeking to elevate the public perception of jazz and to encourage young practitioners to pay attention to the music's traditions, Marsalis put great emphasis on its past masters—particularly in his role as director of Jazz at Lincoln Center. Still, he never advocated mere revivalism, and he has demonstrated in his compositions how traditional elements can be referenced, recombined, and reinvented in the name of individualistic expression. "It's a mistake when people say about Wynton that what he's doing is recapitulating the past," Gerald Early says. "I really think that what he's doing is taking the nature of that tradition and really trying, in fact, to add to it and kind of push it forward." But record executives came away with a different message: that if the artists of the past are so great and enduring, there's no reason to continue investing so much in young talent. So they shifted their attention to repackaging their catalogues of vintage recordings.

Where the young lions saw role models and their critics saw idolatry, the record companies saw brand names—the ultimate prize of American marketing. For long-established record companies with vast archives of historic recordings, the economics were irresistible: it is far more profitable to wrap new covers around albums paid for generations ago than it is to find, record, and promote new artists.

As Bruce Lundvall, the head of the Blue Note recording company, acknowledges, "The profitability of the catalogue is a mixed blessing. Let's say [consumers] buy their first jazz record when they hear Wynton or Joshua Redman or whoever it might be. Then they want to get the history. They start to buy catalogue, and that's exactly what the active, current roster is fighting. I remember [the saxophonist] Javon Jackson saying to me, 'I'm not competing with Joshua Redman so much as [with] Sonny Rollins and John Coltrane and Lester Young and Stan Getz'—the whole history of jazz saxophone players, which is available [on CD]." Jeff Levenson adds, "The Frankenstein monster has turned on its creators. In paying homage to the greats, Wynton and his peers have gotten supplanted by them in the minds of the populace. They've gotten supplanted by dead people."

But dead people make poor live attractions, and thus jazz

clubs have suffered commensurably. "You know, I really love Duke and Louis and Miles and Ben Webster and all those guys, but I like jazz best when I can hear it live—it is supposed to be spontaneous music," says James Browne, who ran Manhattan's Sweet Basil. "They've been saying jazz is America's classical music, and it deserves respect. Well, now it's America's classical music. Thanks a lot. What do we do now?"

No longer signed to major record labels, Wynton, Branford, and other jazz musicians of their generation are taking stock (and they now have the leisure to do so). The focus of the discourse in jazz has shifted from the nature of the art form to that of the artist.

Both Wynton and Branford describe their departures from Columbia Records as an opportunity for self-evaluation. "I'm not with Columbia," Wynton said soberly in his apartment. "It was not vituperative. It's just time for me to do something else. It's just time, and it's a good thing. It's just time for me to figure out how I can forward my identity, to say, 'This is who I am.'

"The record companies should have abandoned us a long time ago. They should have saved us the trouble. It's not going to be healthy for our pocketbooks, but it's healthy for jazz. Through that void there is opportunity. Somewhere in that void is an opportunity for somebody to come up and start signing jazz musicians and letting them make the records they want to make."

• • •

Within Lincoln Center, Wynton Marsalis's jazz program has always had a status much like that of black culture in America: it is of the whole, yet other. Jazz at Lincoln Center began as a way to fill blank dates on the calendar at Alice Tully Hall, the smallest of the institution's four major theaters. "I didn't think it was important at the beginning," Marsalis says. "They called me and said they wanted to do some concerts with dead hall space in

Lincoln Center, and did I have any ideas about what they could do? Because I had played classical music, I was a person to call. So I called Crouch—'What do you think? What could we do?' So we got together. It wasn't that big a deal—it was just three of us in a room [Marsalis, Crouch, and Alina Bloomgarden, of Lincoln Center], talking. Then I started to take it seriously."

Although Jazz at Lincoln Center is now the institutional equal of the Metropolitan Opera, the New York Philharmonic, and the New York City Ballet, most of its concerts are still being held in Alice Tully Hall. Sometime around the fall of 2004 Jazz at Lincoln Center will move into a sprawling multipurpose compound at Columbus Circle, a few blocks south of Lincoln Center proper. There, at the yet unfinished Frederick P. Rose Hall, it will be part of the new AOL Time Warner Center, which will house not only the corporate headquarters of AOL Time Warner but also a hotel, a condominium tower, and various stores and restaurants. It will be the only one of Lincoln Center's fiefdoms to be based "off-campus." Still of the whole, yet other.

Marsalis has been deeply involved in the planning of—and the fundraising for—this new home for Jazz at Lincoln Center, which he talks about with a keen sense of "the spirit of place," the phrase he once used as the title of a concert of Duke Ellington's travel music. In a piercing wind on a January afternoon last year we walked around the construction site, a beam skeleton more than ten stories high at that point, and he described the philosophical underpinnings of the project.

"This is going to be the House of Swing, and we want everything in it to swing, even though the only thing swinging around here now is girders—watch your head," Marsalis said calmly. Against the cold he and I were both wearing long topcoats, woolen scarves, and hardhats, but he looked comfortable; he seemed to know every unmarked area in the maze of steel and most of the men working in it. Marsalis guided me to the center of an open space, about 250 square yards, which would someday be one of Jazz at Lincoln Center's two main performance venues—this one large enough to stage one of Ellington's symphonic suites; the other one about half its size, for small groups and solo recitals. "They're like two sides of the same thing, like night and day or man and woman," he said.

"Sound is very important," Marsalis continued. "So are the people. The people are as important as the musicians here." The stages will be lower and closer to the seats than they are in typical theaters, and the spaces will be designed to carry, not diminish, the sound of the audience. "We want to hear the audience answering us back—the call and response, we want that."

On our way to a makeshift elevator used for shuttling the work crews and materials, a foreman approached Marsalis, accompanied by several construction workers. "Excuse me, Wynton—I want you to meet Moose," the foreman said. "He's a hell of a singer."

A stocky fellow stepped forward tentatively. He had a stiff-lipped, nervous grin that he spoke through. "Hi, Wynton," he said.

Marsalis shook his hand. "Why don't you come over some time and do some tunes with us—sing with the band?" Marsalis said, waving a hand northward in the direction of Lincoln Center.

"No kidding?" the aspiring singer said, still grinning (but less nervously).

"Come on over—we'll do some tunes."

Like Louis Armstrong and Duke Ellington, both of whom toured the world under the auspices of the U.S. State Department during the Cold War, Marsalis has a feeling for people and a passion for his art that in combination make him a potent political force. No one denies his importance as a global ambassador of jazz. "He has never moved me as a trumpet player," Whitney Balliett, a well-known jazz critic, says. "But God—watching him in the Burns thing [Ken Burns's 2001 PBS documentary about jazz], it's phenomenal! All he has to do is open his mouth, and out it comes." According to the composer and conductor David Berger, who has been associated with the Lincoln

Center jazz program since its inception, "Duke Ellington probably had more charisma than anybody I ever met—I mean, he was amazing. But Wynton, he's got it too. When you talk to him, he makes you feel good—just his presence, his energy. It elevates you and makes you want to be a better person."

I accompanied Marsalis to an event at the Cross Path Culture Center to benefit Barry Harris's jazz-education institute, and I lost him in the crowd of several hundred people. Dozens of jazz musicians, including Randy Weston, Kenny Barron, Allan Harris, and Jeffery Smith, were milling around the loftlike open space. When a camera flash went off, I spotted Wynton having his picture taken. Shortly after that another flash popped, ten or fifteen feet away from the first, and I saw Wynton posing again. I realized that all I needed to do to find him at any point during the evening was to look out at the crowd, and a camera flash would mark him.

To an institution like Jazz at Lincoln Center, with a new headquarters under construction and some $28 million left to raise from corporate sponsors, grants, and society donors, Marsalis is an asset of immeasurable value. "What strategy does the board of directors have for raising the necessary funds?" I asked the board chairman, Lisa Schiff, in her office, a few blocks south of Jazz at Lincoln Center's future home. "Wynton," she said.

For years Jazz at Lincoln Center was savaged by charges of mismanagement, racism, elitism, ageism, cronyism, and sexism, but these days it is more inclusive, forward-looking, and professional. Indeed, the concert schedule put together for the 2001–2002 year by Marsalis and his reorganized staff (including Todd Barkan, the artistic administrator, an independent-minded impresario who joined Jazz at Lincoln Center two years ago) was practically a manifesto against canonical rigidity. Emphatically multicultural, eclectic, and even contemporary, the program presented the music of Brazil (Pixinguinha, Cyro Baptista), of women (Abbey Lincoln, Barbara Carroll, Rhoda Scott), of white people (Woody Herman, Lee Konitz), of the French (a tribute to the Hot Club de

France), and of young adventurists (Greg Osby, Akua Dixon). Perhaps Marsalis really did have a plan for Moose the construction worker to sing with the Lincoln Center Jazz Orchestra.

"One of my problems with Wynton used to be that he drew such a hard line many times," the composer and saxophonist Greg Osby recalls. "He doesn't seem to be that firm anymore. A lot of it I recognize as youth. He's a lot more accepting of varied presentation now. Not to say that he loves it, but he's a lot more tolerant of it."

Jazz's public advocates, Marsalis among them, like to talk about the music as a democratic art, a form of communal expression founded on the primacy of the individual voice. In recent years the conversation about the future of the music has focused on the global expansion of the jazz community and the integrity of the voices in that expanded community. But if the effectiveness of any democracy is in inverse proportion to its size, it looks—again—as though jazz may be doomed. That is to say, the music may not survive in the form we now know. Two decades after Wynton Marsalis and his troops took up arms against fusion, world music, the apotheosis of fusion, is at the gate.

"I wonder about the future of jazz, with all the music from other parts of the world floating around more and more and more," Whitney Balliett says. "Eventually that's going to be picked up in jazz. It already has been, and I wonder if there will eventually, in the next ten or twenty years, be a kind of diffusion—if the music will no longer be the jazz that we had ten or twenty years ago."

As for Marsalis, the very subject of globalism and jazz makes him choke on his words. I brought up the topic while we were eating Chinese food on the Upper West Side of Manhattan, after he had told me how much he was enjoying his spicy chicken. "World music"—he coughed out the phrase—"and all that stuff. I like people's music from around the world, and music from around the world belongs in Jazz at Lincoln Center. But for me—my music—I like jazz. I like the swingin.' I loved Art Blakey. I loved Dizzy. I love jazz musicians. Jazz has to be portrayed and brought forward for what it is—and celebrated. It can't be sold by being subsumed into the world-music market, and I'm just not willing to—I'm not willing to compromise my integrity under any circumstances. I wouldn't do it when I was twenty. I'm certainly not going to do it when I'm forty."

· · ·

In 1939 Duke Ellington walked away from his contract with Columbia Records. Coincidentally, he, too, turned forty that year, and was at a career crossroads. After more than a decade of near servitude to his manager, Irving Mills, Ellington ended their association and started rebuilding his musical organization. He hired a pair of virtuoso innovators, the bassist Jimmy Blanton and the tenor saxophonist Ben Webster, and began composing with a new collaborator, the twenty-four-year-old Billy Strayhorn. "Ellington's music was marked by increased rhythmic drive and instrumental virtuosity," John Edward Hasse wrote in a 1993 biography of the composer. "[It presaged] bebop and other musical developments to come, and numerous musical explorations and innovations. With breathtaking originality, Ellington broke more and more new ground." In 1946 the jazz magazines would proclaim, almost in unison, that Ellington was passé again. Ten years after that *Time* would declare "a turning point in [Ellington's] career," saying that the composer had "emerged from a long period of quiescence and was once again bursting with ideas and inspiration."

When Wynton Marsalis turned forty, in the fall of 2001, Jazz at Lincoln Center threw him a surprise party at the Manhattan nightclub Makor, a couple of blocks away from his apartment. I had received an invitation and had been told that the guest list would be limited strictly to those who knew Marsalis well or worked closely with him, but there were hundreds of people sardined into the place: musicians and administrators from Jazz at Lincoln Center; the saxophonist Jimmy Heath; the broadcaster Ed Bradley; and others I could not see, because no one could move. Marsalis entered at 10:30 that evening, accompanied by his father and Stanley Crouch (who lured Marsalis to the club under the pretext of meeting a couple of women). The band struck up "Happy Birthday," New Orleans–style, and Marsalis waded through the crowd toward the bandstand, beaming, his arms raised high in the air.

It took him nearly twenty minutes—and thirty choruses of "Happy Birthday"—to reach the stage. "It really was a surprise," Marsalis said, and he began to cry. "Sometimes you're working so much, and this stuff just unfolds, and—I don't know. I can't say nothing."

The first piece the band played, after "Happy Birthday," was Ellington's "C-Jam Blues" (also known as "Duke's Place"), and the last song of the night was Ellington's "It Don't Mean a Thing (If It Ain't Got That Swing)." Thanking his well-wishers, Marsalis eventually approached my vicinity in the crowd, and I asked him if he knew where Ellington had been on the same day in his life. "In Sweden," he said in half a beat. "Making some music—or making something!" (Ellington had indeed been in Stockholm, on a European tour.)

A few weeks later we were talking about his birthday, and Marsalis brought up Ellington again. "I have so much further to go," he said. "I'm just a baby. I'm just trying to figure out how to play. Like Duke, man—Duke never stopped, never stopped learning. Till the end, man, he was sitting at the piano every night—every night—trying to figure out how to do it better.

"I've had my ups and downs. Everybody does. I don't know what you would say about me right now. But I'm not concerned with that. You have to keep your mind on the issue, and the issue is the music. You have to look at the world around you and the things that happen to you and take them inside yourself and make something out of it. That's what jazz is. That's how I feel."

For Wynton Marsalis, fate is an opportunity for creative improvisation—another ringing cell phone at the Village Vanguard.

Esquire

FINALIST, LEISURE
INTERESTS

The $20 Theory of the Universe

On a spree in New York, Tom Chiarella tests his theory that a $20 bill slipped into the right hand at the right time can make things happen. The result is an article that is laugh-out-loud funny as well as instructive and inspirational for anyone who always wanted to slip a maître d' a few bucks but didn't have the nerve.

Tom Chiarella

The $20 Theory of the Universe

There is almost nothing on earth that cannot be had for a price. The question is, what is that price? And the answer is twenty dollars.

W hen it comes to the language of money, credit cards are nouns. Dull, concrete, limited by rules and restrictions and creepy fine print, credit cards have all the élan of aluminum foil. Personal checks—the coward's stand-in for cash—are ugly and static pronouns. But a twenty-dollar bill, now, that's a thing of beauty. Nothing static about a twenty. Used correctly, a twenty is all about movement, access, cachet. Forget the other bills. The single won't get you much more than a stiff nod and, these days, the fin is de rigueur. A tenner is a nice thought, but it's also a message that you're a Wal-Mart shopper, too cheap for the real deal. A twenty, placed in the right hand at the right moment, makes things happen. It gets you past the rope, beyond the door, into the secret files. The twenty hastens and chastens, beckons and tugs. The twenty, you see, is a verb. It's all about action.

And me, well, I'm all about action, too, because I am the original twenty-dollar millionaire. Give me a stack of twenties and I'll pass them off as well as any mogul. Maybe better. My fortune rises and falls with the double sawbuck. And because of that, I've always wanted to test myself, to establish the weight and worth of a twenty in the world. So last month I took two grand in twenties, rolled them up, and left for New York. I was going to spend three days greasing palms from gate to gate and see what it got me.

I'm not talking about *buying* here, by the way. When it comes to things with a price tag, a twenty doesn't get you much. You could open one of those stores called EVERYTHING FOR $20, and who the fuck would go in there? Who needs a bunch of art calendars and T-shirts? No one wants to *spend* a twenty. It's a fair amount of money, for one thing. And it won't get you much, for another. Not in the way of merchandise, anyway. No, you have to *give* the twenty. Pass it, release it. This is about as much Zen as I can muster: Stuff your pockets full of twenties and doors will open by themselves.

At the airport parking lot in Indianapolis, they offered a car-interior cleaning service for thirty-five dollars. As I was waiting for the shuttle, I started bitching to one of the drivers. "I'd rather pay someone twenty bucks straight cash to get in there and spruce it up for me," I said. The driver stood up on his toes. I asked if he was interested. He'd take twenty now, he said, then talk to the guys in the shop, and they'd put my car in line for detailing so long as I'd slip them another twenty when I got back. So I passed the note and shook hands. Detailing normally costs $120. Fuckin' A. I was *making* money at this point.

When the gate agent wouldn't help me out with my request for the bulkhead seat on my little commuter plane, I set a twenty on the counter. She iced me. An airport is apparently no longer the best place to use a twenty, not since they started x-raying Chuck Taylors. "What's the issue?" she said. I wanted legroom, I told her. She shrugged and shifted me to an exit row. I told her I wanted the front seat, pushed the twenty forward, and she started to look pissed. "I don't want your money," she said. "But I want the seat," I said. "The front one." She said it was assigned and all I could do was ask to trade.

On the plane, I approached the woman in seat 1A and held out a twenty. She asked if I was serious. I said yes. She took it and ran to 9B like her pants were on fire.

On the next leg—Cleveland to New York—I skipped the ticket counter altogether, walked straight into first class, and announced that I'd give anyone twenty dollars for his seat. There was some laughter, some nervous ass shifting, and just when I figured no one would bite, a big guy with a beltful of pagers and cell phones took the deal. The flight attendant jumped me when I sat down, asked if money had changed hands. The guy next to me nodded, and she jabbed me with her finger. "I could have you removed from the plane for that," she said, but the flight was crowded and soon she moved on. The guy sitting next to me said he'd never seen that trick before, and he was going to try it next time he didn't get an upgrade. "The FAA would shit their pants if everyone could do that," he said. "You could auction first class away if you had enough time."

I told him that for a forty-seven-minute flight from Cleveland, twenty dollars was probably about market price. "If I can't get it for twenty dollars," I said, "I don't want it."

He wriggled into his seat and turned away. "Man, there's no price tag on comfort," he said.

I decided right there that this could be a kind of rule for passing the twenty: nothing with a price tag.

The flight attendant, still a little pissed, wouldn't get me my free drink once we took off. So I slipped the guy across the aisle from me twenty dollars to get me three little bottles of single malt. I drank one to flaunt it to the stewardess and pocketed the other two for later.

• • •

A twenty should not be a ticket so much as a solution. You have a problem, you need something from the back room, you don't want to wait, you whip out the twenty.

I could have stood in line at the airport cabstand for fifteen minutes like every other mook in the world, freezing my balls off, but such is not the way of the twenty-dollar millionaire. I walked straight to the front of the line and offered a woman twenty bucks for her spot. She took it with a shrug. Behind her, people crackled. *"Hey! Ho!"* they shouted. I knew exactly what that meant. It wasn't good. I needed to get in a cab soon. One of the guys flagging cabs pointed me to the back of the line. That's when I grabbed him by the elbow, pulled him close, and shook his hand, passing the next twenty. I was now down forty dollars for a twenty-dollar cab ride. He tilted his head and nodded to his partner. I peeled another twenty and they let me climb in. As we pulled away, someone in the line threw a half-empty cup of coffee against my window.

That whole event had been too public, too visible. Another lesson learned: The bigger the favor—which is to say, the more *visible* the favor—the more discreet the pass should be. A security guy elbows his way through the crowd to get you up against the stage at a concert and you slip him the twenty quietly, at belt level. Conversely, the smaller the favor, the bigger the flourish. The bellman brings you a bottle of seltzer on a rainy afternoon, you pass that twenty as if the world were watching.

.　　.　　.

I always grease Bobby H., the bellman at my hotel, and on my first night, within minutes of the pass, he suggested that I might request a room upgrade. He even gave me a room number to ask for. Another twenty at the desk and I was out of two queens, snug in my one king. The next day, we ran the same drill, and *wham*, I was in the minisuite. The twenty after that, I was in a full suite with a view of Times Square. We used a different desk guy each day. When you're passing twenties, Bobby H. told me, you have to spread the wealth. "It's a one-time trick," he said. "You don't want anyone to catch on." Somehow he managed to take a twenty each time, having caught on fully some time ago.

.　　.　　.

In my favorite midtown coffee shop, the Cafe Edison, they maintain VIP seating for a-holes like Neil Simon and August Wilson who supposedly come here to write. They keep the area roped off and generally empty, even at noon while a line stretches out the door. This has always pissed me off. So when I entered at noon one day, I folded a twenty, slipped it to the old lady at the counter, and she waved me into the VIP like she was whacking me with the back of her hand. I paid way over market for that, since the shop was only half full at the time and it was too far away for the waiter to remember to refill my coffee. Still, people left the restaurant peering at me, working hard to figure who in the world I might be.

I wanted to tell them I was the twenty-dollar millionaire. I wanted to tell them how well my twenties were serving me, even in the last few hours. With a bunch of well-placed bills and some fairly precise requests, a maid had left me forty towels neatly stacked in a single tower on my bed, a bellman had carried my laptop on his shoulder for an hour, the janitor had let me into the subbasement where I could see the subway through a large crack in the foundation, and the bartender hooked up the microphone and let me sing in the hotel bar, without accompaniment, all before lunch hour.

At 3:00 that very morning, I had called an Eighth Avenue bodega and told them I'd give them twenty dollars for a pint of milk and a *Hustler* magazine. The guy who answered the phone had a thick Arabic accent. "You are crazy," he said.

"I'm thirsty."

"Come on, mister," he said. "Come on with that."

"Seriously," I said.

"Mister fucking crazy man, we have no *Hustler*!" he continued. "What is your room number?"

Twenty minutes later, the guy was at my door with a quart of 2 percent and a shrink-wrapped valu-pack of three *Hustlers*. He sighed and smiled when I gave him the twenty. "It's snowing," he said, as if to explain his relief. But I understood. The twenty is an important contract and no one, on either end, wants it broken.

•   •   •

A twenty can't buy everything. I failed often enough with my twenties that there were times when I doubted whether they could do anything at all. I tried to get into the Guggenheim when it was closed. I pushed the docent to let me roll one ball in the Frick museum's secret bowling alley. I asked a stripper for a big wet kiss. I tried to get an ABC security guard to show me Peter Jennings's car. I attempted to jump to the head of the rotation at a karaoke place. I tried to get into the premiere of *Analyze That* by passing a twenty folded in the shape of a ticket. The doorman looked at me like I was a mime.

Then I realized something else: Most people aren't willing to lose their job for twenty bucks, but if they have something they already take for granted—a place in line, a seat, a ticket to a show they've already seen—they'll jump on a twenty like a possum on a wet bag of groceries. It's a matter of opportunity. You have to find your moments.

I never developed any tag lines. I generally presented the bill and asked, "How does this help me?" Though at one point I walked into a one-hour photo place, held out a twenty, and said, "Can I now call this a twelve-minute photo shop?" I needed something better than an hour, having just finished a roll featuring photos of me at the wheel of a street cleaner (requiring one twenty and a promise not to take it out of first gear), but I couldn't get the guy to budge off of sixty minutes. As I was waiting, I asked him if he ever developed dirty pictures.

"Sometimes," he said.

"Do you keep a file?"

He shrugged.

"Does this help me?" I said, whipping out the bill, shooting for as much flourish as I could muster.

"What do you wanna see?"

"You know," I said. "I want to see the file."

He picked up the twenty with two fingers and tucked it in his pocket. "I'll show you what I've got." He pulled a manila envelope from beneath the counter and took out four snapshots. The first three were simple bare asses—in a shower, at a kitchen sink, faceup on a couch. Beneath that was an enlargement of a cat licking a woman's nipple. Pretty cool, but hardly what I expected.

"That's it?" I said.

The guy pursed his lips. "That's all I've got this week. That stuff doesn't stay around here long. The master file would cost a lot more than twenty dollars."

Master file! Damn. Clearly, I had priced myself out of the good stuff by coming forward with the twenty too fast. There is a trick to meeting the market: You can pass out twenties endlessly while people reel you in, inch by inch.

It is the sort of thing that often happens at the better restaurants and clubs, where the twenty is the common currency of exchange. That night, I went straight to the sold-out dinner show at the Carlyle Hotel, where Woody Allen was playing, and slipped the guy at the door twenty dollars for a seat at the bar. He took it, guided me to my chair, and, with the twenty long gone, informed me that there was a three-drink minimum. Worse, I was behind a pole. I told him I wanted a table. He said he'd see what he could do. (This was the line I most often heard at good restaurants, like Balthazar, where the woman said, "I don't sell seats, but I'll see what I can do," before giving me a three-top next to Fran Tarkenton.)

As the show began, the floor guy at the Carlyle offered me a seat six feet from the bar. Another twenty. He took the money, then told me that the seat had a seventy-five-dollar cover charge. Fuck me. Then, since the rest of the table was open, he seated a beautiful twenty-two-year-old woman in a hard-on-quality red dress across from me. Good twenty, I thought, good, good twenty. Then her Italian boyfriend joined us. "We were right next to the drums," she told me. "It was very uncomfortable. I had to give him twenty dollars just to get this crappy seat." The only other thing I heard her say in English that night was to her boyfriend, during a lull: "You don't know how bad I want you right now." And me with my little whiskey sour.

Finally, with about thirty minutes left in the show, I figured out that the people who really want the twenty would be the people sitting at the other tables. People getting dunned just like me. As there was an open seat at the stage-front table, I offered a woman sitting there twenty bucks. She said sure. So there I was, three feet from the stage, having dropped twenties all the way from the door, with Woody Allen launching spit all over me through his clarinet. Worst of all, when the check came, there was a space to tip the captain.

·   ·   ·

One afternoon, Bobby the bellman alerted me to a corporate meeting at the dinner club next door. "It's all day," he said. "They have very nice buffets."

I decided to scam a lunch. I walked boldly to the door, leaned toward the doorman—you come face-to-face with a lot of young, large black men when you are passing twenties in New York City—and said, "Is this the lunch?" He raised his eyebrows. "I forgot my letter," I said, holding the twenty pressed flat against the palm of my hand and reaching for the shake. He looked confused; I tried to look equally puzzled and said, "Just give me five minutes." He took my hand and nodded me in. I went in and some wag was talking from a dais to a crowd of about two hundred guys in blue shirts. About six or eight people craned their necks to look at me. I went to the buffet, fixed myself a large plate of tiger prawns. I got a beer out of a bucket of ice and sat, balancing it all in my lap. *Good* shrimp. I got another plate before I left. Every once in a while some hungry young exec would turn for a look at me, me with the shrimp legs sticking out of my mouth, me with the huge can of Foster's, and I would nod. It took me fifteen minutes to realize I was listening to a symposium on corporate ethics.

•   •   •

I pressed on. I bought my way into a good table at a Les Paul show with a twenty. I got an usher at NBC to hold a front-row seat for Busta Rhymes on the Carson Daly show. I got a seat at Dos Caminos, Manhattan's jumpingest Mexican restaurant, in five minutes despite the two-hour wait. I cut to the head of the line at the half-price Broadway ticket booth in Times Square. I got my shoes resoled in twenty minutes instead of two weeks. I got a little love by shoving a twenty into a homeless guy's coffee cup.

Finally, I found myself headed back to the hotel, exhausted and down to my last twenty. At the corner of Forty-seventh and Seventh, a guy handed me a flyer. "Mistress Sandra will give you your future," it read. Ten minutes later, I was sitting in Mistress Sandra's overheated apartment with her kids watching *Sponge-Bob* behind a little fake wall. I felt like dozing, and when I opened my eyes, Mistress Sandra was sitting in front of me. She was a short Mexican woman, mid-forties, wearing a bathrobe. "What are you interested in asking?" she said.

"What can I get for twenty bucks?" I said.

She leaned forward. "What is your real question?"

I repeated myself.

"I do palms for twenty-five dollars," she said.

"Yeah, but I only want to spend twenty dollars," I said, laying the bill on her coffee table.

She shook her head. "Palms must be read together. One palm is no good without the other. Palms cost twenty-five dollars."

The one-palm thing made sense somehow, but I was out of money.

"I can tell you many things," she said. "For instance, you will live to be ninety-seven, God bless you very much."

I was interested now. I fished around in my pocket, looking

for one more bill. When I took my hand out, it was grasping two little airplane bottles of single malt. Mistress Sandra raised an eyebrow. I set them on top of my twenty.

"How does this help me?" I asked, having found my real question one more time.

New York Magazine

WINNER, COLUMNS AND COMMENTARY

My Big Fat Question

Michael Wolff's insight and understanding seem to take on the dimension of sixth and seventh senses. His columns, written in Qatar as Wolff covered the early stages of the war in Iraq, examined the sources from which most of the world got its news of the American invasion. While contrasting the boring generals with the bloody goo, Wolff ends up raising the one question that needed to be asked, and among the answers, came a threat from the military, 3,000 angry e-mails, and a far wiser American public.

Michael Wolff

My Big Fat Question

While the war was raging elsewhere, I was stuck at CENTCOM, where I was supposed to be lobbing softball questions at generals. Naturally, I did the opposite. (Cue hate mail from Rush Limbaugh fans.)

The sandstorms blowing through Iraq left a kind of mustard cloud over the desert flats of Qatar, creating a fair approximation of the end of the earth. Serendipitously, "Midnight at the Oasis" was playing on the car radio as I came up to the camp gate just before 5 A.M.—my tenth day in

Doha. Then the cell was ringing with a nervous producer from CNN in New York (where it was still prime time) trying to figure out where I was—only 200 yards away from the makeshift studio space in the CENTCOM media center. There were rumors that one of the two bomb-sniffing dogs had died—CENTCOM would neither confirm nor deny that this was the first casualty in Doha—meaning the process of getting through the security no-man's-land would be even longer than usual, and, I tried to explain to the CNN person, I might not make it by airtime.

We'd reached the point where reporters were interviewing other reporters in the most media-scrutinized war ever fought. But even among the overexposed, I was—because of the irritable question I'd asked at a daily briefing and over international television—on the verge of a special status: becoming the wiseass of the war.

A television reporter from Istanbul was hotly pursuing me for an interview because I was, apparently, famous in Turkey (a title for a possible memoir). I was very popular, it seems, in France, Canada, and Italy too.

The AP, Reuters, the *Times,* and *The Nation* were calling. What's more, I'd had to switch from the Doha Marriott to the Doha Ritz-Carlton for a faster Internet connection to download 3,000 hate e-mails.

I'd lobbed my big question because it just seemed too obvious not to ask. Everybody here was having the same perfectly *Groundhog Day* experience: You woke up only to repeat the day before, and no matter what you did or said or thought, you were helpless to effect a change in the next day. So every day, everybody asked the same questions about Basra and the supply lines and the whereabouts of the WMDs and Saddam, and got the same answers. They were war correspondents after all (or trying to be). The purest form of reporting: Armies were moved, weapons deployed, kill counts tabulated. Nothing postmodern about a war reporter. Events needed to be confirmed and recorded. But behind this stripped-down façade, invisible to the public, was a secret, very pleasant theater of the absurd.

While the home front saw the unspooling of this war pageant—the green night vision, the small-arms fire, the precision missiles, the Tolstoyan reports of the embeds—radically dissociated from any larger context (the U.S. media had sealed itself off from the almost diametrically opposite view of the war offered by the media in the rest of the world), in Doha, we were in a discrete, amiable, backstage world.

We were in on the joke.

We were the high-school kids who got it. The embedded reporters, on the other hand, were the rah-rah jocks.

"General, is the war going well, or is the war going extremely well?" was the question we all knew we were here to ask.

"In a world where people are being blown up, it is difficult to explain that life at the Ritz is a kind of death, too," said one of the Aussie reporters, contemplating our predicament. "Death by buffet."

Here we were in the world's most boring city, on the world's least enviable piece of earth, in this over-air-conditioned warehouse (a virtual sensory-deprivation chamber), with only microwavable mini-pizzas to eat—all just to wait around for a 45-minute news conference, ably engineered and precisely scripted to tell you as little as possible. Death by banality. General Vincent Brooks, who became the official spokesperson and the face of CENTCOM, was surely the ultimate assistant principal.

Everybody here understood. A roll of the eye. A curl of the lip. A silent scream.

Still, no matter how jaded these reporters were, when the lights went on, they knew their roles. They had producers and an audience. The show must go on. If everybody here seemed privately to accept that the process of reporting war was a crock, publicly they accepted the war as a coherent event that they had some mastery over—they had inside sources, they had the general's ear. They were war reporters.

But I wasn't a war reporter. I didn't have to observe wartime propriety—or cool. I was free to ask publicly (on international television, at that) the question everyone was asking of each other: "I mean no disrespect . . . but what is the value proposition? . . .Why are we here? Why should we stay? What's the value of what we're learning at this million-dollar press center?"

It was the question to sour the dinner party. It was also, because I used the words *value proposition,* a condescending and annoying question—a provocation.

Still, I meant it literally: Other than the pretense of a news conference—the news conference as backdrop and dateline— what did we get for having come all this way? What information could we get here that we could not have gotten in Washington or New York, what access to what essential person was being proffered? And why was everything so bloodless?

My question was met with a sudden, disruptive, even slightly anarchic round of applause—not dissimilar to the whoops when a kid drops a tray in the school cafeteria—and I knew I was in a little trouble.

•   •   •

The question, it turned out, spoke powerfully to people who think this whole thing (not just the news conference but, in some sense, the entire war) is phony, a setup, a fabrication, in which just about everything is in service to unseen purposes and agendas (hence my popularity in Turkey, France, Canada, Italy, and at *The Nation* magazine, as well as among the reporters in the Doha press pool). But it seemed to speak even more dramatically to people who think the whole thing is real, pure, linear, uncomplicated, elemental (lots of, if not all, Americans). For the former, I'd addressed something like the existential issue of our own purposelessness, but for the latter, I seem to have, heretically, raised the very issue of meaning itself.

And seriously compounding matters, there was the rude applause.

It must have seemed like the media was clapping for its own smartness, or smart-ass-ness. By breaking the proscenium like this, by acknowledging the uselessness of these ritualized proceedings, and therefore the artifice, we media people suddenly seemed like a thing apart—apart from the war, and from our audience (and hence from our country too—at least we American media people).

Now, this is a complicated point, because although everybody in the room represented the media (and would, in short order, be recirculating the noninformation and obvious disinformation that was given out), almost everybody in the room saw the media as occurring somewhere else—a confection being created by some unseen hand. Everybody here would step out of the briefing room and look up at the monitors above the makeshift newsroom tuned to the networks and news channels and watch the briefing be reported to the world and share the same reaction: *What bullshit.* (The packaging didn't help . . . MSNBC: OUR HEARTS ARE WITH YOU.)

But as it happens, incredibly, there are many people who believe that these news briefings—getting surprisingly high ratings—are real. That when people in uniform speak, they speak the truth. Really. Truly. (Although in one instance, after showing especially hammy videos of Iraqi citizens receiving humanitarian aid, even General Brooks had to insist, "This is true. Really. It's not coerced.")

What is most surprising about this to me is not so much that there are a lot of people who would mistake a news conference for an actual, transparent, official giving of information but that the Pentagon would be media-savvy enough to understand this. (Certainly, though, they were smart enough to come up with the embed thing—wherein reporters became soldiers and invaders and liberators.) And what's most pathetic was that we reporters could have been dumb enough not to understand that this whole million-dollar business, the plasma screens and such, was not for us but directed over our heads toward the American audience—and not just the American audience but the core Bush American audience.

When I challenged General Brooks, I was unaware of what I was challenging.

· · ·

I only became aware of what I'd done when the Rush Limbaugh thing happened.

Now, General Brooks is a one-star general—hence, the further point of my question, which was about why we were getting briefed by, in effect, middle management. The point was to be briefed by General Franks, the CENTCOM commander, like Schwarzkopf had briefed in Gulf I. To get one star when you were expecting four is something like getting an assistant undersecretary when you're expecting the president. It's a bait-and-switch. And, indeed, Brooks was a stiff, rote briefer. Stonewall Brooks. He relayed information rather than possessed information.

He was, with some critical interpretation, the hierarchical equivalent of the wacky Iraqi Information minister, Muhammad Sa'id al-Sahhaf—both Brooks and the minister had probably gotten more face time than anybody else in this war. And for a while, certainly for the CENTCOM reporters, it seemed to tip back and forth between whose version of the war was wackier.

Except that's not what it looked like on television. On television, I would find out, remote from our Doha reality, Brooks looked fabulous. While daily TV exposure will take anybody from person to personage, there was something else going on here. On the small screen, Brooks had quiet authority, large, sensitive eyes (in person, his eyes seemed hangdog), and a reassuring unflappability (in the room, this seemed like no more than inexpressiveness). On television, what you saw was not just a general but, all the more heroic, a black general.

My question, then, was a challenge to a broad range of certainties. I was suggesting the whole operation was bogus—so I was challenging reality itself. Then I was challenging the ultimate authority—a general in war. This was practically insubordination. And in my bringing up the issue of rank, it must have seemed that, displeased with the service, I was in some sense asking to see the manager.

So, the Rush thing. First it was CNN that replayed my question—the CNN view was, more or less, the liberal-media view: a certain hand-wringing about whether the media was being used. Then it was Fox, with its extreme, love-it-or-leave-it approach to the war, that took me apart: I was clearly a potential traitor.

And then it was Rush.

To his audience of 20 million—pro-war, military-minded, Bush-centered, media-hating, lily-white—Rush laid me out.

I wasn't only a reporter, but one from *New York* Magazine. "New York" resonated. It combined with "media," and suddenly, in Rush's hands, I was as elitist and as pampered (fortunately, nobody mentioned the Ritz) and as dismissive of the concerns of real Americans as, well, Rush's 20 million assume the media to be. Whereas Rush, that noted foot soldier, represented the military heartland. What's more, according to Rush, that great defender of the rights of African-Americans, I was a racist. *Duh*. A white liberal challenging a black general. It's a binary world.

And Rush gave out my e-mail address.

Almost immediately, 3,000 e-mails, full of righteous fury, started to come.

Which all, in some way, helps explain why we are in Iraq.

·   ·   ·

Now, when you suddenly get 3,000 e-mails excoriating you and your fealty, you can begin to think that the media may in fact be a hostile, negative, unloved, and unwanted presence. (My Al-Jazeera colleagues, singled out for showing bloody pictures during war, certainly felt this, too.) But of course, the opposite is true—we are, even Al-Jazeera, a vital, mostly cooperative, part of the war effort. So when, in response to my question, General Brooks said that I was here of my own volition and if it wasn't satisfactory to me, I should go home, this was far from a statement of policy.

You can't have a taping without a studio audience. We were the pretext for the show—and for delivering the message.

So the last thing the Pentagon wanted was for the media to go home. In fact, CENTCOM refused to confirm or deny what everyone could see for himself: that chairs were being removed from the briefing every day (in one day alone, sixteen chairs were removed), so that, as numbers dwindled, empty seats would not be shown to the world. This was a serious problem. What if you gave a war and the media didn't come?

Clearly marked as the rabble-rouser of the get-out-of-Doha movement, I was approached by some enforcer types. The first was a version of a Graham Greene character. He represented the White House, he said. Wasn't of the military. Although, he said, he was embedded here ("sleeping with a lot of flatulent officers," he said). He was incredibly conspiratorial. Smooth but creepy: "If you had to write the memo about media relations, what would be your bullet points . . . ?"

The next person to buttonhole me was the CENTCOM *Über*-civilian, a thirtyish Republican operative (part of his job seemed to be to seed the press pool with specific questions that CENTCOM wanted asked during the briefings, telling reporters, for instance, that CENTCOM wouldn't show the video of Private Lynch being rescued, because it would be seen as "the United States spiking the ball in the end zone," unless reporters asked for proof that the rescue was successful). He was more *Full Metal Jacket* in his approach (although he was a civilian, he was, inexplicably, in uniform—making him, I suppose, a sort of paramilitary figure): "I have a brother who is in a Hummer at the front, so don't talk to me about too much fucking air-conditioning." And: "A lot of people don't like you." And then: "Don't fuck with things you don't understand." And, too: "This is fucking war, asshole." And finally: "No more questions for you."

I had been warned.

.   .   .

I finally got to the x-ray machine on the way through the guardhouse to my CNN interview. Lots of other reporters were arriving at this early hour for their prime-time spots. There was a relaxed attendant at the machine (a private contractor rather than a soldier), and although everybody was always asking to see what the machine saw and getting turned down, this guy let us come around and see our naked selves: It was a flat, shadowy, unflattering rendering, with the buttocks crisply displayed.

Everybody was making Doha jokes. I was talking about my run-in with the scary White House guys. "You've met the Hitler Youth," said another reporter. Everybody laughed. This was grim, but it was funny. The camaraderie of people who understood the joke—who were part of the joke—was very reassuring and comfortable.

Certainly, there was the sense that this, however grim, was a diversion. It wasn't real. We'd go home. Like the first Gulf War, this would be over soon and largely forgotten. Not only are modern wars not very lethal (at least not for us), but they occur at a distance; they don't really disturb (at least not for very long) the larger culture. Militarism and patriotic fervor and all manner of get-with-the-program-ism isn't in the cards for us. Everyone obviously wants to get back to business—getting the great American boom to recommence and roll on. So in some sense, the wiseasses would triumph and the righteous Bushies would falter—or at least there'd be a draw.

But in isolated flashes, during a few moments of quiet on the media bus navigating the security pylons, it was also hard *not* to understand what Rush's people were saying in their violent and bilious e-mails: I wasn't taking this seriously. None of us were. We were the people with the picnic baskets coming out to see the battle of Bull Run.

And this wasn't just a diversion: It was just the beginning. I *had* been warned.

Esquire

WINNER, PROFILE WRITING

The Confessions of Bob Greene

When a man loses everything, does he find his true nature? That's the question explored in Bill Zehme's haunting profile "The Confessions of Bob Greene." This melancholy tale delves into the aftermath of Greene's firing from the Chicago Tribune *for alleged sexual impropriety and looks at how small choices and misguided actions shape, and maybe ruin, a life.*

Bill Zehme

The Confessions of Bob Greene

How far can a man fall? Imagine very far—and then, in the case of this man, keep going.

All you've got is your name, the lost man said in a lost voice. Things for which his name had once stood would never entirely be the same things again—that is what he told himself, that is what he wished not to believe while believing it nonetheless. The weight of penance hung about him, and he wore it calmly, if uncomfortably. He was still the same man he had been before he fell—he looked the same, his feelings and beliefs were still his own, he possessed the same talents—but now he was a fallen man and he had never fallen before and everything was different because he fell. He had, in his triumphant career, frequently observed fallen men, had often written stories about them, stories full of curiosity and compassion. Compassion, by the way, had been one of the many things for which his name had stood. Once, he found a line of poetry to include in just such a story. He has not forgotten that line of poetry. "In my moments of hope, I keep returning to that quote from Yeats," he wrote me in an e-mail note from the new prison of his life. "I had always thought that he was writing about a man who has lost everything—who has tumbled suddenly from the heights and who finds himself back where he began, when he had nothing but himself and his belief in who he is: 'Now that my ladder's gone, / I must lie down where all the ladders start, / In the foul rag-and-bone shop of the heart.' Take everything away from me, the poem seems to be saying—take everything I ever had. And let me find out, once more, who I really am."

Here is who we all are, more or less: We are, each one of us, the sum of many conflicting truths. In our most secret souls, we know—although we'd rather not—that certain of our personal truths might well be seen as dark and shameful truths. When a man falls, without exception, it is only these dark truths that emerge and resonate and expand, eclipsing all other truths that should matter as well but no longer do. We feast on the disgrace of the fallen, feel better about ourselves while doing so, and then await the next fallen one to turn up so as to feast once more. It is, alas, the blood sport of human nature. I will tell you, though, that it is a grim spectacle to privately encounter a shamed man, freshly pummeled in public view. It is heartbreaking as hell, really. And so it was that two weeks into his disgrace—at the first blush of which he had vanished behind a thunderous silence maintained ever since—this particular fallen man began sharing his shattered voice with me over the telephone. In those first two weeks, he had quietly withstood torrents of derision and crushing waves of despair. Friends and admirers, some of them very famous, reached out to him, and he deflected their support. He busied himself with self-laceration while his critics gleefully piled on top. He took his beatings, sometimes hideous in spirit, thinking they would never stop yet also incredulous that they hadn't, two weeks hence. "Let them kick," he said, and this was one of the first things he said to me. "It's like I'm a body in the street, and they keep coming by and kicking until they get tired. They wander away and then they come back and kick it some more and then pour a little gasoline on and set it on fire. But, you know, the body is already dead." This was pure revelation to him, the existential wonderment of a newly fallen man. "Anyway, let them kick," he said, pretending that he meant it.

.   .   .

Bob Greene will not write this story himself, certainly not now, most probably not ever. It is, at core, a heartland Greek tragedy, rife with cruel ironies and tortured plot turns from beginning to astonishing end. It has belonged only to him and, more lamentably, to those closest to him. In a short e-mail he sent moments after our first conversation, he wrote simply: "This is darkness beyond any imagining." Those words came on the first day of October 2002. But it had been at the break of dawn on Sunday, September 15, when his exquisite darkness had fallen like a freight train from the sky. The night before, he had not slept at all because the world as he knew it had just exploded. And so he'd decided to stay awake to await confirmation of his newly scorched reality, which would be dropped outside the door of his high-rise apartment unit in the form of an understated announcement in the lower left corner on the front page of the Sunday *Chicago Tribune*, the newspaper for which he had written a tremendously popular column for the previous twenty-four years. His hometown-sweetheart wife and his sixteen-year-old son had somehow managed to find slumber, even after he had told them the worst thing he could ever tell them; they lay in their beds letting unconsciousness temporarily obscure truth. But he kept his vigil, ruefully remembering the only other time he had ever done this very same thing: Back in the summer of his seventeenth year, he worked as a copy boy for the *Columbus Citizen-Journal* and, one night, had written his first newspaper story on a lark—one paragraph in length, about a man who cut open a golf ball with a liquid center that exploded and squirted him in the eye—and the editor liked it enough to run it under the headline GOLF BALL FIGHTS BACK. And so young Bobby Greene had anxiously stayed up to await that momentous 1964 morning paper delivery, when he would see the words he had written appear in actual news type for the very first time.

Now he was fifty-five and a professional newspaperman and book author, thirty-three years into the big fray, and this nocturnal anxiety was altogether different, and then he heard the paper land, and then he felt the bullet enter his heart, because there it was—a note to readers from Ann Marie Lipinski, editor, in small type, four paragraphs in length, the first of which began: "*Chicago Tribune* columnist Bob Greene has resigned and will no longer appear in the pages of the newspaper. The resignation is effective immediately." Editor Lipinski stated that the resignation had been "sought after he acknowledged engaging in inappropriate sexual conduct some years ago with a girl in her late teens whom he met in connection with his newspaper column." She then said that his acknowledgment came as the result of an anonymous complaint that had prompted an investigation, and upon its completion he resigned Saturday night. "Greene's behavior," she wrote, "was a serious violation of *Tribune* ethics and standards for its journalists. We deeply regret the conduct, its effects on the young woman and the impact this disclosure has on the trust our readers placed in Greene and this newspaper." And that was all she wrote.

All that she had not written was voluminous, of course, and feverish speculation erupted instantaneously and tore across the city and then the nation, while maddeningly few additional details trickled forth in the ensuing days, and while *Tribune* officials refused to disclose the particulars, and while Bob Greene—who had largely lived his life for print as well as in print—had now been all but murdered on page one of his own publication and then gone mute. His telephone began ringing that Sunday morning, and it would not stop, as he did not lift the receiver; the last e-mails he received that day, before his *Tribune* online address was shut down for good, pulsed with inquiries from countless major news organizations. He elected to respond only to the Associated Press. ("It's not like you have a rational thought," he would later tell me. "You're thinking, I'm a dead man, and everything I've ever valued, everything I've tried to be, has just been set on fire.") His message, thus, was a brief one, noting that there were "indiscretions in my life that I am not proud of. I don't have the words to express the sadness I feel. I am very sorry for anyone I have let down, including the readers who have for so long meant so much to me. Today I need to be with my family and loved ones." And that was all he wrote.

The incident in question had occurred not merely "some" years earlier but fourteen years earlier. The girl was of consenting age and one week away from going off to college. And, as the *Tribune* reported on Tuesday the seventeenth, the incident had been a "sexual encounter that stopped short of intercourse." Several months before said incident, on April 5, 1988, Greene had written a puckish column about a senior from a local Catholic girls' high school who had been assigned to do an interview for her journalism class and had chosen him as her quarry. She showed up at his office with her parents in tow, his column revealed, and he submitted to her questions until she asked the Barbara Walters Question: "If you could be any kind of a tree, what tree would you be?" "I don't answer the tree question," he told her, prompting him to call Barbara Walters, who agreed that it was a stupid question, which she had asked only once, of Katharine Hepburn, who had said she felt like an old tree. Greene suggested that the girl ask something else. She then asked, "If you could be any food in the world, what would it be?" And so he sighed grimly and said, "A cheeseburger." And that was that. Weeks later, the girl graduated and secured a summer job downtown, maintaining convivial contact with Greene, who eventually invited her out to dinners and then, at one point, to a hotel room, where whatever happened apparently didn't quite happen the way most people had first imagined. "You should wait to do this with someone you love," he says he told her at the time. And that, again, was that.

She stayed in touch with him, calling at least once a year to say hello or to update him on the progress of her own nascent writing career—nothing more to it than that. Each of their lives continued in separate fashion until a specific call she made to him in July of 2001 took on an ominous tone, which he experienced as blatantly threatening. Nearly a year passed, however, before she called again, last June, at the time of the publication of his twenty-first book, *Once Upon a Town* (a nostalgic elegy about the railroad-station canteen of North Platte, Nebraska, whose towns-people had selflessly served food and offered entertainment to more than six million enlisted men who passed through the station during World War II). But now—at age thirty-two, a girl no more—her tone was, Greene says, more direct as she spoke of making public her version of what had happened fourteen summers earlier, indicating that this could, no doubt, compromise his reputation as a leading chronicler of honor and decency in America. At which point, whiffing the portent of blackmail, Greene placed a call to the FBI. A federal agent then phoned her to explain the penalties inherent in cases of harassment and extortion, without specifically accusing her of such. Greene, knowing of that call, felt relief and embarked on his patriotic book tour. She would wait, instead, until Monday, September 9—after the book had summered luxuriantly in the mid-reaches of the *New York Times* best-seller list, peaking at seventh place—before sending the *Tribune* an anonymous e-mail describing what had happened in the summer of 1988. By Wednesday—September 11, of all days, which would also be the last day that any Bob Greene column would ever appear in the *Chicago Tribune*—the paper's management had made contact with her and asked her to come in for a full-disclosure meeting that Saturday. By Thursday afternoon, Greene was told that the hounds of hell had been unleashed, that corporate cops had opened a file on him, that he was flat-out suspended as of that very minute. So, by all accounts, he immediately told managing editor James O'Shea everything, believing that as he was the largest living star in the *Tribune*'s publishing universe, his company would address this delicate situation protectively and with discretion. "What do you want me to do?" he asked O'Shea. "Should I offer my resignation?" O'Shea told him no. And that was the only time Bob Greene uttered the word resignation. In any case, the resignation that he never tendered was accepted on Saturday night, which he believed to be the worst night of his life as he thus far knew it.

But then, he could not yet know of what lay ahead.

· · ·

"Let's just drive north," he said, furtive as a fugitive. And he did very much look the part, having darted from the low-lit side entrance of his elegant apartment building to my waiting Jeep at the appointed early-evening hour. I had suggested he make an escape from self-imposed confinement, from his vacuum of shame. Postcataclysm, he had not left his home for a public meal in seven weeks; indeed, he had barely left his home in seven weeks for anything more than a daily morning walk to the lakefront, a fairly futile exercise in mind clearing during which he would stroll past all the same doormen he had always passed on his daily walks and imagine what they thought of him now. "How're you doing?" he asked me, climbing into the passenger seat. (He would ask this every time we embarked on what would be a handful of these clandestine escape missions beginning last autumn; inevitably, I would always be doing better than he was.) He wore the same uniform he forever favored prior to life in exile: faded jeans, penny loafers, cotton shirt with sleeves rolled, tie tugged loose, and no jacket other than his weathered beige Burberry trench coat. As ever when out, he carried his battered leather briefcase—*"that goddamned briefcase,"* as one of his friends puts it. He was a man of routine whose routine had ceased to exist, and now he had brought along some vestiges of it, and I understood. We drove slowly around his block in the bustling Streeterville neighborhood and passed a popular Italian steak house he frequented Before All This, and he said, not without drollness, "In a perfect world, we should just be able to walk right in there now." Then he said, "That would look nice—'Greene, after his disgrace, spotted out on the town having drinks and laughing it up and living it up.' How did any of this happen?" (At best, in the realm of laughter, the closest he had come during our weeks of talk was a sardonic chuckle here or there; unfettered cheer had left his wheelhouse completely.) I steered us onto North Lake Shore Drive, and he said, "Why don't we just get out of the city?"

Like most everybody he ever knew, I had not laid eyes on him in his new aftermath. I hadn't seen him up close, in fact, for just about five years, and that had been mere happenstance, a bumping into at a drinking establishment. But now, as he sat beside me, as we piloted northward toward destination/restaurant/reprieve yet unknown, I saw in short glances that he was paler and more sallow than I remembered. His aquiline nose came forth in greater relief. Even his hair, as much as it is hair, which it hasn't been for decades, which is his open-secret life choice, somehow seemed grayer around the edges. Of course, the truth of all this is that, like most everybody else he ever knew, I had never really known Bob Greene much at all, which is how he seemed to generally prefer it. ("I was very good at my work, and I wasn't real good at my life," he had told me weeks earlier, then added, "but I fixed that a long time ago.") The Bob Greene I know has forever prided himself on being unknowable. For certain, he has also been exceptionally pleased to have a well-recognized name, if only because it meant that many people knew his work, but largely he refused to allow details of his personal life to be known much at all by anyone. When his children were born, for instance, his friends and colleagues often found out weeks or months later. For that matter, when his first child was born, many coworkers hadn't even known that he was married, although he wore his wedding band in plain sight.

In Chicago, where we both live, and where newsmen and news-women have long drunk in happy packs at subterranean joints and neighborhood dives, he would more often than not be spotted after work, alone and reading the papers, at the bars of unlikely restaurants along North Michigan Avenue. I used to regularly see him—this was more than twenty years ago—propped at the bar of an upscale deli on the top floor of the fancy Water Tower Place shopping mall: the opposite of a rugged writing-man's watering hole, to be sure, but also maybe a safe remove from the downtime scrutiny of fellow reporters. He had, by then, become the journalistic equivalent of a rock star in the city—the very city of Ben Hecht and *The Front Page,* keep in mind—where he'd been given a column at the youthful and rambunctious *Chicago Sun-Times* in 1971, when he was just twenty-four. Here was a grown boy born of upper-middle-class Bexley, Ohio, a whiz-kid graduate of Northwestern University, hired at this big metropolitan daily straight out of school, then promoted to prominence in record time because of smarts and fierce ambition—it was all a stunning wunderkind paradigm from the get-go. His early stuff had been especially sharp and new and rule busting, and in fairly short order he was considered a worthy peer of (if not eventual heir apparent to) the legendary tough-guy/street-genius columnist Mike Royko, then of the *Chicago Daily News.* And so it was said throughout the seventies: If you were a young writer in Chicago, you more than likely wanted to be Bob Greene. In 1978, he was lured over to the stately *Chicago Tribune,* where his writing would then eventually be syndicated to more than three hundred American cities, and he would become Bob Greene to a wildly receptive nation (contributing, in fact, a regular column to Esquire, American Beat, from 1980 to 1989). Since then, what with Chicago being a small big place, I would accidentally see him on occasion or else phone up for an odd bit of professional advice, and he would be pleasant and supportive. But I saw very little of him in any of those intervening years. Still, I heard things about him, about his penchant for engaging women who admired his writing or his fame, this beginning a very long time back, this coming from those with whom he worked. And now, life being what it is, this was the reason we seemed to be running on the lam, heading north, out of town.

· · ·

In Chicago, a story has circulated among certain pockets of younger newspaper people for years, and it has nothing to do with Bob Greene, and in fact Bob Greene did not know the story until I told it to him. It takes place, circa 1990, at the legendary Billy Goat Tavern on Lower Michigan Avenue, where thousands of ink-stained hangovers were born. Mike Royko sat at the bar, as was his eternal wont, and a young *Sun-Times* columnist a couple of years on the job named Richard Roeper sat at a table with a handful of colleagues, and drinks flowed, as they will, and eventually Royko—the dean among them all, and all else—sauntered over to sit with them. And drinks flowed further, and Royko, who by the way had a grudging respect for Greene and who also loved to tease punks who moved anywhere near his turf, at one point bellowed: "Roeper! What are you doing at my table!" And everyone laughed. And then: "Roeper! Where the hell did you come from, anyway!" Then, minutes later: "Roeper! Do you use your column to get laid?"

ROEPER: "Excuse me?"

ROYKO: "You heard me! Do you use your column to get laid?"

ROEPER: (*half jokingly, keep in mind drinks flowing*): "Of course not. That wouldn't be right!"

ROYKO: (*pounding the table*): "Well, what the hell is the point in having a column if you don't use it to get laid!"

· · ·

"I didn't admire myself," he was saying as we cruised beside Lake Michigan in swift traffic. "I really didn't admire myself. The one thing I know about myself, though, is that I've never intentionally tried to hurt anyone." Of course, he didn't want to talk about what he was talking about—"Let's stop talking about this"—and would frequently change the subject and ask me writer-guy-shoptalk things and excitedly recall many of his own adventures in the trade: the machinations of old book deals or the years spent as a part-time *Nightline* correspondent or the exhilaration of making appearances on the old NBC Letterman show, then flying back to Chicago to watch the broadcasts on the same night. And he would, in those moments, seem to temporarily forget the reason we were leaving the city limits. Until a new wave of shame tugged him back: "I've always been pretty good at standing up for other people. I'm no good at standing up for myself. I just never have been, and I don't have any real desire to. I won't even try. I wouldn't go out on a limb for me."

And so we drove and drove, for twenty-plus Illinois miles, considering and then dismissing various dining possibilities (a decent, dimly lit steak joint seemed to be our lone objective on this, his debut night of liberty), wending eventually onto lakeside Sheridan Road, up into the swank North Shore, through Evanston, past the campus of his alma mater, Northwestern (he averted his gaze there), into Wilmette and Highland Park and then westward to Northbrook and, finally, into the parking lot of a hotel that housed a high-end chain restaurant known for its buttery, sizzling platters of meat. "Let's find a way not to go in through the hotel lobby," he said, and so we found a separate entrance into the steak house, whereupon he immediately headed to the men's room so that I could quietly negotiate securing an inconspicuous booth in the darkened bar before he returned. He is, in this part of the world, accustomed to being recognized, and people I know who have dined with him have told me how he seemed to enjoy sitting in the middle of a room where he could monitor all the action and politely nod and smile back at customers who invariably spotted him, and warmly receive their advances. Now the sociable phenomena that he once enjoyed had become his darkest fear, an anticipation of only judging stares and mutterings. "You think anybody noticed me?" he said, sitting down to his first of two vodka gimlets. I told him, frankly, no, and after he took a few sips, I detected a small sense of buoyancy begin to well in him as he acclimated himself to the room. "Should we get the shrimp cocktail to start?" he asked, leaning forward, rising up a bit in posture, loosening his collar further. He seemed, increasingly, to be a man who was very pleased to be out for a steak dinner in a hotel restaurant—which is what he had been thousands of times in his previous life. He seemed to be a man pleased to make happy chatter again with a waitress—"What's good? I mean, *really* good? I mean, what would you get?" He seemed excited to just be out of the goddamn house and among those who were living lives other than his.

· · ·

I wondered about the briefcase, which never left his side, which rested next to him in the booth. I wondered what a man who habitually carried his briefcase everywhere—and had now spent seven weeks going nowhere—might be hauling around with him, cell phone and hairbrush notwithstanding. "I'll show you," he said, and what he showed me was a time capsule of his life on the day he lost his job. Everything that had been in there then was in there now; there had been no need to do anything with the contents, since there had been no need for him to work again. There were printouts of old columns and assorted correspondence. There were schedules for personal appearances that he had made and for those he had been supposed to make but never did—the ones he had abruptly canceled upon his own cancellation on that weekend in mid-September. He sifted through all these pieces of suddenly irrelevant paper with a mien of bittersweet wonder and strange discovery. "Oh, look at *this!*" he said more than a few times.

.　　　.　　　.

"The funny thing is, I had really been looking forward to that weekend," he would say.

The weekend of September 13 to 15, and on through Tuesday the seventeenth, had been planned for months, it turns out, and it was to be a weekend on which Greene was to have given speeches and been lauded with platitudes and been heroically celebrated by the state of Nebraska, in the state of Nebraska, whose North Platte Canteen he had romantically celebrated in book form and whose state book festival was to kick off in the town of Grand Island with his keynote address. The week leading up to that trip—after which he had intended to claim a good chunk of unused vacation time and disappear for a while—was full of the kind of work momentum he lived for. He had done an MSNBC panel show with Brian Williams on the meaning of September 11 one year later, taped an interview for a PBS biography of the late exiled Ohio State coach Woody Hayes (a longtime Greene specialty topic), cranked out four columns, finished off a new book proposal, done a special live commentary Wednesday night on the *Tribune*-owned TV superstation WGN (on whose newscast he regularly appeared Thursday nights) about the president's speech to the UN earlier that day— the anniversary of the terrorist attacks—which would also be the subject of the column he had roughed out for Sunday the fifteenth. "On the morning of Thursday, September 12," he would recall, "the world was continually this perfect two-lane highway stretching off forever into sunshine."

By late that afternoon, all above had become superfluous. His managing editor called him in and heard him out and suspended him, as an internal investigation had now begun. Greene requested that he be able to honor his weekend commitment and fly to Nebraska the next morning; he was told to go ahead but to be on alert. He went home that night, his brain on fire, his stomach in knots, and shared nothing about what was happening with his wife of thirty-two years, Susan, and his son, Nick—twenty-year-old daughter Amanda was away at college—and pretended his way through the night. "I can't even remember what was going through my mind. All I know is that when I got to O'Hare Friday morning, I hadn't slept." Indeed, all that occurred over the next forty-eight hours would feel as if it were occurring to somebody else.

And so: Walking through the United Airlines terminal, his cell phone rang, and it was managing editor O'Shea urging him to return immediately to the Tribune Tower for a meeting regarding the matter at hand. Greene's luggage, however, had already been checked through, and there was no way to retrieve it, and in our new world, flights can no longer leave with luggage not belonging to passengers aboard. He would have to go to Nebraska and then return to Chicago Saturday afternoon for the meeting, cutting his trip three days short. He flew to Omaha, where he was picked up for the two-and-a-half-hour drive to Grand Island, during which he sat in the car's backseat, signing his name in three hundred copies of his book to be sold at the book fair. That evening, at the festival dinner, he somehow got through his speech—a reverie about wartime North Platte being "the best America there ever was" and how privileged he had been to write its story—and received a standing ovation, the first of his life. "I was looking at those people and thinking, Oh, God, you don't know what's going to happen to me." He returned to his interstate Holiday Inn hotel room, collapsed, spoke again at the fair at eight o'clock Saturday morning, offered his regrets for having to leave so suddenly, and was driven back across the plains to Omaha. He rode again in relative silence and apologized to the driver for being bad company. (On Monday, an AP reporter would track down the driver to inquire about Greene's demeanor on the ride. "Like he was Al Cowlings and I was O. J. Simpson," Greene said to me.)

And so: Flying back to Chicago, whatever denial had thus far allowed him to function dissolved into certain dread. "It sunk in— Why am I being pulled off this trip? Why is it so important to bring me back now?" At O'Hare, as was fairly customary, a few people recognized him and, here or there, said nice things about his work. And again: "I'm thinking and trying not to think it at the same time—*Not only is this going to be the last time this happens to me, but tomorrow I'm going to be someone else.*" He took a cab directly down to the *Tribune* with his luggage and, by late afternoon, entered a conference room where he submitted to a very long inquisition from editors Lipinski and O'Shea and the company's senior legal counsel, Dale Cohen. (At some point, according to *Tribune* sources, he asked O'Shea whether he should have an attorney of his own present for this meeting, and it was suggested to him that things would probably go just as well if he didn't.) He remembers hearing music wafting up from the plaza below and thinking, I want to be out there. What had stuck deepest in management's craw was that Greene had gone to the FBI without its knowledge. ("You don't call the FBI on a whim," he would say to me. "The *Tribune* wasn't being blackmailed—I was.") The session adjourned for a long break, during which Greene was told to wait in his small office. When he was summoned back, Lipinski informed him that his life with his newspaper was over. And she said that fact would be announced on the front page of the morning edition. He remembers there being disgust in Lipinski's voice, there being no room for negotiation, and that it did not occur to him to say, Wait a minute. He got up and left and caught himself heading back to his office and thought, Why?

And so: "I will never talk publicly about what happened specifically when I went home that night, but for any person to have to go home and tell his family that. . . ." His wife was not home and his son wondered why he wasn't in Nebraska, and so he had to tell his son first because his son saw the trouble in his father's face, and then tell his wife after she returned from a movie. He then called his daughter at school. And he woke his eighty-three-year-old mother in Ohio and, at some point, said to her: "Before it occurs to you, even if it never does, you've done nothing wrong to cause this to happen in me. You have been a fine example to me, and a flawless and faultless parent. Don't even spend a second thinking how this could have come upon our family."

And then, when the apartment was still, he sat and waited for the morning paper.

•   •   •

"I still have a bank account, you know," he told me when I paid the check after our first runaway meal. The following week, we repeated the drive north (he scurried once more from the side of his building to my idling car) and returned to the same place—"I'm sorry we're having to get so far out of town again"—and he insisted on forking over his own crisp twenties for our drinks and shrimp and steaks. This time, the bar was full, and, with some trepidation, he had relented to eat in the better-lit and crowded main dining room, walking briskly to our table with his briefcase, past all the other customers, his eyes looking straight through them. He was a little less buoyant this time, self-consciousness on radar as he noticed people noticing him. "What do you think they're thinking?" he said at one point of a table of women dining nearby. Upon leaving, a couple eating in the bar called him over. "Thanks for your work," the man said, extending his hand. They cited one of his columns of distant vintage and made no reference to recent history. Greene seemed happy to engage. "They were very nice," he said to me afterward. "But who knows what they'll say tomorrow?" The hostess stopped him before we reached the exit. "Very good to see you, Mr. Bob Greene!" she chirped. "How are you?" His smile was as wan as wan gets. "Not as well as I'd like," he said.

•   •   •

During these weeks and months, to supplant the urge to write, he began to read over much of his life's work, as if searching for clues.

His books, of course, brim with clues to who he is and why he is where he is right now. With Greene, clues into his shuttered soul must be sought out, since a pathological oath of privacy has kept him from revealing in print—much less in person—the details of his real life, the life he has lived not as a reporter on the loose but as a man with a home and a wife and two children. The lone exception was his seventh book, *Good Morning, Merry Sunshine: A Father's Journal of His Child's First Year,* which became a 1984 best-seller. Not only was this the only instance in his long career when he publicly disclosed the names of nuclear-family members and relatives, but it stands as the first and last time ever that he acknowledged on the page that he was a husband and father, albeit one who wasn't around a lot. "I wish I'd never written it," he has often told me. "It was too big of an opening into my life. I've never said this to anyone, but as soon as it came out, I realized, You know, the reason you've never done this before is because you should not do it. When it went out of print, I never let them reprint it. It just always seemed to me that there's a reason I go through my whole life without opening it up. I'm not sure what it is, but there's a reason."

At his prompting, I also began to pore through his books and excavate pieces to his puzzle, laid out in his own prose. Some were glaringly obvious—recurring and admiring ruminations about the lives of Elvis Presley and Hugh Hefner (he once spent a week living at the Chicago Playboy Mansion for a *Sun-Times* series) or the *Esquire* story titled "The Coolest Guy in the Room," about then–*Monday Night Football* announcer Frank Gifford (about whom Greene wrote, "Women look at Gifford and covet his company; men look at him and suddenly feel too fat or too bald or too short or too pale"). Other times I'd stumble across salient indicators and then tell him what I'd found. Example: From his 1985 collection, *Cheeseburgers* (alas), I divined merely all one needs to know in a piece called "Teen Idol," wherein he tells the story of twelve-year-old Bobby Greene, who, in 1959, sent a short self-description ("I dig Elvis, Kookie and Ricky") and his sixth-grade photograph ("in which I let my eyes half close in what I hoped resembled a come-hither bedroom look") to *Dig* magazine—the *Tiger Beat* of its day—which published both, as well as his address, that summer in its monthly gallery of readers. Once Bobby returned from camp that summer, his father presented him with a box containing four hundred letters from girls who liked his picture; dozens of letters would thereafter arrive daily for months. "There was no getting around it," grown-up Bobby wrote. "At twelve, I was a national sex symbol for young girls. . . . I was a pretty sheltered, innocent suburban kid; what was I supposed to do with all these girls?" And then: "I always knew that other boys might have certain advantages over me—but that they had never been made a teen idol by *Dig*. Somehow it had changed my life."

When I mentioned the story to him, he said simply, "That's it."

•   •   •

I do not know exactly when I realized that I had become his primary link to the outside world. By mid-October, we seemed to be speaking every few days, some chats lasting longer than others, depending on the state of his psyche. "I'm just not having a great day," he would say more often than not. I would regularly ask what he was doing with himself, and he would say: "Nothing. I have no job." In order to initiate our conversations, I would send him an e-mail to say I was around, and then he would call me within minutes. After a couple of months, I finally asked him for his phone number, as the covert nature of all this seemed to feel more melodramatic than necessary. He apologized and gave it to me but said he rarely answered the phone. But I never did call the number he gave me, not wishing to intrude on the fragility of his household or frighten him into thinking that yet another talk-show booker was looking for the exclusive interview. At our second dinner, he told me that he'd actually answered the phone that day and spoken with Matt Lauer, who'd been leaving messages for weeks, offering support while also inviting him onto the Today show; he politely declined.

Support, by the way, issued forth from others who knew the home number. Among the earliest was Oprah Winfrey, on whose show he had appeared to explore the child-abuse cases he had doggedly and passionately written about from the nineties onward (and so often as to incite the eye-rolling disdain of his peers). His first words to her: "I'm sorry I let you down." Paul Harvey, who is to radio what Greene had been to print (i.e., Americana in excelsis), spoke with him at length to remind him of his worth as a human. Bob Costas, on whose NBC *Later* show Greene had been the most frequent guest, came through town in early October and, so as to avoid public scrutiny, just went over to Greene's place to watch the World Series and order in pizza and remind him that he could be present with people who cast no stones. ("Costas would have much rather been broadcasting the World Series than sitting around with me," he said. "I think it was the first time I was dressed. As he left, I said to him, 'Jesus, this must have felt not so much like a visit but a visitation.' It was such a nice thing for him to do.") And then he learned from his book publisher that one George Herbert Walker Bush had been trying for weeks to get his home address from the *Tribune*, but the *Tribune* refused to divulge such to a former president. A handwritten note eventually came, and he learned that the former president didn't like to see Greene take it on the chin but admired the way he had handled himself in the press, no matter that he was paying a tough price, and hoped him to have an exciting future, despite all.

But as I came to understand, he knew nothing of what to do with such support. And yet he also knew nothing of what to make of the silence enveloping him. "There are days I don't hear a fucking voice," he would say. "Because I had managed over the years to construct this wall over my family and my house that if I don't seek people out . . . you know what I mean? It's just odd not to pick up the phone and interview somebody."

.   .   .

As Thanksgiving was now a day away, and as his daughter was returning to an altogether different home, and as he told me that the family would be ordering in their Thanksgiving turkey dinner because simplicity was required as never before, and since he had been rereading his own work to remind himself of who he had once been, he e-mailed me some page numbers to visit in his twelfth book, *Hang Time: Days and Dreams with Michael Jordan*. (Jordan had, most astonishingly, filed a lawsuit a month before against a woman with whom he had had extramarital relations ten years before, whom he claims he had long ago paid $250,000 in "hush money," and who had now reemerged to demand an additional five million.) Anyway, I believe I found the correct exchange between the both of them on the pages that Greene wished me to find:

GREENE: "Think about the things you wake up terrified about in the middle of the night . . . that only you know about yourself. . . . Are any of them the things that other people have said about you?"

JORDAN: "No. The three-o'clock-in-the-morning things are much worse."

GREENE: "I know. It's not just you. It's everyone. The worst things that anyone else could ever say about us don't come close to being as bad as the worst things we think about ourselves."

.   .   .

They had come out of the woodwork, the women had, in that third week of September. The ones he had attempted to charm and the ones he had successfully charmed—they phoned in to Chicago radio shows or wrote in to media Web sites, and they recounted their experiences with him back when they were in their twenties (none younger or much older). Most had sent him a letter complimenting him on a column they had liked and then received a phone call from him and then an invitation for a meal to talk further about whatever the subject of interest had been. One gave an interview to the *Sun-Times*—a woman now in her forties—wherein she blithely recalled exactly the above scenario and how it became a sexual arrangement in 1984, conducted in hotel rooms and lasting a couple of months, until he ended it abruptly. "He was guilty," she said. "He expressed some things about trying to stop this behavior." She also said, "I don't have any bad feelings about Bob Greene. He's a fine person and an excellent writer. The guy isn't a total scum because he has this character defect." And none of these tales were a surprise to his media brethren, although more than a few took immense joy in dancing on his grave. Others, however, came to his defense, none more vociferously than Paul Galloway, a recently retired *Tribune* writer who had started the same day as Greene at the *Sun-Times* in 1969 and remained Greene's closest, if only, professional confidant, which—Greene being Greene—means he knows just a little more about his enigmatic ways than other people. "He's so secretive," Galloway told me with a small laugh. "The privacy thing just became worse and worse over the years. Bob doesn't share too well with anyone. It sounds paradoxical, but he's a very moral guy. He really has a tremendous sense of morality and a great sense of cynicism about himself and what he did. And he turned over a new leaf. He had been getting away from that, I believe, a long time ago."

Because he shares poorly, he can find no way to articulate specifically the nature of what he was getting away from and how he managed to do so. He did say he never wrote about Bill Clinton and the Monica Lewinsky affair because "it would have been the height of hypocrisy. How could I?" And at one point, trying to explain his less-than-noble behavior, he invoked words he attributed to Muhammad Ali, recalling a dark patch of his own: "Everybody gets lost in life. I just got lost, that's all." So, in the early 1990s, he sought and received counseling for his problem. He would address the matter only carefully and cryptically: "It's like if you're an alcoholic or something and you try to get better, then all of a sudden they go back and dig up your alcoholism again. I liked women."

Similarly, he is mortally stymied for words to explain the reason for his departure from the *Tribune* and why he didn't fight harder to defend himself with due process. The guiltiest among us, after all, defends himself. It is what we do. And why, exactly, was Bob Greene fired? Whatever else the episode from fourteen years before was, it was not illegal. And as the young woman was no longer either a subject or source for his column, it is arguable whether what he did was professionally unethical. Clearly, he transgressed his marriage, and not just on that occasion, but that was nobody's business except his own and his wife's. Was he irresponsible? Did he show poor judgment? He is the first to say so. Was the offense punishable? Certainly. But to be terminated and then respond so meekly—that is the hardest thing for him to explain.

The likeliest answer is that, for a man as pathologically private as this man, defending himself could have spurred a torrent of similar complaints and could have resulted in his entire private life being opened to scrutiny. He told me, "I thought if I could protect my family from just one more day's pain by keeping my mouth shut, then it was worth it. They didn't ask for this." And he also said, "I tell myself, If I'd gone in there with a very good lawyer, it would have taken longer for them to get rid of me, and it would have been done more cleanly. But it would have leaked out, and the fact is I'd still be sitting here without a job saying to myself, If only I had gone in there as a human being and tried to explain myself. And that's what I did. It seems to me that if you go in there with an attorney, you've already lost your job." So, instead, from another e-mail: "When Woody Hayes was fired from the job he loved more than anything else in the world, despite all his hurt, he said something I don't think he really believed but that I have never forgotten, because its dignity was so soaring. He said, when he finally had the strength to speak, and when everyone was wanting him to stand up for himself and excoriate the people who had fired him: 'Why don't we just say I got what was coming to me and leave it at that.' I much prefer the sound of Woody's voice back then." On the other hand, I will tell you that he has wrestled daily, sometimes hourly, to grasp exactly why it happened the way it happened. It tortured him from the start and would continue to until events more unfathomable began to unfold. But I did hear him say the following: "Maybe columnists aren't supposed to fuck teenagers. Even though I didn't."

⋅   ⋅   ⋅

We went north again a week after Thanksgiving, but this time not nearly as far north, which seemed a good sign, settling very comfortably into a steak house in Evanston, the town where he had gone to college. He said that he had written Thanksgiving letters to his children (all their lives he has written them letters on their birthdays), but then decided not to hand the letters over. "I thought, Am I doing it for them, or am I doing it for me?" He ate ribs and we tried not to talk about things we had talked about in the past. He seemed to enjoy himself more than on the other nights out. On the ride home, though, out of nowhere, he asked, "What do you think the average person on the street assumed happened in 1988?" When he left the car and walked into his building, I saw that his posture stooped ever so slightly.

⋅   ⋅   ⋅

Then something happened. Something snapped. The new landscape to which Bob Greene was just getting acclimated buckled and split open without warning. It went like this: The second week of December, he went silent on me. He had disappeared all over again. Then he left a voice-mail message on December 13, a check-in call of sorts ("Hey, it's Greene," it began, as all of his calls or messages had), and his tone had never sounded more somber, nor had I ever heard such trembling come from him. I sent him an e-mail the next day, saying that his voice hadn't sounded so good, and he wrote in response, "We'll talk when I can."

•　　•　　•

A day or so later, we spoke and he said his world was collapsing all over again. He gave no further details and got off the line. Privacy, secrecy, et al.

•　　•　　•

December 20, on the phone: "This can go nowhere. My wife is very, very sick. She's likely dying. I don't know what to do. Don't ask any questions, okay? If you were to tell one person . . . That's why I haven't been in touch. It's just—oh, God. I can't go on. My wife, my kids—Jesus . . ."

•　　•　　•

Disbelief came to mind first. But never had I heard such a woeful sound emit from a human throat, much less from one who had fallen so hard already. It had been a long illness, though not always a grave one, and it was now coming to its conclusion. Thus, all that he and I had spoken of to date felt utterly ridiculous. Here then was his family's holiday season. Two days later, an e-mail: "Things are very bad."

•　　•　　•

He had never spoken her name to me in all this time. She was My Wife. Nick Greene was My Son. Amanda Sue Greene was My

Daughter. He could never speak their names. Susan Koebel Greene had turned fifty-five on November 14. He wrote her a love letter for her birthday, the kind of love letter a man writes a wife of thirty-two years, full of appreciation for who and what she was to him. Through these months, he told me, she had been "magnificent." He had said, "You don't know your life has been worth living until the people closest to you treat you with love in a moment like that. It's all I had." Most people who knew Bob Greene had never met Susan Greene or had any idea of what she looked like. Blond, vibrant, playful, smart, it turns out.

· · ·

His brief communications through Christmas remained oblique. I would ask what was happening, and he would say, "You know. Bad, bad." It wasn't until the second day of the new year that he told me what actually had been happening—that she had been experiencing respiratory problems at home, that he had admitted her to a hospital on December 12, three months to the day of his first comeuppance, that he had been by her side ever since. "She has been in intensive care, on a ventilator, for more than two weeks now," he wrote me. "My days and nights have, of course, been devoted only to that—while trying at the same time to be with our children and prepare them for what is to come." A few days later, he e-mailed me the Yeats quote, the one about lying down where the ladders start, about everything being taken away and finding out who you really are.

· · ·

He left the hospital to meet me for dinner the next week. There would be no road trip, as he needed to be near. We met at a downtown hotel and found a street-level steak house there. I forget what he ate. More than a month had passed since we had last done this. He was more pale and more haggard and more gaunt. He said that he had been falling asleep in his clothes a lot. He told me about the health-insurance policy he had thankfully managed to find to replace the one he lost when he lost his job. She had now been unconscious and unable to speak since weeks before the holidays. All he could do was watch her breathe. "There's nothing to do but to do it," he said. His daughter would spend her days doing the same with him. His in-laws as well. His son could not bear to see his mother the way she was. "I keep telling myself, Maybe this means your finest hour finds you," he said. "It doesn't work." His voice contained nothing but resignation, as it were. I drove him back to the hospital and watched him walk inside, carrying his briefcase, striding purposefully and nodding to people who recognized him.

·   ·   ·

Her heart stopped beating two weeks later, on Saturday, January 25. I found the e-mail a few hours after he sent it at 8:19 that night. It said only: "She died today." He wrote some things about her the next day—things about children's charity work she had done and other things about her—so that he could send them to a friend at the *Tribune* for the obituary. He read what he wrote to me and his voice cracked. The obituary ran two days later under the headline SHE GAVE KIDS CREATIVE SPARK, the first four paragraphs of which were devoted to her efforts to teach art to underprivileged schoolchildren. Then:

"Mrs. Greene, 55, died of heart failure Saturday in Northwestern Memorial Hospital in Chicago, where she had been treated for more than a month for a respiratory illness. 'As Susan lay dying during the most painful months of our family's life, she defined, in the eyes of our children and me, the true meaning of strength and love,' said her husband, former *Tribune* columnist Bob Greene. . . . 'In a world that is so often cold-eyed and mean-spirited and unforgiving, Susan was a person of never-ending good-heartedness, charity and mercy,' her husband said." The memorial, the paper stated, would be private.

．　　．　　．

I had sent a note to his former editor, Ann Marie Lipinski, on January 20, saying that I was considering writing the story of Bob Greene's life in exile and requesting an opportunity to, at the very least, informally talk with her about the circumstances of his departure. As the events of that week came to pass, I knew that I would have to tell his story, because it was a story like none other I had ever witnessed. She responded eighteen days later with this e-mail:

"Bill: Bob Greene's admissions and resignation from the *Tribune* were heartbreaking for the readers, for the paper and for me. I can only imagine what this time has been like for Bob and the woman who first came forward, and I would rather not revisit the matter and compound that pain.—Ann Marie"

And that was all she wrote.

．　　．　　．

He waited a week to hold the memorial. The only *Tribune* employees he invited were a few men and women from the copy desk and the writer of the obituary. He wore a dark sport coat and tie and tan pants and, along with his children, greeted people at the door to the service. He smiled a thin smile. When he took the microphone, however, his voice was strong. Until he read the birthday letter he had written to her. Then it shuddered and cracked. Afterward, he stood among the guests and family members, holding his briefcase, accepting condolences, and wishing he were somewhere else. But, of course, he already was.

Zoetrope: All-Story

FINALIST, FICTION

The Only Meaning of the Oil-Wet Water

Zoetrope *offers stories that represent fiction's powerful role as safe ground for theorizing in a complex world. This captivating, original piece investigates the phenomenon of love with the result—disappointment.*

Dave Eggers

The Only Meaning of the Oil-Wet Water

P ilar was not getting over divorce or infidelity or death. She was fleeing nothing. She flew to Costa Rica one day, on two planes, from Champaign, then Miami, because she had time off and Hand, her longtime friend, was there, or near enough. There is almost no sadness in this story.

Pilar: she is not Latin in any way she knows, but since she was very young she's heard from friends and strangers that her name is a Latin or Latin-sounding one. She is always embarrassed to admit, though she's admitted it a thousand times, that she's never looked up the provenance of her name, its meaning or anything else about it. Her skin is the color of blond wood, easily tanning, and her hair is black, which reinforces the assumption of her Latinness, even though she's been told by her parents, always, that she's Irish and only Irish; maybe some Scottish, per- haps a jab of German. Though with her hair in a ponytail and with her long legs, very long for a woman not even five and a half feet tall, she resembles, more than anything, popular images of Pocahontas. She always wanted to have some Native American blood in her, just as everyone does, because with that blood would come nobility as would excuses to do things the wrong way, or not do them at all. But instead she is Irish or possibly even Welsh but not in any tangible sense, and thus born without any sorrow in the lives of her known ancestors, and so she had to smile gratefully and create good things from scratch or just save people from skin disease. Pilar was a doctor, a young one, a dermatologist. Her profession doesn't figure into this story.

PILAR WALKED: with her toes pointing northwest and northeast, like a dancer.

PILAR LAUGHED: in a throaty way, and loudly, while her eyes devoured.

PILAR KNEW: when something would happen, and when something would not.

Hand was in Granada, Nicaragua, for six months and was encouraging all visitors. He was working for Intel, doing something Pilar could never really grasp, even if she wanted to, which she didn't, because her brain, she believed, was meant to be filled with more colorful things. Intel had asserted itself in Central America and was rotating in young Spanish-speaking consultants like Hand for a year or two at a time. Pilar couldn't imagine what Hand would know that Nicaraguan Intel could need, but then again, this was the sort of arrangement he always landed—well-paying, low-commitment, impossible to explain. Pilar accepted Hand's invitation, but they couldn't agree on what the week would entail. Hand, sick of Nicaragua for the time being, wanted a week in Costa Rica, surfing and looking at women jogging across the flat wet sand. Pilar wanted to see Nicaragua, because everyone, it seemed, had seen Costa Rica, but no one she knew had stepped foot in Nicaragua. Nicaragua sounded dangerous; she liked the word. Nicaragua! It sounded like some kind of spider. There it goes, under the table—Nicaragua!

. . .

Hand got his way. They'd be surfing in Costa Rica, on the Pacific Coast. But she didn't mind. She would tell everyone she went to Nicaragua anyway.

In San José the humidity covered her like a net. She rented a car and immediately went the wrong direction, headed straight into the city's center when she wanted to go the opposite way. It was humid and easily ninety degrees and she was in the merchants' district. Cheap electronics, men selling things from white aluminum carts. Rental car agencies and banks and students. Clumps of pedestrians jogging through traffic. Office buildings of the sixties steel-and-glass Erector-set sort, flimsy and forgettable. The road was five lanes wide and was jammed but moving. It looked like L.A., circa 1973. She puttered through San José weirdly horny. The heat maybe. The volume of the sidewalks maybe. She watched women through her windshield and they watched her. She found an English-language station and on it Michael Jackson's "I Want to Rock with You" and she thought she would burst. She was happy, and she'd been for a few years able to recognize it, just dumb happiness, when it came, whatever its cause. When people asked how she was, she said Happy, and this made some people angry. There was traffic heading into town and she was moving, legs and arms and neck, with Michael, who she knew she'd like if she met him. She would understand him and they'd laugh and laugh about nothing, standing in his kitchen.

HAND HAD: loved three of Pilar's oldest friends, and she knew everything.

HAND WOULD: leave this world and everyone in it if given the chance to be in space for just a few minutes.

HAND CRIED: when he read about men falsely imprisoned, freed at age forty, and walking the streets without malice.

. . .

She found her way out of the city and drove straight west, through the tolls by the airport and then around the two-lane bends, hundreds of turns through the hill country, waiting behind so many trucks, everyone so slow. The country was neat and green and lush and everything was for sale. At the airport they had been selling real estate; at the car rental place, at every gas station, slick posters and handmade flyers of properties for the taking, beach-front or lowland country—everywhere along the road, plots and properties available. The Costa Ricans were proud of what they'd created—the most sturdy, predictable, and easily the most tourist-amenable country in Central America—and now that it was ripe, they were bringing it all to market. The highway was tumored with SUVs and buses. Pilar had expected jalopies and wood-fenced fruit trucks, but they were rare. This country was singing with space and sky and bright smooth new cars with clean black tires. There was heat, but between the sun and the treetops were quick-moving clouds, and they dragged black shadows over the leaves.

LOW-FLYING, QUICK-MOVING CLOUDS: I haven't long to live.

TREETOPS, ROUNDED AND ROUGH: That's probably true.

LOW-FLYING, QUICK-MOVING CLOUDS: I won't even make it to the sea.

TREETOPS, ROUNDED AND ROUGH: Self-pity is a fund without dividends.

LOW-FLYING, QUICK-MOVING CLOUDS: You see me like a dragonfly—intriguing maybe, beautiful of course, but soon enough dead. I'm a ghost, an apparition.

TREETOPS, ROUNDED AND ROUGH: Don't be redundant.

LOW-FLYING, QUICK-MOVING CLOUDS: I can already see where I'll end.

TREETOPS, ROUNDED AND ROUGH: I don't know what to tell you.

LOW-FLYING, QUICK-MOVING CLOUDS: But the thing is,

I really love moving like this, and though I know I won't even make it to the sea.

TREETOPS, ROUNDED AND ROUGH: There are advantages to flight.

LOW-FLYING, QUICK-MOVING CLOUDS: But thought is its unfitting companion.

$$\bullet \qquad \bullet \qquad \bullet$$

Pilar was meeting Hand at Playa Alta, because there, Hand said, the waves were forgiving and not too big, the water warm, and the beach almost empty. Even when it's crowded it looks empty, this beach, he said. A big flat playa, he said, and she cringed, because Hand, she knew, would say *playa* when he meant beach, if that beach was located in a Spanish-speaking country.

There is no way or reason to be subtle about why Pilar was in Costa Rica. At thirty-one she was still unmarried and Hand was one of her few old friends also still unmarried, and the only attractive old friend she'd never slept with. So she knew, when she hung up the phone with Hand five weeks prior, that she would sleep with him in Alta, and she knew it on the plane and on the drive to the coast.

Was she in any way saddened by the predictability of the outcome? Was it unromantic? She decided that it was not. Sex and things like sex—things people pretend they regret—weren't about a decision, they were about putting yourself in the path of a decision already made.

She would arrive and hope that he still looked the way she liked him to look—lean, bigmouthed, clean. They would spend the first day pretending to be friends only, barely touching arms. The second night they would drink at dinner, and drink after that, amid shirtless and dreadlocked surfers, and then would sleep together in a tentative and civilized way. That much was assured, because Pilar had done this kind of thing before—with Mark in Toronto, with

Angela in San Diego—and there was never variation in the setup; only the aftermath was changeable. Afterward, with Hand, there could be very little change in their affection and respect for each other: she was too careful, and he was loosely strung. Afterward, with Mark, she'd had to tolerate his frequent references to their weekend, both the almost-funny—"I saw you naked!"—and those helping him achieve a personal sort of release—"What were you wearing that weekend? Tell me again. Wait, hold on . . ."—but again, with Hand, she knew it would be mild, perhaps even forgotten, if it didn't grow into something else. But would they want to continue having sex? That's the simple and only question. And that depended on so many things: Would he do something strange with his tongue? Was his naked body strange in any disastrous way? Was he awkward-moving when naked? Would he cry (Mark) or become callous (Angela)? His legs might be too thin or pale, or his penis purple, or too narrow, his mouth too—

This story is not about Pilar and Hand falling in love.

.   .   .

Once close to Alta, the road devolved from two lanes paved to one lane dusty and everywhere potholed. The cars each way weaved and ducked, passengers inside with their hands braced against the roof. It was ten miles of this, and it felt like hours before the trees and farms gave way to the shanties and shops that announced Alta. A combination juice bar and art gallery called Forget It, Sue. Then a recycling center. More plots for sale. The place was still raw; the road still dust. Barefoot boys on bikes and mopeds outsped the cars, better navigating the road's holes, while women let groceries in blue-striped plastic bags pull their arms earthward. Just past a Best Western and on the right side of the road, a thin wood hid the beach, wide and flat, rippling into a delta berthing small boats of rotting wood.

The hotel where they'd agreed to meet was called the Shangri La, above the main strip, nameless. The town titled none of its streets, but there was a primary artery, the length of three city blocks, with most of the town's shops and restaurants attached. The Shangri La, on the hill, was white, and shone like a monument against a teal blue sky. It overhung a small garden full of iguanas, snakes, and mice, its deck jutting its strong chin toward the ocean.

The owner, a fit and sunburned German named Hans, gave Pilar keys and directions to the room, No. 5, and while walking up the steps, and then along the deck, past the pool, with a preposterous view of the big ridiculous Pacific to her left, the sun teetering above, the waves blithely carrying surfers in, she actually had the feeling, momentarily, that this was not her actually doing, that in fact she was still in Chicago, or even Wisconsin, and was imagining this—that she was just inhabiting a daydream concocted during, say, a dimly lit afternoon salad-bar lunch at Wendy's. It really seemed more plausible than the reality of her inhabiting this moment, of actually walking barefoot around a pool shaped like a curling kitten, bordered in hand-painted tiles of orange and blue, now stepping over two teak-brown surfers on straw mats, on her way to a room, down a long white hallway with geckos scampering on the ceiling above, in a hillside seaside hotel in Costa Rica, which holds Hand, whom she'd known for twelve years, who was still alive, and not only still alive, but here.

·   ·   ·

Pilar was worried that her back was oversoaked from the drive, that Hand would feel her moisture and be appalled. But when she opened the door and they grabbed each other and hugged, he was just as wet as she was. He smelled like pineapple and sweat. His chin was hot on his shoulder, his hair damp.

"No air conditioning here," he said. He said it in a guttural Spanish accent. Pilar hoped he would stop.

"Oh," she said.

"Jesss, it eeez veddy hot here, jess," he said, and then sighed, giving up.

The room was high-ceilinged and open, with a kitchen, a breakfast nook, a bedroom a few steps up. A fan spun overhead, its pull string ticking with every two or three turns. The deck overlooked the pool and the town and then the ocean. She couldn't believe it all.

"This is crazy," she said.

"I know," he said, now speaking like he normally spoke, as he had been speaking since they met, in sixth grade, when their two schools merged and they played silent ball on their sturdy desks, hoping not to drop that damned ball. What the hell was she doing in Costa Rica? How did they get here?

The floor was tile. The whole place was tile. She had come to expect carpeting in hotels.

"That's pretty normal down here, the tile," Hand said. "Anywhere south of Texas is like that."

There was a plunger in the corner of the room, with a handle that looked precisely like a dildo. A gust jumped through the open window and jumbled a chime over the doorway.

She stepped over to Hand and slipped her arms around his waist and smelled his smell. She closed her eyes and pictured her old kitchen and the wallpaper there, a pattern of Disney dwarves bubbled from heat and humidity.

.   .   .

They left their things and they bobbed down the white stone steps. Outside, in the pink light that soon enough, with a shrug, would relinquish the day to night, there were horses. Four, just downhill from the hotel, one standing still in the road, two sitting nearby in the long grey-green roadside grass, the fourth one, white (the others were black), standing by the hotel's straight hedge, just west of the hotel's cherry door. Pilar and Hand looked around for the owners of the horses. They were shod but had no saddles, no bridles. Four horses, all gaunt, alone. Every horse stared at Pilar and Hand, from Wisconsin.

"I almost forgot you were coming," Hand said.

They were standing, talking while standing and while the horses watched.

"What does that mean?" Pilar said. She was scratching the top of her head with one finger, in a circular motion.

"I don't know." He stumbled for a minute, backtracking, explaining that he'd been looking forward to her coming, but that in the past twenty-four hours he'd spaced her arrival.

"You forgot it was today, or forgot completely?"

"Your hair is dark," he said.

"It was winter where I was. You're not going to answer."

"Did it used to be so dark?"

"I don't know. Didn't it?"

They walked by the horses; the horses watched with mild interest. She didn't know what to expect from the horses. There was nothing remarkable about their appearance, but they gave her a chill and she wasn't sure why. She had rarely seen horses unaccompanied or unfenced and they looked huge and sinewy and tightly wound. She was enchanted by them, the novelty of having them by their hotel, but at the same time she wanted them gone because their size made them seem possessing of a wide but focused intelligence—and she imagined that they would break into their room and kill them both.

"There's a woman here who runs on the beach every night," Hand said.

Pilar waited for something else from Hand about the woman, or the running—some point to the story. Nothing came. He looked at her, then down.

"There are some rocks near shore that you have to watch for when you swim," he said. "You want to swim now?" he asked. Pilar didn't. She wanted to eat.

The dirt road was full of small rocks, and huge rocks, and where it was solid it was dusty and uneven. It was not a long walk to the beach, but it was too long. After thousands of miles of travel to reach water, even this, a five-minute stroll, felt cruel. The beach, once they ducked under a tangle of trees, was wide and flat; the tide was out. A woman jogged as her dog bounded near her, like a dog-marionette, by the shore, their reflections loose and interrupted in the wet sand. But otherwise the place was empty, which was good.

"Is that the woman?" Pilar asked.

"I think so."

"Are there other women who run on the beach at night?"

"I don't think so. But it's dark."

Pilar wanted to cut stomachs open with glass.

.　　.　　.

Hand was a thoroughbred. He was tall enough, and built well, with flat strong pectorals and arms that were toned and brown. He'd been a swimmer in high school. But he also had a look of country madness that everyone who knew him noted; it wasn't there all the time—just when a subject had grabbed hold of his mind and he was trying but failing to communicate its urgency, like Lassie and the well. His was a nimble mind, sleeping shallowly when sleeping at all—but there was a raggedness to his brain that contrasted strongly with his attention to what he thought were facts and numbers of great import. Handsome in a way that sometimes looked bland, but there was character there—a faint cleft in his chin, earlobes that drooped though had never been pierced, some grey lines in his blond hair—that gave him advantages and he knew it. The sideburns had come and gone and now were back, and this was a mistake.

He had traveled widely in the past few years, since a trip with a mutual friend of theirs, now dead, had brought him halfway around the world in a week.

They shuffled down the main strip looking for dinner. There was a tiny bodega selling *Miami Herald*s from the previous Friday. Some small homes. A shop selling only towels, most featuring birds and monkeys. They found a restaurant with Christmas lights strung from the roof, full of American teenagers, all of them large, the boys bigger than the girls, huge T-shirts draped over their chests. Pilar and Hand sat down and a cat, gray with luxuriant hair, scooted from their feet and onto the tin roof.

The waitress came. She said *Buenos noches*. They said *Buenos noches* back. Hand said something, in Spanish, that made the waitress laugh loudly. As she was laughing, Hand spoke again, in Spanish, and the waitress laughed more. She leaned against the table for a second with her hand. She looked at Pilar; she was having a great time. Pilar had no idea what was happening. What had Hand said? Hand was a riot.

"What did you say to her?" Pilar asked, after she left.

"Who?"

"The waitress. What was so funny?"

"Nothing, really."

"You were killing her. What did you say?"

Hand wouldn't explain. Pilar let it go, because there were things between her and Hand that sometimes weren't pursued. They ate dinner, chicken and rice, and wiped their mouths with the tiny triangular blue napkins provided. The cat returned and rubbed against Hand's shin, back and forth and again, in a way that began to seem inappropriate.

UNSUNG SONG TO HAND: There are things about you / Like your wide waist, which repel / me, but your lips, smiling / shake me, and your brown shoulders / pick me a few inches off the ground / I want to slap you across the face in the loudest way. CHORUS: I want to jump on your back and ride you like a mule / I want to jump on your back and ride you like a mule / I want to jump on your back and ride you like a mule. You're someone who would lead almost any small nation / if you wanted to, but you don't /

because half of you is odd / but still you have the charm of a lead-ing / man, of an actor who was first a carpenter / someone who still plays lacrosse on the weekends / with the friends he's always had / I think your lips are too thin / your eyes too closely set / our children might be ugly / but you are a man, and there are so few men in the world. CHORUS: I want to jump on your back and ride you like a mule / I want to jump on your back and ride you like a mule / I want to jump on your back and ride you like a mule.

After they'd eaten but before they left the table, Hand said this: "I think I want to make sausages."

Pilar pretended to be watching the cat on the tin roof.

"There are small machines you can buy that make sausage," he said. "You buy the casings and then you stick the meats you want in there. Beef, pork, fat, spices. You ever made a sausage?" Pilar shook her head. Hand fixed her with his look, brilliant and insane and grabbing.

"There are a lot of things like that, things you can just learn how to make. Like pretzels. Or doors. Regular people can learn how to make those things. Pillows. My mom started making pil-lows last year."

. . .

They walked back through the strip. Americans and Canadi-ans and Swiss crisscrossed the street; some stood and watched the TVs positioned above the open-air bars, fuzzy college basket-ball happening, though soundlessly. Sunburned couples in white cotton fondled baskets in the souvenir shops. Surfers waited on benches for one of the two pay phones. Twelve-year-olds sped by on ATVs, three on each bike, huge white smiles.

She counted the reasons she should sleep with Hand: because she was curious about sleeping with him; curious to see him naked; because she loved him; because sleeping with him would be a nat-ural and good extension of her filial love for him; because there existed the possibility that it would be so good that they would change their idea of each other and then maybe think of themselves as a pair; because to deny one's curiosity about things like this was small and timid, and she was neither and didn't ever want to be either; because he had really wonderful arms, triceps that made her jangly in her ribs and tightened her chest; because she was not very attracted to him when away from him—she'd never thought of him while in the tub or flat on her bed—but in his presence she didn't want to walk or eat, she wanted to be nude with him, under a light white comforter. She wanted to hold his shoulders; she wanted to go snowshoeing with him; she wanted to name kids with him; she wanted him to be the father of her children, and also her own father, and brother; she wanted all this while also to be free; she wanted to sleep with other men and come home and tell Hand about them. She wanted to live one life with Hand while living three others concurrently.

At the hotel, the horses: two were sitting in the grass, as if they'd been waiting, patiently but with pressing business, the white one glowing faintly, like a star on the ceiling of a child's bedroom. The third and fourth were standing on the road, by the hedge, their dark hair shining.

HORSES: It's never like we planned.

HORSES' SHADOWS ON DIRT ROAD: I wish I could do more.

HORSES: We want violence, so we can kick and tear the world in thirds.

HORSES' SHADOWS ON DIRT ROAD: I'm helpless to help you.

HORSES: All we need is the spark.

HORSES' SHADOWS ON DIRT ROAD: When it happens, tell me what to do. I'm right behind you.

"Jesus," said Pilar.

"Maybe they live here," said Hand.

The horses had no symbolic value.

·   ·   ·

Pilar wanted to describe, to Hand, how she felt, every twenty minutes or so, about being there with him. They were together in the room, which had a roof and was warm. They were alive, though neither of them could have predicted with certainty that at their age they would both be alive—people flew on airplanes and drove cars after so many drinks, and every time they were away from each other or their family or friends, it seemed very likely to be the last; it was more logical, in some ways, to die or disappear. She had not grown up—her parents stayed home always—thinking that people could go far away, repeatedly, all over the earth, starting and finishing lives elsewhere, and then see each other again.

She wanted to rub herself in bananas. She wanted to open umbrellas into the faces of cats, make them scurry and scream. How could she sleep with Hand in this room? There would be no way. If it would be the only time, she wanted mirrors everywhere, so she could remember it a dozen ways.

But it would not be this night because he hadn't kissed her on the forehead yet. But this would happen. Tomorrow one of them would find a reason to hug the other, and they would hold each other for too long, making sounds about how good it was to be here, and then he would pull away a few inches, to kiss her on the forehead. And the rest would come soon after. She pictured his penis flying across the room and into her, and then shooting in and out. His head on the wall, mounted.

Hand took the couch and Pilar took the bed and they slept to the pulse of crickets and above, the overeager tick-ticking fan.

·   ·   ·

The morning arrived with applause and they made toast. In the sun the dirt road was white. All was white. As if Pilar's eyes had been scrubbed free of pigment.

In a dark shop built to simulate a thatched hut, they rented two surfboards and the woman, orange-haired oval-faced and Australian, pointed them to the nearest path to the water, across the street and beyond the blond sand.

They carried the boards across the white dirt road and onto the path, the sand soft and ashy. Through thin twisted trees and past a tin-roofed house, the beach spread left and right, flat and hard, at low tide a brown-gray parking lot. Close to the water the hard sand was wet, reflecting a blue sky, wide and musical with huge white flat-bottomed clouds.

There were dozens of surfers out already, ten just in front of them, another ten a few hundred yards right. The waves were small, with children playing in the shallows. Rocks to the left, body boarders close to shore. Pilar rubbed lotion on Hand's back and he did hers. Look at him, she thought. His face is strong. What would a man do, she wondered, without a chin! The skin on his back was taut and smooth. His neck aquiline, if that were possible. There was, she felt, a world full of beautiful future leaders, each with a thousand fulfillable promises, in Hand's neck.

$$\bullet \qquad \bullet \qquad \bullet$$

Pilar couldn't surf very well. She could paddle. She could lie on a board and balance and lay her face on its smooth cool wet fiberglass surface and rest. She was good there. And when the waves came she could do a few things. She could get up. She could stand up, turn a little (only to the right) and stand for a few seconds.

But everything closer to shore for her, this day, was more difficult. She worried if she was holding the board correctly. She worried if when she drew the rented board from the rack that she did so correctly. She wondered if she was supposed to carry the board with its slight concavity out, away from her hip, or toward it. She worried if she was supposed to attach the Velcro ankle strap, which was in turn attached to the board and prevents the board from flying away after surfer and board fail, while in the surf shop area, once she hit sand, or when her ankles were wet with water. She didn't know if the board should be set upon the sand bottom-fin up, or down. She was concerned that if she did any of these things wrong she would be laughed at or pointed at.

So she watched. She watched when others rented their boards to see how they drew them from the rack. She watched to see how they held them, carried them, when they strapped on their ankle bungees. And she did as they did, even though, as often than not, they didn't know either. Everyone was an amateur, everyone was trying to pretend grace—that's why they were renting boards and did not own them, and that's why they were surfing here, at Alta, where the waves were small and forgiving.

.　　.　　.

GOD: I own you like I own the caves.
THE OCEAN: Not a chance. No comparison.
GOD: I made you.
THE OCEAN: Prove it.
GOD: I could tame you.
THE OCEAN: At one time, maybe. But not now.
GOD: Are you challenging me?
THE OCEAN: Call it what you will.
GOD: I will come to you, freeze you, break you.
THE OCEAN: I will spread myself like wings. I am a billion tiny feathers. You have no idea what's happened to me.

.　　.　　.

Pilar and Hand walked into the water, same temperature as the air, and Hand bent himself in half, dropping his head in the foam and coming up head-soaked. He pushed the hair back from his face and looked at Pilar and Pilar knew that some people look better wet.

"The water's so warm," she said.

"It's the greatest water I know," he said.

They paddled out past the breaks. The waves were not large but the process was more tiring than she had remembered. By the time they were on flat water again she was exhausted, her triceps aching, shuffling their feet, children in museums.

Pilar and Hand were straddling their boards, watching the horizon for coming waves.

A good wave, five feet, came and with two quick strong strokes Hand was up. Pilar watched him depart for the beach. From behind, it looked like he was riding a very fast escalator. Or a conveyor belt. A conveyor belt being chased by a wave. From behind she saw only the round of the wave's top, and this obscured Hand's lower half. She was watching and he was going and going. He had a nice longboard stance, standing straight up, knees only slightly bent, leaning back, her whole frame one perfect diagonal line.

Then he was back, paddling quickly, smiling. He settled next to her and sat up on his board.

"That was nice," he said.

"It looked nice," she said.

Pilar liked what he had done, but for the time being she was content to sit. Or even to lie down. She had been in this town for half a day, awake this morning for an hour, and was prepared to do more resting, even if it was here, on the water. She stretched out on the board, resting her cheek on its wet cool creamy white, the wax, sand-encrusted, rough on her face. The water came over the board gently and kissed her. She could sleep here. She could probably live here, on this board, her shoulders burning. There was no difference between resting her face here and resting her face on her mother's stomach when she was younger, no difference between feeling her not-large breasts flattened against the board and feeling these not-large breasts flattened against the backs of men. She liked to sleep that way, with men on their stomachs and her breasts on their back. It never worked—she never actually fell asleep in this position, but she liked to try. With one eye she could see Hand, still upright, scanning. To the right of the beach, to the far right, a mountain, the color of heather, lay like a broken body.

"Are you going to take one of these or what?" Pilar said before dunking his head into the sea, coming up again so good, a mannequin's perfect head soaked in cooking oil.

"Right. Sorry," she said.

"Do you need a push?"

"Ha. Yes. Ha."

Now she had to try. She sat up again. They waited, both straddling, watching the blue horizon for a bump.

A bump was on its way.

"Take this one," he said.

"I know," she said.

She turned the board and laid her chest on it and began paddling. Three strokes and she was at the same speed. She let up and allowed the wave to overtake her. The wave came with the crackle of crumpling paper. She rose, one foot, three feet, five. The water brought her into its curved glass and she paddled harder as it drew her up and sharpened itself under her. Then two more strong strokes, both arms at once, and she descended. She knew the descending was key. That if she was not fast enough or her timing was off, the wave would speed below her and she would watch it go under her and then beyond, very much like watching the shrinking back of a missed bus. But if she were fast, or pushed at the right time, she would descend into it, and her board would become a car, a horse, and she would jump to her feet and the board would be solid like a girder of steel, cream-colored smooth, and doublewide.

This wave she took; the board was strong, she jumped up, was standing and traveling with this wave, toward shore—she had gotten on the bus. Beneath her was all chaos, foam and speed, the rush of white pavement. She had one moment of rapture—

up! standing! Look at the sun, the mountains like a body reclining or broken—and then she knew she had work to do. The wave was crashing from her right and she knew she only had a second of straight riding if she didn't try to turn left, to ride the break. If she made the turn she could ride for a minute, a full minute maybe, just stand and ride. She had seen people ride these longboards for minutes, just standing, walking up and back, strolling—the best surfers could join their hands behind their backs and stroll up and back, up and back, considering the issues of the day, so sturdy was a longboard on a good wave, they could set up a nice chair and a rug and sit in front of the fire—and if she could understand the science behind this she would—

She tried to turn left, to follow the still-curved glass away from the breaking, mulching glass, and so she leaned back a little, she weighted her ankles into the board's left side, pushing its edge slightly into the curved glass—

It was done. The board was behind her; she was a cowboy whose horse had pulled up short. She dove into the foam and was under. Her ears exploded with the sound of underwater. It was dark and all violence. She shot up and surfaced in time to see the board, wanting to be free but attached to her ankle, rearing, bucking straight into the sky before it fell again and rested into the now-calm sea of blue-green gel.

But she'd gotten up. A good thing, a bad thing—the rest of the day would be an anticlimax. She'd have two or three more good rides at most, no matter how long they spent out here. Hand was straddling, waiting for her.

This story is equally or more about surfing. People are no more interesting than waves and mountains.

·   ·   ·

In the afternoon, on the hard beach, with the wind snaking at them, hissing and sending sand into their sandwiches, Pilar and

Hand squinted into the sun to see the water. They'd been in the ocean all day and now were watching it like actors would a play going on without them. The ocean didn't need her.

Hand started clapping.

"I'm gonna clap every two minutes for the rest of the day," he said.

There was a surfer out there wearing a cowboy hat.

"What do you do for that company again?" Pilar asked.

"I consult. I brainstorm. They like my brain."

"But why here again?"

"My Spanish. And I volunteered. Down here money goes a long way. We get paid American wages but the costs here are half of what they'd be anywhere else."

"Okay, but why Intel here at all, and not Korea or something?"

"We *are* in Korea. A big setup there."

"Did you just say we?"

"No."

"You did!"

The cowboy surfer was riding a perfect wave, hooting.

Hand had forgotten to clap. Pilar debated whether she should note this, knowing that she might just be bringing on more clapping.

"You forgot to clap," she said.

"Listen. I have no problem with them as a company. They make chips. Chips are good. They're in Granada because the workforce is educated, in the city at least, and they're good workers. The infrastructure's good, airport's good, roads work, communications are good, banks are sound, inflation's fine, conveniences, at least in Granada—and because here Intel avoids the unions on the floor and in trucking, all that. A lot of companies are leaving Puerto Rico, for one because the union activity is getting big down there. Same workforce, basically, as here, but no one sets up in this part of the world to tangle with unions."

Then he clapped for a full minute straight.

·   ·   ·

The horses were outside again, but were loitering down the road, in front of the bucket-blue house with the German woman watering her rock garden. One horse, of the three that were black, was scratching at the road, nodding, as if counting.

"Looking for water," Hand said.

Pilar went back to the room and filled a bowl with water. She came back; Hand's face was skeptical. She walked toward the horse. It backed away and trotted up the hill. She held the water at stomach level.

Hand walked over to comfort her. But just when his arms were supposed to wrap around her shoulders, he knocked the bowl from below, overturning it deliberately, soaking her shirt.

"Oops," he said.

She slapped him hard across the mouth and laughed in one great burst. He picked her up, her waist on his shoulder, and spun her around, and she punched his back.

.　　.　　.

There were animals everywhere. Underfoot there was always something moving—lizards, crickets, mice. There were iguanas. They could see them scurrying through woodpiles and through the forest. In the forest below their hotel they saw an iguana being chased by a yellow truck plowing away the underbrush.

The woman at the mercado had blonde hair like margarine full of crumbs. Pilar and Hand bought ice cream from a freezer in the market. They tore the thin shiny plastic and ate the chocolate first, then the white cold ice cream. The sun made it soft.

.　　.　　.

They jogged through the alley behind the neighboring hotel, El Jardín del Edén, and down the dark dirt road to where the loosely strung Christmas lights smiled between columns, and techno taunted from speakers hidden in the armpits of trees. Most of the restaurants were still open, their attached bars ill attended. At the end of the road, past the pay phones and the surfers waiting patiently in line next to the local women, toddlers at their feet, they stopped into the Earth Bar, its half-heart-half-globe logo hung low over the open doorway.

Inside, people holding drinks. Shirtless thin tan surfers and white men, young, with black dreads were barefoot or wore sandals, always with woven bracelets, beaded necklaces. The women were more varied. Plenty of the surf-girl sort but also backpackers of the Scandinavian breed—white-blond hair and bikini tops, plastic digital watches, reckless sunburns.

Pilar and Hand stood hip to hip by the bumper-pool table and drank very cold Imperials. The first two went quick—they realized how hot it was and how thirsty they were. They took their third drinks onto the deck, facing the black ocean. The darkness was close and concrete. They talked about the babies their friends were having, about Pete and April and their triplets. The last time Hand had seen April and Pete, they'd just left the kids with the fifteen-year-old babysitter and stayed out until 3 A.M., refusing to let go of the night. They'd come home to find the babysitter asleep in their closet, their shoes intermingled and piled up on the side.

"In the closet?" Pilar said, and Hand didn't say anything, or perhaps he hadn't heard. The story was missing many details and it made Pilar angry. But the music was suddenly loud and they didn't say anything for a full minute. A dog ran in circles on the beach, chased by a smaller dog.

Hand pulled Pilar into his body and held her.

"It's good that you came," he said. She murmured her agreement. He kissed the top of her head.

.   .   .

In front of their hotel room there was an anteater.

"It's not an anteater," Hand said, crouching down. "It's a sloth."

"Sloths don't have noses like that," Pilar said, "long noses like that."

It wasn't moving, but from its side they could see it breathing, the rise and fall of its coarse fur.

"They sometimes do," Hand said. "Down here they do. Look at his toes—they're the three-toed things, like—"

"You don't know what you're talking about."

Hand opened his mouth then closed it.

"Maybe it is an anteater," he said.

It was bleeding. From its long snout there was a viscous substance that connected to the tile hallway, a stream of blood and mucus.

Pilar brought a saucer of milk. The animal made no movement toward it.

"It's dying, isn't it?" she asked.

"I don't know. It doesn't look hurt anywhere. Just the blood coming out the snout."

They decided to leave the animal outside. There was no animal hospital in Alta, and it would not be better off inside.

"But how the hell did it get here?" Hand asked. "It can barely move. How'd it climb all these stairs? It must have started weeks ago. And why'd it stop at our door? This is too strange. There has to be a reason. We have to bring him inside."

So they brought him inside. Hand did it.

"Like lifting a very fat cat," he said.

Now the anteater was lying under a chair near the door. Pilar put the saucer of milk near it again, and added another saucer of water. The animal looked dead.

"If it dies tonight, it'll smell," Pilar said.

"It won't die," Hand said.

Hand sat on her bed and Pilar stood before him. He grabbed

her shorts from the front and pulled her toward him. She sat on his lap and leaned into him, but when she wanted to put her mouth all over his, he spoke.

"It's resting. It came here to rest."

.   .   .

The only graffiti Pilar had ever found thought-provoking was the line she'd seen again and again in bathrooms: Sex invented God. Each time she saw those words, for hours afterward, it was the way she saw the world. She loved her life, but the only transcendent experience she'd had began with provocation of her skin.

Pilar and Hand were side to side, and kissing slowly. Pilar wanted to kiss him harder and push him onto his back and stand on his chest and dance, but she didn't, because now they couldn't talk and they were strangers; she continued to kiss him quietly as they lay on their sides, facing each other. They waited for judgment, they wondered if this was working, they hoped they would get excited.

"Hi," she said.

"Hey," he said. "We should leave the door open. In case he wants to leave."

He got up, opened the door a crack, and jumped back to the bed. She swung her leg around him. She was above him, straddling, and from her vantage point Hand looked so far away, so old and dead. She leaned down and held his face in her hands. "This face," she said. It was like holding a rock painted gold.

They took their clothes off and she lay on top of him, placed her ear to his sternum, and the water inside him went shuck-ashucka and kissed her again and again.

.   .   .

Where had she been snorkeling before? Florida, near Pensacola—another place where everything was for sale—when it had rained all day and she and her father had gone in anyway, with rented equipment and just a few hundred yards out.

They hadn't seen anything then, everything so murky there, close to the breaks. But this, here, is what one wanted from snorkeling. The coral was dull colored, and there were no schools of fish. Here the fish traveled alone, loudly blue ones, and very orange ones, small, and there was one with black and white stripes from stem to stern, and red on the hull. There was an especially bright yellow one that wanted to join Pilar inside her mask; it followed her, almost perched on her nose.

They had paddled a shoddy two-person inflatable kayak out to an island in the bay, hoping to watch the sunset here, closer to it. They'd pulled the kayak onto the island, which was not, as expected, covered with sand, but was made of shells. All of its white—the island was white when seen from the beach—was shells. Millions, edges and distinctions worn irrelevant. Pilar and Hand broke a dozen of them with each step. The outermost Pacific-facing side of the island was settled by what seemed to be pelicans but weren't; they were more elegant than pelicans, and numbered about fifty. The surface was lavalike, but was more cartilaginous than that. It was the consistency and color of burned flesh.

From the kayak they retrieved the snorkeling stuff, putting their mouths on plastic mouthed by hundreds before. With the cold fins snug they fell in.

All the fish on the floor were being pushed and pulled by the tide. And though this was their home, it didn't look like they were the least bit accustomed to the underwater wind. They seemed baffled and cautious, like Californians driving cars through rain. Pilar's hands, propelling her forward, appeared in front of her mask, glowing in the sun, angelic. She was an angel, she thought. But what were these fish doing here, where they were pushed and pulled by this bastard tide? This was nowhere to live. The coral was dull colored and barren. But these bright fish, existing only to be looked at, or pushed around, or eaten.

She thought of people she had known; she forced metaphors. The sun shot through the surface like God imagined it, in straight and fabulous rays. The water was full of fish she'd seen in pictures and pet stores.

They had woken up facing opposite walls but their ankles entwined. They smiled at each other and Hand reached over and grabbed her nose, as if to pluck it off. Pilar knew that they would continue to sleep together because the night before had been good, and nothing wrong had happened. It would be this way: at night they would brush their teeth and sit on the bed and pull their legs around and under the thin blanket, and they would scoot toward each other, their hands searching like those of children pretending to be blind.

To Pilar's left came three small sharks, striped, built like jets. They were headed for her. She was calm and knew she could make it safely. She pointed her head toward the shore and with her flippers gave the sharks a flurry of waved goodbyes, the fins like handkerchiefs in a breeze. Close to shore she stood in the warm shallows, feet slipping over the mossy rocks, and looked for Hand. He wasn't anywhere. She wanted him not be attacked by sharks. She wanted to sit on him facing the sunset—it was pink and spreading like spilled watercolors—on this island.

But there was a man on the island. She hadn't seen him before. Or he'd just shown up, and Hand was not visible but the man, not far away, waved to her and stepped toward her. He was about forty, and wearing a small swimsuit and sunglasses, neon-framed, silver and reflective lenses. She jumped back into the water, not fearing the sharks.

On the way back to shore, Hand scolded her for wearing clothes that invited the attention of men in the town whom the two of them didn't know enough about and couldn't necessarily trust.

"I've always wondered what it would be like to be seen as prey," he said.

He went into great detail about what the men in the town had been doing when she'd been walking by. There was the guard in front of the bank, who carried a semi-automatic rifle and, according to Hand, looked Pilar up and down and inside out each time they went into the bank or passed by. How does she decide not to wear a bra? Hand wanted to know. Not to alarm her, he said, but men covet certain women, women they see every day, and assaults usually are committed on women who have some acquaintance with the assaulter. So perhaps it would behoove her—he used this word—to do more to disinvite the gaze of these men. She was speechless; she was furious and confused and ashamed and wanted to club him and kick him and dance on his head.

"I care about you, Pilar," he said. "Don't get pissed. And don't make that face."

Her lower teeth were jutting out, like a piranha's. She knew she did this. More than she was angry about what he'd said, she was angry that this was how it was, and so soon: she was not free. She would be given advice, or whatever it was. And immediately she had to put him in a different category, and it was then obvious that this was what it was, and nothing more.

. . .

In the evenings the sun dropped through the ocean and the sky would darken quickly. Armadillos scurried below their deck, under the streetlamp, their shiny shells sniffling through the high grass. Under the bed where Pilar and Hand slept, platoons of ants circled around crumbs and moved them to the door, under, and on to parts unknown. Geckos squiggled up and down the wall above the screen door, heading to and from what appeared to be their home, in the beam in the center of the room. The dusty white light during the day never wavered; there were three or four clouds all week.

For a few days Pilar and Hand were married. They surfed and rested their boards fin-up on the hard sand, sat on the flat beach, and ate round crackers and drank Fanta. They watched the water, eating nuts and cookies. After they finished eating they would nap, her head in his stomach, and in an hour they would paddle out again. They would stay in the water until the water became black, and then stay until the sun set into it and the black water was striped orange loosely.

At night the surfers roamed the streets barefoot but with hair fluffy from having been finally washed. There was an Internet café run by an Austrian couple. Couples walked, leaning into each other while glancing at people they found more attractive. Or maybe not. There was no way to know what they were thinking.

Every night, after dinner, they bought ice cream from a man who had been burned on half of his face. Burned or perhaps it was coming from below—his face had great growths on it, pink and coarse, like the ass of a boar. Usually the moon was yellow behind Vaseline.

One night they went to see the huge migratory turtles huff ashore and lay their eggs, hundreds of eggs, all of them soft and slathered in gel. They stood behind the great creature as it swept sand into its hole, sprinkling each group of eggs.

Sometimes there was hay on the street. Some days they could hear people playing tennis, but they could not see the court, and even looked for it one day and could not find it. They watched a man painting a picture of the beach; he welcomed their watching and talking. He was from Philadelphia and had had a bad year, a litigious divorce and a friend dead, killed driving to a skiing trip in Tahoe.

They slept together once sober and it was awkward; they were not lovers but friends playing Twister. They went back to their original plan the next night. They drank a bit, and then went to bed, just under the surface of consciousness, feeling no edges. Someone watching them from afar might ask: How did they speak to each other? The answer: With the warmth of very old friends, though they were not yet old. How did he touch her?

Clumsily, for he was clumsy and she was critical. How did she kiss him? Desperately, pulling and pushing, like a woman trying to get to the bottom of a deep pool, without jumping.

When they walked usually there were stones in their shoes, because the road was dotted with pebbles and their shoes were loose.

· · ·

They were leaving Alta the next afternoon—Pilar for home and Hand for Granada; there were no future plans—so they rented boards early and were in the water by nine. It was an uncomplicated day.

Hand was out in the sea before her and she watched him until she was too hot too stay dry. She paddled past the breaks, which meant through four full waves collapsing, like drunks, onto her. Each time she would have to either push the board's nose into the wave and hope she stayed on, or would preemptively surrender, diving off, waiting for the board to bungee away and come back to her. It was exhausting.

Hand soon departed again, on a bigger wave, one that would have crushed Pilar had she tried it. She watched him speed into the beach, looking like he was going faster than the wave. She noticed that people riding waves seem to be moving much faster than waves do when they're traveling without passengers. Hand had caught this one at the perfect moment and was riding it left, on and on, as it sped away and toward the estuary. It seemed endless. Perfect. He waved to Pilar. She waved back. It's weird, Pilar thought, to wave to someone while they're surfing. She saw him wave and continued on, twisting his board a bit, quick, fluid. She maybe loved him.

She sat up again, watching the flat blue for growths.

If there were a question that needed to be answered in this story it would be not one but many, and these would be the questions. How can a world be so good to allow all this? To allow these people to live so long? To travel all these miles south, to a place so different but still so comfortable, and in that place, meet again? To allow them to be naked together for the first time? What would their parents think? What would their friends think? Would anyone object? Who would plan for them? How many times in life can we make decisions that are important but will not hurt anyone? Are we obligated—maybe we are—to say yes to any choice when no one will be hurt? We use the word hurt when talking about things like this because when they go wrong it can feel as if you were hit in the sternum by a huge animal that's run for miles to strike you.

. . . .

In two hours, she had caught two waves. Waves were something she cared about now. But she began to care more about seeing them than catching them, and more about catching them than riding them, and above all she wanted to simply stay out beyond the breaks. Because after each ride, the trip back, past the breaks, was too much.

Her arms seemed so thin, like narrow dowels being pushed through syrup. The ache at her shoulders brought her near tears. It wasn't right that it should be so hard, especially here. The waves would crash ahead of her and the tall strong foam would roll at her, and would then run over her. Knocked off the board, scrape water off face, spit, expel snot, jump back on the board, paddle twice, achieve maybe ten feet of progress out, and then get knocked over again.

She closed her eyes. Opened them, closed them. She could end this world or allow it. She had control over everything, including now, when she could see everything or nothing. This was a moment when a believer, a thoughtful believer, would think of God's work, and how good it was. The waves were perfect to the right and perfect to the left. Far left there were loud long hoots from the man in the cowboy hat, riding a long low slow breaker all the way in. Pilar thought of the man at her church group who taught everyone how to win at pinball. She thought of curved penises. For a while she was enchanted by those who proposed that God was in nature, was all around us, was the accumulated natural world. "God," they would suggest, "is in all living things. God is beauty, God is in the long grass and the foam finishing a waterfall." That sort of thing. She liked that idea, God being in things that she could see, because she liked seeing things and wanted to believe in these things that she loved looking at—loved the notion that it was all here and easily observable, with one's eyes being in some way the clergy, the connection between God and—

She saw Hand, almost at the estuary, finally end his ride, by nimbly stepping off his board and into the water, knee deep where he was. He stood for a second, and adjusted his bathing suit where it held his privates. Then he doubled over again and dumped his head. Had his hair had gone dry during his ride? Incredible. He wouldn't be back for a while.

But a single contained God implied or insisted upon a hierarchy that she didn't accept. That God gave way to a system of extremes, and implied choices, and choices required separations, divisions, subtle condemnations. So there would not be this sort of God in Pilar's world, and thus the transcendental deity—But then why God at all? The oil-wet water was not God. It was not the least bit spiritual. It was oil-wet water, and it felt perfect when Pilar put her hand into it, and it kissed her palm again and again, would never stop kissing her palm and why wasn't that enough?

Her board was pointing almost directly toward the now-dimming sun. The dimming sun made the water seem even more like oil, changing its color to something more golden and green and dark. Where the sun did not highlight the water, the water was black. The sun was large and was more three-dimensional than usual. The water was black where the sun wasn't making it gold. The water was getting warmer and the surfers left and right became with each passing minute more abstract, closer to silhouettes, moving in slow motion.

She sat up on the board, straddling it. She didn't want to surf. She wanted to sit here for a long time, the waves behind her, ridden by the vague black figures. She wanted only to sit and stare ahead and wait for more of the water to go golden.

When the sun fell and the water turned black she would ride the last wave in and sleep. She felt that she knew how her old age would feel. She would be too tired to move much, and she would know that if she rode in she would not be able to ride out again because her arms would feel like dowels.

·   ·   ·

They left the town at dusk. The roped road was potholed completely, full of slow-driving tourists in SUVs, being so gentle to their rentals, like elephants stepping gingerly around puddles. They passed them and left them and drove away from a sunset gaudy with purple. The road went from dirt to gravel to finally pavement unpotholed, but remained two lanes, winding back and forth over hills and down hills and always under a perfect canopy of trees with long fingers overhead laced.

When the night went black they realized their lights were too bright; passing cars thought their high-beams were on, and flashed them. They flashed them back, showing them their real brights, and then, to retaliate, the cars would flash theirs again. It happened a hundred times. They hated the implication of their thoughtlessness, and the strain on their eyes was terrible, all the flashing, all that quick bright anger. But in a second they'd be gone and the road dark again. They drove fast, 110 kilometers per hour, whatever that is in American speed, searing by the people walking and biking on the roadside, the people visible only just before they passed, a headlight snapshot, then back to darkness. They'd likely almost be hit by them. They went around slow cars, trucks, passing without pause, always ducking back into their lane.

·　　·　　·

The night before, it was windy and restless outside, and they had recently fallen asleep and were still lying front to back, Hand's knees behind Pilar's knees. There was a loud thump. Hand sat up and when Pilar moved to investigate, he gestured her to stay in bed. She did because she wanted to see him protect her. Was she scared? She was. Hand had made her convinced—more when she thought about it than when she didn't—that the man from the bank would come, with his gun, and kill Hand and then rape her.

Hand was at the front door of the suite when Pilar looked up and found the origin of the sound. It was a hole in the roof, over the bed, where the skylight once was. The wind had pulled the skylight off, and Pilar could see the clear black night through the square in the ceiling. Hand came back to bed and they were friends in bed together, nude. Hand said he liked going to the door to look for invaders and Pilar said she was glad it was a hole in the roof.

Esquire

FINALIST, FEATURE WRITING

The Falling Man

At first blush "The Falling Man" could be mistaken for a mere 9/11 detective story. But Tom Junod's search for the subject of an iconic image delves into an array of unexpected questions about the grieving process, privacy and America's relationship with photography. His prose is as direct as it is distinctive.

Tom Junod

The Falling Man

Do you remember this photograph? In the United States, people have taken pains to banish it from the record of September 11, 2001. The story behind it, though, and the search for the man pictured in it, are our most intimate connection to the horror of that day.

In the picture, he departs from this earth like an arrow. Although he has not chosen his fate, he appears to have, in his last instants of life, embraced it. If he were not falling, he might very well be flying. He appears relaxed, hurtling through the air. He appears comfortable in the grip of unimaginable motion. He does not appear intimidated by gravity's divine suction or by what awaits him. His arms are by his side, only slightly outriggered. His left leg is bent at the knee, almost casually. His white shirt, or jacket, or frock, is billowing free of his black pants. His black high-tops are still on his feet. In all the other pictures, the people who did what he did—who jumped—appear to be struggling against horrific discrepancies of scale. They are made puny by the backdrop of the towers, which loom like colossi, and then by the event itself. Some of them are shirtless; their shoes fly off as they flail and fall; they look confused, as though trying to swim down the side of a mountain. The man in the picture, by contrast, is perfectly vertical, and so is in accord with the lines of the buildings behind him. He splits them, bisects them: Everything to the left of him in the picture is the North Tower; everything to the right, the South. Though oblivious to the geometric balance he has achieved, he is the essential element in the creation of a new flag, a banner composed entirely of steel bars shining in the sun. Some people who look at the picture see stoicism, willpower, a portrait of resignation; others see something else—something discordant and therefore terrible: freedom. There is something almost rebellious in the man's posture, as though once faced with the inevitability of death, he decided to get on with it; as though he were a missile, a spear, bent on attaining his own end. He is, fifteen seconds past 9:41 A.M. EST, the moment the picture is taken, in the clutches of pure physics, accelerating at a rate of thirty-two feet per second squared. He will soon be traveling at upwards of 150 miles per hour, and he is upside down. In the picture, he is frozen; in his life outside the frame, he drops and keeps dropping until he disappears.

.　　.　　.

The photographer is no stranger to history; he knows it is something that happens later. In the actual moment history is made, it is usually made in terror and confusion, and so it is up to people like him—paid witnesses—to have the presence of mind to attend to its manufacture. The photographer has that presence of mind and has had it since he was a young man. When he was twenty-one years old, he was standing right behind Bobby Kennedy when Bobby Kennedy was shot in the head. His jacket was spattered with Kennedy's blood, but he jumped on a table and shot pictures of Kennedy's open and ebbing eyes, and then of Ethel Kennedy crouching over her husband and begging photographers—begging him—not to take pictures.

Richard Drew has never done that. Although he has preserved the jacket patterned with Kennedy's blood, he has never not taken a picture, never averted his eye. He works for the Associated Press. He is a journalist. It is not up to him to reject the images that fill his frame, because one never knows when history is made until one makes it. It is not even up to him to distinguish if a body is alive or dead, because the camera makes no such distinctions, and he is in the business of shooting bodies, as all photographers are, unless they are Ansel Adams. Indeed, he was shooting bodies on the morning of September 11, 2001. On assignment for the AP, he was shooting a maternity fashion show in Bryant Park, notable, he says, "because it featured actual pregnant models." He was fifty-four years old. He wore glasses. He was sparse in the scalp, gray in the beard, hard in the head. In a lifetime of taking pictures, he has found a way to be both mild-mannered and brusque, patient and very, very quick. He was doing what he always does at fashion shows—"staking out real estate"—when a CNN cameraman with an earpiece said that a plane had crashed into the North Tower, and Drew's editor rang his cell phone. He packed his equipment into a bag and gambled on taking the subway downtown. Although it was still running, he was the only one on it. He got out at the Chambers Street station and saw that both towers had been turned into smokestacks. Staking out his real estate, he walked west, to where ambulances were gathering, because rescue workers "usually won't throw you out." Then he heard people gasping. People on the ground were gasping because people in the building were jumping. He started shooting pictures through a 200mm lens. He was standing between a cop and an emergency technician, and each time one of them cried, "There goes another," his camera found a falling body and followed it down for a nine- or twelve-shot sequence. He shot ten or fifteen of them before he heard the rumbling of the South Tower and witnessed, through the winnowing exclusivity of his lens, its collapse. He was engulfed in a mobile ruin, but he grabbed a mask from an ambulance and photographed the top of the North Tower "exploding like a mushroom" and raining debris. He discovered that there is such a thing as being too close, and, deciding that he had fulfilled his professional obligations, Richard Drew joined the throng of ashen humanity heading north, walking until he reached his office at Rockefeller Center.

There was no terror or confusion at the Associated Press. There was, instead, that feeling of history being manufactured; although the office was as crowded as he'd ever seen it, there was, instead, "the wonderful calm that comes into play when people are really doing their jobs." So Drew did his: He inserted the disc from his digital camera into his laptop and recognized, instantly, what only his camera had seen—something iconic in the extended annihilation of a falling man. He didn't look at any of the other pictures in the sequence; he didn't have to. "You learn in photo editing to look for the frame," he says. "You have to recognize it. That picture just jumped off the screen because of its verticality and symmetry. It just had that look."

He sent the image to the AP's server. The next morning, it appeared on page seven of *The New York Times*. It appeared in hundreds of newspapers, all over the country, all over the world. The man inside the frame—the Falling Man—was not identified.

·   ·   ·

They began jumping not long after the first plane hit the North Tower, not long after the fire started. They kept jumping until the tower fell. They jumped through windows already broken and then, later, through windows they broke themselves. They jumped to escape the smoke and the fire; they jumped when the ceilings fell and the floors collapsed; they jumped just to breathe once more before they died. They jumped continually, from all four sides of the building, and from all floors above and around the building's fatal wound. They jumped from the offices of Marsh & McLennan, the insurance company; from the offices of Cantor Fitzgerald, the bond-trading company; from Windows on the World, the restaurant on the 106th and 107th floors—the top. For more than an hour and a half, they streamed from the building, one after another, consecutively rather than en masse, as if each individual required the sight of another individual jumping before mustering the courage to jump himself or herself. One photograph, taken at a distance, shows people jumping in perfect sequence, like parachutists, forming an arc composed of three plummeting people, evenly spaced. Indeed, there were reports that some tried parachuting, before the force generated by their fall ripped the drapes, the tablecloths, the desperately gathered fabric, from their hands. They were all, obviously, very much alive on their way down, and their way down lasted an approximate count of ten seconds. They were all, obviously, not just killed when they landed but destroyed, in body though not, one prays, in soul. One hit a fireman on the ground and killed him; the fireman's body was anointed by Father Mychal Judge, whose own death, shortly thereafter, was embraced as an example of martyrdom after the photograph—the redemptive tableau—of firefighters carrying his body from the rubble made its way around the world.

From the beginning, the spectacle of doomed people jumping from the upper floors of the World Trade Center resisted redemption. They were called "jumpers" or "the jumpers," as though they represented a new lemminglike class. The trial that hundreds endured in the building and then in the air became its own kind of trial for the thousands watching them from the ground. No one ever got used to it; no one who saw it wished to see it again, although, of course, many saw it again. Each jumper, no matter how many there were, brought fresh horror, elicited shock, tested the spirit, struck a lasting blow. Those tumbling through the air remained, by all accounts, eerily silent; those on the ground screamed. It was the sight of the jumpers that prompted Rudy Giuliani to say to his police commissioner, "We're in uncharted waters now." It was the sight of the jumpers that prompted a woman to wail, "God! Save their souls! They're jumping! Oh, please God! Save their souls!" And it was, at last, the sight of the jumpers that provided the corrective to those who insisted on saying that what they were witnessing was "like a movie," for this was an ending as unimaginable as it was unbearable: Americans responding to the worst terrorist attack in the history of the world with acts of heroism, with acts of sacrifice, with acts of generosity, with acts of martyrdom, and, by terrible necessity, with one prolonged act of—if these words can be applied to mass murder—mass suicide.

.   .   .

In most American newspapers, the photograph that Richard Drew took of the Falling Man ran once and never again. Papers all over the country, from the *Fort Worth Star-Telegram* to the *Memphis Commercial Appeal* to *The Denver Post,* were forced to defend themselves against charges that they exploited a man's death, stripped him of his dignity, invaded his privacy, turned tragedy into leering pornography. Most letters of complaint stated the obvious: that *someone* seeing the picture had to know who it was. Still, even as Drew's photograph became at once iconic and impermissible, its subject remained unnamed. An editor at the Toronto *Globe and Mail* assigned a reporter named Peter Cheney to solve the mystery. Cheney at first despaired of his task; the entire city, after all, was wallpapered with Kinkoed flyers advertising the faces of the missing and the lost and the dead. Then he applied himself, sending the digital photograph to a shop that clarified and enhanced it. Now information emerged: It appeared to him that the man was most likely not black but dark-skinned, probably Latino. He wore a goatee. And the white shirt billowing from his black pants was not a shirt but rather appeared to be a tunic of some sort, the kind of jacket a restaurant worker wears. Windows on the World, the restaurant at the top of the North Tower, lost seventy-nine of its employees on September 11, as well as ninety-one of its patrons. It was likely that the Falling Man numbered among them. But which one was he? Over dinner, Cheney spent an evening discussing this question with friends, then said goodnight and walked through Times Square. It was after midnight, eight days after the attacks. The missing posters were still everywhere, but Cheney was able to focus on one that seemed to present itself to him—a poster portraying a man who worked at Windows as a pastry chef, who was dressed in a white tunic, who wore a goatee, who was Latino. His name was Norberto Hernandez. He lived in Queens. Cheney took the enhanced print of the Richard Drew photograph to the family, in particular to Norberto Hernandez's brother Tino and sister Milagros. They said yes, that was Norberto. Milagros had watched footage of the people jumping on that terrible morning, before the television stations stopped showing it. She had seen one of the jumpers distinguished by the grace of his fall—by his resemblance to an Olympic diver—and surmised that he had to be her brother. Now she saw, and she knew. All that remained was for Peter Cheney to confirm the identification with Norberto's wife and his three daughters. They did not want to talk to him, especially after Norberto's remains were found and identified by the stamp of his DNA—a torso, an arm. So he went to the funeral. He brought his print of Drew's photograph with him and showed it to Jacqueline Hernandez, the oldest of Norberto's three daughters. She looked briefly at the picture, then at Cheney, and ordered him to leave.

What Cheney remembers her saying, in her anger, in her offended grief: "That piece of shit is not my father."

.   .   .

The resistance to the image—to the images—started early, started immediately, started on the ground. A mother whispering to her distraught child a consoling lie: "Maybe they're just birds, honey." Bill Feehan, second in command at the fire department, chasing a bystander who was panning the jumpers with his video camera, demanding that he turn it off, bellowing, "Don't you have any human decency?" before dying himself when the building came down. In the most photographed and videotaped day in the history of the world, the images of people jumping were the only images that became, by consensus, taboo—the only images from which Americans were proud to avert their eyes. All over the world, people saw the human stream debouch from the top of the North Tower, but here in the United States, we saw these images only until the networks decided not to allow such a harrowing view, out of respect for the families of those so publicly dying. At CNN, the footage was shown live, before people working in the newsroom knew what was happening; then, after what Walter Isaacson, who was then chairman of the network's news bureau, calls "agonized discussions" with the "standards guy," it was shown only if people in it were blurred and unidentifiable; then it was not shown at all.

And so it went. In *9/11,* the documentary extracted from videotape shot by French brothers Jules and Gedeon Naudet, the filmmakers included a sonic sampling of the booming, rattling explosions the jumpers made upon impact but edited out the most disturbing thing about the sounds: the sheer frequency with which they occurred. In *Rudy,* the docudrama starring James Woods in the role of Mayor Giuliani, archival footage of the jumpers was first included, then cut out. In *Here Is New York,* an extensive exhibition of 9/11 images culled from the work of photographers both amateur and professional, there was, in the section titled "Victims," but one picture of the jumpers, taken at a respectful distance; attached to it, on the *Here Is New York* Web site, a visitor offers this commentary: "This image is what made me glad for censuring [*sic*] in the endless pursuant media coverage." More and more, the jumpers—and their images—were relegated to the Internet underbelly, where they became the provenance of the shock sites that also traffic in the autopsy photos of Nicole Brown Simpson and the videotape of Daniel Pearl's execution, and where it is impossible to look at them without attendant feelings of shame and guilt. In a nation of voyeurs, the desire to face the most disturbing aspects of our most disturbing day was somehow ascribed to voyeurism, as though the jumpers' experience, instead of being central to the horror, was tangential to it, a sideshow best forgotten.

It was no sideshow. The two most reputable estimates of the number of people who jumped to their deaths were prepared by *The New York Times* and *USA Today.* They differed dramatically. The *Times,* admittedly conservative, decided to count only what its reporters actually saw in the footage they collected, and it arrived at a figure of fifty. *USA Today,* whose editors used eyewitness accounts and forensic evidence in addition to what they found on video, came to the conclusion that at least two hundred people died by jumping—a count that the newspaper said authorities did not dispute. Both are intolerable estimates of human loss, but if the number provided by *USA Today* is accurate, then between 7 and 8 percent of those who died in New York City on September 11, 2001, died by jumping out of the buildings; it means that if we consider only the North Tower, where the vast majority of jumpers came from, the ratio is more like one in six.

And yet if one calls the New York Medical Examiner's Office to learn its own estimate of how many people might have jumped, one does not get an answer but an admonition: "We don't like to say they jumped. They didn't jump. Nobody jumped. They were forced out, or blown out." And if one Googles the words "how many jumped on 9/11," one falls into some blogger's trap, slugged "Go Away, No Jumpers Here," where the bait is one's own need to know: "I've got at least three entries in my referrer logs that show someone is doing a search on Google for 'how many people jumped from WTC.' My September 11 post had made mention of that terrible occurance [*sic*], so now any pervert looking for that will get my site's URL. I'm disgusted. I tried, but cannot find any reason someone would want to know something like that. . . . Whatever. If that's why you're here—you're busted. Now go away."

. . .

Eric Fischl did not go away. Neither did he turn away or avert his eyes. A year before September 11, he had taken photographs of a model tumbling around on the floor of a studio. He had thought of using the photographs as the basis of a sculpture. Now, though, he had lost a friend who had been trapped on the 106th floor of the North Tower. Now, as he worked on his sculpture, he sought to express the extremity of his feelings by making a monument to what he calls the "extremity of choice" faced by the people who jumped. He worked nine months on the larger-than-life bronze he called *Tumbling Woman,* and as he transformed a woman tumbling on the floor into a woman tumbling through eternity, he succeeded in transfiguring the very local horror of the jumpers into something universal—in redeeming an image many regarded as irredeemable. Indeed, *Tumbling Woman* was perhaps *the* redemptive image of 9/11—and yet it was not merely resisted; it was rejected. The day after *Tumbling Woman* was exhibited in New York's Rockefeller Center, Andrea Peyser of the *New York Post* denounced it in a column titled "Shameful Art Attack," in which she argued that Fischl had no right to ambush grieving New Yorkers with the very distillation of their own sadness . . . in which she essentially argued the right to look away. Because it was based on a model rolling on the floor, the statue was treated as an evocation of impact—as a portrayal of literal, rather than figurative, violence.

"I was trying to say something about the way we all feel," Fischl says, "but people thought I was trying to say something about the way *they* feel—that I was trying to take away something only they possessed. They thought that I was trying to say something about the people they lost. 'That image is not my father. You don't even know my father. How dare you try telling me how I feel about my father?'" Fischl wound up apologizing—"I was ashamed to have added to anybody's pain"—but it didn't matter.

Jerry Speyer, a trustee of the Museum of Modern Art who runs Rockefeller Center, ended the exhibition of *Tumbling Woman* after a week. "I pleaded with him not to do it," Fischl says. "I thought that if we could wait it out, other voices would pipe up and carry the day. He said, 'You don't understand. I'm getting bomb threats.' I said, 'People who just lost loved ones to terrorism are not going to bomb somebody.' He said, 'I can't take that chance.'"

•   •   •

Photographs lie. Even great photographs. Especially great photographs. The Falling Man in Richard Drew's picture fell in the manner suggested by the photograph for only a fraction of a second, and then kept falling. The photograph functioned as a study of doomed verticality, a fantasia of straight lines, with a human being slivered at the center, like a spike. In truth, however, the Falling Man fell with neither the precision of an arrow nor the grace of an Olympic diver. He fell like everyone else, like all the other jumpers—trying to hold on to the life he was leaving, which is to say that he fell desperately, inelegantly. In Drew's famous photograph, his humanity is in accord with the lines of the buildings. In the rest of the sequence—the eleven outtakes— his humanity stands apart. He is not augmented by aesthetics; he is merely human, and his humanity, startled and in some cases horizontal, obliterates everything else in the frame.

In the complete sequence of photographs, truth is subordinate to the facts that emerge slowly, pitilessly, frame by frame. In the sequence, the Falling Man shows his face to the camera in the two frames before the published one, and after that there is an unveiling, nearly an unpeeling, as the force generated by the fall rips the white jacket off his back. The facts that emerge from the entire sequence suggest that the Toronto reporter, Peter Cheney, got some things right in his effort to solve the mystery presented by Drew's published photo. The Falling Man has a dark cast to his skin and wears a goatee. He is probably a food-service worker. He seems lanky, with the length and narrowness of his face—like that of a medieval Christ—possibly accentuated by the push of the wind and the pull of gravity. But seventy-nine people died on the morning of September 11 after going to work at Windows on the World. Another twenty-one died while in the employ of Forte Food, a catering service that fed the traders at Cantor Fitzgerald. Many of the dead were Latino, or light-skinned black men, or Indian, or Arab. Many had dark hair cut short. Many had mustaches and goatees. Indeed, to anyone trying to figure out the identity of the Falling Man, the few salient characteristics that can be discerned in the original series of photographs raise as many possibilities as they exclude. There is, however, one fact that is decisive. Whoever the Falling Man may be, he was wearing a bright-orange shirt under his white top. It is the one inarguable fact that the brute force of the fall reveals. No one can know if the tunic or shirt, open at the back, is being pulled away from him, or if the fall is simply tearing the white fabric to pieces. But anyone can see he is wearing an orange shirt. If they saw these pictures, members of his family would be able to see that he is wearing an orange shirt. They might even be able to remember if he owned an orange shirt, if he was the kind of guy who *would* own an orange shirt, if he wore an orange shirt to work that morning. Surely they would; surely *someone* would remember what he was wearing when he went to work on the last morning of his life. . . .

But now the Falling Man is falling through more than the blank blue sky. He is falling through the vast spaces of memory and picking up speed.

·   ·   ·

Neil Levin, executive director of the Port Authority of New York and New Jersey, had breakfast at Windows on the World, on the 106th floor of the World Trade Center's North Tower, on the morning of September 11. He never came home. His wife, Christy Ferer, won't talk about any of the particulars of his death. She works for New York mayor Mike Bloomberg as the liaison between the mayor's office and the 9/11 families and has poured the energy aroused by her grief into her work, which, before the first anniversary of the attack, called for her to visit television executives and ask them not to use the most disturbing footage—including the footage of the jumpers—in their memorial broadcasts. She is a close friend of Eric Fischl's, as was her husband, so when the artist asked, she agreed to take a look at *Tumbling Woman*. It, in her words, "hit me in the gut," but she felt that Fischl had the right to create and exhibit it. Now she's come to the conclusion that the controversy may have been largely a matter of timing. Maybe it was just too soon to show something like that. After all, not long before her husband died, she traveled with him to Auschwitz, where piles of confiscated eyeglasses and extracted tooth fillings are on exhibit. "They can show that now," she says. "But that was a long time ago. They couldn't show things like that *then*. . . ."

In fact, they did, at least in photographic form, and the pictures that came out of the death camps of Europe were treated as essential acts of witness, without particular regard to the sensitivities of those who appeared in them or the surviving families of the dead. They were shown, as Richard Drew's photographs of the freshly assassinated Robert Kennedy were shown. They were shown, as the photographs of Ethel Kennedy pleading with photographers not to take photographs were shown. They were shown as the photograph of the little Vietnamese girl running naked after a napalm attack was shown. They were shown as the photograph of Father Mychal Judge, graphically and unmistakably dead, was shown, and accepted as a kind of testament. They were shown as everything is shown, for, like the lens of a camera, history is a force that does not discriminate. What distinguishes the pictures of the jumpers from the pictures that have come before is that we—we Americans—are being asked to discriminate on their behalf. What distinguishes them, historically, is that we, as patriotic Americans, have agreed not to look at them. Dozens, scores, maybe hundreds of people died by leaping from a burning building, and we have somehow taken it upon ourselves to deem their deaths unworthy of witness—because we have somehow deemed the act of witness, in this one regard, unworthy of us.

• • •

Catherine Hernandez never saw the photo the reporter carried under his arm at her father's funeral. Neither did her mother, Eulogia. Her sister Jacqueline did, and her outrage assured that the reporter left—was forcibly evicted—before he did any more damage. But the picture has followed Catherine and Eulogia and the entire Hernandez family. There was nothing more important to Norberto Hernandez than family. His motto: "Together Forever." But the Hernandezes are not together anymore. The picture split them. Those who *knew,* right away, that the picture was not Norberto—his wife and his daughters—have become estranged from those who pondered the possibility that it was him for the benefit of a reporter's notepad. With Norberto alive, the extended family all lived in the same neighborhood in Queens. Now Eulogia and her daughters have moved to a house on Long Island because Tatiana—who is now sixteen and who bears a resemblance to Norberto Hernandez: the wide face, the dark brows, the thick dark lips, thinly smiling—kept seeing visions of her father in the house and kept hearing the whispered suggestions that he died by jumping out a window.

He could not have died by jumping out a window.

All over the world, people who read Peter Cheney's story believe that Norberto died by jumping out a window. People have written poems about Norberto jumping out a window. People have called the Hernandezes with offers of money—either charity or payment for interviews—because they read about Norberto jumping out a window. But he couldn't have jumped out a window, his family knows, because he *wouldn't* have jumped out a window: not Papi. "He was trying to come home," Catherine says one morning, in a living room primarily decorated with framed photographs of her father. "He was trying to come home to us, and he knew he wasn't going to make it by jumping out a window." She is a lovely, dark-skinned, brown-eyed girl, twenty-two years old, dressed in a T-shirt and sweats and sandals. She is sitting on a couch next to her mother, who is caramel-colored, with coppery hair tied close to her scalp, and who is wearing a cotton dress checked with the color of the sky. Eulogia speaks half the time in determined English, and then, when she gets frustrated with the rate of revelation, pours rapid-fire Spanish into the ear of her daughter, who translates. "My mother says she knows that when he died, he was thinking about us. She says that she could see him thinking about us. I know that sounds strange, but she knew him. They were together since they were fifteen." The Norberto Hernandez Eulogia knew would not have been deterred by smoke or by fire in his effort to come home to her. The Norberto Hernandez she knew would have endured any pain before he jumped out of a window. When the Norberto Hernandez she knew died, his eyes were fixed on what he saw in his heart—the faces of his wife and his daughters—and not on the terrible beauty of an empty sky.

How well did she know him? "I *dressed* him," Eulogia says in English, a smile appearing on her face at the same time as a shiny coat of tears. "Every morning. That morning, I remember. He wore Old Navy underwear. Green. He wore black socks. He wore blue pants: jeans. He wore a Casio watch. He wore an Old Navy shirt. Blue. With checks." What did he wear after she drove him, as she always did, to the subway station and watched him wave to her as he disappeared down the stairs? "He changed clothes at the restaurant," says Catherine, who worked with her father at Windows on the World. "He was a pastry chef, so he wore white pants, or chef's pants—you know, black-and-white check. He wore a white jacket. Under that, he had to wear a white T-shirt." What about an orange shirt? "No," Eulogia says. "My husband did not have an orange shirt."

There are pictures. There are pictures of the Falling Man as he fell. Do they want to see them? Catherine says no, on her mother's behalf—"My mother should not see"—but then, when she steps outside and sits down on the steps of the front porch, she says, "Please—show me. Hurry. Before my mother comes." When she sees the twelve-frame sequence, she lets out a gasping, muted call for her mother, but Eulogia is already over her shoulder, reaching for the pictures. She looks at them one after another, and then her face fixes itself into an expression of triumph and scorn. "That is not my husband," she says, handing the photographs back. "You see? Only I know Norberto." She reaches for the photographs again, and then, after studying them, shakes her head with a vehement finality. "The man in this picture is a black man." She asks for copies of the pictures so that she can show them to the people who believed that Norberto jumped out a window, while Catherine sits on the step with her palm spread over her heart. "They said my father was going to hell because he jumped," she says. "On the Internet. They said my father was taken to hell with the devil. I don't know what I would have done if it was him. I would have had a nervous breakdown, I guess. They would have found me in a mental ward somewhere. . . ."

Her mother is standing at the front door, about to go back inside her house. Her face has already lost its belligerent pride and has turned once again into a mask of composed, almost wistful sadness. "Please," she says as she closes the door in a stain of morning sunlight. "Please clear my husband's name."

．　　　．　　　．

A phone rings in Connecticut. A woman answers. A man on the other end is looking to identify a photo that ran in *The New York Times* on September 12, 2001. "Tell me what the photo looks like," she says. It's a famous picture, the man says—the famous picture of a man falling. "Is it the one called 'Swan Dive' on Rotten.com?" the woman asks. It may be, the man says. "Yes, that might have been my son," the woman says.

She lost both her sons on September 11. They worked together at Cantor Fitzgerald. They worked on the equities desk. They worked back-to-back. No, the man on the phone says, the man in the photograph is probably a food-service worker. He's wearing a white jacket. He's upside down. "Then that's not my son," she says. "My son was wearing a dark shirt and khaki pants."

She knows what he was wearing because of her determination to know what happened to her sons on that day—because of her determination to look and to see. She did not start with that determination. She stopped reading the newspaper after September 11, stopped watching TV. Then, on New Year's Eve, she picked up a copy of *The New York Times* and saw, in a year-end review, a picture of Cantor Fitzgerald employees crowding the edge of the cliff formed by a dying building. In the posture—the attitude—of one of them, she thought she recognized the habits of her son. So she called the photographer and asked him to enlarge and clarify the picture. Demanded that he do it. And then she knew, or knew as much as it was possible to know. Both of her sons were in the picture. One was standing in the window, almost brazenly. The other was sitting inside. She does not need to say what may have happened next.

"The thing I hold was that both of my sons were together," she says, her instantaneous tears lifting her voice an octave. "But I sometimes wonder how long they knew. They're puzzled, they're uncertain, they're scared—but when did they *know*? When did the moment come when they lost hope? Maybe it came so quick. . . ."

The man on the phone does not ask if she thinks her sons jumped. He does not have it in him, and anyway, she has given him an answer.

The Hernandezes looked at the decision to jump as a betrayal of love—as something Norberto was being accused of. The woman in Connecticut looks at the decision to jump as a loss of hope—as an absence that we, the living, now have to live with. She chooses to live with it by looking, by seeing, by trying to know—by making an act of private witness. She could have chosen to keep her eyes closed. And so now the man on the phone asks the question that he called to ask in the first place: Did she make the right choice?

"I made the only choice I could have made," the woman answers. "I could never have made the choice not to know."

. . .

Catherine Hernandez thought she knew who the Falling Man was as soon as she saw the series of pictures, but she wouldn't say his name. "He had a sister who was with him that morning," she said, "and he told his mother that he would take care of her. He would never have left her alone by jumping." She did say, however, that the man was Indian, so it was easy to figure out that his name was Sean Singh. But Sean was too small to be the Falling Man. He was clean-shaven. He worked at Windows on the World in the audiovisual department, so he probably would have been wearing a shirt and tie instead of a white chef's coat. None of the former Windows employees who were interviewed believe the Falling Man looks anything like Sean Singh.

Besides, he had a sister. He never would have left her alone.

A manager at Windows looked at the pictures once and said the Falling Man was Wilder Gomez. Then a few days later he studied them closely and changed his mind. Wrong hair. Wrong clothes. Wrong body type. It was the same with Charlie Mauro. It was the same with Junior Jimenez. Junior worked in the kitchen and would have been wearing checked pants. Charlie worked in purchasing and had no cause to wear a white jacket. Besides, Charlie was a very large man. The Falling Man appears fairly stout in Richard Drew's published photo but almost elongated in the rest of the sequence.

The rest of the kitchen workers were, like Norberto Hernandez, eliminated from consideration by their outfits. The banquet servers may have been wearing white and black, but no one remembered any banquet server who looked anything like the Falling Man.

Forte Food was the other food-service company that lost people on September 11, 2001. But all of its male employees worked in the kitchen, which means that they wore either checked or white pants. And nobody would have been allowed to wear an orange shirt under the white serving coat.

But someone who used to work for Forte remembers a guy who used to come around and get food for the Cantor executives. Black guy. Tall, with a mustache and a goatee. Wore a chef's coat, open, with a loud shirt underneath.

Nobody at Cantor remembers anyone like that.

Of course, the only way to find out the identity of the Falling Man is to call the families of anyone who might be the Falling Man and ask what they know about their son's or husband's or father's last day on earth. Ask if he went to work wearing an orange shirt.

But should those calls be made? Should those questions be asked? Would they only heap pain upon the already anguished? Would they be regarded as an insult to the memory of the dead, the way the Hernandez family regarded the imputation that Norberto Hernandez was the Falling Man? Or would they be regarded as steps to some act of redemptive witness?

Jonathan Briley worked at Windows on the World. Some of his coworkers, when they saw Richard Drew's photographs, thought he might be the Falling Man. He was a light-skinned black man. He was over six five. He was forty-three. He had a mustache and a goatee and close-cropped hair. He had a wife named Hillary.

Jonathan Briley's father is a preacher, a man who has devoted his whole life to serving the Lord. After September 11, he gathered his family together to ask God to tell him where his son was. No: He demanded it. He used these words: "Lord, I demand to know where my son is." For three hours straight, he prayed in his deep voice, until he spent the grace he had accumulated over a lifetime in the insistence of his appeal.

The next day, the FBI called. They'd found his son's body. It was, miraculously, intact.

The preacher's youngest son, Timothy, went to identify his brother. He recognized him by his shoes: He was wearing black high-tops. Timothy removed one of them and took it home and put it in his garage, as a kind of memorial.

Timothy knew all about the Falling Man. He is a cop in Mount Vernon, New York, and in the week after his brother died, someone had left a September 12 newspaper open in the locker room. He saw the photograph of the Falling Man and, in anger, he refused to look at it again. But he couldn't throw it away. Instead, he stuffed it in the bottom of his locker, where—like the black shoe in his garage—it became permanent.

Jonathan's sister Gwendolyn knew about the Falling Man, too. She saw the picture the day it was published. She knew that Jonathan had asthma, and in the smoke and the heat would have done anything just to breathe. . . .

The both of them, Timothy and Gwendolyn, knew what Jonathan wore to work on most days. He wore a white shirt and black pants, along with the high-top black shoes. Timothy also knew what Jonathan sometimes wore under his shirt: an orange T-shirt. Jonathan wore that orange T-shirt everywhere. He wore that shirt all the time. He wore it so often that Timothy used to make fun of him: When are you gonna get rid of that orange T-shirt, Slim?

But when Timothy identified his brother's body, none of his clothes were recognizable except the black shoes. And when Jonathan went to work on the morning of September 11, 2001, he'd left early and kissed his wife goodbye while she was still sleeping. She never saw the clothes he was wearing. After she learned that he was dead, she packed his clothes away and never inventoried what specific articles of clothing might be missing.

Is Jonathan Briley the Falling Man? He might be. But maybe he didn't jump from the window as a betrayal of love or because he lost hope. Maybe he jumped to fulfill the terms of a miracle. Maybe he jumped to come home to his family. Maybe he didn't jump at all, because no one can jump into the arms of God.

Oh, no. You have to fall.

Yes, Jonathan Briley might be the Falling Man. But the only certainty we have is the certainty we had at the start: At fifteen seconds after 9:41 A.M., on September 11, 2001, a photographer named Richard Drew took a picture of a man falling through the sky—falling through time as well as through space. The picture went all around the world, and then disappeared, as if we willed it away. One of the most famous photographs in human history became an unmarked grave, and the man buried inside its frame—the Falling Man—became the Unknown Soldier in a war whose end we have not yet seen. Richard Drew's photograph is all we know of him, and yet all we know of him becomes a measure of what we know of ourselves. The picture is his cenotaph, and like the monuments dedicated to the memory of unknown soliders everywhere, it asks that we look at it, and make one simple acknowledgment.

That we have known who the Falling Man is all along.

Contributors

KATHERINE BOO has been a staff writer for *The New Yorker* since 2003, and a contributor since 2001. Before joining *The New Yorker,* she was a writer and editor for the *Washington Post,* where for a decade she was a member of the Outlook and Investigative staffs. In 2000, Boo received the Pulitzer Prize for Public Service, and in 2003 she was awarded a MacArthur Fellowship to recognize and further her body of work on America's aspiration-rich working poor. She is a senior fellow at the New America Foundation, a nonpartisan think tank on public policy.

MARK BOWDEN is a national correspondent for *The Atlantic Monthly.* He is the author of six books, including the bestsellers *Black Hawk Down* (1999), a National Book Award finalist, and *Killing Pablo* (2001), which won the Overseas Press Club's Cornelius Ryan Award. His newest book, *Road Work,* will be published in fall 2004.

TUCKER CARLSON is co-host of CNN's *Crossfire,* as well as the host of *Tucker Carlson: Unfiltered* on PBS. Formerly a staff writer at the *Arkansas Democrat-Gazette* in Little Rock, Carlson has been a columnist for *New York Magazine* and *Reader's Digest.* He has covered politics and disorder from around the world for dozens of magazines and newspapers, including the *New York Times,* the *Weekly Standard,* and the *Wall Street Journal.* His book, *Politicians, Partisans and Parasites: My Adventures in Cable News,* was published in 2003.

JOHN CASSIDY joined *The New Yorker* in 1995 as a writer covering finance and economics. Since arriving at the magazine, he has written on subjects ranging from the internal culture of the Federal Reserve Board to the economics of film-making. Cassidy came to the magazine after two years with the *New York Post,* and seven years with *The Sunday Times* of London. Cassidy's first book, *Dot.Con: The Greatest Story Ever Sold* was published in 2002.

TOM CHIARELLA is a writer-at-large for *Esquire.* He's the author of three books. His most recent, *Thursday's Game: Notes from a Golfer with Far to Go* is a collection of essays which first appeared in *Esquire.* He lives in Indiana and teaches creative writing at DePauw University.

ANDREW CORSELLO has written for *GQ* since 1995. His first feature for the magazine, about his near-death experience with liver failure, was nominated for a National Magazine Award. His subjects have ranged from foot-and-mouth disease in England, to Frédéric Chopin's Fourth Ballade in F Minor. Two of his pieces—one about a brain-damaged artist, the other about a brilliant teen inventor and his mentor—are currently being developed into motion pictures.

DAVE EGGERS is the author of two novels, *A Heartbreaking Work of Staggering Genius* and *You Shall Know Our Velocity,* and is the editor of the literary journal *McSweeney's* and the anthology *Best American Nonrequired Reading.* He lives in San Francisco, where he runs McSweeney's Books, an independent book publishing company, and 826 Valencia, a nonprofit organization devoted to teaching writing to students ages 8–18.

CAITLIN FLANAGAN, now a staff writer at *The New Yorker* and previously a contributing editor for *The Atlantic Monthly,* began her magazine-writing career in 2001 with a series of extended book reviews about conflicts at the heart of modern life—specifically, modern domestic life as it is lived by professional women. She is at work on a book called *Housewife Heaven* to be published by Little, Brown.

DAVID HAJDU is the music critic for *The New Republic*. He is the author of *Lush Life: A Biography of Billy Strahorn* and *Positively 4th Street: The Lives and Times of Joan Baez, Bob Dylan, Mimi Baez Fariña, and Richard Fariña*, and he teaches at the Newhouse School of Communications at Syracuse University.

SEYMOUR M. HERSH first wrote for *The New Yorker* in 1971 and has been a regular contributor to the magazine since 1993. He has been awarded the Pulitzer Prize, four George Polk Awards, and more than a dozen other prizes for investigative reporting on My Lai, the C.I.A.'s bombing of Cambodia, Henry Kissinger's wire-tapping, and the C.I.A.'s efforts against Chile's Salvador Allende, among other topics. Hersh has published seven books. His latest book, *Chain of Command,* will be published in Fall 2004.

LAURA HILLENBRAND is the author of the bestselling *Seabiscuit: An American Legend*. She has been writing about history and thoroughbred racing since 1988, and has been a contributing writer/editor for *Equus* magazine since 1989. Her work has appeared in *The New Yorker,* the *New York Times, Washington Post, Talk, Reader's Digest,* and *American Heritage*.

TOM JUNOD began his journalism career at *Atlanta Magazine,* before moving on to *Life, Sports Illustrated, GQ,* and *Esquire*. At *GQ,* Junod won two National Magazine Awards, the first for a profile of an abortion doctor, the second for a profile of a rapist undergoing therapy. As a writer-at-large at *Esquire,* Junod has written profiles of Kevin Spacey, Hillary Rodham Clinton, Fred Rogers, and FBI counter-terrorist expert John O'Neill, among others, and reported on American hostages in Ecuador. In all, he has been a finalist for the National Magazine Award eight times.

WILLIAM LANGEWIESCHE is a national correspondent for *The Atlantic Monthly* and a former professional pilot. His *Atlantic* cover story "The Crash of EgyptAir 990" won the 2002 National Magazine Award for Reporting. He is the author of *The Outlaw Sea, American Ground: Unbuilding the World Trade Center, Inside the Sky, Cutting for Sign,* and *Sahara Unveiled.*

SUSAN ORLEAN is the bestselling author of *The Orchid Thief, The Bullfighter Checks Her Makeup,* and *Saturday Night.* She has been a staff writer for *The New Yorker* since 1992, and her articles have also appeared in *Outside, Esquire, Rolling Stone,* and *Vogue.*

GEORGE SAUNDERS is the author of the story collection *CivilWar-Land in Bad Decline,* a finalist for the 1996 PEN/Hemingway Award; *The Very Persistent Gappers of Frip,* a *New York Times* bestseller; and *Pastoralia: Stories,* a *New York Times* Notable book. He teaches in the Creative Writing Program at Syracuse University. His fiction has been published in *Esquire, The New Yorker,* and *Slate.*

CALVIN TRILLIN has been a regular contributor to *The New Yorker* since 1963, when the magazine published "An Education in Georgia," an account of the desegregation of the University of Georgia. His work includes comic casuals and a wide variety of nonfiction, but his principal interest has been reporting on America. For seventeen years, Trillin also wrote a humor column for *The Nation,* and today he continues to contribute comic verse to the magazine. Trillin has published eighteen books, including *Travels with Alice, The Tummy Trilogy, Killings,* and *Messages from My Father.*

MICHAEL WOLFF became a contributing editor to *Vanity Fair* in March 2004. Prior to that, he wrote *New York Magazine*'s "This Media Life," a weekly column about the media. He is a two-time

National Magazine Award winner, and the author of *Autumn of the Moguls* and *The Burn Rate*.

Evan Wright is a contributing editor to *Rolling Stone,* where he was originally known as "Ambassador to the Underbelly" for his reporting on the denizens of American subcultures, from radical environmentalists to drop-out skateboarders, to prison gangs. He has covered the recent wars in both Afghanistan and Iraq, and is the author of *Generation Kill.*

Bill Zehme has been an *Esquire* contributing editor since 1994. His profiles have also appeared in *Rolling Stone, Vanity Fair* and *Playboy.* Among his books are *The Way You Wear Your Hat: Frank Sinatra and the Lost Art of Livin', Lost in the Funhouse: The Life and Mind of Andy Kaufman, Intimate Strangers: Comic Profiles and Indiscretions of the Very Famous,* and *Hef's Little Black Book.*

2004 National Magazine Award Finalists

NOTE: All nominated issues are dated 2003 unless otherwise specified. The editor whose name appears in connection with finalists for 2004 held that position, or was listed on the masthead, at the time the issue was published in 2003. In some cases, another editor is now in that position.

General Excellence

This category recognizes overall excellence in magazines. It honors the effectiveness with which writing, reporting, editing and design all come together to command readers' attention and fulfill the magazine's unique editorial mission.

Under 100,000 circulation

The American Scholar: Anne Fadiman, editor, for Spring, Summer, Autumn issues.
Aperture: Melissa Harris, editor-in-chief, for Spring, Fall, Winter issues.
The Chronicle of Higher Education: Philip W. Semas, editor-in-chief, for June 27, September 12, October 24 issues.
Nest: Joseph Holtzman, art director & editor-in-chief, for Spring, Summer, Winter issues.
Print: Martin Fox, editor, for March/April; Joyce Rutter Kaye, editor-in-chief, for July/August, September/October issues.

100,000 to 250,000 circulation

Chicago Magazine: Richard Babcock, editor, for February, March, August issues.
CIO Magazine: Abbie Lundberg, editor-in-chief, for February 15, March 15, September 1 issues.
Harper's: Lewis H. Lapham, editor, for May, September, October issues.
Harvard Business Review: Thomas A. Stewart, editor, for February, October, December issues.
Time Out New York: Cyndi Stivers, president/editorial director; Joe Angio, editor-in-chief, for April 24-May 1, July 10–17, August 21–28 issues.

250,000 to 500,000 circulation

Bicycling: William Strickland, editor, for February; Stephen Madden, editor-in-chief, for August, November issues.

Budget Living: Sarah Gray Miller, editor-in-chief, for April/May, August/September, December/January issues.

Details: Daniel Peres, editor-in-chief, for June/July, September, December issues.

Teen Vogue: Amy Astley, editor-in-chief, for April/May, June/July, October/November issues.

Texas Monthly: Evan Smith, editor, for March, October, November issues.

500,000 to 1,000,000 circulation

Gourmet: Ruth Reichl, editor-in-chief, for January, March, October issues.

House & Garden: Dominique Browning, editor, for April, July, October issues.

National Geographic Traveler: Keith Bellows, editor and vice president, for March, April, October issues.

The New Yorker: David Remnick, editor, for February 17 & 24, March 31, November 24 issues.

Wired: Chris Anderson, editor-in-chief, for February, June, September issues.

1,000,000 to 2,000,000 circulation

BusinessWeek: Stephen B. Shepard, editor-in-chief, for October 6, December 8, December 15 issues.

Entertainment Weekly: Rick Tetzeli, managing editor, for August 22/29, November 28, December 26/January 2 issues.

ESPN The Magazine: Gary Hoenig, editor-in-chief, for August 18, November 24, December 22 issues.

Popular Science: Scott Mowbray, editor-in-chief, for September, October, November issues.

Real Simple: Carrie Tuhy, managing editor, for April; Kristin van Ogtrop, managing editor, for October, December/January issues.

Vogue: Anna Wintour, editor-in-chief, for March, September, December issues.

Over 2,000,000 circulation

Martha Stewart Living: Douglas Brenner, editor, for April, July issues; Margaret Roach, editor-in-chief, for July, October issues.

National Geographic: William L. Allen, editor-in-chief, for January, September, December issues.

Newsweek: Richard M. Smith, chairman and editor-in-chief; Mark Whitaker, editor, for March 10, March 31, November 3 issues.

O, The Oprah Magazine: Oprah Winfrey, founder and editorial director; Amy Gross, editor-in-chief, for January, March, October issues.

Time: James Kelly, managing editor, for October 6, October 13, December 29-January 5 issues.

Personal Service

This category recognizes excellence in service journalism. The advice or instruction presented should help readers improve the quality of their personal lives.

Consumer Reports: Julia Kagan, vice president and editorial director, for *How Safe is Your Hospital?*, by Nancy Metcalf; *Decoding Your Hospital Bills,* by Amanda Walker, January.

Men's Health: David Zinczenko, editor-in-chief, for *A Tale of 3 Hearts,* by Peter Moore; *100 Ways to Live Forever,* by Adam Campbell and Brian Good; *Death by Exercise,* by Lou Schuler, July/August.

Psychotherapy Networker: Richard Simon, editor, for *Living on Purpose,* by Katy Butler, September/October.

Self: Lucy S. Danziger, editor-in-chief, for its 2003 breast cancer handbook, *Healthy Breasts for Life!,* October.

Time Out New York: Cyndi Stivers, president/editorial director; Joe Angio, editor-in-chief, for *Your New Apartment: From Hunting to Housewarming,* April 24-May 1.

Leisure Interests

This category recognizes excellent service journalism about leisure-time pursuits. The practical advice or instruction presented should help readers enjoy hobbies or other recreational interests.

Bon Appétit: Barbara Fairchild, editor-in-chief, for *Thanksgiving Starts Here,* by Alton Brown, November.

Consumer Reports: Julia Kagan, vice president and editorial director, for *Veterinary Care Without the Bite,* by Jeff Blyskal, July.

Esquire: David Granger, editor-in-chief, for *The $20 Theory of the Universe,* by Tom Chiarella, March.

National Geographic Adventure: John Rasmus, editor-in-chief, for *Ultimate America,* by Tim Cahill and McKenzie Funk, October.

Outside: Hal Espen, editor, for *The 25 Essential Books for the Well-Read Explorer,* by Brad Wieners and the editors, January.

Reporting

This category recognizes excellence in reporting. It honors the enterprise, exclusive reporting and intelligent analysis that a magazine exhibits in covering an event, a situation or a problem of contemporary interest and significance.

The Atlantic Monthly: Cullen Murphy, managing editor, for *Columbia's Last Flight,* by William Langewiesche, November.

Institutional Investor: Michael Carroll, editor, for *Misdirected Brokerage,* by Rich Blake, June.

The New Yorker: David Remnick, editor, for *The David Kelly Affair,* by John Cassidy, December 8.

Rolling Stone: Jann Wenner, editor and publisher; Ed Needham, managing editor, for *The Killer Elite,* a three-part report by Evan Wright, Part I, *The Killer Elite,* June 26; Part II, *From Hell to Baghdad,* July 10; Part III, *The Battle for Baghdad,* July 24.

Time: James Kelly, managing editor, for *The Sum of Two Evils,* by Brian Bennett and Michael Weisskopf, June 2; *The Secret Collaborators,* by Michael Ware, October 20; *Life Behind Enemy Lines,* by Brian Bennett and Michael Ware, December 15.

Public Interest

This category recognizes journalism that has the potential to affect national or local policy or lawmaking. It honors investigative reporting or ground-breaking analysis that sheds new light on an issue of public importance.

The Atlantic Monthly: Cullen Murphy, managing editor, for *The Dark Art of Interrogation,* by Mark Bowden, October.

BusinessWeek: Stephen B. Shepard, editor-in-chief, for *Is Your Job Next?,* by Pete Engardio, Aaron Bernstein, and Manjeet Kripalani, February 3; *The Rise of India,* by Manjeet Kripalani and Pete Engardio, December 8.

The New Yorker: David Remnick, editor, for three articles by Seymour M. Hersh, *Lunch With the Chairman,* March 17; *Selective Intelligence,* May 12; *The Stovepipe,* October 27.

Newsweek: Richard M. Smith, chairman and editor-in-chief; Mark Whitaker, editor, for *The $87 Billion Money Pit,* by Rod Nordland and Michael Hirsh, November 3.

Self: Lucy S. Danziger, editor-in-chief, for *Pharmacy Fakes,* by Katherine Eban, March.

The Washington Monthly: Paul Glastris, editor-in-chief, for *Malpractice Makes Perfect,* by Stephanie Mencimer, October.

Feature Writing

This category recognizes excellence in feature writing. It honors the stylishness and originality with which the author treats his or her subject.

Esquire: David Granger, editor-in-chief, for *The League of Extraordinary Gentlemen,* by Tucker Carlson, November.

Esquire: David Granger, editor-in-chief, for *The Falling Man,* by Tom Junod, September.

Men's Journal: Robert B. Wallace, editor-in-chief, for *The First to Die,* by Hampton Sides, December.

The New Yorker: David Remnick, editor, for *The Marriage Cure,* by Katherine Boo, August 18 & 25.

Popular Science: Scott Mowbray, editor-in-chief, for *Yesterday, They Would Have Died,* by Michael Rosenwald, October.

Profile Writing

This category recognizes excellence in profile writing. It honors the vividness and perceptiveness with which the writer brings his or her subject to life.

The American Scholar: Anne Fadiman, editor, for *The Arctic Hedonist,* by Anne Fadiman, Winter.

The Atlantic Monthly: Cullen Murphy, managing editor, for *Wynton's Blues,* by David Hajdu, March.

Esquire: David Granger, editor-in-chief, for *The Confessions of Bob Greene,* by Bill Zehme, April.

Nest: Joseph Holtzman, editor-in-chief & art director, for *Frances Gabe's Self-Cleaning House,* by Miranda July, Fall.

The New Yorker: David Remnick, editor, for *Newshound,* by Calvin Trillin, September 29.

Essays

This category recognizes excellence in essay writing on topics ranging from the personal to the political. Whatever the subject, it honors the author's eloquence, perspective, fresh thinking and unique voice.

GQ: Art Cooper, editor-in-chief, for *The Vulgarian in the Choir Loft,* by Andrew Corsello, June.

Men's Journal: Robert B. Wallace, editor-in-chief, for *Me and the X Man,* by Paul Solotaroff, November.

Natural History: Peter Brown, editor-in-chief, for *The Pleasure (and Pain) of "Maybe",* by Robert M. Sapolsky, September.

The New Yorker: David Remnick, editor, for *A Sudden Illness,* by Laura Hillenbrand, July 7.

The New Yorker: David Remnick, editor, for *The End Matter,* by Louis Menand, October 6.

Columns and Commentary

This category recognizes excellence in short-form political, social, economic or humorous commentary. The award honors the eloquence, force of argument and succinctness with which the writer presents his or her views.

Governing: Peter A. Harkness, editor & publisher, for three columns by Alan Ehrenhalt, *Devolution's Double Standard,* April; *Republicans Behaving Badly,* August; *Machine Politics,* November.

New York Magazine: Caroline Miller, editor-in-chief, for three columns by Michael Wolff, *Live From Doha . . .,* April 7–14; *My Big Fat Question,* April 21; *Al Jazeera's Edge,* April 28.

The New Yorker: David Remnick, editor, for three columns by Hendrik Hertzberg, *Down to Earth,* February 17 & 24; *Building Nations,* June 9; *Rush in Rehab,* October 27.

Newsweek: Richard M. Smith, chairman and editor-in-chief; Mark Whitaker, editor, for three columns by Fareed Zakaria, *Here's a Bet for Mr. Rumsfeld,* October 6; *And He's Head of Intelligence?,* October 27; *No Way to Make Friends,* December 8.

Sports Illustrated: Terry McDonell, managing editor, for three columns by Steve Rushin, *Fear and Clothing in Atlanta,* February 17; *My Big Fat Sports Wedding,* April 21; *Yule Be Amazed,* December 29.

Reviews and Criticism

This category recognizes excellence in criticism of art, books, movies, television, theater, music, dance, food, dining, fashion, products and the like. It honors the knowledge, persuasiveness and original voice that the critic brings to his or her reviews.

The Atlantic Monthly: Cullen Murphy, managing editor, for three reviews by Caitlin Flanagan, *The Wifely Duty,* January/February; *Housewife Confidential,* September; *Let's Call the Whole Thing Off,* November.

Esquire: David Granger, editor-in-chief, for three reviews by Tom Carson, *Increas-*

ingly Berserk Developments, January; *Back to the Terminator,* August; *Mr. Uncongeniality,* December.

The Nation: Katrina vanden Heuvel, editor, for three pieces by Arthur C. Danto, *Paint It Black,* August 18/25;*Visions of the Sublime,* December 1; *The Abstract Impressionist,* December 29.

The New Yorker: David Remnick, editor, for three pieces by Louis Menand, *The Thin Envelope,* April 7; *The Devil's Disciples,* July 28; *After the Revolution,* October 20.

The New Yorker: David Remnick, editor, for three pieces by Hilton Als, *Glacier Head,* January 13; *Playing for Immortality,* February 3; *Borrowed Culture,* March 3.

Single-Topic Issue

This category recognizes magazines that have devoted an issue to an in-depth examination of one topic. It honors the ambition, comprehensiveness and imagination with which a magazine treats its subject.

Cure: Dr. Vinay K. Jain, editor-in-chief, for its special issue on breast cancer, Fall.

National Geographic: William L. Allen, editor-in-chief, for its special issue on Everest, May.

The Oxford American: Marc Smirnoff, editor, for its *Sixth Annual Music Issue,* Summer.

Rolling Stone: Jann Wenner, editor & publisher; Ed Needham, managing editor, for *The 500 Greatest Albums of All Time,* December 11.

Wired: Chris Anderson, editor-in-chief, for *Kool World,* June.

Design

This category recognizes excellence in magazine design. It honors the effectiveness of overall design, artwork, graphics and typography in enhancing a magazine's unique mission and personality.

City: John F. McDonald, editorial director & publisher; Fabrice Frere, creative director & coo; Adriana Jacoud, art director, for May/June, Summer, Winter issues.

Details: Daniel Peres, editor-in-chief; Rockwell Harwood, design director, for October, November, December issues.

Esquire: David Granger, editor-in-chief; John Korpics, design director, for May, July, October issues.

Real Simple: Carrie Tuhy, managing editor; Robert Newman, creative director for April, May issues; Kristin van Ogtrop, managing editor, for October issue.

Spin: Sia Michel, editor-in-chief; Arem Duplessis, design director, for April, September, December issues.

Photography

This category recognizes excellence in magazine photography. It honors the effectiveness of photography, photojournalism and photo illustration in enhancing a magazine's unique mission and personality.

City: John F. McDonald, editorial director & publisher; Fabrice Frere, creative director & coo; Adriana Jacoud, art director, Piera Gelardi, photography editor, for May/June, Summer, Winter issues.

Details: Daniel Peres, editor-in-chief; Rockwell Harwood, design director; Judith Puckett-Rinella, photography director, for September, November, December issues.

Martha Stewart Living: Douglas Brenner, editor, for April, July issues; Margaret Roach, editor-in-chief, for July, October issues; Barbara de Wilde, design director; James Dunlinson, art director; Stacie McCormick, photo editor, for April, July, October issues.

Nest: Joseph Holtzman, editor-in-chief & art director, for Spring, Summer, Fall issues.

Vogue: Anna Wintour, editor-in-chief; Grace Coddington, creative director; Charles Churchward, design director; Russell Labosky, art director; Ivan Shaw, photo director, for March, September, December issues.

Photo Portfolio/Photo Essay

This category recognizes a distinctive portfolio or photographic essay. It honors either photos that express an idea or a concept, or documentary photojournalism shot in real time.

National Geographic: William L. Allen, editor-in-chief; Kent J. Kobersteen, senior editor, photography, for *21st Century Slaves* and *Inhuman Profit,* by Jodi Cobb, September.

Outside: Hal Espen, editor; Hannah McCaughey, creative director; Susan Boylan, art director; Rob Haggart, photography editor, for *Tigers of the Snow,* by Martin Schoeller, April.

Texas Monthly: Evan Smith, editor; Scott Dadich, art director; Kathleen M. Marcus, photography editor, for *Cuts Above,* by Dan Winters, May.

Time: James Kelly, managing editor; Arthur Hochstein, art director; Michele Stephenson, director of Photography; MaryAnne Golon, picture editor, for *A Soldier's Life,* by James Nachtwey, December 29.

Vogue: Anna Wintour, editor-in-chief; Grace Coddington, creative director; Charles Churchward, design director; Russell Labosky, art director; Ivan Shaw, photo director, for *Alice in Wonderland,* by Annie Leibovitz, December.

W: Patrick McCarthy, chairman and editorial director; Dennis Freedman, vice chairman and creative director; Edward Leida, executive vice president and group design director; Kirby Rodriguez, art director, for *The Kate Moss Portfolio,* September.

Fiction

This category recognizes excellence in magazine fiction writing. It honors the quality of a publication's literary selections.

The Atlantic Monthly: Cullen Murphy, managing editor, for *Happy Hour,* by Alison Baker, January/February; *We Have a Pope!,* by Christopher Buckley, April; *Yao's Chick,* by Max Apple, November.

The Atlantic Monthly: Cullen Murphy, managing editor, for *What is Visible,* by Kimberly Elkins, March; *Monstress,* by Lysley Tenorio, June; *Ghost-Birds,* by Nicolas Pizzolatto, October.

Esquire: David Granger, editor-in-chief, for *Presence,* by Arthur Miller, July; *The Red Bow,* by George Saunders, September; *Rest Stop,* by Stephen King, December.

The New Yorker: David Remnick, editor, for *A Rich Man,* by Edward P. Jones, August 4; *Runaway,* by Alice Munro, August 11; *Debarking,* by Lorrie Moore, December 22 & 29.

The Paris Review: George Plimpton, editor, for *Immortality,* by Yiyun Li, Fall; *The Final Solution,* by Michael Chabon, Summer; *Letter from the Last Bastion,* by Nell Freudenberger, Winter.

Zoetrope: All-Story: Tamara Straus, editor-in-chief, for *The Phrenologists's Dream,* by Karl Iagnemma, Spring; *The Smoothest Way is Full of Stones,* by Julie Orringer, Spring; *The Only Meaning of the Oil-Wet Water,* by Dave Eggers, Summer.

General Excellence Online

This category recognizes outstanding magazine Internet sites, as well as online-only magazines and Weblogs, that have a significant amount of original content. It honors sites that reflect an outstanding level of interactivity, journalistic integrity, service and innovative visual presentation.

Beliefnet (http://www.beliefnet.com): Steven Waldman, editor-in-chief

The Chronicle of Higher Education (http://chronicle.com): Phil Semas, editor-in chief

CNET News.com (http://.news.com.com): Jai Singh, editor-in-chief

National Geographic Online (www.nationalgeographic.com/magazine): William L. Allen, editor-in-chief

Sky & Telescope.com (http://skyandtelescope.com): Richard Tresch Fienberg, editor-in-chief

Slate (http://slate.msn.com): Jacob Weisberg, editor

1966–2004
National Magazine Award Winners

General Excellence

1973	BusinessWeek
1981	ARTnews
	Audubon
	BusinessWeek
	Glamour
1982	Camera Arts
	Newsweek
	Rocky Mountain Magazine
	Science81
1983	Harper's Magazine
	Life
	Louisiana Life
	Science82
1984	The American Lawyer
	House & Garden
	National Geographic
	Outside
1985	American Health
	American Heritage
	Manhattan, inc.
	Time
1986	Discover
	Money
	New England Monthly
	3–2–1- Contact
1987	Common Cause
	Elle
	New England Monthly
	People Weekly
1988	Fortune
	Hippocrates
	Parents
	The Sciences
1989	American Heritage
	Sports Illustrated
	The Sciences
	Vanity Fair
1990	Metropolitan Home
	7 Days
	Sports Illustrated
	Texas Monthly
1991	Condé Nast Traveler
	Glamour
	Interview
	The New Republic
1992	Mirabella
	National Geographic
	The New Republic
	Texas Monthly
1993	American Photo
	The Atlantic Monthly
	Lingua Franca
	Newsweek
1994	BusinessWeek
	Health
	Print
	Wired
1995	Entertainment Weekly
	I.D. Magazine
	Men's Journal
	The New Yorker
1996	BusinessWeek
	Civilization
	Outside
	The Sciences
1997	I.D. Magazine
	Outside
	Vanity Fair
	Wired

1998	DoubleTake
	Outside
	Preservation
	Rolling Stone
1999	Condé Nast Traveler
	Fast Company
	I.D. Magazine
	Vanity Fair
2000	National Geographic
	Nest
	The New Yorker
	Saveur
2001	The American Scholar
	Mother Jones
	The New Yorker
	Teen People
2002	Entertainment Weekly
	National Geographic Adventure
	Newsweek
	Print
	Vibe
2003	Architectural Record
	The Atlantic Monthly
	ESPN The Magazine
	Foreign Policy
	Parenting
	Texas Monthly
2004	Aperture
	Budget Living
	Chicago Magazine
	Gourmet
	Newsweek
	Popular Science

Personal Service

1986	Farm Journal
1987	Consumer Reports
1988	Money

1989	Good Housekeeping
1990	Consumer Reports
1991	New York
1992	Creative Classroom
1993	Good Housekeeping
1994	Fortune
1995	SmartMoney
1996	SmartMoney
1997	Glamour
1998	Men's Journal
1999	Good Housekeeping
2000	PC Computing
2001	National Geographic Adventure
2002	National Geographic Adventure
2003	Outside
2004	Men's Health

Leisure Interests

(formerly Special Interests)

2002	Vogue
2003	National Geographic Adventure
2004	Consumer Reports

Special Interests

1986	Popular Mechanics
1987	Sports Afield
1988	Condé Nast Traveler
1989	Condé Nast Traveler
1990	Art & Antiques
1991	New York
1992	Sports Afield
1993	Philadelphia
1994	Outside
1995	GQ
1996	Saveur

1997	Smithsonian
1998	Entertainment Weekly
1999	PC Computing
2000	I.D. Magazine
2001	The New Yorker

Reporting

1970	The New Yorker
1971	The Atlantic Monthly
1972	The Atlantic Monthly
1973	New York
1974	The New Yorker
1975	The New Yorker
1976	Audubon
1977	Audubon
1978	The New Yorker
1979	Texas Monthly
1980	Mother Jones
1981	National Journal
1982	The Washingtonian
1983	Institutional Investor
1984	Vanity Fair
1985	Texas Monthly
1986	Rolling Stone
1987	Life
1988	The Washingtonian and Baltimore Magazine
1989	The New Yorker
1990	The New Yorker
1991	The New Yorker
1992	The New Republic
1993	IEEE Spectrum
1994	The New Yorker
1995	The Atlantic Monthly
1996	The New Yorker
1997	Outside
1998	Rolling Stone
1999	Newsweek
2000	Vanity Fair

2001	Esquire
2002	The Atlantic Monthly
2003	The New Yorker
2004	Rolling Stone

Public Interest

1970	Life
1971	The Nation
1972	Philadelphia
1974	Scientific American
1975	Consumer Reports
1976	BusinessWeek
1977	Philadelphia
1978	Mother Jones
1979	New West
1980	Texas Monthly
1981	Reader's Digest
1982	The Atlantic
1983	Foreign Affairs
1984	The New Yorker
1985	The Washingtonian
1986	Science85
1987	Money
1988	The Atlantic
1989	California
1990	Southern Exposure
1991	Family Circle
1992	Glamour
1993	The Family Therapy Networker
1994	Philadelphia
1995	The New Republic
1996	Texas Monthly
1997	Fortune
1998	The Atlantic Monthly
1999	Time
2000	The New Yorker
2001	Time
2002	The Atlantic Monthly

| 2003 | The Atlantic Monthly |
| 2004 | The New Yorker |

Feature Writing

1988	The Atlantic
1989	Esquire
1990	The Washingtonian
1991	U.S. News & World Report
1992	Sports Illustrated
1993	The New Yorker
1994	Harper's Magazine
1995	GQ
1996	GQ
1997	Sports Illustrated
1998	Harper's Magazine
1999	The American Scholar
2000	Sports Illustrated
2001	Rolling Stone
2002	The Atlantic Monthly
2003	Harper's Magazine
2004	The New Yorker

Profile Writing

2000	Sports Illustrated
2001	The New Yorker
2002	The New Yorker
2003	Sports Illustrated
2004	Esquire

Essays

2000	The Sciences
2001	The New Yorker
2002	The New Yorker
2003	The American Scholar
2004	The New Yorker

Columns and Commentary

2002	New York
2003	The Nation
2004	New York

Reviews and Criticism

2000	Esquire
2001	The New Yorker
2002	Harper's Magazine
2003	Vanity Fair
2004	Esquire

Single-Topic Issue

1979	Progressive Architecture
1980	Scientific American
1981	BusinessWeek
1982	Newsweek
1983	IEEE Spectrum
1984	Esquire
1985	American Heritage
1986	IEEE Spectrum
1987	Bulletin of the Atomic Scientists
1988	Life
1989	Hippocrates
1990	National Geographic
1991	The American Lawyer
1992	BusinessWeek
1993	Newsweek
1994	Health
1995	Discover
1996	Bon Appétit
1997	Scientific American
1998	The Sciences
1999	The Oxford American
2002	Time

2003	Scientific American
2004	The Oxford American

Design

1980	Geo
1981	Attenzione
1982	Nautical Quarterly
1983	New York
1984	House & Garden
1985	Forbes
1986	Time
1987	Elle
1988	Life
1989	Rolling Stone
1990	Esquire
1991	Condé Nast Traveler
1992	Vanity Fair
1993	Harper's Bazaar
1994	Allure
1995	Martha Stewart Living
1996	Wired
1997	I.D.
1998	Entertainment Weekly
1999	ESPN The Magazine
2000	Fast Company
2001	Nest
2002	Details
2003	Details
2004	Esquire

Photography

1985	Life
1986	Vogue
1987	National Geographic
1988	Rolling Stone
1989	National Geographic
1990	Texas Monthly

1991	National Geographic
1992	National Geographic
1993	Harper's Bazaar
1994	Martha Stewart Living
1995	Rolling Stone
1996	Saveur
1997	National Geographic
1998	W
1999	Martha Stewart Living
2000	Vanity Fair
2001	National Geographic
2002	Vanity Fair
2003	Condé Nast Traveler
2004	City

Photo Portfolio/Photo Essay

2004	W

Fiction

1978	The New Yorker
1979	The Atlantic Monthly
1980	Antaeus
1981	The North American Review
1982	The New Yorker
1983	The North American Review
1984	Seventeen
1985	Playboy
1986	The Georgia Review
1987	Esquire
1988	The Atlantic
1989	The New Yorker
1990	The New Yorker
1991	Esquire
1992	Story
1993	The New Yorker
1994	Harper's Magazine
1995	Story

1996	Harper's Magazine
1997	The New Yorker
1998	The New Yorker
1999	Harper's Magazine
2000	The New Yorker
2001	Zoetrope: All-Story
2002	The New Yorker
2003	The New Yorker
2004	Esquire

General Excellence Online

1997	Money
1998	The Sporting News Online
1999	Cigar Aficionado
2000	BusinessWeek Online
2001	U.S. News Online
2002	National Geographic Magazine Online
2003	Slate
2004	CNET News.com

Best Interactive Design

2001	SmartMoney.com

Essays & Criticism

1978	Esquire
1979	Life
1980	Natural History
1981	Time
1982	The Atlantic
1983	The American Lawyer
1984	The New Republic
1985	Boston Magazine
1986	The Sciences
1987	Outside
1988	Harper's Magazine

1989	Harper's Magazine
1990	Vanity Fair
1991	The Sciences
1992	The Nation
1993	The American Lawyer
1994	Harper's Magazine
1995	Harper's Magazine
1996	The New Yorker
1997	The New Yorker
1998	The New Yorker
1999	The Atlantic Monthly

Single Awards

1966	Look
1967	Life
1968	Newsweek
1969	American Machinist

Specialized Journalism

1970	Philadelphia
1971	Rolling Stone
1972	Architectural Record
1973	Psychology Today
1974	Texas Monthly
1975	Medical Economics
1976	United Mine Workers Journal
1977	Architectural Record
1978	Scientific American
1979	National Journal
1980	IEEE Spectrum

Visual Excellence

1970	Look
1971	Vogue
1972	Esquire
1973	Horizon

1974	Newsweek
1975	Country Journal
	National Lampoon
1976	Horticulture
1977	Rolling Stone
1978	Architectural Digest
1979	Audubon

Fiction & Belles Lettres

1970	Redbook
1971	Esquire
1972	Mademoiselle
1973	The Atlantic Monthly
1974	The New Yorker
1975	Redbook
1976	Essence
1977	Mother Jones

Service to the Individual

1974	Sports Illustrated
1975	Esquire
1976	Modern Medicine
1977	Harper's Magazine
1978	Newsweek
1979	The American Journal of Nursing
1980	Saturday Review
1982	Philadelphia
1983	Sunset
1984	New York
1985	The Washingtonian

Special Awards

1976	Time
1989	Robert E. Kenyon, Jr.

American Society of Magazine Editors

ASME is the professional organization for editors of U.S. consumer magazines, as well as editors of online magazines. ASME's mission is to:

- Bring magazine editors together for networking

- Uphold editorial integrity

- Encourage and reward outstanding and innovative achievement in the creation of magazines and their content

- Disseminate useful information on magazine editing to magazine staff members and others

- Attract talented young people to magazine editorial work

- Defend magazines against external pressures

- Speak out on public policy issues, particularly those pertaining to the First Amendment; and to acquaint the general public with the work of magazine editors and the special character of magazines as a channel of communication.

ASME was founded in 1963, and currently has more than 900 members nationwide.

Permissions